Mother and Me

ESCAPE FROM WARSAW 1939

Julian Padowicz

Academy Chicago Publishers

Academy Chicago Publishers
363 West Erie Street
Chicago, Illinois 60610

First published in 2006
Paperback edition 2008

Printed and bound in the U.S.A.

Library of Congress Cataloging-in-Publication Data
on file with the publisher.

ISBN-13: 978-0-89733-570-6

To my beautiful daughters, Karen, JoAnne, and Nadine,
who knew Barbara as an exciting, glittering woman,
who would not let them call her grandmother.

Acknowledgements

Over the years, many relatives and friends have urged me to put this story on paper, even if only for my children's sake. Without their urging, I probably would not have made the effort.

I am most grateful to my wonderful wife, Donna, who was not only foremost among the "urgers," but who also made it possible for me to give this exercise the time that it needed. I am also grateful to Donna, the first person to read my manuscript, for pronouncing the words every author longs to hear, "You have written a beautiful book."

Memoir manuscripts by non-celebrities are not very popular among publishers. This, I suppose, is because there are so many of them, and because the author of a memoir is not likely ever to write anything else, making him or her a poor publishing investment. Fashioning and then sending compelling query letters to publishers, the vast majority of whom wish you well but don't want to see your manuscript, is a tedious and ego-bruising experience. It was mostly the encouragement of friends who read this manuscript that made it possible for me to continue until Academy Chicago Publishers decided to take a chance with me.

Prof. Jonathan Kistler, my teacher at Colgate University and his wife, Patricia, both dear lifelong friends, were no longer here to cheer me on, but the encouragement and critique they had given me over the years had a strong residual effect. Other friends, whose encouragement made so much difference, include my daughter Nadine Padowicz; my son,

Tom Carter; Tom's grandfather, George Carter; my father-in-law, Alvin Lass; friends Jim Larkin, Marilyn Allen, Gerry and Carol Weiss, John and Jeanine Giddings, Rob Vecchiola, Toby Lester, Donna and Ralph Loglisci, Stella Kiwala, and Arlene and Gerry Donowitz.

Above all, I am grateful to Barbara, without whose vision and courage I would have written a very different story. . . in Polish.

Author's Note

The major events and, above all, the narrator's feelings portrayed in this account are true. Because the memory of feelings and impressions is stronger than the memory of facts, I have had to take liberties to fill in certain facts to make the feelings and the impressions more understandable. Some people, whom I remember as being present, and who were an essential element of the story, cannot be eliminated from the narrative, though I have no memory of their personalities. These have had to be fictionalized. Since this may well do injustice to these individuals, I have changed the names of many characters and some places, and ask that the reader accept this as the somewhat fictionalized account of a true happening.

In addition, in order to give the reader a better flavor of the Polish culture, I have used a phonetic spelling for many proper names. My own name, Julian, for example, though it happens to be spelled the same way in Polish, I have spelled Yulian to approximate the Polish pronunciation. Its commonly used diminutive, as Joe is used for Joseph, would be Yulek. A further diminution, as Joe might change to Joey, is Yulechek or Yul. My last name, Padowicz, becomes Padovich. Where the Polish spelling is *cz*, I have changed it to *ch* to, again, approximate the pronunciation, and so on.

Chapter One

My earliest memories are of my governess—Kiki, I called her. I remember her sitting on a chair by my bed reading to me, her first day on the job. I was, I've been told, four at the time, and it's the earliest memory that I can call up.

I was sick. I was sick, as I remember, on most significant occasions at that period of my life—birthdays, the day I was supposed to have a ride on the carousel, the day we were to go to the circus . . .

Miss Yanka, soon to become Kiki, wears a blue dress with a white Peter Pan collar and buttons up the front. How accurate this memory is, I don't know, but it's as vivid as if it had taken place yesterday. She had a long blond braid which she would wind around her head, and never wore makeup. Kiki never smoked or drank either, except once that I remember her having an earache and Marta, our cook, telling her that smoking a cigarette would help. I don't remember that it did.

There was a photograph of my father on the wall over my bed. He, I had been informed, was in Heaven.

Mother, on the other hand, was usually in Paris or Vienna or Rome or Budapest. Occasionally, I would be told to walk on tiptoe around the apartment and had to wash in the kitchen sink and use the cook's toilet. Then I knew that Mother and my stepfather, Lolek, were back in town and asleep.

Mother, I was told, was very beautiful. Unlike me, she had blond hair, like Kiki's. Sometimes I thought it was even lighter than Kiki's and sometimes darker. She was taller than Kiki and thinner. She had very large, round eyes and full, round cheeks, which reminded me of jelly donuts. I was to learn later that she had had a screen test once to see if she had it to be a movie actress. Apparently, she didn't. It was Kiki, however, with her light blue eyes and thin pink lips, her blond eyebrows and eyelashes under the crown of braids wound around her head, who was my standard of beauty.

Mother, I decided, didn't wear ordinary clothes. Whenever I saw her, she was either in her bathrobe or what I later learned to call cocktail and evening dresses. Her shoes all had very high heels, even her slippers. I didn't like the way she smelled. It was cigarettes and a lot of perfume. Kiki just smelled of soap. Mother's perfume smelled like I-don't-know-what. My stepfather Lolek was very tall and bald, with a lot of black hair on his chest. People said they made a handsome couple, but I thought Lolek was ugly.

I remember asking once why my father never came back from his trip to Heaven the way Mother and Lolek returned from Paris. We were in the kitchen where Kiki was preparing our supper, which we would eat in the room she and I shared. The cook, Marta and Kiki exchanged looks. Marta had very black hair and a big rear end. Her hands were large too, with rough, dry skin, but when Kiki had a day off and she had to wash me, Marta's hands were very gentle. She came from the country. Her father raised potatoes and sugar beets, and they had a cow. Marta told me she had grown up in a house with a thatched roof.

Some time later, probably that same evening or the next day, Kiki sat me down and explained the whole situation. Technically, it seemed, my father was not really in Heaven. My father was dead, like Marshal Pilsudski who, I knew, had recently died, but while Marshal Pilsudski, a Catholic, had gone to Heaven, Kiki did not really know where a Jew would have gone. Having been a very good man in his lifetime, my father had certainly not been consigned to Hell, but she knew that Heaven really wasn't where he was.

Over the next two years or so, I learned from Kiki about God and Mary, their little boy Jesus, and the Holy Ghost. This last, I saw from pictures, was like a white pigeon that they had. This, I supposed, was like the canary that I was going to get some day when I was old enough. The four of them, I learned, as well as the angels and saints, all loved Catholics like Kiki.

How they felt about Jews was another thing that Kiki could not speak authoritatively about. Quite likely, I suspected, they weren't even aware of their existence. Certainly, it was quite obvious that the Jews I sometimes had to sit near, though never next to, on a hot and crowded trolley, in their long black coats and huge hats, with their beards and earlocks, had no place among the white-robed and sandaled Catholic residents of Heaven.

Once I was old enough to do such things on my own, Kiki informed me, I could get christened by a priest and become a Catholic like herself. Then, I too would be loved by God, Mary, their boy Jesus, the pigeon, and all the saints and angels. Then I too could aspire to ending my days in Heaven rather than among the Jews whom I had come to picture as riding sweaty trolleys through eternity.

And if terminal illness should befall me before the age of self-determination, Kiki assured me she was authorized to christen me herself. Against this eventuality, I learned the Lord's Prayer, the Hail Mary, and the Act of Contrition, all of which I recited fervently at bedtime.

I would attend mass with Kiki, say the rosary she lent me, and feel the benevolence of God as He looked down on us from his special perch over the altar. He had his head inclined to one side, which I saw as an expression of kindly concern for our well-being. That he had no clothes on, I took as some sign of purity that, with maturity, I would come to understand.

What I did come to understand was that this was just a statue of God that somebody had made out of stone, like the one of Frederick Chopin in the park. But at the same time that it was only a carved statue, it was also God because God was everywhere. The fact that it was a carved statue and, at the same time, God, who could hear our prayers and our praise of him, was a mystery, which I was very proud that I appreciated. I wondered how many other children my age understood such deep things—certainly not my Jewish cousins.

Then Kiki introduced me to the real world. That was not even God up there, she said, but his other son Big Jesus. And that wasn't a special perch, but a cross he had been nailed to. And it was we, Jews, who had nailed him there.

Now I understood everything. I understood why God didn't allow Jews into Heaven. And I despaired that I happened to have been born one of them. Because questioning God's actions was arrogance of immense proportions, I willed myself into not wondering why God had consigned my soul to a Jewish existence when he could have so easily had me born into a Catholic family. But it was fortunate that I had as my governess someone like Kiki who could eventually bring me into the circle of God's love.

Sin, or rather the lack of it, I understood to be another ingredient in the scheme of things. Catholics, I learned, could get their sins absolved through confession followed by communion. But since this therapy was not available to me, sinning was something I simply had to avoid if I didn't want to end up riding sweaty trolleys.

There were two occasions on which I came close to damning my immortal soul. One was when, for what reason I don't know, I insisted on putting on my blue woolen sailor suit for our daily trip to the park instead of the one Kiki had selected. After an exchange in which Kiki told me the day was much too hot for such a costume, she totally surprised me by not overruling me, but letting me have my way. Walking to the park and sweating from the heat, I felt as though I had broken all Ten Commandments at one blow. If deep contrition could eventually neutralize sin, I must have stored up credit for ten years of debauchery in that one walk.

The other occasion involved the proper replacement of my toys in the space beside the cupboard in our room. Apparently I had not conformed to code and, after reprimanding me, Kiki got down on all fours to make order out of my chaos between the cupboard and the exterior wall.

On sudden impulse, I laid both hands against her bathrobed backside and pushed. Kiki's head banged against the wall in front of her. I was immediately wracked with guilt, though for some reason this act did not have as heavy an impact on my conscience as the issue of the wool sailor suit.

Then there was the terrible secret. This was not a moral issue, but a medical one. It appeared that the smooth, reddish skin on the tip of the organ through which I urinated and which we called my birdie, had the property of causing insanity if touched beyond what was necessary for elimination and hygiene.

"Touching your birdie will make you crazy," I was told. Since this had not been presented in a morals context, but simply as a medical fact, I did not associate the act in any way with Heaven and trolley cars. But lying in bed at night, I simply could not resist slipping my hand below the covers for momentary contact of one fingertip with that dangerous organ. Some day, I knew, as no one else did, I would be as crazy as my Uncle Benek who, must have done the same thing in his youth.

Within walking distance of our apartment there was a public park. This park, I understood, had been a royal residence and contained a palace that one could tour with felt slippers over one's street shoes. Its walls were gilded, and there were paintings on these walls in huge gold frames, depicting a variety of activities featuring either vastly overdressed or underdressed— some even totally undressed—people. Something Kiki must have said, or possibly her body language, led me to understand that there was a significant similarity between the overdressed people and the friends of my mother whom I occasionally saw in our apartment with their hats and veils, jewelry, fur stoles, and cigarettes. They walked funny, and occasionally patted my cheek and gave me smelly kisses. "Painted women," I had overheard Kiki and Marta call them. Overdressing I understood to be pretentious and improper. Because Kiki expressed no opinion regarding the underdressed or undressed ones, I took this as approval. Nor did I miss the connection to the saintly and equally naked Jesus above the altar of Kiki's church.

The painting I remember most vividly is of a king seated on a throne with a sword in one hand and a baby held up side down by one foot in the other. This, I had come to understand, was King Solomon, Poland's smartest king.

Beside a pond in the park, I remember a huge bronze sculpture of the composer Frederick Chopin, seated under a wind-blown willow. Peacocks walked the park paths, occasionally displaying their beautiful tails.

To this park, Kiki and I would walk every morning. Along the way we would stop at a butcher shop—white tiled floor, walls, and ceiling—to have sandwiches made for our lunch. Mine would always be boiled ham, Kiki's sausage. Sometimes, in the park, Kiki would give me a tiny bite of her delicious sausage sandwich, but I understood that it was bad for me.

Along our way, we would pass a stand of doroshkas, the horse-drawn cabs that still served Warsaw, and I would look with envy at the drivers on their tall seats, eating bread and long shafts of sausage. When I grew up, I decided, I would be a doroshka driver.

Sometimes, people in the street would all be stopped, their necks craned and their arms extended upward, pointing. That meant there was an airplane overhead. Kiki and I would crane our necks, too, scanning the sky for the little silver cross. "There it is! Look, there it is!" we would point out to each other.

Usually I went to the park under arms, a sword hanging from my left hip, a pistol strapped to my waist, and a balloon tied to one of the shirt buttons holding up my short pants. In the park, Kiki would sit on a bench and knit a sweater or short pants for me, or she would read from a tiny book. I was instructed to play, but not to get dirty or talk to any children we didn't know. Since I knew no other children besides my cousin Anita, her cousin Andy, and another cousin of mine named Fredek, and since they all lived in a different part of town and came to our park only by special arrangement between governesses, I never did figure out what I was supposed to do.

I would walk up and down the paths and soon find myself not in the presence of the bronze Frederick Chopin under his willow or the blue and green peacocks, but the underdressed men and women of the non-offensive palace paintings. The overdressed ones I had adopted Kiki's distaste for, but the lounging, uncovered ladies would get up from their beds and their chaises and serve me plums and oranges and tell me how glad they were that I had come to visit. Men and women would stop whatever it was they were doing to each other and invite me to participate.

Sometimes I would encounter other children running after each other, shooting their guns and waving their swords. But knowing full well that any disobedience of Kiki was likely to lead to trolley cars, I would ignore them and return to my soft-voiced and soft-bodied ladies and their muscular friends.

On occasions when one of the cousins came to visit in our park with his or her governess, or we went to their park, the governesses would sit together on the bench, and we, children, would be sent off to play, but nicely.

Anita and Andy always came together and had an agenda of their own, to which I could find no access. I would walk or run behind them, but had little understanding of what they were doing. Fredek always welcomed my company to help him get revenge on someone. He would tell me that we must sneak up on some Charlie or Joe, and I must hold him while Fredek kicked him in the belly. Sneak around the park as we might, much to my relief we never did encounter either Charlie or Joe, though on returning to our governesses, Fredek would describe at length and with mounting excitement how he had punished the offender, until his governess acknowledged that it was time they were getting on home.

Marta's niece came from the country to work for us. She must have been in her teens and slept on a cot in Marta's room, off the kitchen. That cot and Marta's bed filled the room practically wall to wall. The girl's name was Susan. She was to do the cleaning in our apartment while Marta tended to the cooking.

I hated Susan. I would punch her and kick her legs whenever she was within reach and no one was watching. One day, Susan was polishing the hardwood floor in the salon with a device that was a broom stick with a heavy, flat, iron weight at the bottom around which you wrapped rags. I went over to her and began kicking her shins. Suddenly the question of why I was doing this occurred to me. Susan had done me no harm. She was just a girl living in a tiny room in a strange family's apartment, trying to make a living, and I was hurting her. Why in the world did I want to hurt her?

The fact that I was hurting an innocent, vulnerable person— she never fought back—hit me like thunder. Why? Why? I was filled with a strange desire to hold her and say comforting things to her. I wished terribly that what I had done could be made not to have happened.

I don't know if there were such things as pet shops in Warsaw at that time. Puppies, however, were commonly sold on the street by men from the country who stood on the sidewalk, holding a puppy, with several more tucked into the pockets of their heavy peasant jackets. Whenever we passed one, my heart would melt at the sight of the puppy's head sticking out from between the man's hands. I knew I couldn't have one, and my soul cried for a puppy to love. I would have settled for a cat, if I had had to, but the hunger for a dog that I could love and hold and stroke was more than I could bear at times. Lying in bed at night, I would sometimes fantasize myself playing with a dog. I could actually feel his soft round head against my palm and his little legs tucked under him in my lap. Then I would break down into tears and turn my mind to prayer to ease the pain.

One day when my grandmother was visiting from Lodz, she accompanied Kiki and me on a walk. I don't remember where we were going, but we came across a man selling puppies on the corner and stopped. How much did he want for the puppy, my grandmother asked. My heart wanted to leap to the sky for joy. But my brain knew better by then. It held my heart in check, knowing well the odds for disappointment. When my grandmother and the man from the country could not come to terms, I was able to walk on.

A major problem was with toothpaste tubes. Every morning and evening, I would carry the toothpaste that Kiki and I shared, along with my toothbrush and towel, to my parents' bathroom, if it was free, or the kitchen sink, if it wasn't. As the toothpaste tube became exhausted, I would be aware of a great sadness. Soon it would be empty and discarded into the trash, and we would start a brand new, strange tube from a box.

As the life of the old tube wound to a close, I would take less and less paste on my brush and perform heroics of rolling, unrolling, flattening, and pressing to extend its life by one more day. I would look down on its flattened, twisted body, knowing that it would soon be going into the garbage, and tears would come into my eyes. When reality could no longer be denied and a sleek new tube replaced the faithful old friend, I was depressed and resentful. I knew how ridiculous this was, but I could not help myself. If ever I needed proof that the abuse of my birdie was having its consequences, I had it in this bizarre response to what I knew to be a natural life process.

I remember a party in our apartment. The dining room table had disappeared and been replaced by several small tables covered with red-and-white checked tablecloths. To our polished wood and silk chairs, had been added other polished wood and silk chairs, but of a different style, and the dining room, as I walked through it on the way to and from the kitchen, was an empty restaurant with unmatched chairs.

For a while, I was a waiter with my handkerchief over my wrist, serving imaginary food with sweeping gestures to beautiful imaginary people. I took orders for chicken and rice with yellow, lemony sauce; cold borscht with sour cream; chopped spinach scrambled with an egg, and sausage, all on an imaginary pad, and then swept up menus with a flourish that impressed even me.

In the park, later that day, I fanaticized being allowed to serve at that evening's party.

Then, after Kiki and I had had our supper in our room and I was in my nightshirt and bathrobe, the guests began to arrive. Because our room was off the entrance hall, near the front door, I could peek (Kiki surprised me by allowing me to do this) through the crack in the not-quite-closed door, at the arrival—the men in identical tuxedoes and the women in sparkling, frilly, floor-length gowns in various colors, with bare shoulders under their fur stoles, and naked backs. Kiki, I remember, sat at our table reading a little book. From the look on her face, I could tell she was in a bad mood.

My mother came into our room at one point, carrying a plate with funny things on it and a glass with wine that had bubbles. She had on a gown of a shiny black material that clung very tight to her body, except that just at the knees it flared out because there were what I now know to be called pleats, with a bright green material on the inside. When she stood still, you could just see a thin green line, but when she walked, the green flashed in a wider or narrower wedge. The stark simplicity of the black dress with its flashing green wedge, topped by

Mother's deep gold hair and emerald earrings, was absolutely the most beautiful sight I had ever seen.

Kiki would not have any of the wine or the funny things on the plate, and she told Mother that I had already had my dinner and brushed my teeth. Then the two of them walked to the window at the other end of the room and started to talk in hushed voices.

Kiki had to look up to talk to my mother. "That's much too late," I heard her say in a very emphatic tone. "Much too late."

I could tell by Mother's body language that she acquiesced, and she left the room nodding her head and carrying the wine and the funny things. Kiki went back to her book.

After a while, a strange woman in a maid's uniform came into our room. "She says to come now," she said over my head to Kiki. Then she pulled up her skirt, adjusted her stocking, and left the room.

"Come here," Kiki said to me, almost as though she were angry at me. I walked over cautiously. She reached for my hairbrush and smoothed my freshly washed hair. Then she stood up, took me by the hand, and we marched out into the hall. I had no idea where we were going.

The guests were all sitting or standing in the salon, and all turned the same way as though for a performance. For a moment I thought someone would be doing magic tricks. But we walked to an empty chair in front of everyone, and I realized I was going to have to recite. Kiki told me to stand on the chair. "Say the poem, 'I'm Not Afraid Of Anyone'," she said.

I had had to recite poems before, for my grandparents or an aunt and uncle, but never for this kind of audience. But I knew the poem well and had been taught to recite in a firm voice its braggadocio lines about even facing down tigers. Kiki didn't need to prompt me even once.

The applause was tremendous and people shouted "encore," which I knew meant more. I knew a song that Marshal Pilsudski's brigade used to sing, which I thought would go well with the tone of the poem, and I began to sing it, but Kiki took me by the hand, dismounted me from the chair, and marched me out of the room. I was still singing as we went out the door.

A few minutes later, one of the ladies with a rouged face, and a frilly blue gown with bare shoulders came into our room with a plate of those funny things again. "You sweet, sweet boy," she said, kissing me. She smelled of perfume, liquor, and cigarettes. She took one of the funny things in her fingers and indicated that I should open my mouth. It was the most awful thing I had ever tasted, but I didn't let on.

"You've done a wonderful job with him, Miss Yanka," she said to Kiki.

"Thank you, Madam," Kiki said. Then the woman placed the plate on the table, kissed me again, and swished out. Kiki picked up the plate and slid its contents into the wastebasket.

My grandparents on my mother's side, lived in the city of Lodz, an hour or so away by an express train called The Torpedo. As I remember, it consisted of just two highly stream-lined, self-propelled cars and no engine. A couple of times a year, Kiki and I would pack our bags and take The Torpedo to spend a few days with the grandparents. I was usually sick the day before departure, and the morning of the trip we would rise early and try to eat breakfast. But the anxiety over not missing the train made me unable to eat, and Kiki and I would sit at the little table in our room as she tried to will the food down my throat, while she continually checked her little gold wristwatch.

This was the one occasion when I would, regularly, see Kiki's will overcome by circumstances. It was not intentional on my part, but I simply could not get the food down, and eventually her anxiety for the train would overcome her resolve, and we would dash for the train station—there to sit on our suitcases as train after train was called before ours began to board.

Grandfather was many years older than Grandmother. He was in a wheelchair, paralyzed from the waist down, diabetic, and attended by a man named Francishek. Poking out of Grandfather's left pant leg was something I first took for the end of a sword scabbard, but realized later it was a rubber incontinence device.

Grandfather was an Orthodox Jew. When he was not at the hosiery factory he owned, he would sit at the dining room table reading what must have been a religious book. Because of this reading and his advanced years, I had to walk on tiptoe all the time I was there. I remember trying to figure out why this was necessary even when he was at the factory and eventually coming to the conclusion that the entire household must have been accustomed to quiet. I was very proud of this deduction.

Every afternoon, Grandfather would ride in his carriage around the park. Grandfather had his own carriage, his own horse, and his own driver named Adam. Kiki and I would accompany him on these rides, Kiki beside Grandfather in the carriage and I on the driver seat beside Adam. Adam was missing most of the index finger of his right hand. I knew instinctively that I shouldn't look at it, but it drew my eyes the same way that my birdie pulled at my hand. I was happy to distinguish this as only a social rather than a mental health transgression.

When we got to the park, Adam would let me hold the reins. I knew no greater happiness in my childhood than sitting beside Adam with the reins in my hands.

One day at the dinner table—Kiki and I ate in the dining room at my grandparents—Grandfather choked on a piece of meat and died. Francishek and somebody else carried him into the next room while Grandmother screamed, and a doctor who lived upstairs was hastily summoned. But Grandfather was dead. It turned out to have been his heart and not a piece of meat.

It was decided that my mother, the youngest of his eight children, should not be told of his passing. I reasoned that by not seeing him or hearing from him for awhile, my mother would gradually arrive at the realization that Grandfather had passed away, without experiencing the shock that a sudden announcing of his death might have caused.

This theory proved pretty much correct when my mother telephoned from Warsaw on the following day and asked to speak to me.

"Don't tell Mother that Grandfather is dead," everyone mouthed as I was handed the receiver, even though I had already been briefed on this conspiracy.

"How are you today?" Mother asked.

"I'm fine," I said. Speaking on the phone was a new experience for me since no one had ever asked to talk with me before.

"And how is Kiki?"

"She's fine too."

"And Grandmother?"

"Grandmother is fine."

"And how is Francishek?"

"Francishek is fine."

"And Adam?"

"Adam is fine."

"And how is the horse?"

"The horse is fine."

Then she blindsided me. "And how is Grandfather?"

"Grandfather is dead," I told her.

I did not need the looks of horror around me to inform me that I had broken down under interrogation.

"Grandfather is asleep," Grandmother mouthed.

"No, no," I corrected myself. "I meant he's asleep. He's sleeping," before the receiver was abruptly pulled from my hand.

I remember no pain at Grandfather's passing. There had been no closeness between us. He was just an old man I was supposed to love . . . quietly. This does not mean that I was a stranger to grief. Every second Sunday, Kiki had her day off. At these times, I was overcome by an emotional agony that

I could neither bear nor understand. I knew that Kiki was coming back that night, but I would still find myself lying face down in the front hall, bellowing out my pain like a cow.

There was no consoling Yulian. However, Mother and one or two of her perfumed friends would sometimes try by taking me to one of the cafes for which Warsaw was famous, and I would be allowed to order any delicacy I chose. Making choices was a foreign experience for me.

The decision always came down to two kinds of cheese-cake, Viennese and Krakow. The former was fairly light with a powdering of confectionery sugar. The Krakow version was richer with some brown pastry strips over the top. All the cafes seemed to carry both varieties and the choice was always dif-ficult, though the decision invariably came down in favor of the native Krakow style.

But even the taste of the cheesecake, consumed in a few minutes, did not cancel my pain. To this day, cheesecake has a bittersweet taste for me.

On several occasions, it was my stepfather, Lolek, who applied a masculine solution to my problem. One time we took a taxi ride into the country and back, which did little for me. Another time, he took me to the movies where two comedians, one fat, one thin, were featured. They were named Flip and Flap, and whether these were Laurel and Hardy dubbed into Polish or a home grown version, I don't know. The results were not much better than with the cheesecake, though I'm not aware of any residual emotions triggered by Laurel and Hardy.

I can remember few other efforts at any bonding between me and my parents. There was the time Lolek returned from some foreign trip with toy soldiers for me. I, of course, already owned a couple dozen three-dimensional lead soldiers, about two inches high in brightly colored uniforms. The ones Lolek had brought me were about half that height and only two dimensional, but there were hundreds of them. My mind arranged them in both parade and battle order as he and I opened box after box of marching, charging, and shooting soldiers on the dining room floor.

I thanked Lolek profusely, motivated by both well-schooled manners and the sincerest gratitude. But I couldn't have them, he said, until I kissed him on the lips.

This was a total shock to me. I had never kissed anybody on the lips, and I found the very idea disgusting. I didn't get my soldiers that day, but they did appear, some months later, in my cupboard. On another occasion, my mother and Lolek tried to get me into bed between them one morning. This was more intimacy than I could handle, and I remember kicking and screaming.

There was also the time my mother was assisting Kiki in giving me a bath, and asked which of them I loved more. "I love you both the same," I pronounced, congratulating myself on my diplomacy, while marveling at Mother's stupidity in thinking that my love for her could, in any way, approach what I felt for my inseparable Kiki.

"You must love your mother more," Kiki immediately admonished me. "You must always love your mother more than anyone else."

On my fifth birthday I remember receiving a telegram from my mother. One hundred years, it wished me, a barrel of wine, and a beautiful wench. In Polish it rhymes and may well be a standard birthday wish under certain circumstances. The next time that my mother and Kiki met, I overheard my governess murmuring something about how madam must have been drunk.

What I remember of summers, Kiki and I spent in a resort town on the Baltic Sea. If we turned right coming out of our hotel, we could walk to the bay. If we turned left, we walked to the beach on the open sea and played in the sand or the mild surf. We would float in the shallow water supporting and propelling ourselves with our hands against the bottom, pretending that we were swimming. When we walked around the town, we would hold pinkies, it being too hot to hold hands.

Recently, I came across a photograph of the two of us in that town. I was surprised to find that, though I was always small for my age, at six or seven, when that picture was taken, I wasn't much shorter than Kiki. The photograph confirms my memory of her long blond braid wound around her head. She has a kindly, but tired face. Though I know she was no more than thirty, she looks older. I suspect her health was not robust.

The start of school was something that I had looked forward to since I could remember. Students wore little navy blue uniforms with colored stripes down the sides of long trousers, and brass buttons on their tunics. They had billed military caps, and they marched in parades carrying flags and singing patriotic songs. Had the afterlife not been so weighty a subject for me at the time, I might now be resorting to the cliche, "my idea of Heaven."

September 1938 came, and Kiki took me by the hand to first grade. And someplace between the dream and reality a cog must have come loose.

It would be fashionable, or perhaps cute, Mother must have decided, if the school I attended were to be French. There was such a school within a few blocks of our house, set up, I presume, for the children of French families stationed in Poland. Because it did not have its own facilities, it rented them from another school in the afternoon, after normal school hours. And in the French fashion, its uniform was not long trousers with a colored stripe down the side and brass buttons, but a black smock with a Peter Pan collar, topped by a beret. A lifetime of dreams was shattered in one blow.

In my black smock and beret I was walked the several blocks to school each afternoon and walked home again, mercifully after dark.

The intent had been that I learn French. But the school did not teach French. It taught the three R's in French to French-speaking children.

I learned a number of things in this school. I learned, for example, that you could roll your pencil down the sloping desk surface, but it was sure to make the boy or girl, sitting beside you in the two-person desk, make a fuss to the teacher, which resulted in your being made to stand in the corner. I learned that if you had a pocket knife, which I of course didn't, you could cut long, sharp splinters out of the desk seat or even carve your own initials in it. I also learned that even though we weren't allowed to use pens, if you dipped your pencil in the inkwell that the morning kids used, you could make ink lines on paper with it. And then I discovered, purely on my own, that if you took chalk dust from the trough at the bottom of the blackboard and mixed it with the ink, you could get paste of various shades of blue, depending on how much ink you used. I also learned one French phrase, "Padowicz dans le coin!" It meant Padowicz into the corner, and I learned it through the technique of repetition. What I had done to merit this on most occasions, I never knew. But one way or another, I had made that part of our classroom my own. And since Warsaw was mostly obliterated by the Germans before the start of the following school year, I can say with reasonable certainty that I was its last occupant.

The other thing I had not counted on at this school was the behavior of children. In my fantasies, we had marched down the city's wide avenues in ruler-straight ranks, our brass shining in the sun, our long trousers in perfect step. But children, it turned out, took your snacks, turned your pencil box upside down, punched you in the arm or other places, pushed you down, yelled French obscenities in your face, and had bad breath. To none of these had I any effective response.

They did, of course, all speak Polish as well, and would do so when a message had to be delivered with particular accuracy, such as, "Go to the devil, you stupid!" And most of the recess-talk in the hall outside our classroom—we apparently did not have a yard—was, in fact, Polish. But they seemed to take great pleasure in addressing me in French, pointing their fingers at me, mimicking my facial expressions, and going into fits of laughter.

At first this surprised me. I knew about witches and giants and evil step parents whose nature—in fact their profession— was to do hurtful things. But the idea of ordinary individuals generating spontaneous anger and cruelty was simply outside my realm of experience. Then, when I noticed how many of them wore crosses and other religious medals around their necks, I finally understood what was taking place. It was not that I accused my tormentors of anti-Semitism—prejudice on a human level was not a concept to which I had yet been introduced. But the Heavenly variety was something with which I, of course, was well familiar. Clear as day, I suddenly saw in their treatment of me, the hand of the Almighty exacting due punishment for what we had done to His Son.

This realization did not mean that I automatically bowed my head to the inevitable. I remember one occasion during joint recess with the second grade, which we did one or two times a week, when I discovered a second grader with shiny metal rods strapped to both sides of one leg. In an effort, I suppose, to join what I obviously couldn't beat, I pointed to him and laughed. "Look at those things on his leg!" I said. I was immediately pummeled for my insensitivity.

When, at home that evening, I explained how I had acquired my bruises, my story apparently prompted a visit to the principal by my mother. I did not know about the visit until my classmates came to advise me of the fact, just before adding some black-and-blue marks to complement the ones that were just beginning to fade.

This time, I reported to Kiki that I had tripped on my way down the stairs and acquired the bruises bouncing off the walls as I tried to maintain an upright position. It was the first time I had ever lied to her. My mother did, however, take some occasion to point out how well the previous matter had been taken care of by my simply reporting it at home, and that this should convince me to continue the practice in the future.

A delegation of girls approached me at recess several days later to inform me in what was obviously a well-rehearsed speech, that they were sorry for Marina, but they were not sorry for me. Who Marina was and how she merited their pity, I do not know to this day. The fact that they did not harbor the same sympathy towards me, I took as a matter of course by then. I had already come to terms with the fact that I was not to be treated like other people. It may even have had some connection with my birdie.

Some weeks later, a chubby girl named Vana did offer me half of her banana at recess. Since I had my own orange, this was quite clearly a gesture of friendship rather than charity. While I accepted both the banana and the friendship, sharing with her my opinion of our fat and homely teacher, Mlle Pro, I could not have much respect for Vana's choice of friends and made no effort to extend our relationship beyond the one-recess stand.

In my parents' bedroom, there stood a radio. It was a magnificent polished wood and cloth structure, about the size of a present-day twenty-one-inch television, with two vertical glass dials. One dial had numbers etched into the glass, the other the names of cities like London, Paris, Berlin, and New York. When the radio was turned on, either the numbers on one dial or the cities on the other would light up. In the center was a round green eye by which you fine-tuned the apparatus. I was not allowed to touch any part of the machine.

When my parents were away, Kiki and Marta would frequently sit by this instrument and listen with great concern to news reports. It seemed that a war was coming with Germany. Sometimes we listened to speeches, on several occasions by Adolph Hitler. None of the three of us spoke German, but there was a hypnotic and frightening quality to his voice.

Marshal Jusef Pilsucki, the George Washington of twentieth-century Poland, had died a few years earlier, and his place as Poland's protector had been taken by a General Ritz-Smigwy. I remember that the general did not inspire in me the confidence that I would have had in the great marshal. Returning from the park where we went before school, Kiki and I would on occasion encounter the general as he walked, presumably to lunch, along one of the boulevards we crossed. In his silver-braided uniform, he would march with military strides along the sidewalk, followed by several officers and two or three men in civilian dress.

One day, it was decided that I should stop him and ask for his autograph. I was horror stricken by the idea, but those were my orders. The year before, Mother had returned from Vienna with a little white homburg for me and a box of visiting cards with my name embossed in letters you could feel with your finger. Mercifully, after being photographed in the homburg, I never had to remove the hat from its box again. The visiting cards remained equally undisturbed until the morning on which I was to confront the general. Kiki and I were instructed by my mother to wait along his route until he appeared, at which point I was to march forward, salute, and say, "Would the general please give me his autograph." Then I was to present him with the back of my visiting card and a pen.

To try and talk my way out of this plan, I knew would be futile. "Little soldiers obey orders," I had been taught, along with, "Little soldiers don't cry." Armed to the teeth with saber, pistol, and rifle, I was propelled at the appropriate moment into the general's path. Quaking with fear, I carried out my assignment without a hitch. The general returned my salute, took the card and the pen, and delivered his signature as requested.

"Thank you, General," I even adlibbed, turned on my heel, and marched back to my beaming governess. As we headed for home, we were overtaken by two of the general's civilian companions who demanded to inspect the card as well as my two firearms before releasing us. That evening, a third man appeared at the door of our apartment and asked numerous questions of my parents.

January thirteenth was my seventh birthday. That morning, a man in the knee-high boots of a manual laborer, was in our salon inflating balloons. In the dining room, the table was removed and the carpet rolled to one end of the room, three or four feet short of the wall, and covered with bed sheets. The carpet pad was similarly deployed at the other end.

Some time in the afternoon, children began arriving. Who they were, I had no idea. I knew Anita, Andy, and Fredek. I hoped none of the guests would turn out to be my classmates, and so far as I could tell, none were.

The same man I had seen earlier inflating balloons came out of the kitchen carrying a large carton. Setting it down, he went back for another. Kiki and Anita's governess reached into the cartons and proceeded to hand each child a rifle and an army hat. These were not the green uniform caps you saw on the street, but the tall red hats with the flaring square tops that the Ulans wore in parades. Then we were told to lie behind the rolled carpet and padding at both ends of the room and shoot at each other. A photographer appeared and took pictures with flash bulbs.

Some days later, I was shown a photograph clipped from the newspaper. It showed my guests shooting rifles from behind the carpet barricade. My mother was in the middle of the photograph, an Ulan hat cocked over one eye, a rifle to her shoulder. I did not seem to be anywhere in the picture.

At the end of the summer following my first grade year, Kiki and I returned from the shore to find Warsaw plastered with posters calling for volunteers for the army and donations of money and metal for armaments. We carried the contents of my piggy bank to a designated place. Whether they would be used to buy bullets or melted down for guns, I wasn't sure. Our car, I overheard, had been requisitioned by the government along with all other private cars. This was the first I had heard of our owning a car.

We were issued gas masks which we were instructed to wear slung over our shoulders in their canisters whenever we went outdoors. They had a hose in front connecting to the canister, the bottom of which must have been an air filter. The pistol and saber I wore to the park were toys, but my gas mask was real.

The reality of the gas mask was emphasized to me when I was told not to play with it. I looked forward to our first bombing raid, when I would be allowed to put it on. It had a terrible rubber smell, but it would be worth it. Then Kiki instructed me that after putting the mask on, I was to close my eyes tightly until the attack was over. She would lead me by the hand to the nearest shelter. This was dreadful news and, I believed, unfair. I had read all the instructions on posters and pamphlets, and not a word had been mentioned about closing your eyes inside the gas mask. I could visualize myself being led down the street in my mask like a blind elephant while others, adults and kids, watched the airplanes dueling overhead.

We tacked black paper over our windows and Marta became an air raid warden with an armband, a whistle, a flashlight, and a helmet in addition to her gas mask. We began digging trenches across our streets. Men and women would show up with shovels to dig into the earth in front of our house. I with my child-sized shovel and Kiki with a dustpan, went downstairs to help. Lolek was there, stripped to the waist in the August sun with the other men, heaving shovelfuls of dirt up onto the pavement. Kiki and I were put to smoothing the walls. There was singing and laughter.

"If the women could take their shirts off," I heard Lolek say, "we'd get this job done a lot faster." There was laughter all through the trench.

I experienced the confusing feeling of embarrassment at the content, amusement at the humor, and pride that it was my stepfather whose words everyone was laughing at. I looked at Kiki and was surprised to see her smile. I wondered whether she really found it funny or was humoring her employer.

Then the announcement came that the Germans had penetrated our border. Immediately there were sirens and more announcements on the radio. "Air raid on the city of Warsaw! Air raid on the city of Warsaw!" the announcer proclaimed. I ran out onto the balcony off our salon to pass the announcement on to people in the street. "Air raid on the city of Warsaw!" I shouted. I looked for airplanes in the sky.

Kiki pulled me by the hand back into the apartment. A reserve officer in the army, as I learned just then, Lolek was about to report for duty at the barracks. As I approached to say goodbye, Lolek caught sight of my wristwatch. It was a waterproof, shock resistant "pilot's" watch with a radium dial. I had received it for my birthday.

"I will need that watch in battle," Lolek said. "Mine is gold and could get damaged." With great reluctance, but knowing it my patriotic duty, I unbuckled my watch.

"Yulian has a knife," my mother said. She was referring to the small hunting knife in its leather sheath that I had been recently given as a symbol of trust in my maturity. "He would love for you to have it." I was sent to fetch that as well. The last time I saw Lolek for the next nine years, he was standing in the elevator strapping on my waterproof, shock resistant, pilot's watch with a radium dial, the handle of my hunting knife sticking out of his suit coat pocket.

We didn't go to the park any more. The following day Mother was up by the time Kiki and I had our breakfast. She was fully dressed in a dress that was attractive, but plain at the same time. I had seen Mother in a cocktail dress, a long evening gown, or a bathrobe, but never anything like this. She was on the telephone a great deal. Kiki's attention was fixed mostly on things other than me, and I felt a totally new sense of existence. Where I had been the epicenter of a small satellite world, I now felt a part of the real one. The loss of my wristwatch and hunting knife, the two symbols of my manhood, was no longer a factor. They, I knew, had only been symbols. This was reality.

I watched my mother, Kiki, and Marta packing cartons of canned and packaged food for storage in each of the apartment's rooms. This, I had been told, was in the event that the other rooms were destroyed by bombs or somebody was trapped in one room. The three women (I don't remember what had become of Susan) apportioned the food with great care, maintaining equality among the boxes' contents. Dried fruit, cellophane bags of bread, tins of meat and vegetables, jars of water, were all sealed with a wide tape and packed carefully. It was actually Marta who seemed to be directing the operation, my mother asking for and following instructions. There seemed to be a mutual respect among the three women that gave me a strange feeling of security and pleasure.

The air raid siren sounded several times that first day after Lolek's departure, and we moved in an orderly way into the front hall, the only room without windows, to sit on the floor and wait for the all-clear. Nobody needed to tell me what to do, and nobody tried.

We heard a rumbling in the distance. "Bombs," Marta said. It didn't sound anything like what I expected bombs to sound like. I had expected individual explosions, like the ones my cousin Fredek made with his mouth, not a continuous sound. It was the distance, I decided.

"Is it the barracks?" Mother asked.

"No," Marta assured her. "The barracks are in a residential area. It must be the factories."

"You're right," Mother said. "If they bombed the barracks, they might hit civilian homes." If they didn't bomb civilians, I wondered why we had packed those food boxes so diligently.

I knew I shouldn't be wishing for bombs to fall closer to us, and I struggled not to, with only partial success. I waited anxiously to go out after the air raid and see the damage, but Kiki said no to my suggestion.

Actually, it may have been voicing that wish that became my undoing. As soon as the air raid ended, Kiki set me to work writing a letter to my newly departed stepfather. While I had not learned much in my first year of school, Kiki had taught me the alphabet, and theoretically I was capable of scratching out a three-sentence letter on my own, an activity that would keep me occupied the better part of the next hour.

This brought my new reality of belonging and maturity to a sudden end. As I sat at the little table in my room and worked to shape the letters that would spell out the compulsory sentiments, I fanatisized a future relationship between me and Kiki in which I, a good six inches taller than she, announced my decision to take a walk to inspect the bomb damage, and Kiki, a paid employee after all, had little choice but to put on her sweater and accompany me.

My fantasy and my letter writing were both interrupted by Marta's announcement that the airport, only a short distance from our house, was on fire. We rushed, I with a newly found freedom, onto the balcony to see a huge cloud of black smoke floating towards our street.

As the four of us stood on two balconies, Kiki and I on one, my mother and Marta on another, I felt a presence in this dark, churning mass approaching our street. I saw it quite clearly as a masculine presence coming into my life. War was waged by men, and already this war had begun to loosen the controls with which women held me. Two days ago I would not have been permitted to dash that way from my letter to the balcony. Nor, I realized, would I have had the courage to try. In Kiki, standing beside me, I could see fear. I had never seen fear before, but in her face, as she looked at the on-coming cloud, I recognized fear.

Nobody told me to finish my letter, and I never did.

The telephone rang, and it was Lolek. They had not bombed the barracks. But they had destroyed some buildings nearby, he said.

"My God, they bombed civilians?" I heard Mother ask. They agreed it must have been a mistake. Kiki, Marta, and I stood in her bedroom as Mother sat on the bed and talked on the phone.

"When are the British and the French coming into the war?" she asked him. The answer didn't reassure Mother. "But they have to," she said. "They signed a treaty. People are being killed." It was common knowledge that as soon as Britain and France honored our mutual defense treaty and declared war on Germany, Hitler would back off.

That evening Kiki and I ate dinner with Mother in the dining room. We had eaten in the dining room before when certain guests were there, but this was the first time that it was just the three of us. We sat at the polished wood table with round ends and a carved edge. It must have seated six, and had extension leaves. There was a sideboard with the same carvings and a long, gilt framed mirror over it, suspended by cords from the molding at the top of the wall. The chair seats were padded silk and slippery.

As we waited for Marta to bring out the food, Mother said, "Let us ask God to watch over us and our loved ones at this time." She folded her hands and bowed her head. I saw Kiki cross herself and then do the same. Instinctively; I followed Kiki's example. Then, looking down into my folded hands, I realized what I had done in front of my mother. I did not look up again until I heard Marta come in with a tray.

I knew that Mother knew that I frequently accompanied Kiki to Mass. How much she had known about my being a closet Catholic, I had no idea. What she was thinking now, I had no idea.

Then I thought of the early Christian martyrs who, Kiki had told me, had gone gladly to be eaten by lions rather than deny their faith. And here I was afraid of risking my mother's displeasure on account of mine. This crossroads, I realized, was an opportunity—an opportunity to prove my faith to God. I raised my head. I had no idea what Mother would make of this, but, for the first time in my life, I knew God was on my side.

Come to think of it, Mother's reference to God was surprising. By now I knew that Jews sometimes went to a place called Son of Gaga to pray, ignorant of the deaf ear God turned in their direction, but I had never known them to pray at home like Christians. Was Mother committing blasphemy? Should she be confronted? Would true faith require me to defend God against such outrage? Then I realized that Kiki had not confronted Mother on this, and one could do worse than follow Kiki's example. I decided to let the matter drop.

But how can you deny the existence of a situation involving God? If I finked on my Christian duty, God would know it. Right then He may have been waiting for me to act. Oh Lord, he may even have instructed Kiki to be silent so as to test me.

I was totally willing to do the right thing, if I only knew what the right thing was. Was Mother using the Lord's name in vain? Was she pretending to be a Christian now when there was danger? What sin might that be? I wondered. Was she trying to get into God's favor now, while I had to prove my faith over and over with rosaries and abstinence from sin— while I had endured the taunts of my classmates and teacher?

No, I finally realized. Mother may be trying to win the favor of God, but God knew. He knew how I lived and how she did. Or in turning a deaf ear to Jews, did he also turn a blind eye?

"Why are you crying, Yulian?" Kiki said. I had no idea I had been crying. "He's tired," she said to my mother.

"Why isn't he eating?" Mother asked.

"It's been a very upsetting day," Kiki explained. I began to sob uncontrollably.

"Little soldiers don't cry," Mother said. She didn't say it unkindly.

"Let's go to our room," Kiki said. "We'll have our dinner there." She stood up and bent down to pick me up. I put my arms around her, and she lifted. But I was too heavy for her, and we fell to the floor together. There was a very long silence.

I looked at Kiki. "You're too big for me to carry any more, you big horse," she said.

I began to laugh. Kiki laughed. "I'm too big for you to carry any more," I repeated proudly.

"You big horse," she added.

"I'm a big horse, and you can't carry me any more," I said.

"You're too big for me to carry any more, you big horse." Then, instead of laughing, Kiki was crying.

Later, when she had tucked me into bed, Kiki sat down beside me and repeated what she had said that other evening in the bathroom. "Yulek," she said, "you must always remember to love your mother more than anyone else." Then she hugged me and left the room

When I woke up the next morning, Mother was in my room. She was having a cup of coffee and a cigarette at the little green table where Kiki and I ate our meals. She sat sideways to it like Kiki, because her knees wouldn't fit underneath. Mother's knees, in their silk stockings, showed when she sat like that. Kiki's dress always covered her knees.

"Where's Kiki?" I asked, already fearful of the answer.

"Well, Yulek, Kiki has had to go home to pack some things. She'll join us in a few days."

I fought back the tears that wanted to gush forth. After the burning airport experience yesterday, after the dinner table matter, I must never, never cry again. "J-join us?" I repeated.

"We're going to the country," Mother said. "Until the war is over. Kiki will join us on the way. You're going to have to be a very brave little soldier now."

There was no ignoring an appeal to God or to country. I got out of bed and stood stiffly at attention waiting for orders. "What should I put on?" I asked.

"What do you normally put on?" I had taken Mother by surprise.

"Kiki always tells me what to put on."

"Well, why don't you decide. You're a big boy now."

I had never had to make such a decision before. I opened my green cupboard and confronted a stack of neatly folded shirts. I had no idea I owned so many. Thankfully the under-wear was all the same, making decisions unnecessary. As I buttoned my underpants to my undershirt, I contemplated the stack of shirts. I finally settled on a blue one because it was on top. Applying the same reasoning to my selection of shorts—I owned no long trousers—I was soon in the kitchen washing. Marta had oatmeal ready for me when I finished. I sat at the enameled kitchen table forcing down the food. My heart was in tears over Kiki's departure, but my face remained at attention.

"My God, Yulian, you can't wear those green pants with that blue shirt!" Mother said, coming into the kitchen. "After breakfast, go back to your room and change." She refilled her coffee cup from the pot on the woodburning stove. "Marta, go back with him and find him something proper to wear."

"I think you look just fine," Marta muttered under her breath as I followed her back to my room after breakfast. "Where does she think you're going, to the opera?" The opera was Marta's expression for putting on airs. Going to the opera, making an opera, looking like an opera, dressing like for an opera, all described states of existence for which she held scorn. As she moved hurriedly through the apartment ahead of me in house slippers, a damp rag in her hand, I realized that Marta had begun to waddle.

She selected a tan shirt for me. "Here, put this on. Tan goes with everything." I put the shirt on while she folded the blue one and put it back in the cupboard. She couldn't fold it as neatly as Kiki.

"Here, let me fix your hair," she said. She took the comb from the shelf and proceeded to flatten my cowlick. "Oh Christ," she said when it wouldn't stay down. She put two fingers in her mouth, and applied saliva to my cowlick. "There, go show your mother." I hurried to my mother's bedroom for inspection, conscious of Marta's saliva on my head.

Mother was on the telephone facing away when I came in. She turned when she heard me. "Oh, good," she said. Then she gave a sigh of resignation. "Oh, nothing," she said into the telephone. "Marta just dressed Yulian up in a summer shirt and winter pants. Well, we all have to do the best we can." She turned back to me and placed a hand over the receiver. "Go pack, Yulian," she said. Then she yelled out, "Marta!" and then back to the telephone. "Sorry, dear. I was just calling Marta. She's going to stay in the apartment, you know. Marta!"

Marta waddled into the room. "Marta, be a dear and get a suitcase for Yulian. A small one."

I sat on my bed staring at the empty suitcase, the tears making my eyes blurry. There was a white cross in the paint on the wall above Kiki's bed where her crucifix had hung. The hairbrush my mother had given her for Christmas was gone from the shelf. She would brush out her braids every night, and her long hair would lie in soft gold waves over her shoulders and down below her elbows. It made her look like one of the saints, and I had begged her to wear it that way sometimes, but she never would. Sometimes when we were in the country in the summer, I could get her to weave it into one thick braid and let it hang down the middle of her back. Otherwise it was always in two braids wound around her head. She said she had never cut her hair in her life, except to trim the ends and make it even.

The picture of the two of us at the beach was gone too. We had been seated on a wooden crocodile, me in a white cotton beret, Kiki in a beach jacket over her bathing suit.

It was all right for me to cry, I decided, as long as no one saw me. No, it wasn't a matter of doing it in secret. Not crying in front of people was the most you could expect of someone my age. While I was too old to cry publicly over Kiki's departure, I was, after all, a little soldier, not a grownup one.

"Oh, my God," Mother said, coming into my room. "Didn't she teach you to pack?"

"I know how to darn my socks and wash them," I retorted. "And I can crochet." I was lying. I could only crochet a chain; Kiki hadn't yet taught me to do rows. But Mother wouldn't know that. "Kiki also taught me all the letters and two times everything." She had also taught me how to brush her hair, counting one hundred strokes on the right and one hundred on the left, but I had a feeling that that skill would not be accredited.

"All right," she sighed, squatting by the open suitcase. "Bring me your underwear."

"What should I do now?" I asked when the suitcase was full and snapped closed.

"I have to make some phone calls," Mother said.

This did not answer my question, but she left the room. I ran after her down the hall. "What should I do now?" I repeated.

"I have to make some important phone calls now, Yulek," she said over her shoulder.

"But what should I do?!" I demanded.

"Go back to your room and read," she said. I turned back to my room.

I had a bookcase of books in my room, from many of which Kiki had read to me. Many I had received as gifts to be appreciated in future years. Most of these were in leather bindings with gold letters, and either had no pictures in them or, if they did, they were just black and white sketches.

I stood in front of the bookcase and realized that I had never selected a book before. What, I wondered, was to stop me from selecting one of the grown-up ones, one I hadn't already heard several times? I pulled one out at random and began sounding out the words. To my surprise they were no more difficult than the words in the books Kiki had given me to read before, except that the letters were smaller. I had never read with no one in the room before. "It was," I began aloud, "the best of times." I flipped back to see if I had missed something. I hadn't. The book began with, "It was the best of times." All right. But then it contradicted itself. "It was the worst of times," it said. I closed the silly book and put it back on the shelf.

I took out the one about the poor woman with the three sons and no food. But I had already heard that one so many times. I looked over the grown-up books again. One was larger than the others, but thinner. Large pages usually meant pictures. I pulled it out and opened it. There was a colored picture of a sailing ship, leaning down so low it looked like it was going to roll over. It literally made me lose my breath. The sails were so full of wind and the waves leaping so high, like wolves trying to get at the sailors. And the ship looked as if it was sailing faster than it was ever supposed to sail. I spent a long time feasting on that one picture. There were little, tiny sailors up in the rigging, I noticed. How windy and slippery it must be up there.

When I finally turned the page, the next picture was of medieval soldiers in battle. There was silver armor shining in the sun, several men on horseback fighting a lot of men on foot with swords and spears. The horses had huge round muscles, and their necks were arched so their chins almost touched their chests. One soldier, I saw, was lying on the ground dying. He had his hand up to protect himself, but a horse was about to back over him. I didn't like that picture at all. The one after that was another battle scene, and I flipped past it quickly.

The next one was of a lady with no clothes on lying on a bed, having something done to her toenails. It was like the ones in the palace in the park, and I immediately felt comfortable with it. I felt what a special lady she must be to let herself be seen without her clothes, when I couldn't stand to have anyone but Kiki or my mother see me naked, and the way Kiki used to cover up if she and I had to change in the same room at the beach. I had a strong desire to touch this lady. She would feel so soft, and I knew she would be kind. She would invite me to have some of whatever it was that she had in her cup, unless, of course, it was wine or beer. But I had the feeling that with her it would be hot chocolate or tea with honey and milk in it—certainly not lemon. She would tell me a story about a beautiful princess and a handsome prince, and there would be no witch or stepfather or giant or dragon or evil magician, knight, or king. It would just be about a prince and princess who met and fell in love and lived happily ever after in a beautiful castle.

She and I would both live in the castle, except that I'd be grown up, and we would walk around the gardens together, and the prince and princess would be like our children and we would watch them as they played, and sometimes we would take them to the beach and she and I would sit under an umbrella on a blanket as they built sand castles. The waves would come up on the beach and wash the castles away, and we would tell them not to cry and help them build a new castle up above where the waves couldn't reach it.

And then the air raid siren sounded. Mother's high-heeled footsteps were in the hall. "Come in here, Yulian!" she called.

I was immediately back from the beach and terribly aware of Kiki's departure. I walked into the hall and sat in one of the chairs that someone had placed there. I was not going to cry.

"Why don't I tell a story!" Mother said. She bounced up and down on her chair in enthusiasm. I didn't say anything, and Marta mumbled a few words about how nice that would be. Mother proceeded to tell the story of the Three Little Pigs. But she got it wrong. She had the wolf go to the house built of sticks first and then the one built of straw. And she didn't even know the little rhyme the wolf recited each time he went to blow down one of the houses. And at the very end, when the wolf is in the kettle of boiling water under the chimney and the Three Little Pigs are playing their fiddles, she had one playing the drums and another playing the organ. It's one of the Seven Dwarfs in Snow White who plays the organ.

I sat in my chair scratching my knee, my elbow, the side of my leg, my head, all to show her that I wasn't listening to her story.

"Yulian, don't scratch," Mother said. I dropped my hands by the sides of the chair.

Each time the bombs rumbled somewhere, Mother would stop and take a deep breath. She would tighten her lips and turn her eyes towards Marta, without shifting her head, as though I couldn't see what she was doing. Then she went on to do Jack and the Bean Stalk, and totally left out the Magic Harp. I sucked on my upper lip, making quiet sucking noises and examining a scab I had just rediscovered on my knee. I realized that I actually found great pleasure in her getting the stories all wrong. I presumed Marta recognized her mistakes as well.

"Stop picking your knee!" Mother said, louder than I'm sure she meant to. I swung my feet back and forth above the floor and switched to sucking my lower lip.

Then we heard a loud whistle. It was followed by a loud crash, and our three chairs lifted a little ways off the floor. I knew all about bombs. Kiki had told me about the exploding shells the cannons fired in the Big War twenty years before. Her brother had been a soldier then and buildings that he was in shook just like this.

"My God! What are they doing?" Mother said. She ran through the salon and began opening the balcony doors. I saw Marta take off after her, and I ran after Marta. She held Mother around the waist and was pulling her away from the doors. Marta, I realized, was much bigger than Mother. I had always thought of Mother as tall, because she was taller than Kiki.

"Madam must come away from the balcony," Marta was saying in the awkward, third-person way that Polish grammar does those things. I was in a bind. I was wishing Mother would open the balcony doors with their blackout paper so I could see what was happening in the street. On the other hand I was happy to see Mother admonished. Then I remembered Kiki's command to love my mother, and I realized I wasn't doing that.

Then our house shook again. The sound and the shaking were bigger than before. A chunk of plaster, the size of my green table, fell from the ceiling between me and the two grownups. I looked at Mother and Marta standing there together and they looked at me as though there were a crater between us. None of us seemed able to move.

Then I was the one who had crossed it. I had crossed the three or four feet of salon floor and crumbled plaster that had separated us and I was kicking at Mother's legs.

"What are you doing? Yulian, Yulian, what are you doing? Stop that, Yulian! Yulian, stop it!" Mother and Marta were both shouting. I remembered the way I had been kicking Susan in that same room when I was smaller, and I stopped and ran back to my room and jumped onto Kiki's bed. I was crying from the pain and from the embarrassment, and I had my eyes shut tightly. There were hands picking me up, and when I smelled my mother's perfume close to me I pushed away. I didn't want to be hitting her any more, but I was pushing with my hands wide open in the dark behind my closed eyelids. Then she released me, and I felt Marta's large, dry hands on my sides, and I let her pick me up and hold me to her.

I pressed my face hard against her neck and wondered why I had done what I had. Why did I hate my mother so? Why did it please me when she told stories wrong? Why was I happy to see Marta holding her and her thrashing around like that? And, of course, why had I started kicking her legs without any thought even about what I was doing? I knew it wasn't a Christian thing to do—I would be punished for it some day. Was it because I was really Jewish, and I could pretend to be a

Catholic, but could never really be one because Jews had bad in them? Or was it from touching my birdie?

Kiki would explain it all to me when she joined us. I had never told her about touching my birdie. How do you explain to someone why you persisted in doing something that gave absolutely no reward, but only did something terrible, like make you go crazy? It was a crazy thing to do, and to do it, you had to be a little crazy already. So maybe it was the Jewish that made you a little crazy to start with—crazy enough to touch your birdie when you knew it would make you more crazy. But then, if that were so, then all Jewish men would be crazy. How did I know they weren't? The only Jewish men I knew were Lolek and my late grandfather. Was Lolek crazy? He certainly wasn't crazy like my Uncle Benek—I had forgotten that I knew Uncle Benek too, and he certainly was crazy—everyone knew that. But then, my grandfather certainly hadn't been crazy. So I figured that theory wasn't right.

But I would tell Kiki when I saw her tomorrow or the next day. And I would stop touching my birdie. Yes, that was what I would do. I could do it. Poland was at war. Soldiers were marching into battle to be shot at, maybe killed, by the Germans. They were sleeping in tents on blankets on the ground. I could certainly discipline myself enough to never touch my birdie again. Then I could help Kiki serve food to soldiers at the railroad station, as she had done during the World War. I would not go crazy, but be available to serve my country.

No, I would not tell Kiki about touching my birdie. As long as I was going to stop it, it would be all right, and I wouldn't need to talk to anyone about it, would I? And it would remain my great secret.

The all-clear had sounded some while ago, and I realized Marta must be tired of holding me. Besides, I was, in a sense, a soldier now on a special, secret mission. I disengaged myself from her arms, and she lowered me to the floor. Mother was not in the room.

I had not asked God for a sign. I hadn't known that to be negotiable. Nevertheless, I received one. On our dining room table, rested a street lamp.

Our dining room table was on the floor now, or most of it, anyway, one leg still upright and the tracks connecting the two sliding halves and supporting the leaves, shattered. And on top of our splintered table lay a street lamp.

We were on the fourth floor, and it had found its way to our dining room window and landed on our dining room table. It wasn't the entire street lamp. But it was the important part, the part that actually lit up and was so high above the sidewalk that you could never hope to touch it. And there it was with its iron parts that you could never get close enough to see properly, shaped to look like leaves along a tree branch and the glass globe all broken, and thick, golden wire in colored wrapping, and the remains of the biggest light bulb I had ever seen.

I knew it was for me—what would either Mother nor Marta want with a street lamp? God had found my new determination pleasing, and was both telling me so and rewarding me for it. Marta was already sweeping up the broken glass and wood, but I knew she wouldn't be able to move my street lamp.

There were pieces of glass, curved ones from the lamp and flat ones from our window, imbedded in the plaster walls. It was so real.

I approached the street lamp for a closer look. "Don't touch it!" Marta shouted. "It could still have electricity in it!" I backed off at her command, though I doubted her reasoning. It could not have flown all this way from the street, crashed through our window, shattered our dining room table, and still have electricity left in it. Besides, God would not have given it to me in that condition.

On the other hand, it suddenly occurred to me, maybe that was exactly what God was doing. I had resolved not to ever touch my birdie again, and God was testing me by giving me something which, if I touched it just the slightest, would kill me. It wasn't that God was trying to kill me, I understood. What God was actually doing was showing His confidence in me by tempting me with something that would not just make me crazy some time in the future from excessive touching, but could make me dead on the spot. And He knew and I knew that I would not touch it.

I watched Marta sweep carefully around it, leaving a shadow of debris on the floor where she would not let her broom come too close. My fingers ached to run over the carved metal, my eyes to feast close up on the broken giant light bulb. But I knew I must resist it. Whether it had electricity in it or not, I did not know. But I knew God wanted me to perform this exercise. If Kiki only knew! I couldn't wait to tell her.

Then I helped Marta clean up the room. We leaned the broken parts of the tabletop against a wall, and Marta found a box to hold all the splinters. We put new blackout paper over the broken window. When it was all done, I went back to my room. I didn't need anyone to tell me what to do this time. I lay down on my bed and thought about my street lamp and God and his testing of me and my vow and my new awareness of my sense-less hostility towards Mother which I was about to change, and how grown up I had become in that one morning.

Marta woke me up for lunch. She had set places for the two of us at the kitchen table. Mother ate off a tray in her bed-room. It occurred to me to feel sorry for her eating alone after the way I had treated her. I couldn't tell whether I was actually feeling sorry for her or just knew that I should be. I wondered when we were supposed to start our trip, and when Kiki would be joining us.

It was almost my bedtime when Mother and I finally left the house. She had two suitcases, I had the one she had packed for me. Marta had come out and found us a doroshka. It had taken her some time. With cars, including taxis, all mobilized for military use, doroshkas were in great demand. Then Marta had hugged me, and she and Mother had even hugged each other briefly.

There were no lights on, and it was difficult to see anything. There were holes in streets and buildings. Some buildings, I could see, had spilled into the street, and there were always people doing something there. As we passed one place like that, Mother said, "Don't look, Yulian," and covered my eyes with her hand. I struggled to see, but couldn't see anything anyway. In one street we had to turn around and go a different way because the street was blocked by fire trucks and a crowd of people.

I was pretty sure we weren't heading for the railroad station. Then I recognized where we were; we were at Fredek's house. In some way, I knew, Fredek, the one whom I always had to help catch and hold people in the park so he could kick them in the belly, but never could find, was my cousin, though how we were actually related, I had no idea. If we were going on a trip with Fredek, I wasn't happy at the prospect. I just hoped his governess, Miss Frania, hadn't gone away too.

Fredek's apartment was full of people. Two or three were men, and I wondered why they weren't in the army fighting the Germans. The rest were all women. When the doroshka driver had dropped our bags in the hall and Mother paid him, Auntie Edna, Fredek's mother, came into the hall to greet us. She was much taller than Mother, with a long face and black hair rolled around her head. She and Mother didn't kiss. "Sasha and Renia are here," was all I heard Auntie Edna say in the way of greeting. She said it in a low voice as though it were something private between them. Mother said, "Good." Auntie Edna didn't seem to take notice of me. Mother was holding my hand.

The others stood in groups talking. Nobody sat. They talked in urgent voices, and some people would move from one group to another and continue talking as though they had been there all along. I wasn't hearing words, but only the urgency. Mother and Auntie Edna separated, joining different groups. Mother and I walked up to one group in the dining room, and no one seemed to greet us, but Mother was immediately in the conversation. Everyone seemed to be smoking. I didn't see Fredek anywhere, but with all the adults standing, I wasn't surprised.

There was one man sitting down. He was very old and bald, and had a little black cap, like the one my grandfather had used to wear, on the back of his bald head. He was sitting at the dining room table eating boiled chicken from a soup bowl. His hands shook. I had never seen that before and watched him with interest. He smiled at me with gold teeth and beckoned with a bony, shaking finger. I turned away pretending I hadn't seen.

Then Mother and I moved to another group. "Edna and I are going together," I heard Mother say. "I think Renia will come with us." Suddenly panic gripped me. She had not mentioned either me or Fredek. Would we be left here with the strangers? I began listening intently. "We have a truck," she went on. "It's a van from the factory. Lolek didn't give it to the army. He told them it was on a trip to Posnan and hadn't come back."

"We're going with the Rosenbaums," a woman said. "They have a carriage, and the army didn't know they had a horse."

"Which way are you going to go?" somebody else asked.

"We're going south, Fina and I," the woman said. "Boris called me from the barracks and said to go south."

"Bolek said we should go east," another woman said.

"Toward Russia?"

"The Russians aren't going to do anything—they're afraid of the English."

"The English, the English. Chamberlain won't do anything."

"They have to. We have a defense pact with them."

"England and France will declare war on Germany tomorrow, you'll see."

"Lolek said we should go south too," Mother said. She and the woman who was going in the carriage immediately moved away from the group and formed a group of their own.

"Major Solecki and his wife are going south too," the woman said. "He has to report to the barracks in Lublin."

"Are they here?" Mother asked. I was listening carefully for any mention of me.

"They're in the living room," the woman said.

Then Fredek was suddenly by my side. "That's the German ambassador," he said. I looked around in surprise. Then I saw him indicating the old man eating the chicken. "We're holding him prisoner until they return our ambassador from Berlin. Then we'll shoot him."

I knew Fredek was making it up, but I glanced at the old man again. He gave me another gold-toothed smile and held up a dripping chicken leg. I quickly turned away.

"He wants you to eat that chicken leg," Fredek said, "but it's poisoned. Go take it from him and pretend like you're eating it while I sneak up behind him with a gun. My father gave me a real gun before he went to the war. They gave him two guns by mistake, and he gave one of them to me."

Fredek's victims were always imaginary, but this one was real. I didn't want to go near the old man. "Mommy says I can't let go of her hand," I lied.

"Auntie Barbara," he said referring to Mother, " is a German spy. Germans always use women as spies because no one suspects them. We'll shoot her together with him. We'll ask if they want blindfolds and cigarettes, and if they say yes, we won't give them any."

The part about blindfolds and cigarettes I didn't understand, though I realized that my knowledge of things like executions was not as thorough as my cousin's. I wondered if Fredek knew what the plans for us were.

Then I felt someone take my free hand. Looking around I saw a woman I had never seen before holding my hand in one of hers and Fredek's in the other. She had on a brown wool skirt and a light brown sweater.

"Yes, please take him, Miss Bronia," Mother said.

I was gripped by terror. There had been a story that Kiki had told me once in which a wicked stepmother took her daughter by the hand into the woods and then gave her to an old couple to be their servant. "Here, take her," Kiki had her saying.

"No!" I screamed and pulled my hand free. I wrapped my arm around Mother, still clutching her by one hand. I buried my face against her side. "Get away from me, you witch!"

The room must have grown silent. "Miss Bronia's not a witch," Mother said, laughing.

"Don't touch me! Don't touch me!" I screamed in terror.

"Yulian!" Mother said sharply. "Yulian, control yourself!" She was squeezing my hand hard and she was hurting it, but it didn't matter.

"It's all right, Madam," I heard the woman say behind me. "He's upset like everybody else."

I felt Mother's hand loosen on mine immediately. The woman's voice was very gentle. Of course she wasn't a witch. There were no witches—I knew that. And I was suddenly terribly embarrassed by my outburst. I had made people think I still believed in witches.

"Yulian," my mother said. The sharpness was gone from her voice, but her tone said, now behave properly.

"It's my fault. I surprised him," Miss Bronia said.

I turned my head enough to look at her with one eye.

"Just give him a moment to adjust."

She had brown, wavy hair, cut short, and there was a kind expression on her face. At her throat, she wore a little gold cross on a chain.

Of course she wasn't going to take me away from Mother. She must just be somebody's governess, and she was going to take me and Fredek to some other room while the grownups talked. Fredek was still holding her hand and must obviously have known her.

"I'm Sonya's governess," Miss Bronia said to me. "I don't know if you remember Sonya. She's Fredek's other cousin. I know Miss Yanka," she added, referring to Kiki. "Now do you want to come with us to Fredek's room?" she asked me. Her tone implied that I was perfectly free to refuse. It was a totally novel experience, and, of course, I would not refuse that kind of appeal. She took my hand again, and the three of us went down the hall to Fredek's room.

Fredek's room was dark, except for the light coming through the partially open door. Somebody was lying on Fredek's bed, and Miss Bronia led us directly to the other bed in the room. "Take off your shoes," she whispered, "and lie down on the bed. Fredek at this end and Yulian at that end."

She spread a blanket over us and gave Fredek a hug. I both wanted a hug from Miss Bronia, too, and didn't want one. I didn't know if I would ever get used to war.

Miss Bronia whispered something to Fredek then came to my end of the bed. I was too embarrassed to hold my arms out for a hug as I did every night for Kiki. Miss Bronia sat down beside me. Then she reached down for my shoulders, and I knew she would hug me. I sat up, and she held me to her for a much longer time than I could ever remember being held by Kiki.

She was soft, and she smelled of a gentle cologne, not the strong perfume and cigarette smell that Mother had or the soap smell of Kiki. I was crying again, quietly, and I didn't think she heard me, but if she did, I sensed that it would be all right.

Chapter Two

I remember waking for a few seconds as someone was carrying me in the elevator going down. I could tell by the scent that it was a man. Then I remember the dark inside the truck. It was totally dark. It was a dark I had never seen before. They had seated me in the corner, supported by walls in back and on my right. I was sitting on some kind of bench with a blanket wrapped around me. The truck was moving in the direction I was facing, over rough pavement, probably cobblestones. I didn't know who else was in the truck with me. I remembered Miss Bronia and hoped she was in the truck. I sniffed for her cologne, but smelled only cigarette smoke and heavy perfume.

Then I heard voices whispering. I couldn't make out the words. Sometimes the truck made a turn, and I'd have to catch my balance. There was a lip to the bench under me that I could hold on to. The truck, I sensed, must be moving very slowly. Sometimes it would stop. If it stopped for a long time, someone would groan, and someone else would go, "Shshshsh."

When the truck was moving again, a woman said, "When we're stopped, we've got to be absolutely silent. There's not supposed to be anyone in the back of this truck. It's supposed to be a supply truck." It was an older woman's voice, I was sure.

"We're supposed to be cabbages," my mother said. I recognized her voice. There was quiet laughter. It was the way kids laughed behind their books in class so the teacher won't hear. I had never heard adults laughing that way. Then the truck stopped, and everyone was quiet again. I was back asleep before we were moving again.

Later, when we were once more underway, I heard Fredek's voice. "I have to go to the bathroom," he said aloud.

"Did you bring something for him?" another woman asked.

"Like what?" I recognized Auntie Edna's voice in the dark.

"Each woman was supposed to be responsible for her own child," the voice said. "Bronia doesn't know what you packed. She doesn't even know Yulek." The mention of Miss Bronia's name was music to my ears. I had been afraid she wasn't along.

"What did you want me to bring?" Auntie Edna asked.

"All right, I have a hot water bottle," the voice said, "but you'll have to buy me a new one."

"You brought your hot water bottle?"

"It's for Sonya when she has cramps."

"Sonya has cramps?" Auntie Edna said. "She's only five years older than Fredek."

"Five and a half. And she does have cramps."

"The hot water bottle will be fine." That was Miss Bronia's voice, and it was honey to me. Now I heard some moving around in the dark.

"It's in my bag here somewhere."

"I have to kaka," Fredek wailed.

"God damn! Stop the truck! Somebody stop the damned truck!"

Somebody started banging on the front wall. I sat in my corner, wrapped in my blanket and the darkness, glad that it wasn't I who needed to go to the bathroom.

I felt the truck pull to one side, the side I was sitting on. Then it began to incline considerably. "We're going to roll over!" Auntie Edna cried, but at that moment it came to a lurching stop.

"I have to kaka," Fredek sobbed as we waited for someone to open the door.

"For godsakes hurry up and open the door!" a voice said.

Then we heard somebody working the latch, and finally the door opened. A man's head and shoulders appeared in silhouette in the opening. I recognized the shape of a four-cornered, military hat on his head. "Is something wrong?" he asked in the formal tone of an employee.

"The children have to go to the bathroom," a voice said. I recognized myself included in the statement and resented it. It was the voice of the one with the hot water bottle. "Sonya, do you have to go too?" she asked.

The answer came from a form sitting at the other end of my bench. She sat in the front corner of the truck box, wrapped in a blanket much like I was. "No, Mother," she said sleepily. "I just want to sleep." I saw Miss Bronia and Fredek scrambling down from the truck together.

"Yulek, you'd better go too," Mother said. In the dim light from the open door, I could see that she was sitting on a bench on the other side of the truck, between the woman who must have been Sonya's mother and an older woman. Auntie Edna was kneeling on one suitcase and opening another in a pile of leather bags in the middle of the truck's cargo box in which we all sat. A cardboard carton contained our gas masks in their green, metal canisters and canvas pouches. I did not have to go, and, like the girl Sonya, would have preferred to sleep, but I was accustomed to following orders in this regard. Besides, I certainly didn't want to leave myself vulnerable to Fredek's undignified plight. I would pee by myself against some tree or bush, as I knew how to do. I would not do the other thing without more suitable privacy.

The light was gray, outside the truck. The sky was gray, and everything else seemed gray. I realized it must be early morning. I carefully clambered down from the formidable height that the truck bed represented to me. And suddenly I felt the warm, breathy proximity of a horse. Only inches away from my face was the muzzle of a horse, dapple gray with a white star

on his forehead and a bewhiskered chin. He was hitched to a
wagon on the seat of which three people sat, huddled together
sleepily. Behind them, the wagon was loaded with boxes and
bundles, and behind the wagon, what I had not been able to
see from the interior of the truck, was a parade.

I knew that this was not a parade in the usual sense of the
word. These were not soldiers in dress uniforms or students
with shiny brass buttons marching for the benefit of onlookers.
But parade was the only concept I had for long files of people,
filling a road, all heading in the same direction at the same
pace. At the moment, that pace was virtually zero.

Some were on foot, some sitting in wagons, some in carriages—I even recognized one as a doroshka. Two men in suits
and gray felt hats were asleep behind the driver, a blanket over
their legs. I saw a few cars in the long line of not-moving people.

I reached out for the horse's nose, which I knew would be
soft and velvety. I held my hand out the way Grandfather's
coachman, Adam with the missing finger, had shown me, palm
up, fingers bent back where the horse could not nip them. He
nuzzled my hand. Assured that he would not bite, I bent my
fingers to feel the soft nose. Without anyone's permission, I
reached for the soft underside of his neck. It was warm and
soft as I had also known it would be. The large, trusting eye
was looking at me, and he rubbed his muzzle against my chest,
clanking his bit. I started to reach for his ears.

"Yulek, get away from that horse!" I heard my mother
shout. Startled, the horse and I both moved apart.

"I'd better see if there's some place for me to weewee too,"
Auntie Edna was saying behind me.

"You'd better take Yulek with you," I heard Mother say.
"Yulek, wait for Auntie Edna!"

I clenched my teeth in rage at my mother. I was perfectly
capable of going to the bathroom by myself, but beyond that,
the thought of sharing bathroom intimacies with Auntie Edna
repelled me.

"Give me your hand, Yulek!" Auntie Edna sang out merrily, "I'm afraid of the dark." I could tell by her tone that this was a joke veiling a command. I took her hand obediently and we made our way down into a ditch beside the truck.

What terrified me, I realized, was not the idea of Auntie Edna seeing my birdie, since only a little of it would be exposed out of the leg hole of my short pants and I could easily turn away from her, but rather the thought of seeing Auntie Edna squat there with her bare bottom exposed and her seeing me seeing her—even if I didn't really see her. We climbed up the other side of the ditch and into the brush beside the road.

"You go around that side, I'll take this side," Auntie Edna sang out again when we came to a particularly large bush. "Meet me back here when you're through." I breathed a huge sigh of relief and decided that I liked Auntie Edna. Auntie Edna, I now remembered, was Lolek's sister. She was tall for a woman, as he was tall for a man.

"Yulian and I are committed to each other now," Auntie Edna said when we were back at the truck. I did not understand her meaning except that it somehow implied to the others that what I had feared most had, indeed, happened, though it hadn't. It would be best, I decided, to pretend total ignorance. I hoped I wasn't blushing or that, if I was, it would not show in the half-light. Maybe I wasn't going to like Auntie Edna that much after all.

The parade had begun to move again, and the horse and wagon had gone on ahead. Mother and Sonya's mother stood in the open truck door smoking and looking out over the parade. I watched it move past. A man and a woman were pushing a white baby carriage along the road. There were cartons in the carriage, and I wondered whether there was a baby inside as well. One man was pushing a wheelbarrow with someone in it. A girl about my age in the back of a wagon, held a cage with a canary on her lap. Another wagon had a cow tied to the back with a length of rope. I had never seen a cow that close. I was surprised that she had no horns. She kept swishing her funny, brush-ended tail back and forth against her flanks. As she passed by, I noticed how strained with milk her udder was. I knew that you had to milk a cow early every morning and in the evening, and it was easy to see that this one was due.

Then Miss Bronia and Fredek came walking along the side of the road. They held hands and were laughing.

"We found a stream and washed our hands and everything," Miss Bronia said.

"I stepped on a frog," Fredek said.

"You did not," Miss Bronia said, laughing. Fredek laughed in response. "And are you all right, Yulek?" she asked.

"Yes," I said. "I went by myself," which was absolutely true.

"But I saw a frog," Fredek insisted. "I did. I saw three frogs."

Miss Bronia looked at him with a bemused look of disbelief on her face.

"I did," he said.

I was sure Fredek was making it up, but I realized that he knew that there was no way Miss Bronia could say she knew for sure that he hadn't. The look of triumph on his face confirmed my suspicion.

"All right," Miss Bronia said, "you saw a frog."

"I saw three frogs."

"You saw three frogs? You did not."

"I saw four frogs."

"Sure you did."

Fredek laughed at his victory, and Miss Bronia, instead of being angry, laughed a beautiful merry laugh with him.

This wasn't right. Fredek was lying, and Miss Bronia was making a joke of it as though lying wasn't wrong. Why would she do that?

I looked toward the front of the truck. I saw that the man in the army hat, who had opened our truck door, was leaning against a front fender, smoking. He had on an army coat as well, but it was open and his shirt and trousers were civilian. Next to him stood a man in a proper uniform, but without either hat or coat. He had major's insignia on his collar. I guessed he must be the Major Solecki someone had mentioned to Mother at Fredek's apartment. The other man must be the driver from Lolek's factory, wearing the major's coat and hat to look like a soldier. I noticed the truck was painted the same funny green that they painted army trucks.

They were doing this, I understood, to get past military barricades. But that was not right either. What they were doing was not right. What we were doing was not right. Lying to your own soldiers was traitorous. I wondered if it was a Jewish thing. Catholics would not do something like that, particularly in a time of war. I would ask Kiki when she rejoined us.

The older woman I had seen inside the truck was standing with the two men. I guessed she must be the major's wife. I saw her drop her cigarette butt on the ground and grind it into the dirt with her foot. They said something to each other, and then she came back to the rear of the truck. "We must get going," she said and began to climb into the truck. We all followed. Miss Bronia pulled me up by my hands. "Up, Yulian!" she said merrily. The driver came to close the door.

"Just let us get settled, Dembovski, before you close the door," my mother said.

"Yes, Missus," the man said and waited with the door.

"Yulek, go back to your place," Mother said. I returned to my corner. I saw Miss Bronia tucking the blanket around Sonya, apparently asleep at the other end of our bench. Then she sat down next to Fredek who stretched to whisper something in her ear. Miss Bronia laughed again.

"Is everyone settled now?" Sonya's mother asked. There was no answer.

"All right, Dembovski," Mother said, and the man closed the door, putting us in the dark again.

"Now remember, no talking when we stop," the major's wife's voice said in the dark. "And the children aren't to talk at all." I felt the engine start up, and the truck lurch forward.

The darkness was not complete, I realized now. High up on the opposite wall, just below the ceiling, there was a line of little circles of light. I guessed they must be holes—air holes, I deduced. I hadn't seen them before because of the darkness outside, but now that it was morning, the light of the sky was showing through. Occasionally, the first light, the one nearest the front would go out. Then the next one would be darkened and then the one after that, while the first light went on again. I decided that we must be passing trees. I counted the lights. There were twenty-seven of them. I guessed that there must be a similar line of holes on my side of the truck, but I couldn't see them by looking straight up. The light didn't come down to where we were. Maybe a little did because sometimes you could just barely make out the shapes of people in the dark.

"I could use some coffee," Auntie Edna said after a while.

"I have a thermos of cocoa," Miss Bronia said, in her melodic voice. "It's for the children, but we can all take a few sips."

"Yuck," Auntie Edna said.

"I want some cocoa," Fredek said.

"The children aren't to talk!" the major's wife snapped.

"Here, feel for my hand," Miss Bronia said. "But be very careful—it's hot." I heard some movement on the bench beside me.

"Yulek, if you want some cocoa, slide over here," she said. I would have liked some, but I couldn't drink out of the thermos after Fredek. "No thank you," I said.

"Sonya," Miss Bronia went on, "if you want some, just slide over here."

"I had Marta make some sandwiches here," Mother said. "There's sausage and some nice boiled ham for the children."

"Maybe later," Sonya's mother said.

"I think the children should go back to sleep," Auntie Edna said.

"That's a good idea," Mother said. "We don't know what we'll have to deal with later. Children, go back to sleep now."

I tried to wrap myself up in the blanket and the darkness the same way I had before we stopped, but it wasn't working the same way. Miss Bronia and Fredek were whispering again, and I was jealous. I understood that Miss Bronia knew Fredek a lot longer than she knew me, but Fredek told lies and always talked about killing or hurting people, while I loved God and tried very hard not to sin.

Then I realized that I had not said my prayers the evening before. It was the first time since Kiki had taught me to pray that I had failed to say my evening prayers.

But God would surely forgive me under the circumstances—wouldn't He? Of course, the saints prayed even when they were about to be eaten by lions. My plight certainly fell short of that. On the other hand, I was only seven years old, and God would make allowance. But then, as an unchristened Catholic, I carried a greater burden of proof.

What was I doing worrying about not praying, when I should be making up for that dereliction? In the name of the Father and the Son and the Holy Ghost, Amen. I crossed myself in the darkness. Our Father who art in Heaven, hallowed be Thy Name. Thy Kingdom come, Thy Will be done . . . I clasped my hands together, shut my eyes tightly despite the darkness, and mouthed the words that I knew would bring me back into contact with God. God knew that at heart I was Catholic. I loved Him and I loved Jesus and Mary and the Holy Ghost—which, I knew now, wasn't really a pigeon, but something more complicated—and because of my love for them all, they must love me too. Of the group of us in the back of the truck, God loved me and Miss Bronia, and I wasn't sure about the major's wife or Sonya and her mother. Miss Bronia, of course, had no way of knowing that I was Catholic like her, but when we met in Heaven, some day, and she saw me there, she would know. Hail Mary, full of Grace, the Lord is with Thee . . .

*   *   *

The truck lurched, and I realized I had been asleep again. From the sound, I deduced we were moving faster now. Somebody was snoring the way I had heard Lolek snore sometimes. I didn't know who it was.

"No, she has no idea," I heard whispered on the other side of the truck. It was my mother's voice, and she was talking in the loud whisper you use when you don't want to wake someone, but you're not talking directly into the other person's ear. "She showed up at the Boleskis' last week in the most awful hat. Zosia was so embarrassed for her, though I don't know why she should worry about what Lara was wearing."

There was silence for a few minutes, except for the snoring. Then I heard Auntie Edna's voice. "Who do you think Fela Eldmann saw together at Sobinski's?" I had heard of Sobinski's as a cafe that Mother and her friends went to a lot.

"Who?" Mother asked immediately.

Auntie Edna didn't answer.

"All right," Sonya's mother said after a while, "so are you going to tell us?"

"Michael . . ." Auntie Edna said.

"Michael Kopievich?" Mother said.

"No, Michael Shchepanski."

"Michael Shchepanski," Mother repeated. "Michael Shchepanski and who?"

"Michael Shchepanski and . . ."

"And . . . ?" Mother said.

"Mina Boleska," Auntie Edna finally told her.

"Michael and Mina?" Mother said, "I don't believe it."

"Mina Boleska and Michael Shchepanski are an old story," Sonya's mother said, sounding bored. "He's been blah-blahing her all summer." She used a word I didn't know. It sounded Yiddish.

"Everything's an old story with you," Auntie Edna said. "You always say that. You can never admit you didn't already know something."

Now there was silence.

"Wasn't Mina seeing that Belgian lawyer, what's-his-name?" my mother asked after a while.

"That's long over with," Sonya's mother said. "He's gone back to Brussels, and I don't remember his name either."

"Tadek Potanski is in love with you, you know, Basia," Auntie Edna said, using the diminutive of Mother's name.

"Every man in Warsaw is in love with beautiful Basia," Sonya's mother said in a very serious voice. Then I heard all three of them laugh.

"What about Richard—Richard Cypronek?" Mother said, still laughing some. "Isn't he in love with you, Edna?"

"With me?" Auntie Edna said. "He's five years younger than I am."

"More like ten years," Sonya's mother said.

"He is not!" Auntie Edna said, in an angry tone that I suspected was make-believe, and Mother and Sonya's mother laughed a little at this. "But he did drink champagne," Auntie Edna continued, "out of my slipper at the Orphanage Ball, you know."

"Everybody knows that story," Sonya's mother said.

"Well, he said I had very clean feet." And again the three of them laughed.

"We were all very drunk that night," Mother said. I wondered if that was the night Mother sent me that birthday telegram that Kiki got so angry about.

Then nobody said anything more, and I was soon envisioning tall Auntie Edna standing in one shoe while her friend held the open toe of her other shoe above his upturned mouth like a funnel, and a waiter poured champagne into it from a bottle.

I must have fallen asleep again because the next thing I heard was the major's wife. "There are some nice pensions," she was saying. "This won't take more than a week or two, but there's no point spending the money on a good hotel when you have the children with you, and I wouldn't stay at a second-rate hotel under any circumstances."

I heard a buzz from Miss Bronia and Fredek. They were whispering again.

"Basia, I think I'll have one of those sandwiches of yours now," Auntie Edna said when the major's wife paused.

"Anyone else hungry?" Mother asked. "Yulek, you have to eat something now," she added. I didn't need prompting, nor, it seemed did anyone else. "Just a minute," Mother said, and I heard the rustle of paper-wrapped sandwiches being unpacked. "Here," she said, "you have to feel around for my hand. These are boiled ham for the children."

I moved towards the center of the truck box and felt out-stretched hands and arms. There was a wrapped sandwich in my hand, and I felt my way back to my seat, bumping my shoulder against someone in the process. And then, for the second time in as many days, God sent me a message of approval. Into my hands He had placed a sausage sandwich.

Sausage would make me sick, Kiki had admonished on more than one occasion. But not, I was sure, if it came from God. Of course, Kiki could not have foreseen the use of sausage as the medium for sacred communication. And if it did make me sick, then that was obviously God's will too. The priest at mass had told about God speaking to someone by setting a bush on fire, which obviously would not have worked in this situation. And there were the stone tablets with His commandments written on them that He had given Catholics. But here He had found a way to speak quietly to me to just let me know that He was watching out for me. In the very unlikely and highly disappointing event that this had been a human mistake, I ate my delicious sandwich very slowly, which, I knew, would minimize the risk of its making me sick.

I felt myself lean forward, away from the wall, and realized that our truck must be braking. It didn't stop, but continued at a slower pace. "Maybe they found someplace we can stop for coffee," Auntie Edna said.

"That sausage made me thirsty," Sonya's mother said. "If you packed sandwiches, why didn't you pack something to drink?"

"I told Marta to make sandwiches," Mother said. " I really didn't think she had to be told to pack something to drink too. She's not very well trained. I could use a cigarette." Sensitized, as I now was, to matters divine, I hoped that God took note of Mother's talking that way about Marta.

"My ham was very good," the major's wife said. "It wasn't salty at all." I tensed, waiting for Mother to ask what child had eaten the major's wife's sausage, but she didn't.

"Mummy, can we stop somewhere I can take a bath?" It was Sonya's voice. "It's hot and sweaty in here." I realized that I had no idea what Sonya looked like. And it was getting hot.

"The children are not to talk," the major's wife repeated.

"Sonya isn't a child," her mother responded. "She has breasts."

"She does not," Auntie Edna said. "If she's an adult, why does she need a governess?"

"She does so have breasts. I bought her a bra this summer. And Bronia is not a governess, but a companion. She speaks fluent German. Sonya, dear, say something in German."

"Oh, Mummy!" Sonya complained.

"Oh, go ahead," her mother coaxed."

"Blah, blah, blah," Sonya said, the words sounding like the German that I had heard on the radio.

"I don't dare imagine what she just told me," her mother said, laughing.

"Yulek speaks excellent French," my mother said.

I was prepared to say, bon jour Madame, if called upon, but Sonya's mother said, "I think languages are so important. I wish I had learned French or German as a girl."

"I wonder where we are," Miss Bronia said quickly. "Anybody got any idea?"

Then the truck came to a sudden stop, and I almost fell off the bench. I heard somebody fall on the suitcases. "Merde!" she said. It was a French word I knew. The voice was Auntie Edna's.

"What happened?" Sonya's mother asked. The major's wife immediately shushed her. We waited to see if we would start up again.

Then the door opened, and my eyes hurt from the sudden light. The driver was shaking his head. "The children probably shouldn't come out," he said.

"What is it?" Mother and Auntie Edna asked together.

The driver was shaking his head. "They've been bombed," he said.

Now the major was at the door too. "They've been strafed," he said. At first I wasn't sure what strafed meant, but Fredek immediately made a machine gun sound reminding me. Over the two men's heads, behind us, I could see a wagon on its side in the road. A chestnut horse was lying and not moving on the ground.

I had seen dead horses before. In the city occasionally a worn-out horse collapsed in its traces. More than once, Kiki and I had cringed at the sight of a driver whipping an animal trying desperately to rise, while a crowd gathered. This one lay lifeless on the pavement.

"Look, a dead horse!" Fredek cried.

"Haven't you seen a dead horse before?" Sonya said. She had unwrapped the blanket from around her, and I could see her for the first time. But my attention was on the scene outside. "It isn't nice to look," she admonished Fredek.

"Oh, my God!" Auntie Edna said, stepping to the open door. "They've been shot."

Suddenly Fredek had slipped out onto the ground, and Miss Bronia was following after him. "Catch him! Stop him!" Auntie Edna called. Now Mother was climbing down from the truck and Sonya's mother after her. Then the major's wife sat on the edge, and the major helped her down. Auntie Edna still stood at the door, motionless, and Sonya had wrapped herself back up in the blanket. Nobody seemed at all concerned with me, so I moved to the door and slid to the ground as well.

The reason we had stopped, I realized, was that a large car stood across our path. I could see no one inside, but there were lines of what had to be bullet holes down its side. I could see no people anywhere. Further ahead on the road there was another wagon. This one was standing, but I couldn't see the horse. He, too, may have been lying dead in front of it. It was very, very quiet.

The major and the driver walked up to the car. They looked inside. Then they came back and talked to the women, in front of the truck. Miss Bronia stayed with Fredek and me by the back of the truck. I realized she had taken my hand. Sonya was sitting on the back of the truck, dangling her legs. It was the first time I had seen her properly. I saw she had light brown hair pinned up in some way, but a lot of it was hanging down. She had a round face with a short, up-turned nose. There were a few pimples on her face. If she had breasts, I couldn't tell.

Fredek was very quiet, which surprised me. "Are they dead?" he whispered to Miss Bronia, though he did not need to whisper. "Are they all dead?"

Miss Bronia was looking at the bullet-ridden car. "I don't know," she said vacantly. I could tell that the sight upset her. I nestled my hand inside her warm, soft one. Her skin wasn't dry like Kiki's. I was reminded again of Kiki and felt proud of how grownup I was and how well I was dealing with her absence.

Then I saw the adults walk to the car. They each looked inside first, except for Auntie Edna, then they gathered at the back to try to push it off the road. It wouldn't move. Our driver reached inside the driver-side door and did something. Now they were able to push it into the ditch. Whether there was anyone inside, I still didn't know.

Everybody walked back to our truck. "Do we still need to keep the doors closed?" my mother asked. "It's getting pretty hot, you know."

The major and his wife walked aside a bit to confer.

"Why does she have to be the one telling us what to do all the time?" Auntie Edna asked, referring to the major's wife. Nobody answered her, but I saw Mother bite her lower lip.

"My husband says it's all right to tie the door open," the major's wife said when she came back. When we had all climbed back into the truck, she and Miss Bronia tied a length of cord between the two double doors. One door was bolted in place; the other could open for the length of the cord. Then the truck started up again.

Now I could see inside the truck. Sonya's mother sat diagonally across from me, at the front corner on the other side. Her hair was light brown, like Sonya's, in braids that were pinned to her head, which was something like Kiki's, but not as long or as thick. Her face was round, like Sonya's, with the same up-turned nose. Auntie Edna sat a little distance from her, towering over the others. My mother was next, and she, I noticed, was the smallest of the women. The major's wife, with graying brown hair pulled back severely and the body roundness of an older woman, sat directly across from me in the back corner. They all seemed to be sitting evenly spaced apart, each with her hands in her lap, except for the major's wife, who had her arms crossed. All seemed deep in thought. The noise of the engine and the road came in through the open door.

"Was there anyone in the car?" Fredek asked in an uncharacteristically small voice. Nobody answered him.

"I don't know, Fredek," Miss Bronia said after a while. "I didn't look."

Then the loose door began to bang. It would rest at the end of the rope for a moment, then, for no apparent reason, work its way in to darken our compartment and finally crash against the other door. "Somebody's got to do something about that damned door!" my mother yelled above the noise.

"If somebody has something I can wedge it with, I'll try to stop it," Miss Bronia said.

The women all looked at the pile of baggage in the middle of the truck.

"Whose green canvas bag is that?" the major's wife asked.

"You can't use that," Sonya's mother said. "That's my knitting."

"It won't hurt your knitting," the major's wife said.

"It'll bend my needles."

"It's wartime," the major's wife said. "Miss Bronia, please wedge that bag against the door."

Miss Bronia looked up at Sonya's mother. Sonya's mother nodded her head, and Miss Bronia moved cautiously in the swaying truck to where the bag was.

"I'm going to help you," Fredek said.

"No, you stay there," Miss Bronia said.

"You'll fall out the door," Auntie Edna said.

"I will not," Fredek argued.

"Sit down, Frederick!" the major's wife commanded. Fredek resettled himself on the bench.

"Be careful of my needles," Sonya's mother said.

"We should have used Paula's douche bag," Auntie Edna said under her breath, laughing. I didn't know who Paula was or what a douche bag was either.

"It's not a douche bag. It's a hot water bottle," Sonya's mother said.

Mother and Auntie Edna both laughed.

Now I knew Sonya's mother's name. She was the Auntie Paula who knitted me sweaters for which I had to sweat out thank-you notes. As for the douche bag, I remembered now seeing a hot water bottle-like thing with a rubber tube coming out of the bottom, hanging on the door in my parents' bathroom and speculated that that must be what they were referring to. Kiki had been quite vague about explaining its purpose to me, so I was sure that it had to do with female hygiene and asked no further.

With the door wedged open, I could now see the road behind us, and suddenly I was aware of traffic moving the opposite way from us. At first there were a few carriages and wagons, but no cars. Then there was one car that sped by. It was painted green like our truck, with soldiers inside. It weaved in and around the wagons and disappeared out of my sight. The grownups, sitting on the side of the bolted door, could not see the road.

Then the traffic was becoming heavier again. Our truck slowed down, and we could now hear the noise of feet and hooves and wheels and creaking axles, and the hum of voices.

"What is it?" Auntie Edna asked, and then stood up to look through the door. "They're all going the other way now," she said. The other two mothers and the major's wife crowded to the opening, blocking my view. I felt the truck move slower and slower.

"Where are they all coming from?" Sonya's mother, Auntie Paula, asked. I didn't hear an answer. "We're stopping," she said. Almost at that same moment we came to a stop. "We've stopped," she said. The truck moved forward a little bit and then stopped again. Somebody was shouting angrily outside. We moved ahead a little more and then stopped again. Somebody banged on the side of the truck a few times. "What are they doing?" Auntie Paula said.

We stayed stopped for a while, and the grownups, except for Miss Bronia, got out.

"Yulian, do you know how to do cat's cradle?" Miss Bronia asked. She was tying a loop of string.

"A little," I said.

"Come over here and let's all do it together."

I did as I was told.

"Sonya, come help us," Miss Bronia said.

Sonya didn't move. "I don't think I want to," she said. I saw she had a nail file and was shaping her nails the way I had seen Mother do.

"All right," Miss Bronia said, "we'll do it without you, won't we."

I slid over on the bench, not wanting to show my surprise, but the idea of Sonya saying no to her governess was totally novel to me.

Fredek had already erected the starting cradle on his hands with the string. "Yulian, do you know the next figure?" Miss Bronia asked. I did, and I eagerly demonstrated, moving the string structure to my own hands.

"That's very good, Yulian," Miss Bronia said. But she said it as though I had done something very difficult, which I certainly hadn't. Kiki and I knew a lot of cat's cradle figures. "Fredek, do you know what to do next?"

Fredek did seem to know the next figure, but I could see he wasn't as sure of it as I was. At one point, Miss Bronia almost began to help him.

The moment Fredek had finished, I reached quickly for the figure and began converting it. But Fredek released his too soon, and the whole structure collapsed in my hands.

"Oh, you almost had it, Yulian," Miss Bronia said. It sounded as though she thought it had been my fault and was trying to make light of it. "Well, let's try it again, and this time I'll help you a little."

"I don't want to," I heard myself saying. I don't think that I had ever put that particular combination of words together before, and I was suddenly gripped by shame for what I had said. I quickly slid back into my corner.

"That's all right," Miss Bronia said. "Is there something else you'd like to do?"

I suddenly remembered the blue wool sailor suit that I had insisted on wearing to the park some time ago and I felt that same guilt again. I stood up and looked sightlessly through the open door.

"I want to see," I heard Fredek say behind me.

"No, we'll just play another game. What would you like to play?" Miss Bronia said.

"How come he can look and I can't?"

There were tears running down my face, surprising me. I wiped them away with my sleeve and tried to concentrate on what I was seeing. The road behind and around us was full of people and animals. There were wagons and horses and cows and goats, all of them creeping along in the opposite direction from us. People on foot bent forward with sacks over their shoulder. People in wagons looked at our truck and at me as they passed by. Only, they moved so slowly that we seemed to stare at each other for ever.

There were people with babies in their arms, and cats and dogs. There were children holding dolls and toys. A man pushed a wheelbarrow with a woman in it. I laughed at the sight. The woman looked up at me. I didn't know if she had heard me laugh. A man was walking a bicycle. Two women struggled with a wheelchair like Grandfather's, piled with boxes. It didn't seem to want to go straight ahead. I wondered what had happened to the person it belonged to. Another woman led a cow along. And all seemed to stare at me and I at them as they crept past us. Our grownups stood in a little group beside the truck, smoking and talking.

Then I saw that behind us two open-bed trucks were trying to make their way towards us, against that current. They were full of soldiers, I saw, and several soldiers were walking in front of the first truck, trying to clear a path. But the headway they were making was even slower than that of those going in the other direction. One soldier was standing on the running board of the first truck waving at the people to make way.

Suddenly, the hum of the voices and the road noise became louder. I saw people turning away from looking at us to look over their shoulder. People started to get down from wagons and make for the ditches alongside the road. Our own grown-ups turned back to the truck shouting, "Out of the truck!"

"Everybody out of the truck!"

"Bronia, get the children out of the truck!"

Our driver grabbed me around the waist suddenly and pulled me down from the truck. Mother grabbed my hand. "Under the truck! Under the truck!" the major was shouting. We were crawling under the truck bed.

Now there was the roar of airplanes—not the faint hum of a plane above the clouds, but the quickly growing pounding of nearby machines. It was a sound I had never heard before, but there was no mistaking it. My mother was on top of me under the truck. I raised my head to see, but she pushed it down.

I heard a blast of air and engines, feeling it with my whole body and sensing the truck over me swaying. "Stay down! Stay down!" the major shouted. The roar grew fainter and stopped. There was a moment's pause when everything was silent. I could hear nothing except my own feet scratching against the ground as I tried to change my position.

I wanted to see the planes. I had never seen an airplane up close, and these, I knew, must have passed close enough to even see the pilots.

Then I could hear the sound again. First a hum and then it growing into the roar. Mother's arm pushed my head down again. Now there was a new sound. Another sound I had no trouble identifying. It was machine gun fire.

It was a terrible noise. It was nothing like the *a-a-a-a-a* we would emit in make-believe. It was a noise of metal tearing and rocks jumping and people crying out.

The noise of the planes and the wind and the creaking of the truck blew over us one more time, and then, again, it was still.

"Stay down. Stay down. Everybody stay down," the major was saying.

We lay very still, and there was the sound of crying from around us. People were crying and animals were crying.

"Everyone all right?" the major asked, cautiously.

"I'm all right, dear," his wife answered

"Yulian and I are fine," Mother said.

"We're fine!" Fredek said.

"I'm all right," Auntie Paula said.

"And I." It was Miss Bronia's voice.

"I'm all right," Auntie Edna said. Everyone answered except Sonya.

"Sonya! Sonya!" Auntie Paula suddenly shouted. "Where are you?"

"Oh, I'm fine," Sonya answered from somewhere behind me. "I'm just fine."

"All right," the major said. "I think they've gone."

"Next time they come, everybody immediately under the truck," his wife said.

I could hear people under the truck begin to move. There were strangers under our truck, and they were beginning to crawl out.

"Oh my God!" It was Auntie Edna's voice. "Oh, my God."

"Oh, heavens!" Auntie Paula said. "Sonya, don't look."

"Really, Mother."

"Don't look," my mother said to me. I tried to see, what it was I wasn't supposed to look at, but with my mother's weight on my head, all I could see was a piece of Auntie Edna prone beside me.

"Oh, my God, what have they done to her?" I suddenly heard Auntie Edna say. Mother raised her head, so I was able to raise mine as well. Mother quickly pushed me back down. But what I saw in that moment was a woman in a babushka, the colored kerchief Polish women frequently wore on their heads, sitting beside the truck holding a bloody glove hanging from her hand for us to see.

"Quickly, we have to fix a tourniquet," I heard the major say. There were the sounds of people moving rapidly from under the truck. I caught sight of Auntie Paula moving towards the woman with Fredek crawling on all fours behind her. I wanted to go too, but my mother held me down.

"Fredek, come back!" Auntie Edna cried, then after a moment began to crawl after him, clearing my field of vision. The major, his wife, Auntie Paula, Fredek, and some other people were all crowding around the woman, hiding her from my view. Auntie Edna had stopped part way there. She was on her hands and knees and might have been throwing up.

"Keep her upright till I've fixed a tourniquet," the major was saying. "Fredek, give me your belt." I saw Fredek pulling his cloth belt out of its loops. I was deeply envious.

Suddenly it dawned on me. That had not been a glove in her hand. There had been no hand. That had been her hand and wrist, hanging by strands of flesh from her forearm.

And I suddenly saw my field of view narrowing, like in a tunnel, and felt a numbness coming over my body.

"Yulian! Yulian!" my mother was shouting. "You're all wet!"

For a moment I thought I had wet my pants. But I realized I was wet all over.

"You're all sweating," Mother said.

"Get off him," I heard Miss Bronia command. "Give him some air."

I had a great feeling of shame. Fredek was helping to tend to the wounded woman, and I, who was six months older, who had talked so much with Kiki about going to care for the wounded, was lying here under the truck feeling faint. And I didn't even have a belt for a tourniquet—my pants were held up by buttons on my shirt.

Mother crawled off me. "I'll take him," Miss Bronia said. She put an arm around my shoulders and tried to ease me towards the back of the truck. I didn't want to go. I didn't want to go and be taken care of while Fredek was helping take care of wounded people. I hid my face in the crook of my elbow.

"Let's just stay here awhile, then," Miss Bronia said. I felt her cover me with her cardigan sweater.

Lying there, I realized now that there were many voices crying, voices helping—Here, let's turn him over gently . . . Help me lay her down . . . Hold your hand like this . . . and then, Oh, he's dead . . . No, he isn't . . . Where is she? What happened to her? Oh, my God! . . . The bastards. They're shooting at civilians . . . They want to kill us all . . . Hail Mary full of grace . . .

After a few minutes I let Miss Bronia help me back into the truck. She had me sit on the bench beside her and held her arm around me. "Here, drink some cocoa." She held the thermos up and then wiped the mouth of it with the hem of her skirt. I took a sip. "Would you like me to tell you a story?" she asked. I was not in a mood for giants and witches, but I didn't want to refuse her offer. I nodded my head. Then Miss Bronia proceeded to tell a story I had never heard before. It was about a toy stuffed bear and the boy who owned him and some other toy animals including a pig, a tiger, and a donkey. But there was no witch or jealous stepmother or evil king or hungry wolf in this story, and not one of the characters wanted to cause harm to any of the others—not even the tiger—except that once the bear wanted some honey that wasn't his. I had never heard a story like that before. I couldn't wait to tell Kiki about it.

And then I realized that Kiki, too, may have been machine-gunned on her way to the city where we were scheduled to meet. Kiki would be coming by train. Did they machine-gun trains. Did bullets penetrate the sides of railway cars? Did they drop bombs on trains?

The idea of something befalling Kiki on her way to our rendezvous now occurred to me for the first time. Suddenly a wave of fear moved outward from somewhere between my heart and where I believed my stomach to be.

"Yulian, you're shaking," I heard Miss Bronia say, and she sounded as though she were on the other side of a closed door. I felt a blanket being wrapped around my shoulders. I realized my teeth were chattering and I was suddenly cold. And I was sweating again.

"He's so delicate," I heard Mother saying apologetically. Miss Bronia was cradling my head and shoulders in her arms like a baby, and I realized I must have fainted completely. I tried to sit up, but Miss Bronia held me down. "Just rest a little longer," she said.

"He was just very scared," I heard Auntie Edna saying. "You see, he's just fine now. Bronia is a genius with children."

"He is all right, isn't he?" I heard Mother ask.

"Yes, Mrs. Waisbrem, he's all right. He's just very upset," Miss Bronia said.

"Miss Bronia, I will give you a hundred zloty if you stay with him."

"That's not necessary, Missus," Miss Bronia said. I could tell from her tone that Miss Bronia was impatient with Mother the way Kiki sometimes was. "I'll just hold him for awhile," she said.

Then I realized that the truck was moving again. Mother crawled back to her seat over the bags. Across the way, Fredek was sitting beside his mother with spots on his shirt that I realized were blood. He made no effort to wipe them off. Nobody was talking.

I started to sit up again. "Just rest awhile longer," Miss Bronia said in her kind voice. I closed my eyes and let her hold me.

*   *   *

Then I was sitting beside Miss Bronia again, as the truck made its wobbly way forward. Mother had sat down now beside Auntie Edna. The major's wife and Auntie Paula, I realized, were not with us. Had something happened to them? No,

I had seen them both after the attack. Had there been another attack while I was unconscious? That would have been too embarrassing. Or were they sitting up front with the driver and the major? Held tight against Miss Bronia's side, I could not see out of our partially open door. Fredek kept lowering his face to look at the blood spots drying on his shirt.

I was aware that I had not experienced any more feelings regarding Kiki since regaining consciousness. Kiki might already be dead, I said deliberately in my own mind. But, strangely, the words had no impact. She might have had her hand severed by machine gun bullets like that poor woman— or a foot, or a leg. I tried to make myself visualize these conditions, but, still, I had no feelings about it. That wave of fear for Kiki's safety that I had felt before falling unconscious, I could remember it, but I could no longer feel it. Why was that? What was happening to me?

After a while, the truck stopped again. Auntie Paula appeared at the rear of the truck. "I told Dembovski to stop here so he could rest," she explained. "He drove all night and now all morning."

"That's a good idea," my mother said.

"Besides which, I need my cigarettes," Auntie Paula added. She laughed as she said it, but it didn't sound as though she really found it funny.

There were trees beside the road. "Everyone find a bush," Auntie Edna was saying as we climbed down from the truck. There was a jolly tone to her voice too, and it didn't sound any more real than Auntie Paula's. "Fredek, stay close," she added.

"Yulek, stay close to Fredek," my mother called.

I saw Fredek heading into the trees and followed. He stopped by a large tree and began digging into the leg opening of his shorts. Not wishing to intrude on his privacy, I walked to a tree a few yards further. In a moment, I saw Fredek walk past me to a still further tree. It took me a moment to understand his purpose—he wanted to go further from the truck than I did. Unlike the matter of helping the wounded, this was only a silly game. I let him have his silly way. When I had finished, I simply turned around and walked back.

"Where is Fredek?" his mother asked when I came back to the truck.

"He's going to the bathroom, Auntie Edna," I said.

"Weren't you two together?" my mother asked.

"Well, yes, but he went farther than I did."

"Farther?" Auntie Edna asked.

"Well . . ."

"Fredek!" Auntie Edna called. The alarm in her voice was real. "Fredek, can you hear me?!"

"For godsakes, Edna, he'll be right out," Auntie Paula said.

"Would Missus like me to find him?" Miss Bronia asked.

"That's nonsense," Auntie Paula said. "He'll come out by himself when he's through doing his business."

"Why didn't you stay with your cousin?" my mother asked.

"I'll go look," Miss Bronia said.

"There may be animals," Auntie Edna said.

"Don't be stupid," Auntie Paula said. I didn't like Auntie Paula.

Miss Bronia took me by the hand. "Show me where you went," she said. I headed straight into the trees, the way we had gone before.

"I think it was this tree," I said, pointing to the one I thought he had stopped at first. Sure enough, it was still wet. "I went to that one," I said, pointing to my tree, "and then Fredek went to that one."

"He did?"

"Yes." I didn't want to go into explanations.

"Oh, I see," she said. "Fredek! Fredek!" she called, "it's time to go back!"

We waited in vain for a response. "Fredek, I'm not playing now!" Miss Bronia called, her voice more serious than before. There was still no answer.

"Fre . . ." she began again, but was cut off by the a-a-a-a-a! of Fredek's machine gun sound behind us.

"You're both dead!" he said as we turned to face him. He had stepped out from behind a tree, an imaginary sub-machine gun shaking in his hands.

"That's not funny, Fredek," Miss Bronia said. It was the first time I had heard her disapproval. "Do an about-face right now and forward march!"

Fredek turned on his heel and began marching back toward the road. As we saw him walk out into the clear, I felt Miss Bronia squeeze my hand a little. "What were you doing, Fredek?" she whispered in a shrill little, make-believe cry, just for me to hear. "I was so worried!"

Immediately we heard Auntie Edna's voice. "What were you doing there? We were all worried something had happened to you!" Miss Bronia and I both laughed silently. I laughed out of happiness because I knew now that Miss Bronia didn't really like Fredek more than me.

*   *   *

When Miss Bronia and I came out of the trees, Auntie Edna was leaning with her back against the truck and her fingers against her forehead. The other two mothers had their backs to us and were saying something to her. Fredek was just disappearing inside the truck.

The road was full of people, as before, with wagons and people on foot, all moving at the same rate, and in the same direction as we were pointed. In the distance there was the now-familiar pop-popping of guns or bombs or both. A man in suit pants and an undershirt passed by at a brisk walk holding a suitcase on his head. I couldn't help laughing. He looked at me reprovingly as he hurried by. I saw Mr. Dembovski, our driver, checking something on one of the rear tires of the truck. He had a cigarette between his lips. I wondered what had become of the major and his wife.

Suddenly, I saw Mr. Dembovski jump onto the running board of our truck. In an instant he had opened the door and was inside the cab. The truck rocked slightly, and then Mr. Dembovski backed out again. He was pulling someone with him. He had the man by the coat lapels, and he dragged him out onto the dirt and almost into the drainage ditch. Had the man been trying to steal our truck?

Lying on the ground now with Mr. Dembovski kneeling over him, the man held his hands up in surrender. He was breathing hard and I thought he looked very frightened. Mr. Dembovski got to his feet shaking his head. The other man didn't try to get up. He had on a gray tweed suit with knickerbockers and high socks, a common fashion at that time. He had a longish face and straight dark hair parted on one side and pomaded in place. Now some of it hung over one eye, not unlike the pictures we had seen of Adolph Hitler, except for the little mustache. I saw that he was talking quickly. Our driver said something and jerked his head to one side in a gesture clearly directing him to leave. The man got to his feet, pulled a cap of the same gray tweed from an inside jacket pocket, placed it on his head with both hands, and proceeded to brush off his knickered trousers. He said something more to the driver, who made the same head-jerking gesture as before. The man said something again, and I saw our driver make a fist and shake it at the man.

"What is it, Dembovski?" I heard my mother's voice behind me. She and Auntie Edna were standing by the back of the truck. I saw Fredek and Sonya standing together and laughing.

The man in the knickerbocker suit turned his head towards my mother. He whipped the cap from his head and quickly walked towards her. "My name is Herman Lupicki, Missus, and I am the second assistant manager in the Shoe Store of Goldfarb," he said. "I thought your truck had been abandoned. I simply desire transportation with you, esteemed ladies, because my home, as well as the store have been bombed." He spoke quickly, without pause, as though afraid of providing an opportunity for a negative response. "I have no money to pay for such transportation, but I can provide additional protection, since there are unscrupulous people who are forcing their way into vehicles along the way."

"Who is this man?" Auntie Paula asked. She and Miss Bronia had just come up.

The man turned to face them. "My name is Herman Lupicki, Missus, and I am the second assistant manager of the Shoe Store of Goldfarb," he repeated. "I desire transportation with you in your vehicle. I will sit up front with your driver and provide added protection against ruffians who are right now forcing their way into slow-moving vehicles and taking them over."

"I was sitting up front," Auntie Paula said.

Mr. Dembovski, I saw, was standing by the front of the truck, lighting another cigarette and keeping a watchful eye on this Mr. Lupicki.

"It is really dangerous for fine ladies like yourselves, and with small children, to be traveling in such a truck with just one man to protect you," Mr. Lupicki went on. "They see just one man, and they try to take advantage. I, myself, thought your truck had been abandoned." The women were surrounding him now, and, crushing his cap in both hands in front of his chest, he turned from one to the other as he spoke.

"We had another man with us," Mother explained, "an army major even, but he was under orders to report to Lublin."

The man waited patiently while Mother spoke, but went on again as soon as she had finished. "Just my presence in the front seat, Missus, will be a deterrent. I am also skilled at driving an automobile. I can assist your driver, and in the event of a burst tire I can be of quite valuable help as well."

"Where is it that you want to go?" Auntie Paula asked him.

"Esteemed lady, I want to go where everyone is going, far enough from the city to be out of the way of the bombing. They are bombing the cities, you know, to make people leave and fill up the roads so the army can't travel. They bomb and strafe us along the way to keep us moving. Your truck can't move any faster than people on foot right now, which, of course, is exactly the goal the Germans want to achieve. But when you get further from the city, you will be able to roll faster, and you can eventually get to where you are going. And you, esteemed ladies, can drop me anywhere along the way that you wish or, if you desire it, I shall stay with you to your final destination. As I said, I have no specific destination of my own."

"If he sits up front with Dembovski . . ." Mother said. "He's right. People will see him through the window sitting there. And having a second man along can always help."

"How do we know we can trust him?" Auntie Paula asked.

"Esteemed lady, I am the second assistant manager of the Shoe Store of Goldfarb. I am accustomed to serving the feet of fine gentlemen and ladies. I assure you of my total benignity."

"I think it will be all right," Mother said.

"I no longer own anything except what I carry about my person," he quickly added. "I had a suitcase, but I had to drop it when the German Stukas came and we ran for the woods. And when it was over, my suitcase was gone."

"All right," Mother said. "Go sit up front with Dembovski."

"Basia, you shouldn't have done that," Auntie Paula said when the man had gone. "I don't trust him—he doesn't look right to me."

"Eh, it's wartime," Auntie Edna said, with a wave of her hand. "Nobody looks right."

"Well, it's done," Mother said. "So shouldn't we be on our way again?" We climbed back into the truck.

"We need to talk about how we make decisions," Auntie Paula said when we were moving again.

"Not in front of the children," Auntie Edna said.

"It won't hurt the children to hear this," Auntie Paula said. "We are three adult women, mothers, each with a child to take care of, and there is a war going on. None of us knows what's going to happen next or what's the best thing to do about it."

"Yes, but please not in front of the children, Paula."

"It'll do them good to hear this. It's a lesson about life."

"What Paula is trying to say," my mother said, "is that she wants to be the one to make the decisions."

"Please, Basia," Auntie Edna said, "we'll talk about all this later."

"I heard you complaining about how Mrs. Solecki was giving all the orders," my mother went on, ignoring Auntie Edna. "Mrs. Solecki is the wife of a major and she's lived through one war already. But Paula couldn't stand Mrs. Solecki giving directions."

Even though Auntie Edna didn't want us to hear what they were saying, I understood that this was a grownup conversation and they had a right to their privacy. I was rather proud of reaching this conclusion and tried not to listen.

But that was hard to do. I heard Auntie Paula say to my mother, "You think you're a princess because everyone has always treated you like one. Well, this is a different world."

"For heavensakes, Paula!" Auntie Edna said.

For a while, nobody said anything. Though I had decided to give the mothers their privacy, I could not help thinking about how much nicer Auntie Edna, who didn't want to argue, was than either Auntie Paula or my mother.

"He's got a gun," I heard Fredek say.

"What did you say?" his mother asked.

"He has a gun," Fredek repeated.

Auntie Edna looked at Auntie Paula, then at Mother.

"Who has a gun?" Auntie Paula asked.

"That man, Mr. Lupicki. I saw it inside his coat. It's very small and has a white handle."

"You didn't really see it," Miss Bronia said with a little laugh in her voice. But I could tell by her tone that she wasn't really sure.

"Yes, I did," Fredek insisted.

"I don't believe him," Auntie Paula said.

"If Fredek says he saw it," Auntie Edna insisted, "that means he saw it."

"Fredek is very creative," Miss Bronia was saying in a tone that I could tell was meant for Fredek's benefit. "He's very good at making up wonderful stories, aren't you, Fredek?"

"Yes," he agreed.

"And this is one of them, isn't it?" Miss Bronia said. "You made it up for our amusement on this long hot trip."

"No," he said. "I saw the gun."

"What are we going to do?" Auntie Edna said.

"Fredek is lying," Auntie Paula said.

"Fredek doesn't lie," Auntie Edna answered. "Like Bronia said, he is very creative and makes up stories sometimes."

"And this is one of them."

"He said it isn't," his mother insisted, "and I believe him." But I wasn't sure that she did. "Basia?" Auntie Edna said.

"What?" my mother asked. "Now you're asking me what to do? A minute ago you two were saying that I wasn't qualified to make decisions about my own truck, and now you want me to decide whether Fredek is telling the truth?"

In the first place, Auntie Edna hadn't said anything of the sort—she had been trying to stop them from arguing. And in the second place, Auntie Paula had said that none of them knew what the best thing to do was. What she had meant, of course, was that they should make decisions together. Mother was being unfair to them both.

"What I propose we do," Mother was saying, "is forget the whole issue for the moment. We let Lupicki ride with us for protection, and if he does have a gun, that makes him even better protection, doesn't it? And if he means to use the gun against us, there is nothing we can do at the moment anyway. But if that does turn out to be his intent, I'm sure I can talk him out of it. He's only a shoe store clerk."

"Do you agree with that, Paula?" Auntie Edna asked.

I looked over at my cousin Fredek. With his index finger extended, he held an imaginary pistol and was quietly and repeatedly executing each mother in turn. Sonya was huddled in the corner, her legs drawn up on the bench. I expected that she was asleep.

Suddenly the truck lurched violently.

"What was that?" Auntie Edna cried.

Miss Bronia, who could see through our partially open door because she sat on my side said, "We've left the road. We seem to be in a field of some sort."

"It's Lupicki!" Auntie Edna shouted.

The truck was rocking back and forth as we drove. Craning my neck to peer around the partially open door, I could see the road that we had been on to our left. A big crater cut the road in two, and people were making their way around it. Some people were lying on the ground.

We passed fairly close to several. I didn't think that anyone besides me and Miss Bronia could see them.

"Are they dead?" I whispered to Miss Bronia.

"Nobody's dead," Auntie Edna snapped. She hadn't been meant to hear my whisper, and from where she sat she couldn't see out the door, but I could tell from her tone that her comment was rooted not in fact, but in expediency. It was, I realized, like my grandmother trying to keep Grandfather's death a secret. Miss Bronia didn't say anything, but gave me a little squeeze with the arm she held around me.

"Children," Auntie Paula said suddenly, "there is a war going on and some people are being killed. We may all have to see some dead people before it's over."

"Don't say that to the children," Auntie Edna admonished her. "Children, it's true that sometimes people get killed, but you're not to look at them. Sometimes we may have to tell you to close your eyes."

"What nonsense are you telling them now?" Auntie Paula said. "We may get to see a lot of dead people, and the children will have to learn to look at them too. We may be killed ourselves."

"What are you saying?" Auntie Edna demanded. "What are you saying? Children, we're perfectly safe in this truck. It's bulletproof, and nothing will happen to us."

I heard Auntie Paula give a loud snort.

The truck gave another big lurch and then smoothed out. We were on the road again. We were moving faster than before. I could see that we were passing people on foot. They were dressed in work clothes and business suits, in dresses like my mother wore and long peasant skirts with kerchiefs around their faces like the woman who sold vegetables down the street from our house or the one who had had her hand shot off. Some rode bicycles and one man was riding a donkey with his feet almost dragging on the ground.

I wished I had more time to see the people as they passed my slot in our partially opened door. I wanted to look longer at the man on the donkey and the red-faced woman in the kerchief, the long skirt, and the boots, as she leaned forward against the weight of a large bag on her back. But they all flashed by too quickly, whipping backwards out of sight.

"Where are we going anyway?" It was Sonya's voice.

"We're going to a farm, dear," her mother answered. "Remember Irenka's parents, Mr. and Mrs. Metner? Well, they have an estate—it's a farm where they grow . . . well, I don't know what they grow, but they have peasants who raise things to feed people in the cities . . . people like us. And they have cows and horses. It's away from the city so it won't get bombed, and they're letting us have one of their cottages till this is over."

"Will Irenka be there?"

"I don't know. I suppose so. I don't suppose the Metners will want to stay in Warsaw either."

"Irenka has a brother your age, boys," Miss Bronia said. "He has a pony, I hear, and maybe he'll let you ride it sometime. Maybe they even have more ponies and you can ride together."

I was immediately envisioning Fredek and me and our young host, each mounted on a pony and led around by a man in a cap and high boots, the way they did in the park. Kiki and I had passed those ponies millions of times, me waiting anxiously for my eighth birthday, which was when I was to have my first ride and which wasn't due until the coming January. And now, months before my birthday, I would be riding a pony, not just for one ten-minute ride as a birthday special, but daily. And by the time we went back to Warsaw, I would be able to get up onto the pony by myself and control him by myself too. Then, when I finally got my birthday ride, I would surprise Kiki as well as the pony-rides man by jumping up on the pony, myself, and galloping around the park.

"I know how to ride horseback," Fredek said. "I can gallop and jump and everything. I'll draw my sword, hold it over my head like this, and charge!" He followed this by making hoof-beat sounds.

I doubted strongly the veracity of Fredek's claim. But I did realize that our rides were not going to be as idyllic as I had first fantasized. Fredek would, right away, be wanting to race and attack cows and things. And the men in caps and high boots who led the ponies, would think Fredek was brave and I wasn't because I just wanted to ride the pony. Now I hoped they only had one pony, and Fredek and I wouldn't be invited to ride it.

The three mothers were all sitting very quietly now, and Fredek was still making his galloping sounds with an occasional, "Charge!" or a horse's neigh thrown in. I returned to my private theater on the other side of our half-open door, watching the endless variety of people whip in and out of my life for two seconds, moving backwards.

"Somebody's crying," Auntie Edna said suddenly. I listened, but couldn't hear anything. And then I did, but it wasn't a person.

"It's a scream," Auntie Paula said, because it was quickly growing louder. I felt the truck suddenly speed up.

"What is . . . ?" my mother began, but the scream became deafening.

There was a crash, a sudden wind inside the truck, and the truck rocking left and right as though it would topple over. We were all on the floor suddenly, and the truck was speeding now, still oscillating from the concussion.

Auntie Edna screamed, "Oh, my hand! Oh, my hand!" The explosion had torn the cord and blown both doors open. As they banged back and forth, I could see a big cloud of dust in the road we had just passed. One of our suitcases fell out and bounced along the road. Beyond the cloud of dust, an ugly airplane was flying away from us, low to the ground. Its wings looked like they were broken. They came out of the fuselage at a downward angle for a foot or two and then turned upward. Its landing gear, which other modern planes tucked up into their body, hung down like the stumpy legs of a dwarf. Then it pulled up and disappeared.

I was lying across the legs of some woman who turned out to be Auntie Paula. Miss Bronia was across my legs, and Fredek seemed to be hugging my mother. Only Sonya seemed not to have been dislodged from her corner seat.

"My hand! My hand!" Auntie Edna cried again, as we began to untangle ourselves.

"Is . . . is everyone else all right?" Auntie Paula asked. Nobody else complained.

"What's wrong with Missus's hand, Mrs. Tishman?" Miss Bronia asked, making her way over the tossed-about luggage on hands and knees.

"I fell on it."

Miss Bronia knelt in front of Auntie and took her right arm and hand in both of her hands. "Can Missus move the fingers?"

"Ow, it hurts."

"Missus should try."

"Yes, ow, I can. It's moving."

"All of them?"

"I don't know."

"Mrs. Tishman should try them all."

"Let me see . . . ow . . . yes, that one and, ow, that one and, yes, I think I can move them all."

"All right, then I don't think it's broken. It's probably badly sprained. Missus should sit back up on the bench . . . here, I'll help Missus. That's it, and now Missus should rest her arm on her lap for support. I'll find something to wrap it with."

The truck slowed to a stop. Mr. Dembovski and Mr. Lupicki appeared at the open doors. "Is everyone all right?" our driver asked.

"Yes," my mother answered. She didn't even mention Auntie Edna's hand.

"He missed us," Mr. Dembovski said.

"He was diving down right at us," Mr. Lupicki said, "and when Boleswav speeded up suddenly, I think he couldn't make the adjustment. It was a Stuka."

I had heard that name before.

"They make a horrible sound," Auntie Edna said.

"I'm afraid they may try again," Mr. Dembovski said. "They think we're an army truck."

"Yes, because we're painted green," Auntie Edna said.

"Maybe the ladies should get out and walk," Mr. Lupicki said. "That way, if we hear them coming again, you can run away from the truck. Boleswav and I can jump out into the field." Mr. Lupicki seemed to suddenly become aware of his loosened collar and tie, which he now proceeded to adjust. His pomaded hair, however, was still all in place. I looked at his tightly-fitting jacket, and it didn't seem to be concealing any gun.

"What if the airplanes come and machine-gun us again?" Auntie Edna asked.

"It's easier to crawl under the truck from the road than from inside," Auntie Paula answered her.

The stream of people parted to pass around us as we stood behind the truck. Somewhere behind us, I realized, there must be a big hole in the road where the bomb had landed, and the people must be circling it the same way, but I wasn't tall enough to see over their heads.

"Are you going to walk on this road in those heels?" Auntie Paula asked Mother.

"I don't have any others."

"You didn't pack any other shoes?"

"I don't have any flats."

"You didn't bring any flats?" Auntie Edna asked.

"I don't own any flats."

"What did you plan to wear at the Metners' farm?" Auntie Paula asked. I smiled inwardly. Then I remembered Kiki's charge.

"Maybe mine will fit Missus," Miss Bronia said. She began digging in her suitcase.

In a moment Mother was standing in a pair of brown sandals, and I noticed with pleasure that she wasn't taller than me by as much as before. Being happy to find myself nearly as tall as Mother, I reasoned, was not breaking God's Commandments.

"Why don't the ladies walk in front of the truck," Mr. Lupicki said. "That way, Boleswav and I can keep an eye on them."

I could tell that the mothers were beginning to like Mr. Lupicki.

"We're just out for a country walk," Auntie Paula said. "Give me your arm, Sonya." She and Sonya hooked arms and stepped into the stream of walking people.

"Hold my hand," my mother said, the way she did when she took me out on the street on Kiki's day off, even though Kiki had not made me hold her hand for over a year, except when we crossed the street. Mother's palm was smooth and soft as a silk cushion.

"Here," Mother said, taking the gold lighter from Auntie Edna, who was struggling to light it with her left hand. Mother lit Auntie Edna's cigarette for her.

"Do you want one?" Auntie Edna asked.

"I left mine in the truck," Mother said. I watched Auntie Edna reach her left hand into the sling that Miss Bronia had fixed for her and produce a box of cigarettes for Mother. Mother took both the cigarettes and lighter from her and lit up.

"It hurts like the devil," Auntie Edna was saying. "Bronia says she has some powders for the pain, but there's nothing to wash them down with except the children's cocoa."

Walking in front of us, Miss Bronia held Fredek's hand, and I could see them talking to each other and wondered what they talked about. I could not imagine Fredek carrying on a conversation about anything other than guns and shooting people. I looked at Miss Bronia's free hand with longing.

"Are we going to walk all the way to Metners'?" Auntie Edna was saying.

"When it's dark it should be safe to get back in the truck." Mother answered.

"I suppose so," Auntie Edna agreed. Then her tone changed and she began speaking French.

"*Julien parle Francais*," Mother answered. It meant Yulian speaks French, and it was one of the few things that I could understand in that language. "Go walk with Miss Bronia and Fredek," she said to me. Without further prompting, I rushed ahead and claimed the free hand.

"Hello, Yulian," she greeted me. "You're going to walk with us?"

I nodded my head enthusiastically. We walked on in silence, but the hollow of Miss Bronia's palm spoke volumes to my hand.

Nearly everyone, I realized, was walking at the same pace. A little ahead, on my right, a man and a woman were not keeping up with the others. They were older than Mother, but not as old as my grandmother, and they were walking arm in arm. They wore city clothes. The man had taken off his jacket and rolled it on top of a bag that he had tied to his back with two neckties. His shirt was sweat stained under the arms. The woman had on a brown wool skirt and a beige blouse. It, too, had little damp stains under the arms. I felt sorry for the embarrassment she must be feeling. She had a kind, round face with brown hair streaked with gray. A widow's peak made her face look like a heart. I saw that she was having difficulty walking and she was leaning heavily on his arm for support, as they drifted backwards in our stream.

The man, too, I saw, was laboring under his extra load. Then, suddenly his face had turned dark red, and he stopped, there on the crowded road, and began tugging at his shirt collar, which was already unbuttoned. The woman had turned to face him and was saying something to him. Then, as we moved further ahead, I saw the man just get shorter.

Several other people were surrounding him now, and I could just see his red face as they held him up. His eyes were rolling back and forth as though looking for a way out of their sockets.

We continued walking. I didn't think that either Miss Bronia nor Fredek were aware of the happening. I wanted to see more, but I didn't want Miss Bronia admonishing me not to look, so I turned away as we walked on.

Then I heard Mother's voice. "Miss Bronia, the truck's stopped for something!" she called.

"Oh, we'd better wait," Miss Bronia said. "Mrs. Herbstein!" she called to Auntie Paula, up ahead, "the truck has stopped!"

Auntie Paula and Sonya stopped. "What is it?" Auntie Paula asked.

"They just put a man into it," Fredek said.

Auntie Paula and Sonya walked back to where we were standing. "What's happening?" Auntie Paula asked.

"I don't know," Miss Bronia said.

"They put a man in our truck," Fredek said.

"A man fainted," Auntie Edna said.

"And they put him in the truck?" Auntie Paula said. "Our things!"

The three mothers ran back to the truck. Fredek tried to go after them, but Miss Bronia held him by the hand. "We'll just wait here," she said.

"Mother doesn't need any help," Sonya said, laughing.

Then I saw Mr. Dembovski standing on the running board. "Is anybody a doctor?" he yelled out. Nobody responded, as people kept walking past.

After a while, Auntie Edna and Auntie Paula came back to where we were standing. "He looks like he had a heart attack," Auntie Paula said to Miss Bronia. "Mrs. Waisbrem is staying in the truck with his wife. It's dangerous to stop here." Then the truck began to move again and we resumed walking.

"What's a heart attack?" Fredek wanted to know. I knew what a heart attack was. I had seen my grandfather die from one. I wished I had said so before Miss Bronia began telling Fredek about the heart stopping to pump the blood. But then I thought about the poor woman with the heart-shaped face, whose husband was right now dying in the truck, and felt ashamed.

"What songs do we all know?" Miss Bronia asked. Without suggesting any songs, Fredek immediately launched into a soldiers' marching song, which Kiki and I knew very well. Miss Bronia joined in, but I didn't feel like singing. That poor woman in our truck was right in the process of losing her husband who was dying because he had been helping her walk. I had a good sense of how awful she must be feeling.

"Do you know the words, Yulian?" Miss Bronia asked.

If I said yes, she would ask why I wasn't singing, and if I lied and said no, that would be even worse. Besides, she would probably tell me to listen to Fredek sing them again. I realized that of the options open to me, the most expedient one under even these dire circumstances was to just join in the singing. I did. It was, after all, wartime.

*   *   *

In a while the road went into a forest, and people were sitting and lying down under the trees. There were wagons, carriages, bicycles, and all sorts of handcarts pulled off the road. Some had no people near them and looked as though they may have been abandoned there. When we found a spot big enough for our truck, Auntie Paula and Sonya turned off the road, and we all followed. In a moment the truck followed us onto the grass.

"Is anybody a doctor?" Mr. Dembovski shouted again from the truck as soon as it had stopped. He turned and repeated it in the other direction. Nobody answered.

"A man's had a heart attack!" Mr. Dembovski said.

Miss Bronia led Fredek and me a distance from the truck, and we sat down. "Anybody have to go to the bathroom?" she asked. I had to a little bit, but I didn't say anything.

"I'm hungry," Fredek said. I was too, but I figured it wouldn't help any to say so.

"Who knows the story about the rooster and the pig?" she asked.

"I do," Fredek said.

"Would you like to tell it?" she asked.

"No. You tell it." I was sure that Fredek didn't really know it. I didn't either, but my attention was still on the poor woman with the limp and the face like a heart and the sweat stains, whose husband was in the truck dying.

Then I saw a woman, sitting on the ground not far from us, urging the man sitting with her to come forward—I couldn't hear them, but I could tell by their gestures. Finally, he got up and came towards the truck. He had on a white shirt and gray suit trousers. He was bald with just a horseshoe of gray hair and a gray mustache. "I was a dentist. Maybe I can help," he said.

Mr. Dembovski led him to the back of the truck, and they disappeared inside. Other men were now gathering around the rear of the tuck and stood looking inside. I remembered how in Warsaw people would crowd around to look when a horse fell in the street. My mother, my Aunties, and Sonya were standing at the front of the truck talking together.

Then a man who had been watching walked away, saying, "He's dead. The dentist says he's dead."

Miss Bronia stopped her story and all three of us watched the goings-on at the back of the truck.

After a few more minutes, Mr. Dembovski got down from the truck and began talking to the people standing behind it. Then the group broke up. Mr. Dembovski went to the side of the truck now, opened a compartment, and brought out a shovel. Then another man came walking back carrying a shovel. And finally, a third man showed up with a shovel as well.

"They're going to bury him," Fredek said. He stood up and started to run towards the truck.

"Come back, Fredek," Miss Bronia called, but he didn't. Instinctively I braced myself for her reaction. But Miss Bronia didn't do anything, just let him disobey her. I could have run with Fredek and watched them bury the man. But I didn't do it and now, again, he was there and I was sitting here.

"I saw my grandfather have a heart attack and die," I told Miss Bronia.

"Did you, now?" she said. "Would you like to tell me about it?"

Her curiosity over the matter surprised me.

"Did you love your grandfather?" she asked.

"Yes," I fibbed. Then, feeling that it needed elaboration, I added, "He gave me a red tricycle to have when I visited them in Lodz." What I didn't say was that I hadn't yet ridden it because I wasn't allowed to ride it either around the apartment or out in the street.

"Tell me what it was like when he died."

"Everybody was calling for a doctor and crying."

"And what was it like for you?"

I knew what she meant. I realized that somebody must have told her about my blowing the whole secret of his death on the phone with Mother. The story must have made the rounds of the family.

"Pretty awful," I said.

"Did you cry?"

"No." Then I corrected myself. "Yes, I did," I fibbed again, remembering that she seemed to be in favor of crying.

"You were afraid to have anyone see you cry," she said. But she said it kindly, not accusingly.

I nodded my head. It was actually true what she said, though crying had not been an issue at that time.

"Would you like to cry now?"

"Yes," I said, surprising myself. She reached out and drew me against her. I cried deliciously against her neck, though it wasn't for Grandfather and, maybe not even for the poor man in the back of the truck nor his poor widow.

"That's just fine," she soothed, stroking my head and shoulders. "Crying is good for you. Any time you feel like crying, you can come to me." I had had no idea that life could be this good.

After a while I noticed that Mr. Dembovski and some other men were digging a hole next to a bush. Fredek was standing there watching. I quickly turned away before Miss Bronia could catch me looking.

"It's all right to look," she said. "They're digging a grave for the poor man who died. We may see more graves before this is over. If you want to go over there with Fredek and look, it's all right."

I wanted to go look, and I wanted to stay in Miss Bronia's arms. But I realized that not going over to gawk would be more grown-up. "That's all right," I said. "I don't need to look."

"Do you want to tell me more about your grandfather?"

The extent of Miss Bronia's curiosity regarding this matter surprised me. "Well, of course he was very old and he couldn't walk," I said, beginning with the main thing I could think of about him.

"He was very old and he couldn't walk?" she asked.

"Yes," I said, surprised now that she should know about my blunder on the telephone, but not about his paralysis.

"Yes. He was paralyzed and had to be pushed around in a wheelchair." I knew it would be inappropriate to tell her about the incontinence device sticking out of his pant leg. But there wasn't much else I knew to tell her about my grandfather.

"He was paralyzed and had to be pushed around in a wheelchair," Miss Bronia repeated after a while.

That was what I had said. Now I wondered why Miss Bronia had to have it repeated. She certainly was very nice, but now I wondered about how bright she might be. Marta, our cook, was like that. Things had to be explained to her.

Then my thoughts were interrupted because Auntie Edna and Auntie Paula came over to us. They carried a wooden chest with handles between them, and water was dripping out of the bottom.

"Mr. Lupicki brought us this," Auntie Paula said to Miss Bronia, setting down the chest. "Don't ask where he got it," she added with a tilt of the head towards me.

I understood that signal. Mr. Lupicki had probably gotten it from a car with dead people in it. I wondered if Miss Bronia understood. I would make sure she did, later.

Auntie Edna opened the lid, and I saw that the chest had a tray with what looked like sandwiches and things wrapped in wax paper. Under the tray, there were two small cakes of ice. Two bottles with what looked like water rolled around the bottom as well.

Miss Bronia unwrapped a sandwich, sniffed it, and handed it to me along with its waxed paper wrapper. I bit into it eagerly. It tasted like chicken.

Later, when it was dark again, we all got back into the truck. I was surprised to see the poor woman whose husband had died, still sitting there. It seemed that she was going to come along with us. She sat between Mother and Auntie Edna as though they were holding her up, and Auntie Edna had an arm around the woman's shoulders. The woman cried gently into a handkerchief. The rest of us were all quiet. Fredek and Sonya were playing some kind of silent game with their fingers. It was one I had never heard of, but they seemed to find it very entertaining.

I knew that I shouldn't be staring at the poor woman in her grief, but it was difficult to keep my eyes off her. She was the only person I had ever seen, other than Grandmother, who had been so bereaved, and I understood myself to be in the presence of something momentous.

This woman was very different from Grandmother. Grandmother had carried on, walking aimlessly from room to room, twisting a kerchief in her hand and saying, "Oh, my God," in Russian over and over. Kiki had wiped the makeup off Grandmother's face with cold cream and the polish off her finger and toe nails. She had looked as though she didn't have any face. This woman just sat there between Mother and Auntie Edna and sobbed quietly into her handkerchief. She reminded me of a little girl I had seen sitting between her parents on a park bench eating a banana.

"He was helping me walk," she said after a while. "Our car had burst a tire, and Anton was trying to fix it, but we were blocking the road, and some men came along and we thought they were going to help us, but they just pushed the car into the ditch and we had to walk."

I was horrified by what those men had done, but the woman didn't seem at all angry at them. She must have been an extremely kind woman, I concluded—saintly, even.

Auntie Edna made a soothing clucking noise.

"Then I twisted my ankle, and Anton was helping me walk. He was such a strong man. When he was young he was an athlete. When the war is over, we'll come back and bury him in the cemetery, won't we?"

"Yes, we will," Mother said. But I knew that she didn't mean it.

"You're very good to take me in your truck," the woman went on. "My cousins will be so grateful to you. . . . oh, I hope the Germans haven't bombed them too. Do you think they have?"

"There aren't any people on the road now," Mother said, "so I would guess they haven't been bombing here."

"Oh, that's good, and you can stay with them as long as you want. They have a house. We just had an apartment, you know, but the German planes dropped a bomb right on it. Anton said we should go into the basement as soon as the sirens sounded, and he was so right. It saved our lives. Oh, God, poor Anton. He was an accountant, you know, for Zielenski Brothers, a very careful man. Everything had to be done just so. He was a wonderful man, too. So kind and so gentle. You're all very kind too. My cousins will be so grateful to you for helping me.

"We used to have a little dog," she began, and I was suddenly gripped by the fear that it had been in the apartment when it was bombed or in the car when they pushed it into the ditch. "His name was Kropka, and we took him everywhere we went. He had a little pillow that he lay on in our car. He would beg for his food and roll over and always come when you called him. But he died last year, and Anton was so upset."

I was much relieved. Then she went on to tell us about the company her husband had worked for, that built apartment buildings. I don't think she stopped talking until the truck stopped.

Then we were at the house of her cousins who lived in a two-story house on a winding, hilly street in the outskirts of a town. Getting out of the truck, I had seen the tall three-and-four-story buildings and the high church spires of the main part of town downhill from where we stood. Their house was actually two stories at the uphill end and three on the downhill side.

The cousins were very happy to see our passenger, but not so happy to see the rest of us. They clucked and cried at the sadness of her husband's death and then the woman spread her hands out, palms forward, and explained that they had no room for us. There were four of them, mother, father, a girl around my age, and a toddler of indeterminate gender. The mother was in a blue bathrobe, the children in nightgowns. The girl my age held her hands out from her sides like her mother. The toddler pressed against his or her mother's leg and sucked her or his thumb. The father had on a blue shirt with white pin stripes, but without its detachable celluloid collar. Gray suspenders held up his gray trousers.

"Oh, but you have to put them up for the night," the woman who had lost her husband said. "They were so kind to me, and they buried poor Anton. And they're going on to Durnoval tomorrow." We were all standing in the dining room, except for Mr. Dembovski and Mr. Lupicki who waited in the truck. Fredek and I were each holding one of Miss Bronia's hands. I recognized a picture of Jesus on the wall.

"The army has taken over the hotel," the father said to us, but I think he meant that for his wife. I had the feeling that he really wanted to let us stay.

"They can sleep on blankets on the floor," the woman whose husband had died said. "They're tired, and the children . . ."

"We have no food," the other woman said. She had a heart-shaped face like her cousin's, but she was shorter and stouter. "The stores are all empty, and you have to go directly to the farmers and pay a terrible price. And who knows how long that will last. Many of the farmers have been taken into the army." The buffet behind her was stacked high with jars and cans of food.

"We can pay," Auntie Edna said.

The woman brought her hands to her temples. "What good is money?" she said. "They're bombing people in the cities. They'll be bombing here next. The army took our automobile."

"Let's go," my mother said.

"The children need to eat and to sleep," Auntie Paula said. Then to the woman she said, "You have children."

"I'm not staying in this woman's house," my mother said and turned toward the door. Auntie Paula grabbed her by the wrist to stop her.

"Marinka, these are children," the woman who had lost her husband said.

"Then do what you will," the other woman said. She wrapped an arm around the shoulders of her cousin and led her quickly into the hall and up the stairs. Her two children hurried after them. I never saw any of the four of them again.

The man stood there looking very uncomfortable. For the second time that day, I was reminded of the time I had put on the blue wool sailor suit to go to the park and knew how the man must feel.

"I'll help you bring your things in," he finally said. "We'll lay some blankets out in the parlor."

"We have blankets," Auntie Edna said.

"There are two men with us," Auntie Paula said, "The driver and another man. They can sleep in the truck."

"They can sleep in the kitchen," the man said. Suddenly people were bringing things in from the truck.

"There are eggs," the man said, "we have chickens. And there's ham and potatoes." This was very different from what his wife had told us. "Our cook has gone home," he added.

My mother and the Aunties all looked at each other. "I can fry eggs," Auntie Edna said.

"I'll do it, Mrs. Tishman," Miss Bronia said.

"You have such beautiful children, Mr. Halpin," I heard my mother say. "They resemble you more than your wife."

"She's very upset," he explained. "Her father was killed by the Germans in the last war, and now her brother is at the front. I'm not in the army because of my liver, but she's afraid that if things get bad enough, I will have to go too."

"I know just how she feels," Mother said. "Our husbands are all at the front. There is nothing left of our apartments in Warsaw."

Then, Miss Bronia, Mr. Dembovski, Mr. Lupicki, Fredek, and I ate at the long kitchen table with its thick, bare wood top. My mother, my Aunties, Sonya, and Mr. Halpin were in the dining room. I could hear their voices, and sometimes they would all laugh.

In the kitchen, Mr. Lupicki entertained us with magic tricks. He made little balls out of bread and made them disappear and appear out of Fredek's ear. He borrowed Miss Bronia's ring and made it appear under my arm and pulled a long, colored handkerchief out of Miss Bronia's hair, and all of it without saying a word. We sat and watched and laughed, and at some point I must have fallen asleep.

In the morning, Miss Bronia woke me up to give me a bath. I discovered that Fredek and I had been put to bed under the dining room table. Fredek was still asleep, curled up on his side. Miss Bronia had put a washtub on the kitchen table, and I had to take my clothes off, climb up on the table and into the tub. I was embarrassed to undress in front of Miss Bronia, but knew it had to be. I kept myself turned away as I climbed up and in so that she would see only my behind.

Her hands were gentle with the strange-smelling soap. "Here, wash yourself while I go get a towel," she said, handing me the soap and washcloth. The moment she stepped out of the room, I got up onto my knees and washed my privates. I was seated again when she returned, and the water had grown opaque.

Fredek came into the kitchen bragging that he had had his bath the night before when I had fallen asleep. I hoped he would leave the kitchen before I had to get out of the tub.

Then a woman I hadn't seen before came in with a broom and a dustpan full of sweepings which she poured into the flames in the stove along with some additional sticks of wood from a cubbyhole in the wall. She was stout, with white hair pulled into a bun and, like Marta our cook, didn't wear makeup. She wore a gray dress and man's shoes.

"All right, you big fish," Miss Bronia sang out. "It's time to get out."

The woman was stirring a pot on the stove with her back to me, but she might turn around at any moment. I shook my head. "Hey, slippery fish, we have to get going," Miss Bronia said cheerfully. I found myself clutching the edges of the tub as I shook my head again. Miss Bronia held up the towel as a screen between me and the cook. I stood up a little, and Miss Bronia immediately had the towel wrapped around me. She had her own head turned to the side, but I didn't really mind her seeing my birdie. Wrapped inside the big towel, it felt wonderfully soft and warm.

Fredek, Sonya, and I ate some sort of oatmeal and bread with honey at one end of the dining room table while Miss Bronia packed suitcases and folded blankets. Sonya had coffee with her breakfast. Mother and my Aunties sat at the other end talking in low voices. Then I saw the cook come in with a cup of tea for Mother. "Thank you so much, Helga," Mother said to her. "Now, would you be a dear and toast this bread a little for me."

"Certainly, Missus," the cook answered with a little curtsey. Auntie Edna and Auntie Paula exchanged looks. Mrs. Halpin, her cousin, and the two children were nowhere in sight.

When we went out to get back into our truck, I saw that it had been painted a bright yellow. Fredek, who was already outside looking at it when I came out, explained that it was so German airplanes wouldn't mistake us for army and attack us again. I, of course, could figure that out on my own and ignored him.

"It was the only paint we could get, Missus, and it's still a little wet, but the wind will dry it," Mr. Dembovski explained to Mother. He was carrying suitcases out of the house.

"I think Lupicki stole it," Auntie Paula confided to Miss Bronia.

"What did he steal, Auntie?" Fredek wanted to know.

"Nothing," Auntie Paula said.

"I told you he was a crook," Fredek said to me. Mr. Halpin had come out to say goodbye, and I saw Mother hand him a fold of money. "Oh, I couldn't," I heard him say.

"It's wartime," my mother told him. "We must all carry our own weight when we can." She pressed the money into his hand. "Please thank your wife for us, and may God watch over you all." Mother's reference to God surprised me.

Suddenly I heard Fredek cry out in pain. "Look what you've done!" his mother was shouting. She had Fredek by the ear with her one good hand. "Those pants came from Vienna!"

"Ow!" Fredek was crying while Auntie Edna looked as though she were trying to lift him off the ground by that ear.

"Look at that," Auntie Edna was saying to the group, turning Fredek around by his ear. On the seat of his gray shorts there was a smear of yellow paint. "We brought these pants back from Vienna last winter, and we've waited all this time for him to grow into them. Now look what he's done."

"Let it go, Edna," Auntie Paula said. "It isn't important."

"Do you know what Morris paid for those pants?" Auntie Edna said.

"It isn't important," Auntie Paula repeated. "You're hurting him."

"Ow! Ow!" Fredek repeated. I saw his face was red and he was in tears. Auntie Edna let him go. Fredek rubbed his ear and continued crying.

"He makes me so mad," Auntie Edna said. "Always tormenting me with his guns, his spies, his . . . his I-don't-know-what's."

"He's a boy, Edna," Auntie Paula said.

"Look how well-behaved Yulek is. He sits quietly, and answers politely, doesn't make trouble, obeys. . . ." Auntie Edna was saying.

Suddenly I felt very embarrassed—embarrassed and pleased at the same time. I knew immediately that I should feel sorry for Fredek, but I was pleased instead.

"In front of the children!" Auntie Paula admonished her.

"I know, I'm a terrible mother."

"Edna!"

Auntie Edna was crying as she stepped on a box to get into the truck, and I felt sorry for her. We all followed in silence.

"Basia has a new conquest," Auntie Paula said, laughing, as soon as we pulled out into the street.

"That anti-Semitic bitch," Mother said.

"Anti-Semitic?" Auntie Paula repeated.

"That's why she didn't want us in the house," Mother said.

"Really, Basia," Auntie Paula said.

"This isn't Warsaw, you know. Small town people aren't like the people you know in Warsaw."

"I've never seen . . ."

"No, Paula, you don't see it, first because you don't travel, and second because you don't look Jewish. Edna is a beautiful woman, but she's a beautiful Jewish woman. Look at her nose. With that nose and her black hair, she could be the queen of Palestine. I have a nose, too, but I dye my hair." That was news to me. "In America they do operations now where they change your nose," my mother went on. "Everybody has it done. Lolek and I were going to go to New York next summer. Now I don't know what's going to happen."

"Paula, look what's happening in Germany." Auntie Edna spoke up for the first time.

"But this is Poland," Auntie Paula said.

"You think it's that different in Poland?" Mother said. "Because we have money, we're accepted. We can go to fine restaurants and hotels. But have you ever tried to get a table at Bolecki's? 'I'm sorry, Mrs. Herbstein, but we have no tables this evening.' Try to enroll Frederick Tishman or Sonya Herbstein in the Kormanevich school."

"That's right," Auntie Edna said. "Basia's right. You and Felix don't look Jewish. Only your name gives you away, but you don't travel."

"What do you mean we don't travel? We came back from Paris just last month."

"That's not the kind of travel Basia is talking about. First of all, people who travel don't go to Paris in August, and second of all . . ."

"Felix had to go there on business."

"All right, on business. And where did you stay, at the Plaza?"

"Isn't that where you and Morris stay?"

Auntie Edna began to laugh. "From now on, we all hide behind Paula," she said. "And Bronia," she added.

"Why don't you dye your hair like Auntie Barbara?" Fredek asked his mother. The three mothers all burst out laughing.

Miss Bronia quickly reached into her purse and brought out the knotted string we had played with the day before. "Let's do cat's cradle," she suggested.

"I want to do cat's cradle with Fredek," Sonya suddenly announced.

"We'll all take turns," Miss Bronia said.

I didn't want to play cat's cradle, and I exercised my newly-discovered right to voice it. Something far more important was forming in my mind. How could I best love and help Mother, as I knew I was supposed to at this difficult time? The answer was simple—by converting her to Catholicism. Then her Immortal Soul could go to Heaven for the rest of eternity, and that would be a much more valuable thing than anything else I could ever do for her. Suddenly I was very excited. How I would go about doing this, I had no idea. But if I had faith in God, He would show me. Hadn't He already shown me signs of His approval?

*   *   *

That day was mostly uneventful. There were no people on foot on this road, and only an occasional farmer's wagon passed by. Once some cars and trucks carrying soldiers zoomed past us, going the other way.

But there were thoughts rushing through my head. I could see myself going to mass with Kiki and Mother after the war. I was the tallest of the three, and I would prompt Mother on her prayers. Kiki would be so proud of me and would hold my arm tightly. I was on a mission now. God had sent me on this adventure with these five Jews and Miss Bronia for a purpose.

Did that mean that I was supposed to convert all of them? God would tell me. If I had faith, God would tell me His intentions in His own time.

The three mothers talked little and slept a lot. Fredek and Sonya huddled in one corner whispering and laughing. Mr. Dembovski had tied both doors wide open and there was plenty of light now. Miss Bronia would ask me occasionally if I wanted her to tell me a story or something. But there was too much in the way of stories going on in my head to warrant troubling her. I realized by now that God was not really an old man with a long white beard and sandals, but lacking a more current image, I envisioned His bearded presence praising me for my missionary work.

We stopped at a farmer's house and Auntie Paula went to the door and bought bread, cheese, and milk for our lunch. We made some bathroom stops, one by a stream where we washed our hands and faces. Mr. Lupicki made us laugh by pulling a stone out of my ear and then doing funny things with his hands by bending his fingers in ways that nobody else could. I noticed that he had taken off his jacket and even his hair was a little messy.

Turning to the mothers, Mr. Lupicki pulled a well-worn deck of cards out of his back pocket and proceeded to do some card tricks that I couldn't follow, where he guessed what cards they were thinking of. He finished by fanning the entire deck out and then making them all fly through the air in some way that landed them neatly stacked in his hand.

"What clever hands Mister has, Mr. Lupicki," my mother said to him. "Such supple fingers. Let me see them." She held her hand out, palm up.

Mr. Lupicki carefully laid one of his hands in Mother's. He was a small man, and his hand wasn't much larger than hers. "You can tell so much about a man by looking at his hand," Mother said, turning his hand over. "I don't tell fortunes, but I see courage and great cleverness in that hand." Mr. Lupicki blushed. "When this is over," Mother went on, "Mister should look into something more ambitious than selling shoes in someone else's store. Maybe Mister should come to see us in Warsaw."

"Thank you, Missus." Mr. Lupicki withdrew his hand as carefully as he had placed it.

"Why are you turning poor Lupicki's head?" Auntie Paula asked when we were back in the truck, rolling down our empty road again.

"Lupicki's very resourceful," Mother answered her. "It's good to have his good will."

"Isn't that a dangerous way to do it?"

"Why?"

"He's a simple man, and you're putting wrong ideas in his head."

"Because I told him to have bigger ambitions than clerking in a shoe store?"

"You know what I mean," Auntie Paula said.

"For heavensakes, Paula."

"Paula's right," Auntie Edna said. "It's not a good idea to be putting ideas in these people's heads."

I had no idea what they were talking about.

"I'm not putting ideas in anyone's head. He's an intelligent man, who's just never thought he could do better than be a shoe-store clerk."

"It's just dangerous, particularly at a time like this," Auntie Edna said. Then they all stopped talking.

I thought my mother was right. If Mr. Lupicki was as smart as she said, then he should certainly do something that paid him more money than being a shoe-store clerk. What was dangerous about that, I could not understand.

Later that afternoon we pulled to a gradual stop without pulling off the pavement, which seemed to concern the grown-ups. "Why are we stopping here?" Auntie Edna asked.

Mr. Lupicki's dark head and shoulders immediately appeared at the back of our truck. Just some soldiers with car trouble, blocking the road, he assured us. Then he helped us all to the ground.

Looking around the side of the truck, I could see three cars and three trucks, all different shapes, but all painted the same green that ours had been until this morning, stopped in the other lane of the road. Soldiers stood all over the road, and some were peering under the hood of one of the trucks. They had helmets on their heads and carried rifles. Some had back-packs. I could see one young soldier, without his jacket, his shirt sleeves rolled above his elbows, a large screwdriver in his hand, talking to Mr. Dembovski at the front of our truck.

"What is it, Dembovski?" Mother said, walking up to the two of them. I found myself following her, though the others stayed at the back of the truck.

"They want to take Missus's truck," I heard Mr. Dembovski say.

The young soldier's face suddenly turned a dark red. "I am First Lieutenant Yan Tchymanchek," he said, and I could see how nervous he was. "One of our trucks has broken down, and I have authority to commandeer Missus's truck for military service."

"This is Senator Nathan Padovich's truck," my mother lied. That had been my father's name. I didn't know what a senator was.

"I am Mrs. Senator Padovich," she said. In Polish the wife of a doctor was addressed as Mrs. Doctor, and this must have been the title for a senator's wife. "I'm taking my family to Durnoval."

The young lieutenant pulled to attention. "I am sorry, Mrs. Senator, but I have orders."

"What kind of orders?"

"Orders to take my men to Warsaw for defense of the city. My orders . . ."

"I understand," Mother cut him off. "What's wrong with your truck?"

"We don't know, Mrs. Senator. It just stopped."

"Maybe my driver can fix it."

"We haven't the time, Mrs. Senator. We have already been delayed."

"And you want to leave us out here on the road? We have children," she said.

Suddenly I was frightened. I could see us all standing in the empty road with the broken truck as the soldiers drove off in ours.

The lieutenant's face got still darker, and now he was sweating. But he didn't have an answer for her. He had dark wavy hair and a little mustache.

"Go see what's wrong with his truck," Mother said to Mr. Dembovski.

"Y-yes, Missus . . . Mrs. Senator," Mr. Dembovski said, touching his forehead as in a salute. He walked over to the truck, and the soldiers made room for him at the engine. Mr. Lupicki quickly joined him.

"He's an expert mechanic," Mother said. "But tell me, Mr. Lieutenant, where is Mister from?"

"Oh, from Lvow, Mrs. Senator."

"I hear it's a beautiful city," Mother said, "though I've never been there. Is Mister married?"

"Yes, Mrs. Senator."

"And children?"

"One little girl." And now he was smiling.

"Does Mister have photographs?"

"I have some in my tunic in the truck."

"I would love to see them. This is my son Yulian."

I stood to attention and saluted.

"My father's in the Air Force," I heard Fredek say behind me.

"Fredek, come back here!" Auntie Edna said. I saw Fredek head, instead, towards the broken truck.

"Fredek!" Auntie Paula commanded. Fredek turned back.

"Come with me, Yulek," Mother sang out and reached for my hand. I sensed there was a purpose in this invitation and took her hand obediently. We followed the lieutenant to the truck where Mr. Dembovski and Mr. Lupicki were both tinkering with something under the hood. A soldier was in front of the truck fitting the crank into its receptacle under the grill.

The lieutenant brought his tunic out of the cab and pulled a photograph out of an inside pocket.

"Oh, aren't they beautiful," Mother said. "The little girl looks just like Mister. And Mister's wife looks so young. Look,

Yulek, aren't they a beautiful family?" I understood that I was to agree, although the faces in the picture were small and dark. "Yes, Mummy," I said. I was surprised that the lieutenant didn't see that we were putting on an act for him.

"Is the little girl strong?" Mother asked.

"Strong?"

"I mean, is she in good health?"

"Oh, yes."

"Then Mister must thank God for it. Yulek is so fragile. Every little thing upsets his little system."

In the context of the situation, I didn't consider this a put-down. "Oh, the poor boy," the lieutenant said. I coughed, and Mother looked at me out of the corner of her eye.

"In Warsaw he was under a pediatrician's care."

"Maybe he will grow out of it."

"Yes, his father and I pray for that. Is Mr. Lieutenant a career officer?"

"Actually, Mrs. Senator, I'm an architect. I am in the reserve."

"Then, after this is over, Mister will have to come to Warsaw and visit us. We're in the telephone book, Padovich, you know. My husband is in charge of some important building projects, and there will be a lot of rebuilding to do."

Mother was telling one lie after another. But this, too, I supposed, was part of its being wartime.

Then there was some shouting among a small group of soldiers, and the lieutenant excused himself to tend to the commotion. Immediately, Mr. Lupicki was at Mother's elbow.

"Boleswav says he can't fix their truck. It's something electrical," he said in a whisper that I could hear. "He says that we should all, very quietly and quickly, get back in Missus's truck."

I saw that Mr. Dembovski was still working under the hood of the soldiers' truck. Mother didn't answer Mr. Lupicki, but took my hand again and began to lead me with quick steps

back to our truck. The rest of our group, who had been standing at the back, were not in sight.

Mr. Lupicki helped Mother and me climb up, and I found
everyone else in the truck already.

"We're not supposed to speak," Fredek whispered as I took
my seat next to him.

"Shish!" Auntie Edna hissed.

"Shish," Miss Bronia said quietly. We sat in silence. Then I
heard the engine start up, and we began to move. People were
holding their breath.

After we had passed the soldiers in the road, I could see the
lieutenant standing alone, looking after us.

"Do you think they'll come after us?" Auntie Edna whispered.

"No," Mother said. "He wouldn't leave women with children out in the road."

"Well done, Mrs. Senator Padovich," Auntie Edna whispered,
as we watched the lieutenant in the road growing smaller.

Relieved as I was to be on our way, it wasn't without some
pangs of guilt. It was only when I realized that it wasn't the lie
about who we were that had let us escape, but the lieutenant's
unwillingness to leave women and children stranded on the
road, that I felt better. I chose not to pursue the matter further.

*   *   *

In a while we made another stop so people could go to the
bathroom. Again, we had stopped by some trees and a stream.
The three mothers and Sonya walked a way along the side of
the road to stretch their legs. When I had rinsed my hands in
the stream after going to the bathroom behind a bush, I saw
Mr. Lupicki standing behind me.

"Would you like to learn how to do a magic trick?" he suddenly asked me.

"Yes, please," I answered him, surprised that he should single me out for this attention. Mr. Lupicki put the cigarette between his lips and proceeded to show me how he flicked a coin into the palm of his hand as he pretended to throw it into the air. He gave me a coin, a smaller one, and had me try it. I, of course, immediately dropped the coin, but he urged me to try it again, and after awhile I got so that I could actually hold it without its looking like I was holding anything.

"You keep the coin and practice," he told me, "and tomorrow I'll show you how you can turn your hand over and still hide it." He held his head cocked to the right and squinted his left eye to avoid the smoke while he talked. Then he patted me on the head and walked back to the truck cab where Mr. Dembovski stood smoking.

Back in the truck, I practiced my new skill . . . until I dropped the coin.

"Yulek, where did you get that money?" my mother asked with alarm as she saw me retrieving it. I explained that Mr. Lupicki had given it to me.

"What did he do to you?" she asked, her alarm compounded.

"He showed me how to do coin tricks," I said, puzzled and somewhat frightened by her alarm.

"Give it to me," she said. I stepped across the space between us and handed her the coin.

"You are never to accept money from strangers," she said.

"All right," I conceded.

Nobody in the truck said anything for a moment, then my mother asked again, "Are you sure he didn't do anything to you? Did he touch you?"

"He patted me on the head."

"On the head?"

"Yes."

"You are never to speak to him again, ever," she said.

For the life of me, I could not imagine in what way either one of us had transgressed.

To my Aunties, my mother said, "The next time we stop, that man is getting out of this truck."

"All he did was teach Yulek some coin tricks," Auntie Edna said.

"Why would he do that? Fredek, did Mr. Lupicki teach you any tricks?"

"No, Auntie Barbara," Fredek said.

"So why just Yulek? Why not both boys? Why single out Yulek?"

"Because you were nice to him, Basia," Auntie Paula said. "He was being nice to Yulek in return. You brought this on yourself."

"Well, I don't want Yulek taking money from strangers."

"He didn't give him money." Auntie Paula said. "He gave him a coin to do tricks with. With that, he couldn't buy a chocolate."

"I don't trust that man," Mother said.

"Do you hear what you're saying?" Auntie Paula asked her.

"What? I said I saw courage and cleverness in his hand. That doesn't mean I trust him. Yesterday you were the one telling me you didn't trust him."

Auntie Edna said, "We'll be in Durnoval tonight, and he'll be going his way."

"I just don't want Yulek taking money from strangers," Mother repeated. "Miss Yanka should have taught him that. Didn't Miss Frania teach Fredek that?"

"I don't know," Auntie Edna said.

"Fredek," Mother said, "are you supposed to take money from strangers?"

"Oh, no, Auntie Barbara, Miss Frania taught me. . . ."

"What stupidities you ask, Basia," Auntie Paula interrupted. "What do you expect the child to say?"

"The truth," Mother said. "Fredek always tells Auntie Barbara the truth, don't you, Fredek?"

"Oh, yes, Auntie Barbara."

"This is total nonsense," Auntie Paula said. "Don't you understand children at all?"

"Of course I understand children. Fredek is a very intelligent boy, and he and I get along . . ."

"Why don't we just all sing?" Auntie Edna interrupted. "Bronia, start a song."

Miss Bronia looked confused for a moment, as though her mind had been far away. "Yes . . . yes, a song," she said. "How about . . . ?" It took her some time to think of a song for us to sing.

I still didn't like Auntie Paula very much—she wasn't kind or gentle—but she did make a lot of sense when she talked. And my ability to see her in these two different lights, I considered, a very grown-up observation.

*   *   *

That night we had a proper supper and slept in real beds in the house of some people who had been expecting us, though we didn't actually know them. Their house was in what looked like a real city with cobblestone streets, sidewalks, and street lamps.

They were an elderly couple, and there was a woman about the same age as Mother and the Aunties, who must have been their daughter. There was also a cook named Maria who limped, and I saw that one of her shoes had a much thicker sole than the other. Auntie Paula, who appeared to be the one who had made the arrangements in the first place, introduced us all in the entrance hall, except for the men, who were bringing in the bags. When she introduced Fredek, I saw him pressing a little against Miss Bronia and recognized it as shyness. This inspired me and, when it was my turn, I imagined Kiki telling me that I must step up and shake hands with each of our hosts and look them in the eye, just as she had ordered me to march up to the marshal earlier that year and ask for his autograph. With that self-inflicted spur in my side, I crossed the hall and offered a firm handshake to each one.

Stepping back, I could see my mother beaming. She didn't know that it was Kiki for whom I had done it.

These people, it turned out, were friends, or maybe some kind of employees, of the Metners to whose farm we were going. They had heard on the radio about what was happening in the north and were full of questions about what we had seen. The grownups sat around the dinner table talking, late into the night.

After dinner, Miss Bronia took Fredek and me outside for fresh air and some exercise. Sonya opted to accompany us rather than talk war and politics with the adults. She held Fredek's hand and they walked on ahead up the street, while I had Miss Bronia to myself in the evening's half-light. Unlike Warsaw's five– and six-story buildings that were familiar to me, here none seemed over three stories high. The street was narrower than the ones I knew, and there were no cars or even doroshkas.

As in Warsaw, the windows were now covered with black-out material on the inside, and the street lamps were dark. In a little while, I knew, the street would be completely dark.

Fredek and Sonya walked several steps ahead of us, engaged in some sort of conversation. It was warm and Miss Bronia's hand and mine both grew damp. Instinctively and unconsciously, I slid my palm out of hers and hooked her little finger with my own pinkie.

This was what Kiki and I used to do when our hands grew sweaty. I realized that I had lost track of the fact that this wasn't Kiki. But the maneuver had worked with Miss Bronia as well, and suddenly I realized that Miss Bronia had replaced

Kiki in my life and that I would probably never see Kiki again. Or if I did, we would be much older people—if not chronologically, then in life experience.

And at once I was in the grip of a great sadness, the sadness that I had fully expected yesterday in the truck, but had not felt then. Now it was finally there, and I began crying there in the street.

Miss Bronia called to Sonya and Fredek to stop and then squatted down in front of me. She didn't ask what I was crying about, as Mother would have. And it was good that she didn't, because I would not have been able to tell her—not because I didn't know, but because I did. Because part of my grief was that I knew that I was now in love with Miss Bronia fully as much as I had ever been with Kiki. I was grieving the loss of one woman and that my fickle heart had given itself away to another. Fortunately, she was Catholic too.

Miss Bronia held me to the softest part of herself, and I let my tears flow freely as they never had in my life. Greedily, I found her cheek with my wet mouth and kissed it passionately. In a minute or two it was all over, and we headed back before it would get dark.

Chapter Three

"It's all right," Kiki was saying as she held me against her blue bathrobe. "You just had a bad dream."

Only it wasn't a blue bathrobe, it wasn't Kiki, and it hadn't been a bad dream. It was Miss Bronia, with her brown knit sweater over her nightgown. She was sitting on the side of my bed, holding me in her arms, and telling me that I had had a bad dream. My mother and Auntie Edna were standing there, too, and suddenly I was very embarrassed at having to be comforted one more time by Miss Bronia.

"He's fine, Mrs. Waisbrem," Miss Bronia was saying over her shoulder. "It's just a bad dream."

"He shouldn't have eaten that pear after supper," Mother said.

I could taste the salty tears in the corner of my mouth, but my dream had not been a bad one. Kiki and I had simply been on our way to the park. It had been a very short dream—we came out of the house, walked down to the corner, crossed the street, and then gone into the butcher shop for our sandwiches. That was all that had been to the dream. Why had that made me cry and whatever else I had done to wake people up? Fortunately, Fredek was still curled into a ball at his end of the bed, sound asleep.

"Are you sure he's all right?" my mother was asking. "Should he have something for his stomach?"

"No, he's fine, Missus. It's just a dream. He's had a few very difficult days."

"Why doesn't Fredek have bad dreams? Why doesn't he faint?"

"Yulian just has a different blah-blah-blah. He's all right, I assure Missus. I'll stay with him."

"I will pay Miss," I heard Mother say, as she and Auntie Edna shuffled out.

I wondered if I should tell Miss Bronia that I hadn't had a bad dream. Would she think something was the matter with me? What would she think of me then? I decided against it and hoped Fredek wouldn't wake up.

The next morning, Mr. Dembovski drove us out to the Metners' farm where we had been given the use of a cottage. It had a thatched roof that was bigger than the rest of the house and made me think of a giant, rectangular mushroom. There was even a bit of a mushroom scent about it. I had seen such cottages from a distance and in pictures, but I had never been inside one.

This one had walls painted white on both the inside and the outside. The front door opened into a large room dominated by a huge wood-burning stove, several times bigger than the one in our own kitchen. Against one wall was a large sink made of wood and a hand pump with a gracefully curved blue handle for pumping the water. There was also a large table flanked by two benches and some chairs. Doors at the back of this room opened to other rooms and a staircase led to a loft.

When our belongings had been brought in from the truck, Mr. Dembovski and Mr. Lupicki began saying goodbye to the rest of us. I had no idea this was going to happen. The women all offered their hand to Mr. Dembovski, who, I could see, was not comfortable doing this. Mother even gave him a quick, stiff hug. Mr. Lupicki kissed the hands of all four women. Then he patted my head, and the two of them drove off. Mother, it seemed, had given the truck to Mr. Dembovski. I was sad to see them leave.

The cottage proved considerably bigger on the inside than it had seemed from the outside. "It's like a good pair of shoes," Auntie Edna said, "bigger on the inside than on the outside." I found the idea hilarious, though no one else seemed to. Each mother had her own bedroom, Miss Bronia and Sonya shared a room, and Fredek and I had an incredibly soft mattress on top of a surface they used for kneading bread dough, in a corner of the big room. On the front wall, between the sink and the door, hung a wooden icon of the Blessed Virgin.

Behind the cottage, there was the tiniest house I had ever seen. All it contained was a wooden seat with a hole in it and a very bad odor. In time, I would become very intimate with this little house, though I never enjoyed the relationship.

As the mothers bustled about with sheets and pillowcases, Miss Bronia set to lighting a fire at one end of the big stove. "We have to wash all the dishes," she said to Sonya, who now surprised me by immediately gathering the dishes and flatware and setting them beside the wooden sink. I had not credited Sonya with such energy. Then I watched with fascination as Miss Bronia picked a tumbler of water up off the counter and poured it down into the hand pump. The first few pumps of the handle produced only noise, but eventually, water began to flow. Miss Bronia filled an iron pot and set it on the stove to heat, as Marta had always done.

"Let's go find us some Germans in the woods" Fredek now said to me. He, too, had watched the pump-priming procedure with interest.

"Miss Bronia is washing dishes," I answered.

"We don't need her," he said.

I had never gone outdoors without supervision. "What if we get lost?" I said. In my realm of experience, children outdoors on their own usually got lost and encountered evil of one sort or another.

"I've never been lost," Fredek said. In truth, I could have made this same statement. Now I realized that farm children must go outdoors quite frequently without adult oversight. Some even herded sheep.

"All right," I said, though I really would have preferred to dry dishes for Miss Bronia as I used to do for Kiki. But I knew that my little-soldierhood demanded my preference for this activity. "I'll just ask Mother," I said.

"In the country, you don't need permission."

I understood that this wasn't to be taken as an absolute, but that a certain context was implied. What he meant was that in the country a number of the laws that proscribed our lives were suspended. I recalled hearing that Fredek and Miss Frania had spent summers in the country, while Kiki and I had been at the beach resort. I followed Fredek into the sunlight.

A dirt road ran in front of our cottage with a field on the other side. To our right, it rose uphill a little.

"They went this way," Fredek said, turning up the rise in the road. I followed. He found a stick beside the road and it immediately became his sword. "Better arm yourself—they're dangerous," he advised me. I was already picking one up. It was vaguely in the shape of a rifle, and I put it over my shoulder. Fredek was waving his and he had begun to skip. "That's no way to carry a sword," he said.

"It's not a sword. It's a rifle."

"What are you going to do with a rifle on horseback?"

"What horseback?" I asked.

"I'm on a horse. If you don't get mounted, you won't be able to keep up."

There was no refuting his logic. I began to skip as well and turned the rifle into a rather awkwardly shaped saber. With our sabers pointed up at forty-five degrees, we cantered on up the hill.

Over the rise we almost ran into two real horses coming towards us at a walk. They were in harness, followed by a man on foot holding the long reins. He had an unbuttoned vest on over his shirt and boots up to his knees. As we passed, he smiled and said something that I didn't catch. When he had passed the man, Fredek turned and slashed his saber viciously toward the man's back. I was struck by the humor of the situation in which we, on imaginary horses, had just passed a man riding in an imaginary wagon.

When I had caught up to him, Fredek demanded, "Why didn't you help me finish him off? Now he's escaped and he'll tell the others that we're here."

"No he won't," I ventured. "The others will capture him. He's riding into a trap." Fredek didn't know that I could make things up as well.

Fredek cocked his head to one side. "What are you talking about?"

"The other troops," I said uncertainly.

"What other troops?"

"The rest of our brigade?"

"They've all been gassed. You and I are the only survivors." Then he clucked to his horse and galloped on down the road. I followed.

We were now between two fields, both covered with the stubble of some recently harvested crop. Ahead of us a large piece of farm machinery stood on the side of the road.

"A German tank," Fredek said out of the side of his mouth as I pulled my mount to a stop beside him. "Here's what we do," he continued. "You pretend to surrender. Put your hands up and walk slowly toward him—slow enough to give me time to sneak up behind him. Then, when he sticks his head and shoulders out of the turret to come out and handcuff you, I'll shoot him with my rifle."

I could have reminded him that soldiers didn't handcuff each other or that he had a saber, not a rifle, but I didn't see what that might accomplish. So I dropped my weapon, raised my hands, and began to walk slowly, hoping there was no one around the machine to see me. Fredek, in the meantime, crouched down and ran forward, through the stubbled field, holding his former saber in both hands.

Then, as I got closer, I began to hear voices. Some men, I realized, must have been doing something on the other side of the machine. Embarrassed, I put my hands on top of my head which, I knew, was still a legitimate surrender signal but could also be seen as just somebody strolling along.

I saw that Fredek had come to a stop and stood frozen in the field beside the road. I continued walking.

Then I began to distinguish individual words. But I couldn't understand them. The men weren't speaking Polish. Fredek was moving back towards me now, bent over. In a moment he had broken into a run. "Run!" he said as he passed me, "Run! They're Germans! Real Germans!" I wasted no time following Fredek's example.

"The Germans are here! The Germans are here!" Fredek shouted as we ran into the cottage.

Mother and Auntie Paula, who were in the big room washing and wringing clothes, stopped to look at each other.

"Fredek?" Auntie Paula said after a moment.

"I heard them too," I said. "They were speaking German!"

"They're miles away," Mother said. "They're fighting west of Warsaw. They couldn't be here."

"Downed pilots?" Auntie Paula said.

"German spies?" Fredek suggested.

"German spies?" It was Auntie Edna standing now in the doorway to her room. "Somebody saw German spies? Where?"

I could hear the fear in her voice. "We didn't actually see them—we only heard them," I said in an effort to mitigate the disaster.

"There's a big farming machine up the road," Fredek said. "They were hiding behind it."

"Hiding behind it?" Mother said.

"Yes," Fredek said eagerly. "We never saw them."

"Yulian, were they hiding?" Auntie Paula asked me.

"I guess not. They weren't whispering or anything. They were just talking," I had to admit. And as I spoke, I began to become aware of the illogic of our conclusion.

"But they were speaking German," Fredek said. His tone was definitely defensive now.

"How do you know it was German?" Mother asked. Neither of us had an answer.

"They were speaking Ukrainian," Auntie Edna said, her face brightening.

"Of course," Mother said.

"What's Ukrainian?" Fredek wanted to know. I knew that the Ukraine was a separate country that had been divided between Poland and Russia after the big war. But I had no idea that that was where we now were.

*   *   *

There were no ponies on the Metners' farm, that we knew of. In fact, the Metners weren't there either, except for Mrs. Metner's mother, who made her home on the farm. I never actually saw her—we called her the old woman—but Miss Bronia and Sonya would go to her house every morning to buy milk and eggs from her cook at the back door of the Big House. Meat, bread, and vegetables we bought from some of the peasants who lived in cottages like ours, but usually smaller.

The bread came in large round loaves, about two feet across. Miss Bronia would hold the loaf against her chest as she buttered the cut end, before cutting off a slice. It was either black bread or a gray color, and, with butter or butter and cheese, both were delicious.

One day Miss Bronia and Sonya carried home between them a crate of live chickens, which they installed in a little shed with a fence around it behind our cottage. They were to be Sonya's charge, and Fredek and I were given strict instructions to leave them alone. That was all right—I had no affection for chickens. Had they been rabbits, for instance, this would have been a different issue.

We had a wooden icebox for which we had to fetch a cake of ice from the icehouse every other day. The melted ice dripped into a large, shallow pan under the icebox and had to be emptied twice a day. It was Auntie Paula's idea that Fredek and I be made responsible for the ice and its subsequent residue.

We were both thrilled. This was the first time I had ever been given a job other than things like washing out my socks under Kiki's supervision. Fredek told me he had had lots of jobs before.

Durnoval, where we had spent the night before arriving here, I learned, was ten kilometers away. On our second day on the farm, my mother hitched a ride into town on one of the farm wagons. I watched her step on a wheel spoke, as we had all seen drivers do, and then transfer her weight hesitantly onto the seat beside the driver. As I watched her in her blue dress, silk stockings, and high heels next to the driver in his coarse wool vest and cap, I reminded myself that it would have been un-Christian to gloat at her awkwardness.

She returned that evening on the same wagon with a carton of canned fruit, a woolen sweater for me, several packs of cigarettes, and a pair of tennis shoes for herself, which she said were a size too large, but the last pair of flats in town. She also had news. The Germans were nearing Warsaw, and there was no sign of the English or the French. The stores in town, she told us, were mostly empty. The canned fruit and cigarettes she had bought from women selling them in the street at several times their store price.

While my mother was in town, Fredek and I had spent a good part of the day pushing each other around in the wheelbarrow. By the time my turn to wheel the cake of ice home from the icehouse arrived, the magic associated with the activity had worn off. And after several shaky, four-handed trips from the icebox to the wooden sink with the pan of water, the bloom quickly faded from this activity as well. After a few days, Fredek approached me with a proposition. He was perfectly willing, he said, to relinquish his share of both activities to me. In exchange for this, I would owe him a favor to be named at some later time.

I could see quite clearly through this arrangement. But the idea of being the sole custodian of the icebox operation had, for me, a certain attraction that went well beyond the actual act of pushing a wheelbarrow or emptying the water pan. I couldn't quite understand why it seemed so attractive, but it did, so I said that I wasn't interested.

Fredek's disappointment was very clear. "But I'll tell you what I will do," I said in response. "I will take over responsibility for the icebox if you will clear my plate from the table to the sink every evening after supper." Clearing our own plates from the dinner table was a duty assigned to us just that day, and the only thing I could think of to barter with. He would, of course, still have to help me carry the slippery cake from the wheelbarrow to the icebox.

Fredek had to think a moment about this. I understood that he didn't like the idea of having to clear my dinner plate. On the other hand, he could also see that this would take much less effort than the icebox obligation. He agreed to my terms, and I immediately asserted my stewardship of the icebox by emptying the pan, even though he and I had done it together not two hours earlier. I wanted to start with a clean slate.

This made me, Miss Bronia, and Sonya the only ones with an actual responsibility. As the only person in our group who knew how to cook things like meat and vegetables or even work the wood stove, Miss Bronia was in charge of buying the food and preparing the meals. Sonya assisted her in this and took care of the chickens. The two had taken to wearing long, peasant skirts and kerchiefs over their hair, tying the kerchiefs behind their heads instead of under their chins.

Miss Bronia had little time to give to me, but I found that wrapping my arms around her waist for an occasional hug on the go, reinforced the sense of our relationship. The rich Ukrainian earth was very child-friendly, providing beach-like digging, construction, and fantasizing opportunities. Augmented by rocks, pieces of scrap lumber, and Fredek's endless imagination, the place left me little time to worry over issues of the heart.

Also, I had found a round piece of metal, like a coin but with a hole in the center, lying on the road near our cottage. This, I quickly discovered, I could palm the same way I had palmed Mr. Lupicki's coin. I slipped it into my pocket and, when I was alone, would practice the tricks he had shown me.

The mothers did decide to take on the responsibility of drying the dishes after Miss Bronia washed them. They had originally intended to wash the dishes as well, but Miss Bronia said that the harsh soap available to us would harm their hands and ruin their nails, so she would not at all mind washing the dishes herself. As for the laundry, there was a woman at the Big House who could be negotiated with.

Our second evening on the farm, Auntie Edna heated a kettle of water on the stove and directed Fredek to take off his clothes and climb into the wooden sink. Hearing this, I quickly turned my back and feigned great interest in the plaster of the cottage wall. As I listened to the water sounds and Auntie Edna telling the assembled audience how good it made her feel to give her son his bath and how she would frequently tell Miss Frania that she would take on the task that evening, I could not help feeling terribly sorry for Fredek, who was suffering such humiliation. Not for a moment did I dream that immediately following the sound of Fredek's descent from the sink, I would hear my own name called by my mother.

"Let me bathe him for you, Mrs. Waisbrem," I heard Miss Bronia interject. I remembered how cleverly she had

protected my privacy the other morning, and my hopes rose
for a moment. Under different circumstances, I am sure that
my mother would gladly have let Miss Bronia relieve her of
the task, but after Auntie Edna's confession, I knew that my
chances were slim.

"Thank you, Bronia," Mother said, "but I enjoy bathing
Yulek." This was a vicious lie. I had no recollection of her ever
doing more than assisting Kiki in this work. "Come on, Yul,"
Mother summoned.

"The boy is very shy," Miss Bronia said.

"Well, he has to learn not to be," Mother said. Then, to
me, she added, "You know, soldiers sleep in barracks and take
showers together." I had no choice but to come forward, step
up on the chair, and allow my mother to begin removing my
clothes.

"Let's go to our room," Miss Bronia said to Sonya, who sat
at the table reading, with her back to the sink.

"No, Bronia," Mother insisted. "Don't coddle the boy.
Yulian has to learn. It's wartime, and he needs to be a little
soldier like Fredek. Everyone should stay, and this should be
settled once and for all."

I closed my eyes so that I would not see them seeing me.
Closed in my darkness, I was unconscious of anything happening in the room. Instead, I was back in that darkening street,
hand-in-hand with Miss Bronia.

When it was over, and I sat wrapped in a large towel beside
the stove, I knew that my dream of saving my mother's Immortal Soul had been just that—a dream. And, while working to
save every soul was the duty of every Catholic, my own soul was
currently filled with too much anger to be in any way effective.

As for the others, they apparently did their washing at the
sink when Fredek and I were asleep. One night, though, I did
see Auntie Edna step out of her robe in the empty, darkened
room. I quickly closed my eyes and covered them with my
fists. My mind, however, kept returning to the image of Auntie

Edna's smooth curves and I realized afterwards that, with my eyes half open, I could have watched through my eyelashes, and she would never have seen me seeing her.

*　　　*　　　*

When I arrived at the icehouse by myself for the first time, the attendant asked where my friend was. This was the first time I had heard him speak, and he spoke with a strange accent. I realized that this must be because he was Ukrainian. He was an old man with a mustache and he shuffled his left leg when he walked.

I told him that I was in charge. This wasn't a lie, and I hoped that it implied that Fredek worked under my supervision.

"That's good. That's very good," he said. "You are the head iceman."

I accepted the title with unconcealable pride.

"You live in Warsaw," he said.

I confirmed that we did.

"Your father, what does he do?"

I told him that Lolek had a factory that made shirts, but he was my stepfather.

"A big factory?"

"I don't know."

"He has a car?"

I said I wasn't sure.

"He's fighting the Germans now?"

"Yes, he went in the army a few days ago."

"And your real father."

"He's in heaven," I fibbed. Kiki had been pretty certain that Jews didn't go there, but I wanted the man to think of me as the Catholic that I was at heart. In recent days, I realized, I saw myself as more of a virtual Catholic than the wannabe I had been before. In actuality, only the technicality of a baptism separated me from the legions of true believers.

"And the others?" he asked.

"Oh, they're all . . ." I began, but stopped myself, realizing that he wasn't asking about their religion.

"They're rich too?"

"They're my Aunties, their son and daughter, and a governess."

"A governess?"

"Yes, Miss Bronia."

"You all live together in Warsaw?"

"No, we live in different apartments."

"What do the other husbands do?"

"I don't know," I admitted. But I was also growing uneasy with this line of questioning. "I have to get back with the ice," I said.

"That's good. That's very good. You're a responsible boy, the head iceman." He patted me on the head.

I smiled and left with my cargo. On the road back, I saw a man's head, then his shoulders, and finally his whole figure rise up over the hill in front of me. In a moment I could see that he was a priest in his long black cassock. He was tall with a thin waist cinched by a brown leather belt, a long, blond beard, and hair down below his collar. As he walked, a gold cross on his chest swung left and right from behind his beard.

Coming closer, I saw that the cassock had been mended many times and a stitched-on, dark-blue hemming tape bound the bottom of the cassock. There were grease stains on the black gabardine. His eyes were large and round. His blond hair and beard were streaked with gray. I had never been that close to a priest before. As we passed, I bowed my head in respect and received another pat on the head.

Remembering how upset Mother had been at my encounter with Mr. Lupicki, I decided to tell no one about either of these encounters.

One day it was determined that Fredek's, Sonya's, and my schooling was suffering, and lessons were organized for us. We had no books, so it was decided that Auntie Edna would teach Fredek and me the multiplication tables while my mother taught French to Sonya. It turned out, though, that Fredek already knew the multiplication tables, all the way up to twelve times twelve, which was further than his mother could go, while I had trouble with anything beyond the times-two table.

It quickly became evident that Fredek and I were not well matched as classmates, at least in the math department. To remedy this situation, Fredek was transferred along with Sonya to French, which met under a large tree near our house, while Auntie Edna was to bring me up to speed with the multiplication tables, a project that she assured me would take no more than a week or two.

Auntie Edna made me repeat the times-three table several times with her, but the moment I was launched solo, I was lost. She then made me copy it out ten times, which helped a little—I realized that it was just a matter of adding three to the previous answer, and was finally able to pass an oral test, as long as I could count on my fingers under the table. Auntie Edna was quite proud of my achievement and, much against my better judgement, made an announcement to that effect that evening at dinner.

"What's three times seven?" Fredek asked me, and, as I had feared, Auntie Edna's structure showed itself to be the house of cards that it was.

Fredek, on the other hand, had his own difficulties. His acquisitive mind clamped itself around the French words with admirable speed. By the second day, his vocabulary must have surpassed mine by a considerable multiple. Unfortunately, though, coming out of his mouth, the words sounded no more French than their Polish equivalents.

Unlike Auntie Edna, my mother had little patience for his tin ear. Her remedy, it seems, was to present Fredek with the correct pronunciation in ever-louder tones, which Auntie Edna and I could soon hear at our table inside the cottage. Finally,

Auntie Edna excused herself and went out to confer with her son's teacher. Through the window, I could see the two of them standing in the stubbled field talking for quite some time. When Auntie Edna came back into the cottage, I could tell that she had been crying. She told me to go out and play because there would be no more school that day.

At the dinner table that evening, when Auntie Paula, who had admitted at the outset that she did not have sufficient patience to teach small boys, tried to resolve the issue of Fredek's difficulty, it was discovered that when he wrote the words down at Mother's instructions, his spelling was nothing like the proper French spelling. When he asked Mother what the proper spelling was, it turned out that she didn't know how to spell French words either. School was not resumed the following day.

There was some discussion among the mothers about the idea of Miss Bronia teaching us German, but it was deemed inappropriate under the circumstances. Besides, as the only member of our party who knew how to cook or deal with the farm people over provisions, she hadn't the time. She did teach us to pluck chickens, an activity I found loathsome, but also very grown up.

As for Sonya's schooling, she learned many practical things assisting Miss Bronia, and in the evenings the two of them would get together to discuss some books that Miss Bronia had brought for her to read.

What else happened over the next few weeks, I can't fix into proper chronological order. Every two or three days one of the mothers would ride the wagon into town for news. We didn't have a radio and without electricity we could not have used one anyway.

The news was always bad. The Germans were moving further and further east, closer and closer to us. Oddly enough, there was no sign of them in our sky. While we had seen German bombers and fighter planes bombing and harassing towns and roads in advance of their troops further north, here in southeastern Poland, it was as though the Germans had no interest in us.

And where were the French and the English? We had heard that they had declared war on Germany, in accordance with their mutual defense pact with Poland, but so far there had been no sign of their involvement. Our own army, Auntie Paula explained, was losing ground because the surprise German attack had disrupted our transportation and communication, but the French, she said, had a mighty army on Germany's western border that simply needed the order to advance. Once they did, this whole thing would be over in a few days.

One evening, six peasants showed up at our door looking for shelter. They spoke Polish without the Ukrainian accent. Then it turned out that under their peasants' clothes they had on army uniforms. Their unit, they told us, had been wiped out and the city they were defending to the west of us, overrun. Polish defenses, they said, were helpless against the German tanks, our airplanes outclassed by the Messerschmitts. They were cut off from other Polish forces and were now on their way east to Russia where our army would regroup with arms borrowed from the Russians, and liberate Poland. It sounded like a good plan to me.

Two of them had wounds, hastily bandaged, and the mothers cleaned and redressed them with a torn-up sheet. Miss Bronia went around to the back of the cottage and killed two more chickens; Fredek and I then set about plucking under Sonya's supervision. The soldiers spent the night on the floor in the loft and were gone when I woke up the next morning.

On another evening, there was a knock on our door and a tall man fillied our doorway. My heart leaped as I recognized the priest I had passed on the road back from the icehouse. He wore the same mended cassock, or one equally mended and equally stained.

"I am Father Chernievich," he said in a booming voice as he stepped into the big room. "We will say the rosary."

That was something I was very familiar with, having said the rosary with Kiki, using her beads, and having also participated in a rosary led by Kiki's priest brother at the wake for their Uncle Bolek. There were parts that the priest spoke alone and parts where everybody joined in.

Mother and Auntie Edna were there in the big room with Fredek and me, and what was on the mothers' faces could have been taken for nothing but panic. I could not help enjoying Mother's discomfort, even though I knew this to be not only un-Christian, but counterproductive to my missionary assignment.

Mother was the first to recover her composure. "We don't have our rosary beads with us, Father," she said in a remarkably calm voice. "We had to leave Warsaw in a hurry." This, of course, as any Catholic knew, was nonsense since holding beads was not necessary to saying the rosary, and I was afraid that Mother had blown her cover with her very first line.

But Father did not seem to notice her ignorance. "Just kneel down," he said with evident impatience. I knelt immediately at his instruction and watched to see what Mother and Auntie Edna and Fredek would do.

At that moment, Miss Bronia who had evidently heard this from her room, came out. "Good evening, Father," she said, stepping quickly past both Mother and Auntie Edna to place herself between them and our visitor. She knelt down, and Mother and Auntie Edna followed her example. Fredek knelt too, and, out of the corner of my eye, I could see Sonya peeking around the door of the room she shared with Miss Bronia.

Father turned around to face the icon of the Blessed Virgin on the wall beside the front door. It was obvious that he knew his way around this cottage. "In the name of the Father, the Son, and the Holy Spirit," he intoned. Miss Bronia and I crossed ourselves. There was a flurry of noncommittal hand motions on the part of Mother and Auntie Edna. Fredek watched wide-eyed.

"Amen," Miss Bronia and I chorused.

"Our Father who art in heaven, hallowed be Thy name," Miss Bronia and I said, following Father's lead. I could tell that Miss Bronia was praying extra loud to sound like three people. I, on the other hand, made sure that she could hear me. After the first few repetitions of the Hail Mary, I could actually hear Mother and Auntie Edna chiming in. I could see them smiling to each other. While it was probably no sin for a non-Catholic to recite Catholic prayers, Mother was making a joke out of it. She saw me looking at her and quickly turned serious and indicated that I should face the front. By the time we reached the second Decade, I could hear Fredek's voice as well, and I could even discern a certain bounce of enthusiasm in our praying.

"Hail Mary, full of grace, the Lord is with Thee. Blessed art Thou amongst women and blessed is the fruit of thy womb, Jesus," Father led, and we followed with our "Holy Mary, mother of God, pray for us sinners now and at the hour of our death, Amen." Only in the stand-alone Our Father did we lose my relatives.

My own joy, of course, knew no bounds. Mother was now on my turf, and while she might be fooling Father, there was no pulling the wool over God's eyes. And Miss Bronia, too, could not have missed my Catholicism.

But on one's knees, even pious ecstasy can grow wearisome, and Father Chernievich's knees were, obviously, better conditioned for this activity than ours. Mother and Auntie Edna had begun to rock from knee to knee, and even Miss Bronia was fidgeting. I tried hard to maintain soldier-like discipline, but found that not only were my knees betraying me, but my mind was wandering from the Divine to the temporal. The soles of both of Father's boots had holes part way through them. The one on the right was shaped like an egg, the left could have been a rabbit without ears.

Auntie Paula barged in through the front door and froze in her tracks. Father took no notice of the disturbance, but behind his back, Mother made a face and pointed to the floor indicating for Auntie Paula to join our ranks. I saw Auntie Paula shake her head and remain standing by the door, a strange expression on her face. We plowed on.

When there was a knock on the door, all of us, except Father, looked hopefully in that direction. Auntie Paula, standing by the door, opened it, and a rotund little woman with a gentle face and the long peasant skirt and kerchief stood in the doorway. Excusing herself, she turned directly towards Father, still on his knees before the Blessed Virgin. "Come, Sasha," she said, using the diminutive form of the name Alexander, "it's time to come home to supper." Her voice was as kindly as her face, but quite firm.

Father turned his bearded face from the icon up to the woman.

"We have to go now," she said. Father Chernievich made the sign of the Cross and rose to his feet.

The woman apologized for disturbing us. Then, taking the tall priest by the hand, she led him outside.

When they had gone, Auntie Paula leaned her back against the closed door and began to laugh. "So you've all done rosary with Father Chernievich," she said.

Mother and Auntie Edna did not grasp her humor.

"You know who he is, don't you?" Auntie Paula went on.

We all looked at her without understanding. Auntie Edna was massaging a knee.

"He's Renia's uncle. . . . Renia Metner," Auntie Paula said. "Renia tells stories about him sometimes. He thinks he's a priest and lives here on the farm."

"Renia's Uncle Sasha?" Auntie Edna repeated. "They let him go around impersonating a priest?" And she began to laugh too.

"He doesn't cause any harm, she says," Auntie Paula said, "so the Polish people around here let him do rosary with them as long as he doesn't try to do Mass or confessions. The Ukrainians are some other kind of Catholic, you know."

This took a moment to sink in. "Well, it was a good rehearsal," Mother said. "We may have to do this kind of thing again. Bronia's going to have to teach us."

There was general agreement to this. "I realize now," Mother went on, "that real Catholics wouldn't have left Warsaw without their rosary beads. We should get some."

"I'll see about getting some at the church," Miss Bronia said.

"Get them from Father Chernievich," Auntie Edna laughed. I could already envision myself teaching them to cross themselves and to recite the Act of Contrition.

*   *   *

The very next afternoon, Auntie Edna came back from town with wonderful news. People were actually dancing in the streets, she reported, over the news that the Russians were coming to our aid. They had crossed our eastern frontier with their tanks and their guns, and the people along the way, she had heard, were showering them with flowers. They would be here soon to help stop the Germans some place on the other side of Durnoval.

This was the relief we had looked for all along, even though from an unexpected direction. The grownups drank vodka after dinner and wondered how our various apartments had fared after we left Warsaw and what else awaited us on our return. I could not totally rule out the idea that God's pleasure at the sight of three and a half Jews saying the rosary together was, somehow, linked to this new and totally unexpected development. The fact that "Father" Chernievich was mad only reinforced this speculation, since God was reputed to work in strange and mysterious ways.

The next day Auntie Paula rode the wagon into town to find out more about how soon the Russians might be expected to pass through and make us invulnerable. Fredek and I were Russian soldiers roaming the fields around our cottage, look-

ing for German deserters to take to our prison camp behind
the house, currently occupied by the chickens who Fredek said
were really German spies. The script was all Fredek's, but this
time even I took pleasure in the activity as we probed with our
shoes and our bayonets under the large leaves of ground-hug-
ging squash or pumpkin plants, or whatever they were, for the
hated Nazis cowering in the field.

In this mode, we were only slightly surprised by our encounter with two elephants driving a wagon along the dirt road,
pulled by an elderly, bony horse. The elephants were singing
in Ukrainian. Their voices were muffled coming through their
trunks, which had originally been gas masks, but had had their
air hoses disconnected from the canisters that filtered out the
gas, and now hung loose in front.

The wagon stopped in front of us, and the elephants invited
us on board in young, accented voices. That I clambered up as
eagerly as Fredek, would surprise me later—it was not in my
character. But the joyous war news must have worked to permit
me to get into our make-believe to a degree that bypassed my
customary shyness. Before I knew it, Fredek and I were seated
on top of the cabbages behind the elephants, who now sang
their song in Polish. It didn't rhyme in Polish, but it praised the
strength of Marynka who could pull a wagonload of cabbages
and two elephants. Fredek and I joined in the song.

The kids in the gas masks seemed to be about a year or two
older than we were, and the one driving had braids down her
back. After several repetitions of the song, I volunteered the
addition of ". . . and two soldiers," to the verse, which was
immediately incorporated.

We rode past several cottages. There were people outside
some of them, and they waved to us. There were women in
their long skirts and kerchiefs, with hoes or babies or baskets
of wash. "Hey Marynka!" they called to our horse. We waved
back. In the fields, there were men with teams of horses and
farm machinery, and some of them waved to us as well.

After awhile, we pulled up in front of a barn and stopped. It was built of stone, and I could see no windows in it, but a large open door on the second floor. The two on the driver seat jumped down and removed their gas masks, transforming themselves into a boy and a girl, and began unfastening Marynka's harness.

Inside, I was struck by the smell of the place. Horse manure and hay were smells you encountered on any street in Poland, but here they were an intense mixture that surrounded and permeated you.

There were several stalls in a row here; they weren't the roomy stalls my grandfather's horse had lived in, but were only wide enough for the horse to stand. I remembered that horses slept standing up. The stalls were all empty, except for Marynka's.

Past the stalls, the boy began to climb a ladder that went straight up the wall into the loft above. I followed. I had never climbed a ladder before. Up in the loft, the smell was different again, with the hay smell much more intense. As my eyes got used to the semi darkness, I could see a mountain of hay filling a great portion of the floor. Several wide beams ran across the width of the barn, and the boy was walking along one of them.

Suddenly the boy was gone from the beam. I looked down in alarm. There he was, on his back, lying in the pile of hay. "Jump down!" he called merrily.

I would have preferred not to. I understood that it must be fun to do and evidently harmless, but then I saw the girl coming up the ladder to our beam with Fredek behind her. I tensed for the jolt and jumped.

The jolt didn't come. Sinking into the deep hay was softer than jumping into water or onto a mattress. But the free-fall itself was the most astonishing feeling I had ever experienced. It was, for that split moment, as though all that I was ever anxious about had dissolved.

In a moment, the other two had joined us in the hay. The older boy was already climbing back up the ladder, and I ran after him compulsively. "My airplane's on fire, and I have to bail out!" he said before jumping. I followed right behind him, spreading my arms like an airplane. As I fell into weightlessness, I heard a cry of joy escape my mouth. It surprised me completely, and I knew I was blushing when I landed. The boy and the girl laughed. Fredek made the sound of a gun firing, staggered, and fell backwards off the beam.

We had done several repetitions of this delicious jump when I was suddenly gripped by terror. We must be, I realized, long overdue for lunch. But I had no idea how to go about telling our hosts that we had to terminate this delightful activity. It was a situation I had never been in before.

I sidled up to Fredek in the hay and whispered that we had to go home. Fredek though about this for a moment.

"We have to go home," he announced.

Without objection, our host and hostess led the way back downstairs. "You can come back tomorrow if you want to," the girl said to us.

They walked us out to the front of the barn. "Your cottage is over there," the boy said, pointing in the direction of some thatched roofs in the distance. "Follow this road till you can make a right turn."

"Goodbye and thank you," I said, as I had been taught to do. It felt so grown up. We began running down the road.

I knew there would be anger when we got back, maybe even spanking—something I had never experienced—but the good feeling I now had, somehow made all that seem irrelevant.

In the distance, we could see Auntie Paula standing outside the door of our cottage, shading her eyes with her hand. We could tell she was looking for us, and, when she saw us across the field, she went inside.

As we came through the door, she just said, "Go to my room and sit there quietly. No talking." Her tone was ominously quiet, implying that at least part of our punishment would take the form of our contemplating the trouble and worry we had caused everybody. "Miss Bronia is looking all over the farm for you," she added. She gripped Fredek's shoulder and propelled him towards her door.

As we crossed the room, we suddenly heard sobbing coming from Auntie Edna's room. Through the doorway, we could see Auntie Edna lying on the bed, a wet cloth across her eyes, and my mother sitting on the side of the bed facing her. Fredek broke from Auntie Paula's grip and ran to his mother. His sudden concern for her surprised me. I saw Fredek's mother remove the cloth from her eyes, reach her arm out, and draw him to her. Only she didn't stop sobbing now that we were back, but just sobbed louder.

"They're civilized people," I heard my mother say. "My mother, you know, is Russian."

Auntie Edna made an effort to stop crying and sat up in bed. She and Fredek had their arms around each other with his head tight against her breast. "It's going to be all right," she said to him.

Auntie Paula's interest in my punishment seemed to have waned because she now followed Fredek to his mother's room. "That was twenty years ago," she said to Auntie Edna.

"It was in nineteen twenty-four," Auntie Edna corrected her.

"All right, fifteen years ago, but don't forget, he was a Count. We aren't nobility. We are three simple women with children and a servant living on a farm."

"And our husbands are in the army and own businesses," Auntie Edna answered. "Lolek even owns a factory."

"They don't know that," my mother said. "We are three women with husbands in the army. We are no different from most of the women in Poland."

I had not the faintest idea what they were talking about, except that I was suddenly reminded of the conversation I had had with the man at the icehouse.

Auntie Edna didn't say anything more, probably because Fredek and I were in the room.

"Basia, you'd better tell him," Auntie Paula said. Of course she meant me.

"Why don't you tell them both," my mother suggested. Her voice was suddenly like a little girl's.

"For godsakes, Basia, he's standing right here," Auntie Paula said. I could tell she was impatient with my mother, and I was pleased—at the same time that I was desperate to know what it was that no one wanted to tell us.

"Well, somebody has to tell the boys," Auntie Paula finally said. "They'll be finding out soon enough. Frederick, Yulian, this morning I heard in town that the Russians aren't coming to fight the Germans. They're coming to occupy this part of Poland. Do you know what occupy means?"

"Like before Marshall Piwsudski," I volunteered. I knew that not many years ago Marshal Piwsudski had saved Poland from Russian occupation.

"That's right," my mother said quickly.

Auntie Edna pulled herself up higher on the bed. "There will be Russian soldiers telling people what to do," she said in a weak voice, "and we will have to do what they tell us."

"Or they'll shoot us," Fredek said.

"No, darling, they're not going to shoot us," his mother said.

"I won't let them shoot us. I'll kick them in the shins where it hurts a lot, and then I'll hit them in the head."

"My little patriot," Auntie Edna said, smiling through her tears.

"No, we're not going to do that," Auntie Paula said sternly. "The patriotic thing to do will be to get through this as safely as we can until the French and the English come."

The mothers spent much of the rest of the day cutting collars off their dresses and letting down hems. Auntie Edna even turned one green dress inside out and held it up to herself for approval. Mother and Auntie Paula approved. When Miss Bronia came back with Sonya from looking for us, she was relieved to see us and probably assumed that our absence had already been dealt with, because she said nothing about it.

The following morning, when Miss Bronia went up to the Big House for milk and news, she told Sonya not to come with her. Auntie Paula drew a line in the dirt outlining a few hundred square feet in front of the cottage, and Fredek and I were told to play inside that area. We immediately began construction on a stockade of imaginary logs and boulders.

When it was time for my trip to the icehouse, Auntie Paula came with me. But nobody was there to cut a piece off the big block for us, though we did manage to find a few small pieces of ice that would do in place of our one big one.

When we got back, Miss Bronia was telling her experiences at the Big House, and she started from the beginning again for Auntie Paula's benefit. It seems that there had been no one to answer her knock on the kitchen door, but the door had been open, so she had gone inside. There, she found Mrs. Metner's mother and several others with their arms in the air while a number of peasants with red armbands brandished rifles. These were not local peasants, but from another town, and they were collecting money and valuables for redistribution among themselves.

Asked for her money and jewels, Miss Bronia explained that she had none, since she worked for a woman in a cottage nearby. "Then you're a worker like us," they told her and gave her a red armband and a costume brooch before sending her back with a container of milk for the "sick child" she cared for.

That day, the sewing that Kiki taught me was put to use as the mothers pried their valuable gems out of their settings and we sewed them up in layers of cloth as buttons for our jackets. I could see that my stitches were tighter and neater than Mother's. Only Fredek refused to touch needle or thread.

Money and small jewelry pieces were wrapped in cloth and sewn into jacket linings. A bracelet of Auntie Paula's went into a thermos and laid among the cooking utensils. A brooch of Auntie Edna's became a bright green pincushion.

Finished by early afternoon, we settled down to wait for our expected visitors.

"This isn't the place for them to find us," Auntie Edna suddenly said. "We should be where all good peasant women are, out in the potato field." Mother and Auntie Paula agreed. "And Yulek can be the sick child Bronia told them she was caring for," Auntie Edna added. "Bronia can be reading to him. It'll make them sympathetic." They agreed with this as well.

Then Auntie Edna turned to me. "This is a game we're going to be playing," she said. "Some people will come here, and you're going to pretend that you're sick. We know you aren't really sick, but they won't know that."

I knew very well why I had to pretend to be sick, and didn't need Auntie Edna to explain it to me. But I let her go ahead and explain it anyway. In a few minutes, the three mothers and Sonya had marched into the potato field across the road and Miss Bronia was left to care for the sick child. Fredek was posted as lookout, and, on his signal, I was to jump into Auntie Edna's bed and act weak. I knew I could do better than that. I had offered to moan and cough, but the offer was turned down on the basis that I would not carry it off believably. I did, however, determine secretly that I would roll my eyes and drool, as I had seen a beggar do in Warsaw.

Fredek sat by the window and I sat near the door to his mother's room, while Miss Bronia read what had become my favorite story, the one about the toy bear, donkey, and tiger, and the little boy named Christopher. Fredek's signal was to be a sneeze, and when it came I dashed into the bed and pulled the comforter up to my chin.

"Give me your jewels!" came the command, but the high-pitched voice was Fredek's.

Miss Bronia explained, very seriously, that this was not a game and had to do with our safety. Chastened, Fredek returned to his post.

Looking over Fredek's shoulder, I could see four figures in the potato field crawling around on hands and knees. There seemed to be a familiar pattern to their movement, and I finally deduced that they were playing some sort of tag.

Then Fredek sneezed again, and once more I dove into bed. This time Fredek apologized, claiming that there was a breeze coming through the window. Miss Bronia sent him to her room to sit on the bed where she could see him through the open door, while I lay in bed and was read to.

We had no visitors that day. At suppertime, the women came in from the potato field, covered in dirt, laughing, and calling each other Comrade Barbara and Comrade Edna.

That evening, men in blue uniforms came to our door. They were Polish border police escaping from the Russians. They had a car full of guns and ammunition, which they spent several hours burying around our cottage. The women set to work removing the insignia from their uniforms and replacing the metal buttons with buttons that had themselves been replaced on our own clothes that morning by the ones we had fashioned out of diamonds and emeralds. The men spent the night in our loft and drove away before I was awake.

Later, Fredek found one of their uniform caps under the stairs. He put it on and began parading around the table, humming a marching song. Auntie Edna came out of her room, tore the cap off his head, and slapped his face before dropping into a chair and beginning to cry. After a moment, Fredek continued his march around the table, but quietly, on tiptoe, without the cap. I tiptoed outside.

Miss Bronia ventured again to the Big House. There were no armed peasants this time, and the occupants were unharmed, though dispossessed of some jewelry, mostly costume. This time she brought back some peasant skirts and boots. With the top cut from one of her dresses, the deep blue, flowered, full skirt that Miss Bronia had brought, and two of her own scarves, one orange, the other yellow, Mother immediately fashioned what Auntie Edna called a stunning outfit and Auntie Paula declared not appropriate for the occasion. Of the boots, not one pair was small enough for my mother's tiny feet, so her peasant's outfit, minus the two scarves, began with the tennis shoes she had bought on her visit to town.

We saw our first Russian soldier that day. He galloped past our house on a rather small horse. He had on a green felt cap with a point on top, like some of the German soldiers wore in photographs from the Big War. His helmet was strapped to the back of his saddle and a rifle rested across the front. He didn't stop.

Then, as we ate supper that evening, our front door burst open and five men and one woman stood in our big room. The men had rifles, the woman a pistol strapped around her large middle. They all wore red armbands and helmets over their caps. One, I noticed, had trouble seeing from under his. Another, I recognized as the man from the icehouse.

"We are the Village Census Committee," one of the men said in the heavily accented Polish. "How many people live here and what are they called?" Auntie Paula gave him all of our names, which one of them wrote down in the margin of a folded newspaper page. He and the man from the icehouse seemed to be consulting on the spelling, though they didn't ask us. With erasing and refolding the paper for more writing space, the process took some time.

"How much money do you have?" the woman asked. Auntie Paula said that we had just enough to buy food. The scribe seemed to be writing this down as well.

There was some consultation among them, and the man who had spoken first said, "You are rich Jewish bourgeois women from Warsaw—your husbands own factories. Where is your money?" My heart sank as I realized where this information had come from.

"Our money was all in the bank," Auntie Paula said. "When the Germans started to bomb, the banks closed and we couldn't get our money out." This was written down as well.

The man who had trouble seeing from under his helmet kept pushing it up with his finger, but it kept sliding down. I saw him pick up a candle off a table and slip it into his pocket. I knew that I should not say anything. I looked over at Fredek. With one eye closed, he was taking dead aim with his extended index finger at each of our visitors in turn.

"And your jewelry?" the spokesman said. I noticed that he had a sword in its decorated scabbard strapped to his side. In the Polish army, the officers wore swords. He also had a mustache that hung down below his chin.

Auntie Edna held up her two hands, denuded now of all but her wedding band. "Our jewelry is all in the bank too," she said.

There was more consultation while Auntie Edna's answer was duly recorded. I saw the man who had taken the candle edging toward Sonya's orange pincushion. It wasn't the one with the brooch. This one was in the shape of a mouse.

"We must search the house," the leader said. "We are under orders. Your belongings will be respected." Sonya's orange-mouse pincushion had vanished.

We stayed at the table as our visitors scattered throughout the cottage. Very much aware that it was I who had supplied the information about Lolek's factory, I kept my eyes on my plate.

Within a minute or two, the search was concluded, and the visitors had reassembled in our big room. "You have passed the census inspection," the man with the sword declared. "We will be in contact." Then he aimed his index finger at Fredek, fired an imaginary shot, and they were gone.

"They took my pincushion," Sonya said.

"I know, dear," her mother said. "You'll get another one."

"No, that's not what I'm saying. I was just so surprised."

"Well, they're not real soldiers, you know. They're just Ukrainian peasants who don't like Poles very much and they're taking advantage of the situation. The Russians, you know, are Communists."

Sonya knew that, but for Fredek's and my sake, Auntie Paula explained about Communism and how the peasants here now felt that they could rise up against the landowners and others they considered rich, and whom they called bourgeois. I had never heard of Communism, though I didn't let on in case Fredek had, but my sympathies did rest with the poor people like Kiki's family and Marta, our cook, and Grandfather's coachman, Adam.

While Auntie Paula was explaining all this, Mother wrapped a stained rag that we used for dusting around our green pincushion with Auntie Edna's brooch inside. This, as she explained, was to make it less attractive. I found the idea of making something less attractive, funny, but I understood what she was doing. Miss Bronia said that these were local peasants and not the same ones she had seen at the Big House the day before.

That night we heard several gunshots. Next morning at breakfast Auntie Edna reported that her alarm clock had disappeared in the search. Mother said that her orange and yellow scarves were missing as well. Before we could leave the breakfast table, three members of the previous evening's Census Committee returned and demanded to know who had been shooting. They were again led by the man with the long mustache and the sword, but this time they presented themselves as the Village Security Committee, and they weren't wearing their helmets.

Auntie Paula said that we had no firearms. They had searched our cottage last night, she reminded them.

"We will search again," the leader announced. "Everybody must go outside."

"What a beautiful sword you have," my mother said from her seat at the table. The man looked down self-consciously.

"My father had a sword from the last war," Mother went on. "Did you fight in the last war?"

"In the Lancers." He drew himself up stiffly.

"You have the look of a cavalryman," Mother said.

The man blushed. Then he said something in Ukrainian to his companions, and they headed for the front door. Their leader pulled off his wool cap. "Goodbye, Comrades," he said before following his men out the door.

"What did they want?" Auntie Edna said.

"You sure got rid of them, Aunt Barbara," Sonya said admiringly. Mother laughed.

"You're playing a dangerous game," Auntie Paula said. "That man has a lot of power."

Mother laughed again. "He's only a peasant with a sword and an armband," she said. "That's how Yulek goes to the park every day with Miss Yanka. Tell Yulek he looks like a cavalryman, and he'll do anything you want."

I didn't like her saying that about me, but on reflection I realized that she was probably right.

I could tell that Auntie Paula still wasn't happy about Mother speaking that way to the man, but the talk turned to a discussion of whether they should go out into the potato field again. Auntie Edna said that there wasn't any point to it since the peasants all knew that they were from the city, and Auntie Paula reminded her that the Russians didn't know that, and who knew when they were going to show up. Auntie Edna started crying again, but she stopped after Mother told her that we all had to be brave.

It was decided that we would be safest with the mothers in the potato field and me sick in bed. Miss Bronia gave Fredek one more chance to prove his reliability as a sentry.

We saw no Russians that day, but that evening, after Fredek and I had been put to bed in our corner of the big room, there was a knock on the door, and I saw two of the men from that morning's Security Committee come in. Comrade Tishman, they said, was wanted at headquarters.

Auntie Edna was very frightened, but she didn't cry this time, and Mother demanded to know what it was about.

"Comrade Konievik says you must come," the man said.

"What for?" Auntie Paula said.

"Comrade Konievik says you must come," the man repeated. He raised his rifle a little to show the seriousness of his intent.

Auntie Edna stood up slowly. "I'll come with you," Mother said, standing up beside her.

"No, you come alone," the man said.

"I'm coming with her," Mother said.

"No, no," the man said in sudden confusion. " Missus . . . I mean Comrade must sit down," and he motioned to Auntie Edna to sit. Then he pulled a folded section of newspaper with last night's notes from inside his jacket. Both men looked at it.

"Which one is Comrade Tishman?" he finally asked.

Auntie Edna looked at Auntie Paula. "I am Comrade Tishman," she said.

"The pretty one," the man said, "you," indicating my mother with his free hand. "What is your name?"

"I am Comrade Waisbrem," Mother said.

The second man was crossing something out in the newspaper margin. "You come, Comrade," the first man said to Mother. Now he was sweating. "Comrade Konievik says you must come. Don't be afraid."

Fredek and I had both been pretending to be asleep, but now we sat up with unconcealed interest.

"What does Comrade Konievik want with Comrade Waisbrem?" Auntie Paula asked, speaking very slowly and deliberately.

"Don't be afraid," the man repeated. I thought that now he was more afraid than anybody. "He wants to talk about his sword."

"His sword," Mother said, her voice turning suddenly melodic. "I'll be happy to talk to Comrade Konievik about his sword." Then, to the Aunties she said, "I'll be right back." The second man held the door open for her.

"Don't you harm her!" Auntie Paula warned the two men.

"We don't hurt her," the first man assured her.

"Comrade Konievik likes swords very much," the second man added.

"You boys go to sleep," Auntie Paula commanded when they had gone out the door. Fredek and I quickly lay down again. The Aunties, Miss Bronia, and Sonya began whispering at the other end of the room.

I woke up a little while later when they were talking loudly again. My mother was back already. "I slapped his face, of course," she was saying. Apparently I had missed something.

"You couldn't leave his sword alone?" Auntie Paula was saying angrily.

"Men like to be flattered," Mother said. "He's a man, isn't he?"

"So you found out," Auntie Paula said. "This may not be the end of it, you know." Then they dropped their voices before I could find out why Mother had slapped his face.

When I woke up the next morning, the committee members were back in our house.

"Get dressed quickly," Miss Bronia was saying to Fredek and me, and there was anxiety in her voice.

"Please, can we give the children their breakfast first?" Auntie Paula was asking the man who seemed to be in charge. He had a red scarf around his neck in addition to his armband. The man with the sword wasn't there.

"You will pack and go immediately," he commanded.

"But the children," Auntie Edna said. Mother was not in the room.

"We will be back in an hour," he said. He pulled up his right sleeve to look at his watch. He was wearing at least three.

"Then you will get in the wagon and go to Durnoval." He left the cottage, followed by the others.

I understood that we were being forced to leave and was sure that it had something to do with Mother's slapping the man's face last night.

I didn't want to leave this place. I didn't want to go back to Durnoval or anywhere else. Being able to go outside without supervision, to roam and pretend with Fredek, to take the wheelbarrow by myself to the icehouse, and to go back to that stone barn where the boy said I could come and jump in the hay, were all things I wanted to keep doing. I wanted to do that even more, I knew, than I would have wanted to go back to Warsaw if the war ended tomorrow.

Mother came out of her room sliding a suitcase along the floor. Auntie Paula looked at her, and I could tell she was angry at my mother. "They'll be back in an hour with the wagon," she said to Mother. "You'd better just stay out of their sight." Mother didn't say anything.

"Where are we going to live in Durnoval?" Auntie Edna said.

"We can ask the Roseviches to help us find a place," Auntie Paula assured her. That was the name of the people at whose house we had stayed before.

"I tell you," Mother said, "that the reason that they want us out of the house has nothing to do with last night. They want us out of here so they don't have to share the land with us when they divide up the estate by Soviet law. What happened last night just gave them a convenient excuse."

"Just stop giving them excuses," Auntie Paula said angrily. "You put ideas into a simple man's head, like you did with Lupicki."

I wasn't following any of this. I did know that it was Mother who had made the man angry at us by slapping his face and with her silly talk about Grandfather's sword from the Big War. Grandfather was an old man, paralyzed from diabetes;

Francis, his attendant, had to give him injections every day, and he had not fought in the Big War. And, I was sure, he didn't own a sword.

When they came back for us with the wagon, two men carried our belongings out to the wagon. It was the same wagon that Fredek and I had ridden in with the elephants and the cabbages, but pulled by a different horse. An old man with a white beard drove us to Durnoval.

Nobody talked much on the way, except for Miss Bronia and Sonya who got to dangle their legs over the back end of the wagon and whispered and laughed together. Auntie Edna and Auntie Paula sat with their backs against one side of the wagon, my mother against the other. A large wooden box that Miss Bronia had filled at the last moment with pots, bowls, and other utensils from the cottage, clanged in the center of the wagon. Fredek and I were sitting up with the driver—one on either side—but that didn't really matter to me at the moment. I was jealous of Sonya for Miss Bronia's company. I thought about the way Mother had gotten us kicked off the farm with her silly lies about Grandfather's sword and how she had undressed me in front of everybody and I came to the conclusion that making a Christian out of her was something that neither I nor, probably, anyone else could do.

I watched the driver take out a small square of yellow paper from inside his jacket, form it into a kind of trough with one hand, pour some tobacco into it from a little pouch, and then roll it into a cigarette. He licked the end of the paper, where there must have been some glue, to complete the cylinder, and placed the cigarette between his lips. He then pulled a match out of his pocket with the same hand, lit it with his thumbnail, and raised it to the cigarette.

In a moment, Mother's head and shoulders were between me and the driver. "Would you roll one for me, please," she asked. Without a word, the driver produced another piece of paper and proceeded to repeat the process.

"Yulek, change places with me," Mother said. I didn't care about sitting up with the driver right now, but I resented her making me get down. But I did change places, and in a moment she was asking him questions about his wife, his children, and whether he had fought in the Big War. With each question, I saw Auntie Paula roll her eyes.

"You look like an artillery man," Mother said.

I was mortified.

Chapter Four

Somebody was playing a radio very loud when we rode into town in our wagon. A woman was speaking in what I took to be Ukrainian. But, instead of getting louder and then fading after we passed it, the voice followed us along the street.

"They set these up yesterday," our driver said to Mother, pointing his whip at what I recognized as a loudspeaker attached to a lamppost on a street corner. There was another loudspeaker on the next corner and the one after that.

"She's speaking Russian," Auntie Edna said, "but I can't make out what she's saying." Russian was what my grandmother spoke, and I understood a lot of the words, though what the woman was talking about didn't make sense to me either.

Mother turned in her seat. "She's saying what a paradise the Soviet Union is," she said.

"Who's she talking to in Russian?" Auntie Paula said. "Aren't the Russians already supposed to know what a paradise they have?"

"Look at the Russian soldier. There's a Russian soldier over there!" Fredek said, pointing. There was a Russian soldier standing on one corner. He had on the same pointed green hat as the one I had seen galloping by our cottage. His rifle was strapped diagonally across his back with a length of packaging string. On the front of his cap was a shining enamel red star. Another soldier and another loudspeaker stood on the next corner.

A line of people stood outside a bakery shop. They must have very good bread or cakes or something to attract so many people, I reasoned.

There was nobody home at the house where we had spent that night on our way to the farm. I remembered that we had been expecting them to help us find a place to stay.

With servants in the household, it was unusual to find a house completely empty, but no one answered the doorbell, and the window shutters were pulled shut.

The wagon driver had already begun unloading our things onto the sidewalk. "Just a moment," Auntie Paula said. "There's nobody here."

"I have to go back," the old man said. "I have to go back to the farm."

"But we have no place to go," Auntie Paula said. "We expected to be able to stop here, but there's nobody home."

"I have to go back," the man said, continuing to unload our suitcases and boxes.

"Mr. Koblonski," Mother said. I noticed that she called him Mister and not the Comrade they were all calling each other now. "Mr. Koblonski, you aren't going to leave women and children out on the street with their suitcases, are you?"

The old man sighed and began putting the suitcases and boxes back in the wagon.

"I don't think they're coming back soon," Auntie Edna said. Auntie Paula agreed.

Mr. Koblonski drove us to a little hotel, but the rooms were all taken by the Russian army. They did, however, let us wait in their lobby with our baggage while the three mothers went looking for a place for us to stay. Before leaving, Auntie Paula gave us a strong admonishment about being well-behaved and quiet. Here, in the presence of real enemy soldiers, we needed little persuasion.

I saw Mother walk quickly towards the front door and I could tell by the deliberately slow pace of the Aunties that they were still mad at her. The lobby of this hotel wasn't like the one Kiki and I had stayed in at our resort. It didn't have marble floors with oriental carpets, palm trees in enormous pots, or uniformed bellboys. The hotel was no wider than a town house, and the lobby had room for only one sofa and three armchairs around a coffee table. The walls were covered with a gray paper that had a burlap-like texture. The man who had permitted us to stay was doing paperwork behind a counter at the side of the lobby. A uniformed attendant operated a small elevator behind us, and a bathroom, Fredek and I had been shown, was behind that.

From the armchair that we had been told to share, Fredek and I watched as soldiers in green tunics and dark blue trousers walked in and out through the lobby in twos and threes. They looked different from Polish soldiers. They seemed, for the most part, not as tall and heavier set, with round faces. Some were darker skinned, with oriental eyes. They didn't have swords, like Polish officers, but like Polish officers, they did wear pistols at their sides. Many carried briefcases as well.

One soldier, coming into the hotel, stopped in front of Fredek and me and smiled. His round face and short-cropped hair made me think of a snowman. "Ah, little boys!" he said in accented Polish. He seemed delighted with his discovery. I saw Miss Bronia lean towards us from the sofa she shared with Sonya. The Russian fished in the pocket of his loose-fitting trousers and, after a moment's search, came up with two lumps of sugar in their paper wrappers. Hotel Grand was printed on each wrapper. He held them out to us, one in each hand.

We had all been warned, in the weeks before the war, about German planes dropping poisoned candy, and neither Fredek nor I reached out to accept his gift.

"They are not allowed to eat sugar," Miss Bronia interjected. "It rots their teeth."

The Russian broke into another big smile, revealing a number of steel teeth. "Ah, the momma," he said, then added, "and the big sister."

The smiling Russian dug into his pocket again. This time he produced a button. It was a large blue button with some design molded into its surface. He held it out to Sonya, who looked at it blankly.

"Go ahead, take it, dear," Miss Bronia urged her. To the Russian she said, "Thank you for your kindness, Comrade," as Sonya reluctantly accepted the gift. The man patted Sonya's cheek, winked at Fredek and me, and walked on.

When he had gone, Miss Bronia explained to us that Russia was a very poor country, and things like sugar cubes and fancy buttons were special to them. The man was trying to be friendly, and, as long as the Russians were our occupiers, we should take care not to offend them.

Miss Bronia had packed some bread and cheese, which we ate for lunch soon after settling into our chairs in the hotel lobby. She had also dug in the boxes and suitcases that the elevator man had neatly piled behind our armchair, to produce some books for us to read silently to ourselves. The books, mine about a talking rabbit and Fredek's about a boy in America who delivered newspapers on his bicycle, we had read many times before, and they held little interest for us now. Sonya was knitting under Miss Bronia's close supervision.

As the afternoon wore on and grew into evening, boredom and hunger had taken up residence inside me. I had made two trips to the little bathroom under the stairs and Fredek had made four or five. After one of them, he whispered to me his discovery of a secret room with a short wave radio where a Russian soldier was listening to everything that was being said here in the lobby and reporting it to Moscow. In view of our need not to cause a disturbance, I thought it best to pretend quiet interest.

I would have liked to practice my coin-disappearing with the coin substitute I had found—Miss Bronia had told me it was something called a washer—but that required a certain arm movement that I did not believe appropriate under the circumstances.

When Mother and Auntie Edna returned without Auntie Paula, it was well past suppertime, and the lateness of the hour was gnawing at my stomach. The way they walked together didn't look as though anyone was mad at anyone else anymore. It seemed that they had been unable to find a proper place for us to stay, but they had found one where we could spend the next night or two in until they could find us something better. Auntie Paula was cleaning the place out now.

We left some bags in the care of the hotel desk clerk and carried what we could the several blocks to our new temporary home. Fredek's question about supper, as we walked, was answered by his mother's un-reassuring, "We'll see."

The place was two large rooms on the ground floor of an apartment building built around a courtyard. They were connected by an archway and had windows on the street. The outer room must have been at least twenty-five feet by twenty, and the inner room even bigger. Although the autumn chill had not yet set in, these two rooms were cold and damp, and there was a strong odor. The beige paint was peeling off the walls, and there was mildew near the ceiling. I had never seen walls like that before.

"Smell the wall," Fredek said, standing with his nose to the wall.

"Get away from that wall!" his mother said.

An electric light bulb hung on a cord from the middle of each ceiling. A stove stood in the first room for cooking and heating. The toilet and the water pump were down the hall to be shared with other tenants. The furniture was one chair and a pot on the stove.

"This is just for one night," my mother said. "Tomorrow we'll find something much better."

For supper, we had a basket of very large carrots that the mothers had bought from a peasant woman—there had been no food in the shops. By noon, the food stores are empty, they had been told.

Miss Bronia broke up the one chair to burn in the stove and cook the carrots. Never a fan of carrots, I was hungry enough to find these palatable. After dinner, we unpacked the suitcases to make one large sleeping pallet out of all the clothes. That night we all slept fully clothed, side by side on the common pallet, covering ourselves with coats and jackets. I had my mother's mink jacket, which kept me warm, but did not keep out the damp.

There was nothing for breakfast the following morning. Fredek complained of being hungry. I could not understand his persistence since we all knew that there was nothing to eat.

"Yes, yes, dear. I know and I'm sorry," Auntie Edna kept telling him, and I could see that she was on the verge of tears. She walked back and forth nervously, waiting for her turn at the wash basin. When it was her turn, she washed Fredek's face rather roughly, making him cry out. "I'm sorry, dear, I'm sorry," she kept saying. I didn't know why she did it in the first place, since Fredek and I had washed ourselves every morning at the cottage. To her credit, Mother let me do my own face washing this morning.

Miss Bronia had taken water from the pump in the hall, in a pitcher that we had brought with us from the cottage. We washed ourselves in the pot we had cooked the carrots in the night before, carrying it to the toilet to empty. When Mother told me to go to the bathroom, as I did every morning, with a sheet of newspaper that wasn't for reading, I found the toilet, a board with a hole in it in a closet off the hallway, too foul smelling to do more than pee in it, which I could do without stepping close to that hole, though I did wet the board liberally. When Auntie Edna led Fredek there by the arm, we could hear his muffled protests even inside our apartment.

With our morning toilet finished, Auntie Paula laid out a plan for attacking our problems. A bakery two blocks away would be open at eight. That would be in fifteen minutes, and somebody should, right now, go and get in the line that was probably already forming. Actually, two people should go so that one could come back to give the rest of us an idea of how long the wait might be so that we would know whether to wait here for breakfast or go out foraging for the other things we needed. Once we had had breakfast, or learned that it would be too long a wait, Auntie Paula said, we should break up into teams to look for firewood, meat and vegetables, and other quarters.

"Bravo Paula!" Mother said, when Auntie Paula had finished presenting her plan, and I, too, was impressed. Miss Bronia quickly volunteered to go to the bakery, and Sonya said she would go with her. The two left immediately. I got the sense that Mother was making a special effort to be nice to Auntie Paula.

Auntie Edna said she would go apartment hunting. "Fine," Auntie Paula said. "You and Fredek can start looking in that section on the other side of that little park that we didn't have time to get to yesterday. Barbara and Yulek can go left from the front door, looking for food and firewood. Sonya and I will turn right from the front entrance, and Bronia can try the big avenue. Everyone buy whatever they can find in the way of food or firewood. How's that?"

"Paula, you're like a general," Mother said.

"Why don't you take Fredek with you, and I'll take Sonya," Auntie Edna said to Auntie Paula.

"Maybe Fredek can go with Bronia," Auntie Paula said. "He can help her carry things. You won't have anything to carry."

I could tell that neither one of my Aunties wanted Fredek with her, and I felt sorry for him. Fredek didn't seem to care. "When do we eat breakfast?" he asked.

"In a little while, dear," his mother said. Then, turning to Auntie Paula and Mother she said, "I never thought that the time would come when I didn't have one scrap of food to give to my child for breakfast."

"Don't be an idiot!" Auntie Paula snapped. "This is only a temporary situation. We have money, and you can do anything you want when you have money."

I decided once more that I didn't like Auntie Paula. I could see that Auntie Edna was in pain, but whether I liked her or not, I wasn't sure.

In a few minutes, Sonya came back to say that Miss Bronia was just four people from the door to the shop and that it wouldn't be long now. Then, a few minutes later, Miss Bronia came back with a large round loaf of black bread. "Only one loaf per customer," she said. The bread would have tasted better with butter, but it was warm and soft and moist and delicious.

Out in the street, a woman with a Russian accent was speaking in Polish over the loudspeakers. The Soviet Union was a paradise where the stores were full of wonderful things, she was saying, and everyone was given as much money as they needed. I wondered what exactly the Soviet Union was. If it was a shopping area somewhere here in town that she was advertising, I wondered why Mother didn't pay more attention to it—it sounded like just the answer to our needs. And the bit about being given money, I didn't understand at all.

"Take my hand," Mother had said as we first came out of the dark hallway of our building into the not much brighter daylight in the street. In Warsaw I would have taken her hand automatically, knowing I had no viable option. Now I sensed that if I refused, Mother would have a difficult time enforcing her command and there was probably too much going on for her to make an issue of it later. On the other hand, this was wartime, and my making an issue of so petty a matter would have been wrong in terms of the urgency of the times. Realizing quite well how this reasoning distinguished me from my cousin Fredek and maybe anyone else my age, I opted to take Mother's hand.

As we walked in our assigned direction, looking for a greengrocer, a butcher, a baker, or firewood, I realized that Mother and I were almost the only people walking. There were others in the street, including a Russian soldier with a rifle on almost every corner, but most people did not walk, but stood or sat. They stood in small groups talking, the men with cigarettes and pipes, wearing the flat caps that, to me, implied working class, in contrast to the fedoras and bowlers that one saw on the streets in Warsaw. Women, mostly in black coats and kerchiefs, stood in little groups of their own. Some people sat alone on chairs in doorways. I had the feeling that everyone and everything seemed sad. Mother had exchanged her peasant skirt and blouse for a gray tweed suit and, once more in her own high-heeled shoes, towered over me again.

Most of the stores we passed were closed, their lights off and the steel grates pulled across the glass windows. In one store that wasn't closed, I could see several Russian soldiers lined up at the counter, but couldn't tell what they were buying.

"Oh look, Yulek!" Mother said suddenly. "In that next block there."

Looking ahead, I could see a line of people outside a store of some sort. "Let's see what they're selling," Mother said, breaking into a fast walk; I had to run to keep up with her.

This queue was about as long as the one outside the bakery that I had seen from the wagon yesterday. I counted thirty-eight people standing against the wall outside the door.

"What are they selling?" Mother asked the woman at the end of the line.

"Sausage," came the answer, "one ring to a customer. And they have soap and cigarettes. They had butter for a while, but it's gone."

My outlook brightened at the thought of sausage. The food situation being what it was, Mother was not likely to refuse me sausage—unless of course Auntie Paula or Miss Bronia came up with ham. We joined the end of the line.

The woman, whom Mother had asked the question, was only a bit taller than I was, in a gray coat and a little basket of artificial flowers in the way of a hat. She was older than Mother, and a partially filled cloth bag hung from her arm.

"Missus is not from here," she said to Mother, turning to face us.

"No," Mother said. "We're from Warsaw. And Missus?"

"I live here. My husband was a captain in the police, but the Russians detained him night before last. There's a place out in the country a few kilometers away where they've taken a number of men, nobody knows why. My husband didn't do anything. He was just a policeman doing his job, but they just came to the house and took him. I'm trying to get a permit to go see him, but you have to stand in line for that too, and I have a son and a daughter to feed in the meantime."

"I'm sorry," Mother said. "My husband went into the army when the war started, and I don't know where he is."

The woman clucked her tongue. "One must survive," she said. "Missus has her boy to take care of. I don't let my daughter out of the house as long as they are in the streets." Her head made a little nod towards the Russian soldier across the street.

As they talked, we advanced a few places toward the entrance door. A man stood on the other side of the glass door, unlocking it to let each customer out and a new one in.

"Missus doesn't have a shopping bag," the woman said to Mother.

"No, it's our first day here. We were on a farm. There was no shortage of food there."

"Missus will need to sew herself a bag. You never know how many lines you'll stand in and how long you'll have to wait."

"Yes. Thank you for the advice. What's happened to all the food anyway?"

"The Russians take it all. Their army, you know, doesn't carry provisions. They just live off the land. Everything's stopped since they got here. The stores have nothing to sell.

The soldiers go crazy buying up trinkets, watches, mechanical children's toys. When a store does get some supplies, you stand in line like this."

There was an old man in line behind us now. He had a white mustache, a little white goatee, and very large ears. "Have you been waiting here long?" he asked me.

I tugged on Mother's sleeve. "Don't do that," she said, turning away from her conversation.

"Mummy, the man wants to know if we've been here long," I said, mindful of admonitions against speaking to strangers.

"So tell him."

I was pleased with this change of policy. "A few minutes," I said to the man.

"A few minutes?" he repeated. "Do you have a watch?"

I was puzzled by this question. "I do have a watch, but not on me. It's my father's gold pocket watch."

"Then how do you know it was a few minutes?" His tone and his face were extra, extra serious, and I suddenly realized he was joking. "I counted the seconds," I said.

"Now, that's a very good way to tell the time when you don't have a watch," he said in a grave tone. "Do you know how many seconds are in a minute?"

"Sixty."

"That's very good. And how many minutes in an hour?"

"Sixty."

"And I suppose there are sixty hours in a day?"

"Of course. And sixty days in a week," I said laughing.

"And sixty weeks in a month."

"And sixty months in a year."

I had never had a nonsensical conversation like this before, and, for some reason, it made me feel very grown up.

"Do you know how many years in a century?" he asked.

I was afraid that if I said sixty again, he might think that I didn't know the real answer. "One hundred," I finally said.

"Very good. And do you know what century this is?"

"It's the twentieth century and this is nineteen thirty-nine."

"That's excellent. Here's your reward," he said, reaching into his coat pocket. Here I was concerned. While the ban on my speaking with strangers seemed to have been lifted, I doubted that it also applied to accepting presents, and I did not want to bring this very weird and funny conversation to a premature end by refusing his gift. The old man fished around in his pocket for a moment, then extracted his hand holding nothing, which he held out to me proudly.

With great relief I accepted the imaginary object, placed it carefully in my mouth and began to chew.

"Oh no, no, no!" he said in mock alarm. "You don't eat it—you wear it on your head like I do." There was, of course, nothing on his head other than a little black skullcap to keep his bald spot warm, like Grandfather did.

"I am terribly sorry," I said in equally mock regret. I took the object out of my mouth, blew on it, and carefully put it over my head. The man cocked his head back a little and looked at me. "I think I would wear it a little more over the right eye."

I adjusted the imaginary headgear.

"No, maybe over the left eye," he said. I adjusted it again.

Suddenly there was a loud, collective groan from the people making up the queue. "I've been waiting over an hour," somebody said. Now I saw that a hand-lettered sign had been put up in the glass door. "Closed—out of stock," it said.

"Is this what happens?" Mother asked the woman in front of her.

"It happens all the time."

"I wasted half an hour," Mother said.

The line was quickly dissolving. The man with the white goatee and the skullcap behind us curled his fingers around an imaginary object. I guessed it was a sausage. He took a bite. "Not up to pre-war standards," he confided to me, "but actually quite decent. Now I have to find some bread to go with it."

I followed his example. "Not as good as we had in Warsaw, but eatable," I acknowledged. Remarkably, I could actually almost taste the spicy meat.

Suddenly I felt Mother's hand sliding down my arm. "Give me your hand," she said. We walked quickly on down the street; Mother's heels clicking angrily on the sidewalk. "I can't waste my time like this," she said, though I wasn't sure she was talking to me. I looked back for my new friend, but I couldn't see him.

It wasn't long before we spotted another queue on the other side of the street. It was even longer than the first one. Like the other one, it was mostly women in kerchiefs or little flowered hats with shopping bags hanging from their arms. Some of the bags had lumps in the bottom—many hung down empty.

"It's a butcher shop!" Mother said in a triumphant tone when we could distinguish the empty steel hooks in the window and the tiled interior walls.

Edging toward the curb, where the line ended, I felt Mother pulling me, instead, towards the shop door. "Adam, Adam Starecki!" she called, when we were a few yards from the waiting people. In a moment I could see that she was addressing a man, three people from the store entrance, about a head taller than the women in front and in back of him. In a blue, pinstripe, double-breasted suit, like the ones men wore in Warsaw, he looked like someone not from here. He had a long, thin face and a neatly trimmed little dark mustache. His hair was neatly combed and brushed back, and held in place with hair oil. He certainly could have been one of Mother and Lolek's Warsaw friends, except that he didn't respond to the name and he certainly wasn't Adam Starecki, whom I knew because, when he came to our apartment, he often brought a box of chocolates for Kiki and me. And he wasn't as tall as this man and was nearly bald.

"Oh, I'm so glad to see you safe," Mother said as we kept approaching.

Finally, the tall man realized that it was he who was being addressed, made a little bow with his head and said, "I am sorry, Missus, but my name is Rokief, Roman Rokief."

"Oh, I'm so sorry, Mr. Rokief," Mother said, stopping short and holding a hand up to her face. "Yes, yes, I can see now that Mister is not Judge Starecki. But from a few meters away Mister looks just like the judge. And Mister has the same bearing. I would guess that Mister is also a judge. Am I right?"

"As a matter of fact, I am an attorney," he admitted, "but, I'm afraid, not yet a judge."

"But Mister is not from Durnoval."

"No, my wife and I came here from Krakow when the fighting started. I have a bad heart, so they wouldn't take me in the army, and I wanted to get my wife and daughters out."

"My brother lives in Krakow. Maybe Mister knows him, Pavew Rogacki. I don't know what happened to him. I'm so worried."

My uncle Pavew's name was Rozenfeld, not Rogacki, and he lived in Lodz where he ran Grandfather's stocking factory.

The man thought for a moment. "No, I don't know that name," he finally said.

"My name is Barbara Padovich," she said, and there she was with that Padovich again. I realized that I resented her taking over my name that way.

"My little son and I are from Warsaw," she went on, "and we've had just an awful time getting here. We were bombed on the road and then, when we finally found a little cottage on a farm near here, the peasants turned Communist and threw us out. My little son is sickly."

I was damned if I was going to cough for her this time. While she was telling lies to a total stranger for some bizarre reason, several people had already joined the line ahead of where we should have been, and the man who wasn't Judge Starecki was almost ready to go into the store.

"Mister really does have the bearing of a judge," Mother repeated now, and made the man smile self-consciously. Then, a man in a white apron unlatched the shop door from the inside, indicating that Mr. Rokief should come in. Mr. Rokief quickly took Mother's elbow and the two of them stepped inside the butcher shop together, pulling me along by the hand.

"You can't do that!" I heard a woman say, who had been standing behind Mr. Rokief, and suddenly the purpose behind Mother's entire charade revealed itself to me. I ducked my head in shame as the glass door shut behind us.

"I would like some beef, please, a nice cut," Mother said to the woman behind the counter.

"All we have is lamb and pork," the woman said. "Quarter kilo to a customer." Like the people in the butcher shop in Warsaw, she had on a white apron over a white smock and a white cap on her head.

"My husband and two children are home sick with nothing to eat," Mother said.

"All I can sell you today is a quarter kilo. I sell you more than one package, and he'll arrest me," she said, indicating a Russian soldier sitting in a chair, which he rocked back against the wall, at the side of the store. A rifle stood against the wall. He yawned without covering his mouth. "Come back tomorrow. Lamb or pork?"

"Lamb," Mother said a little uncertainly. The woman reached into a box and handed mother a little package in white paper.

Mr. Rokief leaned forward across the marble counter. "And a quarter kilo of lamb for the young man," he said.

"A quarter kilo per customer is all I'm allowed to sell," the woman said.

"He's a customer!"

"He's a little boy."

"He's a big boy, who came here and waited in line to buy some of your lamb." He said it quietly so the soldier wouldn't hear, but very forcefully.

Looking sideways at the yawning soldier, the woman quickly thrust a white package towards me as well. I took it before I realized what I was doing. Involuntarily, I also glanced at the soldier, who seemed to have seen nothing.

Mother quickly paid for our purchase, Mr. Rokief paid for his, and in a moment we were standing outside the store with our white-paper-wrapped packages.

The people in the line were all looking at us. "They cut into line," one woman said. "Dirty cheaters!" someone added.

Mother and Mr. Rokief ignored them. "Thank Mister so much for Mister's kind help," Mother said to him. "I'm living now with two sisters-in-law, their two children, and a governess. This half kilo isn't going to go very far, but a lot further than a quarter kilo."

"Line cutter!" somebody said. The package in my hands seemed as though it were the size of a soccer ball. I stepped around to Mother's other side, away from the queue.

"With some vegetables, they'll make a nice soup," Mr. Rokief said.

"I suppose I overpaid several times," Mother said, laughing. "I have no idea what a quarter kilo of lamb is even supposed to cost. At home, my husband pays all the bills. I don't even know what cut this is."

"The commissar won't let them overcharge. That's why the soldier's there. He's a good man."

"Where can I find a greengrocer?"

I realized that Mother hadn't even bothered to tell Mr. Rokief that Lolek wasn't really home sick. That was because he would already know that. He would know that she didn't really have a sick husband and probably that she hadn't really mistaken him for Judge Starecki either. He and Mother had never met before, but they immediately recognized in each other their common dishonesty. It was that Jewish thing.

"There's a greengrocer around the other side of this block. I don't know if they're still open," Mr. Rokief said. "I'd take you both to a café, but there aren't any open—there's no coffee. Coffee is probably the most precious commodity in town." I just wished we would go anywhere else.

Mother laughed. "I'd invite Mister and his wife for cocktails, but we have no cocktails." They both laughed at this.

"Stop that, Yulek!" Mother surprised me. I hadn't realized that I had begun to tug at her sleeve. "He's anxious to get going," she explained to Mr. Rokief. "Does Mister have a telephone?"

"We have two rooms in a kind lady's apartment. Let me write her telephone number down for Missus." He wrote a phone number with a little gold pencil on a pad of paper in a little leather folder. Mother explained that we were staying in an awful place for just a night or two, they shook hands, and we finally walked down the street and around the corner.

The line at the greengrocer's was very short. We bought some vegetables and headed for home. It must have been lunchtime by now, because I was hungry. But I knew it would do no good to mention it. I remembered Fredek's wailing this morning.

I also noticed that all the people that I had seen standing in the streets were now gone. Except for the Russian soldiers on the corners, Mother and I were practically the only people in the street. The voice on the loudspeaker was telling us that in the Soviet Union everyone was equal.

Back at our building, there was a new problem—we had no key to our apartment. Miss Bronia had been entrusted with our only key, and she was to pay frequent visits to the rooms in case somebody came back early.

A little hallway, running past the water pump, the toilet, and the door to our rooms, connected the courtyard at the center of the building with the street. One step led down to the sidewalk. Parts of three hinges from an absent iron gate were embedded in the masonry.

The hallway was too dark and malodorous from the toilet and the courtyard too strewn with garbage for us to wait there.

We went back out to the street, put our packages down in the hallway, and waited. I sat down on the step and Mother told me to stand up because it wasn't nice to sit on the step and I would get my pants dirty. Then she changed her mind and said it was all right for me to sit.

The loudspeaker said that the Red Army had brought equality to us. "Equality" seemed like a big thing to these people. I guessed that Red Army was what the Russians called their army, since their flag was red, but the equality issue concerned me. Not that it really mattered, but it was something to ponder while we waited. I wondered whether those soft little spikes on the soldiers' hats had something to do with equality. Were shorter soldiers issued hats with longer spikes?

I saw two soldiers with rifles across their backs approaching along the sidewalk. One was taller than the other, but the spikes on their hats seemed to be of the same length. So that certainly wasn't it. As they approached us in our doorway, they smiled. Instinctively, I smiled back, but immediately realized that I was smiling at the enemy.

They stopped and greeted us in Russian. They seemed quite friendly. Mother answered them in Polish. The taller one bent down and patted my cheek. The other was saying something I couldn't hear to Mother. It sounded like a question. He continued smiling.

"I don't understand," Mother said in Polish. "I don't speak Russian," which wasn't true.

The soldier put his elbow against the side of the building, leaned closer to Mother, and said something else.

"I don't understand," Mother repeated.

The soldier reached for Mother's hand. She drew back, shaking her head. "No, no," she said.

The other soldier held a piece of candy out to me. I shook my head. "It's good," he said in Russian.

"No!" Mother said in a much firmer tone than before. The soldier's tone sounded like he was pleading. His hand reached up to touch her cheek.

"No!" she said again, pushing his hand away.

The soldier shrugged his shoulders and said to his companion, "She must be waiting for an officer to come along." They both laughed. Then they walked on.

"Standing in the doorway like this, I look like a blah-blah," Mother said, using a word I didn't know. I could tell she wasn't really talking to me. She gave a little private, dark-sounding laugh.

"What did he want?" I asked. I sensed that this had been one of those things that adults didn't like to share with children, and it gave me a perverse pleasure to ask.

"About buying cigarettes," she snapped.

"What?" This was new and scary ground for me.

Mother's voice grew much calmer. "He just wanted to know where he could buy cigarettes."

I knew this wasn't the truth. "Why did you say you didn't speak Russian?"

"I just didn't want to be nice to them."

I knew she still wasn't telling me the truth, but I didn't want to push further. I let it go.

"Let's walk up and down the street a little," Mother said. "Pick up your package, and we'll just walk back and forth a little until Miss Bronia comes."

"I'm hungry," I said maliciously.

"Little soldiers learn to accept hunger sometimes," she said. It wasn't an answer I had expected, and I had no response to it. Now I wished I hadn't said it. I was being like Fredek. I stood up.

But just then, we saw Miss Bronia and Fredek come around the corner. Each carried an armload of firewood, and they were singing a song I didn't know, something about tents and campfires.

"There was a truck full of firewood, and the soldiers were giving it away to everybody," Fredek said.

"If we had had something to carry it in, we could have gotten a lot more," Miss Bronia said, out of breath. "Mrs. Herbstein found two more loaves of bread and some cheese. I'm afraid there's no butter. Missus didn't find any, did she?"

"We got some lamb," Mother said, holding up a package. "And some more carrots and spinach."

"Wonderful, I can make a stew," Miss Bronia said, leading the way into the building. We were immediately enveloped by the smell of mold and the toilet.

*   *   *

Auntie Edna wasn't back by suppertime. Auntie Paula and Sonya had brought back potatoes and roses. "A poor old woman was trying to sell flowers, and nobody was buying, so we bought some," Sonya said.

"Anything to make the place smell better," Mother said, and they laughed. Then we sat around on suitcases and boxes while Miss Bronia dealt with supper.

"Where's my mother?" Fredek asked.

"She'll be home soon, dear," Auntie Paula said.

"She'll be home soon," Mother repeated.

"Your mother is out finding us a nicer place to stay," Auntie Paula said. "You don't want to go on staying here, do you?"

"I want my mother," Fredek wailed. Fredek was not a little soldier.

"So, Basia," Auntie Paula said cheerfully, and I could tell it was for Fredek's benefit, "you and Yulek really did well. Sonya and I stood in line at a butcher shop too, but they ran out of meat long before we could get in."

"There was a soldier in the store to make sure they didn't sell more that a quarter kilo to a customer. A very pleasant lawyer from Krakow made them give Yulian a quarter kilo too."

"When is my mother coming home?" Fredek whined. He had curled up on our sleeping pallet and was sucking his thumb.

"She'll be home soon," Auntie Paula said again, but without her earlier cheer. Then, to Mother, "How did you meet this very pleasant lawyer?"

"He was standing in line, and you could tell that he wasn't from here. So I walked up and started a conversation. And when he went into the store, we just went right in with him."

Auntie Paula found that amusing. Of course Mother did not tell her about pretending to mistake him for Judge Staretski, but I was just as glad not to have to relive that experience.

We ate out of an odd assortment of bowls. I didn't like the lamb stew and would have filled up on the delicious bread and cheese, but Mother made me eat some. "Who knows when we'll have meat again," Auntie Paula said. Miss Bronia tried to coax some stew into Fredek, but he made a terrible face after his first sip. "It is pretty bad," Miss Bronia said to Auntie Paula, and they agreed to let him abstain.

"The people are saying that the farmers are all selling their meat on the black market," Auntie Paula said. Putting two and two together, I reasoned that black market must be another name for that Soviet Union where, the woman on the loudspeaker said, you could go and buy anything you wanted.

"We'll have to find out how to contact them," Mother said. I wondered why the Russians would go to the trouble of setting up loudspeakers to advertise the Soviet Union without telling you where to go and find it. I had heard that the Russians were stupid.

Miss Bronia was now sitting beside Fredek in the back room, holding his head in her lap. The rest of us had gravitated to the proximity of the stove.

"Do you think something could have happened?" Auntie Paula half whispered.

"Some soldiers tried to blah-blah me," Mother said, again using a word I didn't know. "But it was an honest mistake.

Standing in the doorway in my heels and stockings, I must have looked the part."

They both gave a little laugh. Sonya laughed too, but louder.

"I think they're trying hard to keep order," Mother said. "Edna can take care of herself."

At that moment, Auntie Edna came in the front door. She stood there looking down on all of us on our boxes and suitcases. Fredek ran to her side and buried his face in her suit jacket.

"You have no idea," she finally announced very slowly, "how lucky we are to have found this place. There is nothing out there— absolutely nothing. There are people sleeping in the park."

I visualized my park in Warsaw with people sleeping on the benches. I wondered what was left of the park.

Miss Bronia was the first to speak. "I have a bottle of disinfectant," she said. "We can scrub this place clean. We can air it out and the fire will dry up the dampness."

Nobody said anything for a while. The prospect of staying where we were, however disinfected and dehumidified, took us all a bit of time to digest. Finally Auntie Paula said, "Bronia's right. We can make this place habitable. Tonight we'll make a list of things we need. Tomorrow we'll figure out how to get them. We saved you some lamb stew, Edna."

Auntie Edna just shook her head as she stood there. You could tell how tired she was.

"You have to eat something," Auntie Paula said. Auntie Edna stood there, holding Fredek to her and not saying anything.

*   *   *

In the days that followed, Miss Bronia, Sonya, Fredek, and I washed down every surface of our two rooms with the disinfectant. Opening our windows wide during the day and maintaining a small fire in the evenings, seemed to get rid of much of the dampness. When Auntie Paula and Sonya returned to the corner where Miss Bronia and Fredek had gotten the firewood, there was no more wood, and no one knew when or where another army truckload of wood might appear. When one of the mothers encountered a man or woman carrying firewood, they would ask where the wood had been obtained and sometimes would arrive at that corner while wood was still being distributed—sometimes not.

The same method was applied to the procurement of meat. "They have chickens at such-and-such butcher shop," would initiate a rush to that location. A queue meant that there was still merchandise. Whether there would still be some when your turn came, was a different issue. Bakers and greengrocers seemed to have a steadier supply. If you lined up early enough in the morning at the baker's, you could usually count on being rewarded with a loaf of bread, though what flour they had received to bake with, varied from day to day.

Foraging for supplies was pretty much a full-day occupation for the mothers. My mother preferred going on her own, while the Aunties usually went out together, though they often split up eventually, according to the opportunity. I definitely did not want to go with Mother again and was allowed to help Miss Bronia with the housework. Fredek was, sometimes, invited to accompany our Auntie Paula, which he enjoyed. I don't remember him ever asking to go with his own mother. Sonya sometimes accompanied either of the Aunties. As for me, I just didn't feel comfortable enough with either of my Aunties to go out with anyone but Miss Bronia.

Miss Bronia and I sewed pallets out of old curtains, sheets, and tablecloths that Auntie Edna had found somewhere. It seems that nobody ever asked where such items came from. Fredek, who wouldn't touch a needle and thread, stuffed the pallets with straw. A universal packing material, straw was available for the asking from almost any store. The pallets turned out to be quite comfortable, except that each movement raised a small could of dust.

One time, I went out early in the morning with Miss Bronia to wait in the bread queue together. Miss Bronia got into a conversation with two women standing in front of us. She seemed to know one of them from other queues—or maybe the same queue on other days. The other woman had come from another town where there weren't any queues because the food stores had nothing to sell. The farmers came into town and sold food out of their wagons at many times the normal price. The woman had heard that the commissar commanding this town didn't allow things like that.

Somehow we acquired several chairs in the next few weeks, two tables—one slightly higher than the other—that, fitted together, could seat all seven of us. Two people sat on nail kegs and Fredek and I shared a steamer trunk at the end. We even got a bed. The mothers took turns sleeping in it, one week at a time. Fredek and I shared a large pallet.

"No talking," Auntie Paula had told us on our second night there, when Fredek and I were put to bed in the back room where we all slept, while the older people had their tea around the table in the front room. Prior to arriving at our former residence, the cottage, I had never had anyone in my room to talk to at night, and in the cottage our bed was only a few feet from the center of after-supper life. It had never occurred to me that anything like talk was appropriate in bed, unless you were there because you were ill or unless you were married people who read the paper and ate breakfast in bed.

No sooner had Auntie Paula given us her admonition, turned out the light bulb hanging from the ceiling, and gone into the front room, that I heard Fredek's whisper in my ear. "If we whisper," he said, "they can't hear us in the other room."

I considered the statement for a moment and realized that it was probably true. "What . . . should we whisper about?" I asked. Fredek had no ready answer, but took it under advisement. Before he could formulate a reply, I heard the deep breathing that indicated he had fallen asleep. Relieved, I turned my back on my sleeping bedfellow.

*   *   *

"Tomorrow a whole train of firewood is arriving at the station," Auntie Paula announced one evening, coming in with a headless chicken wrapped in a newspaper under her arm. "We should all go and carry home as much as we can." The days and nights were colder now, and the supply of firewood was growing sparse. The truckloads brought in by the army and dumped on street corners seemed to have stopped, and the price that the peasants asked for wood they sold from their wagons was linked inversely to the mercury in the thermometer. It may have been my imagination, but I was sure I had seen Auntie Paula eyeing Fredek's and my wooden steamer trunk.

The next day was overcast and damp as we all walked the few blocks to the train station, each of us equipped with a cloth shopping bag. There, we indeed found a train of open cars stacked high with the split yellow firewood. It stood on a side track beyond the platform and, as we had expected, a queue paralleled the cars, veering only to skirt the puddles from the night's rain.

To our right, three cars were empty and soldiers stood on top of the pile in the fourth car, throwing the wood to the ground. The pieces bounced and somersaulted in all directions while six people at a time were permitted by armed guards to pick up as much as they could carry, while dodging the tumbling pieces. As each moved away with his or her load, the guards would let the next person in line have his turn. To our left, the train and the queue extended several car lengths, until they both curved away and disappeared from view.

Auntie Paula led the way, as we began following the line to its end. The track curved gently in front of us, revealing another railroad car and more waiting people with each few steps. A guard stood at the front of every car, keeping the queue separated from the train by several yards.

Gravel crunched under our feet as we walked. I held Miss Bronia's hand. Fredek and Sonya walked on ahead, deep in conversation. As on other such occasions, I wondered what the two of them talked about so intently. The three mothers led the way. Their conversation didn't interest me, but I gloried in the feel of Miss Bronia's soft hand around mine.

The end of the line had finally come in sight, still several cars ahead of us, when it began to drizzle. Anticipating rain, we had put on raincoats this morning. Mine was a cape with a hood and a heavy rubber smell.

"I'm not doing this," I suddenly heard Mother say, as she stopped in her tracks. "Yulek, give me your hand," she commanded. I obeyed and, to my embarrassment, we began walking back towards the station. Long and wet as the wait in line promised to be, I understood it to be her and my duty to our "family." To enjoy the firewood that they had waited all day for and we hadn't, was simply unthinkable. As we walked back, I realized that while Mother's skin was actually softer than Miss Bronia's, her grip wasn't so much one of affection as of possession.

Mother was walking very fast again, and I was, again, running to keep up. But where I had expected her to turn right to head back home, we continued on towards the head of the line. My heart sank even further as I realized that instead of going home, we were about to crack the line in some way again.

We approached one of the guards where they were throwing the wood down from the train, and Mother spoke to him in Russian. I heard her explaining that I was sick and that she wanted to talk to the commander.

The guard indicated two other soldiers, standing off to one side, one considerably taller than the other. Their uniforms were no different from the others', but, by the pistols at their belts, I took them to be officers. I heard the guard say the name, "Comrade Captain Vrushin."

Mother thanked the soldier with a big smile, and we made our way over the gravel to the two officers. The rain was growing heavier. Mother's smile didn't leave her face.

"Comrade Captain Vrushin," Mother said as we approached the two. I didn't think she knew which of the two he was.

The look of delight that suddenly came over the faces of these two officers was actually comical. I understood the taller one express surprise at Mother's fluent Russian, to which she answered that her mother was from Moscow. Then I heard her go into her "sick little son" routine and immediately straightened up to look as strong and as healthy as I could. I certainly was not about to collaborate in her charade to wheedle the enemy into giving us special favors at the expense of my countrymen waiting in line for their firewood. The eyes of the two officers, however, were not on me.

Mother talked about her brave husband fighting the Germans and about not knowing what had become of her little mother and how much she wanted to see Moscow and the Soviet Union. This, at least, clarified one thing for me. The Soviet Union, I now concluded, was a department store in the Russian capital, not here.

The rain had become quite heavy by now. Mother and I were in our hooded rain capes, but the two officers were both bareheaded and wore no rain gear over their uniforms. The rain matted their hair down and washed down their faces. The one who turned out to be the comrade captain was the tall one with a long thin face and cheekbones that looked as if they might poke through his pale skin. The other man had dark skin and looked something like the pictures I had seen of Eskimos. I noticed that their tunics must not have been intended to be cinched by leather gun-belts, because they hung in folds below the waist.

Suddenly I saw the smile on Comrade Captain Vrushin's face turn to alarm. Following his gaze, I saw that black rivulets had begun running down Mother's face from her eyes. I immediately realized that this must be from the black makeup Mother applied to her eyelashes in the morning, but the comrade captain didn't seem to make the connection. Mother saw his alarm, but not the reason for it, and I could see the confusion on her face. "What's wrong?" she asked. The smile on her face wasn't real.

Capt. Vrushin pointed to mother's face and she touched her hand to her cheek. Seeing the black smudge on her finger, she began to laugh. "It's my eye makeup," she said. She took a compact from her rain-cape pocket and looked at herself in the mirror. She tried to wipe her cheeks with the back of her wet fingers.

The relief on the captain's face, I saw, was very real. It was quickly replaced by one of embarrassment. Mother laughed that light, bouncy laugh she sometimes used. The comrade captain now pulled a neatly folded handkerchief from his tunic pocket and, with an awkward little bow, handed it to her.

Mother thanked him. But as she wiped, the black rivulets continued to flow. She looked like she was crying black tears at the same time that she was laughing. Capt. Vrushin was looking embarrassed again. The shorter man maintained his seriousness. In another minute, the eye makeup was gone from Mother's face, and the captain's handkerchief was black.

"Oh, I am so sorry," Mother said. "I will wash it and bring it back tomorrow."

"I will wash it myself," Capt. Vrushin answered. He reached out and took the handkerchief from her. "Comrade Lt. Grunsky will get you some wood." He turned and spoke to the man beside him, who immediately headed for the wood train.

"You are very kind, Comrade Captain," Mother said. "My son and I are very grateful."

"You must dry your son in front of the fire when you get home. And give him hot tea with honey."

"I would," Mother assured him, "but we have no honey. But you speak as though you have children of your own."

"I am not married, but I have younger brothers and sisters."

"Do you have photographs of them?" Mother asked.

The comrade captain said that he did not, but he did have one of his dog, which Mother admired greatly. Then Lt. Grunsky returned. With him were three soldiers, each with a bulging potato sack over his shoulder. The sacks were filled with firewood.

Mother didn't seem terribly surprised by this. "Thank you so much for your kindness, Comrade Captain," she said. Then, to me in Polish, she said, "Say thank you."

I liked the man's open face and the very genuine concern that he had shown for Mother's distress, and I didn't mind thanking him. "Thank you, Captain," I said in Polish. Now I wondered whether Mother actually knew how much Russian I had picked up from Grandmother. Something told me that this ability might be something worth keeping secret.

Mother and I walked home, followed by the three soldiers. Mother gave them each some money when they had stacked the wood beside our stove and lighted a fire in it.

It was after dark when the others returned. The room was warm, and some stew from last night simmered in the pot. Mother sat at the table doing her solitaire. Each of the arrivals carried a shopping bag filled with firewood. They looked tired and their shoes squished water. Auntie Edna and Auntie Paula did not look happy to see us.

"There's last night's stew on the stove," Mother said. Fredek and Sonya immediately moved to the stove to warm themselves. Neither Auntie said anything as they hung their wet coats over the backs of chairs.

"I didn't want Yulek catching pneumonia out there," Mother said. "But you'll notice that I did bring some wood home." Mother used the word some, but what the Russian soldiers had carried for us was several times as much as the others had brought home. I saw Auntie Paula notice our stack of firewood for the first time. There was a flicker of real surprise on her face for an instant, but her expression quickly returned to its previous disdain.

"Oh, look at all that wonderful firewood!" Miss Bronia said. "Look, Mrs. Herbstein, Mrs. Tishman." Since our first visit from the Village Census Committee, Miss Bronia had been instructed by the mothers to address them by their first names, but she had not found that easy.

"How did you get it all home, Aunt Barbara?" Sonya asked. Neither of the Aunties said anything, but I saw them both pause, presumably to hear Mother's answer.

"Some soldiers carried it for me," Mother said.

"You're so blank-blank-blank, Aunt Barbara," Sonya said. I didn't understand the words she used, but I could tell that they were complimentary. Neither Auntie Paula nor Auntie Edna spoke to my mother for the rest of the evening.

The next morning Fredek had a sore throat. "Yulian had better not sleep with Fredek until he's better," Mother said, which made Auntie Edna cry. "I'm sorry," Mother said, not sounding at all sorry, "but without proper nutrition or medicines, we all should be extra cautious."

It was Auntie Edna's turn to sleep in the bed that week, and she made Fredek lie in it and drink hot soup or tea, which she brought him almost every hour. This made Fredek go to the bathroom a lot, and Auntie Edna made many trips to the toilet with a glass jar into which Fredek had no objections to peeing, while his mother held it for him, in sight of everyone.

"You might have him wear wool socks," Mother said, when she came home with a ring of sausage and cigarettes that evening. This made Auntie Edna upset again. "He doesn't have any wool socks," she finally said, at which point Mother produced a pair from her shopping bag. Auntie Edna snatched them from her angrily and went to put them on Fredek's feet.

"I'm just afraid his asthma will come back," she said, her back to us. I knew about asthma—Kiki's niece had died of it. I knew that it stopped you from breathing. I didn't want that to happen to Fredek.

After supper that evening, which Auntie Edna had spoon-fed to Fredek, sitting on the edge of his bed, Sonya surprised me by asking if I wanted her to read to me. There had been occasions when Miss Bronia had asked Sonya to read to both Fredek and me, but her volunteering to do something with me alone surprised me. I understood that her mother must have told her not to go near Fredek with his sore throat.

I accepted Sonya's offer. I had found sounding out words to be hard work, especially since I had a tendency to reverse letters or simply mistake them for letters that weren't even there. Fredek didn't seem to have this problem. Sonya had a very pleasant reading voice. She was reading from a book Miss Bronia had bought for Fredek and me about knights in armor.

Then, as she and I sat at one end of the table in the front room, we were all startled by a knock on the door. I saw Auntie Edna and Auntie Paula look at each other. Auntie Paula pulled her knitting close to her chest and Miss Bronia looked up from the stocking she was darning. Mother was sitting cross-legged on her pallet in the other room, doing a solitaire. Sonya paused in her reading.

Nobody moved toward the door, and the knock came a second time. Finally Miss Bronia went to the door, unlocked it, and opened it a crack. I couldn't see who it was, but I heard a man's voice say something in Russian.

"Mrs. Waisbrem!" Miss Bronia called, Mother being the only one with a good command of Russian.

My mother walked to the door. I saw Miss Bronia plant her foot on the floor behind it to prevent its being opened further.

"Ah, Comrade Captain!" Mother said, recognizing the visitor. She did not sound at all surprised. Miss Bronia seemed reluctant to remove her foot from behind the door, as Mother opened it wide. The comrade captain from the train station stood there in a freshly pressed uniform. He wasn't wearing his gun belt, so his tunic hung straight down without the silly-looking folds. His black hair, dry now, was like a cap of curls on the top of his head. In one hand he held his hat, in the other, a small bouquet of evergreen sprigs. "It's so good to see you," Mother said.

As Capt. Vrushin stepped into the room, I saw Auntie Edna jump to her feet and cross right in front him to disappear around the corner into the inner room.

There was a moment's silence, then Mother said in Polish, "This is the very nice officer who sent us the soldiers with the firewood, Comrade Captain Vrushin." I suppose because of the similarity of the two languages, Mother spoke in the formal tones that she would have used had everyone spoken the same language. Then she introduced Auntie Paula, Sonya and Miss Bronia to the captain. I was very pleased when she called Miss Bronia, "my friend."

The captain made a stiff bow to each of the three in turn, turning all the way around to bow to Miss Bronia at the stove. Miss Bronia returned the bow with her head, and Sonya curt-sied. Auntie Paula did something I had never seen another person do—she raised one eyebrow. I immediately tried to imitate it. It didn't work, but my face was all screwed up when I heard the captain pronounce the Russian version of my name. My training overcame my embarrassment, and I crossed the room to shake hands. Pinning the hat to his side with his left elbow and still holding the evergreen sprigs in the other hand, the captain wrapped his huge right hand around mine. In his quiet voice, he asked Mother about my health, and she answered that, thanks to God, I was all right. But Fredek, she said, pointing to him lying in bed in the back room with a wet cloth over his forehead, had fallen ill from the rain

"Do you give him hot tea with honey?" the captain asked.

"We can't get honey," my mother answered.

A smile lit up the captain's long face as he reached his free hand into his tunic pocket and produced a jar of what certainly looked like honey.

"Oh Comrade Captain, you are too kind," Mother said.

"And an egg," the captain said. "Do you have eggs?"

Mother shook her head. For a moment, I though he would pull an egg out of his pocket as well.

"I will get you eggs."

"Won't the comrade captain sit down and have tea with us?" Auntie Paula said. My mother immediately translated the invitation into Russian, indicating Auntie Edna's vacated chair beside Auntie Paula.

Instead of sitting down, the captain quietly said something to Mother, who answered him, and he laughed. Then he said something else, and she laughed. It was what I would later learn to call her "social laugh." Now he indicated with his hand that she should translate it for the rest of us.

"I told the comrade captain that Edna had gone to make herself beautiful, and he says we are the four most beautiful women in the city."

"Five," Capt. Vrushin said, holding up five fingers and indicating Sonya.

"Five," Mother translated, though the Russian word was almost exactly the same as the Polish.

Auntie Paula laughed a little, making a gesture with her hand indicating that she didn't believe him, but at the same time her other hand moved to the braid pinned around her head.

"Are those for us?" Mother asked, indicating the evergreen bouquet.

"Oh yes, yes," the captain said. I could see that he was embarrassed at having forgotten to give them to her. He clicked his heels together and handed them stiffly to Mother. "I am sorry they aren't flowers," he said.

"But there are no flowers, Comrade Captain. How clever of you. They're beautiful." Then Mother held them out to Miss

Bronia. "Be a dear," she said in Polish, "and put them in water. And take the comrade captain's hat too." I could see that the captain understood what she had said, because he held his hat out to Miss Bronia.

In a moment the captain was seated in Auntie Edna's vacated chair and Miss Bronia was pouring water for tea from the kettle.

"Give the captain his tea in a glass," Mother said to Miss Bronia before taking her own seat beside the captain. From a glass, was the way I had seen my Russian grandmother drinking hers. Then Mother apologized for our lack of sugar, at which point the comrade captain held up his hand in a clear indication that this was not a problem. Reaching inside his tunic, he produced a little bundle of brown-stained paper, which he carefully unwrapped to reveal the stumpy, brown remnants of a sugar cube. This he laid on the table in front of him. I had seen Grandmother sip her tea through a sugar cube held between her teeth and watched it turn brown, though I never saw her wrap what was left of the cube for future use.

Now Capt. Vrushin placed the cube between his own teeth and was about to raise his glass, when he must have realized that he was the only person with sugar for his tea. I saw his face grow red suddenly and watched him quickly re-wrap the cube and put it back in his pocket.

"Oh please," Mother said, "we have become accustomed to drinking our tea without sugar."

Capt. Vrushin raised his hands and said something to Mother. He was almost whispering. "Capt. Vrushin says that sugar rots your teeth anyway," she translated. Then the captain pointed to mother's eyes and said something else, and now they both laughed again. Mother's laugh sounded even less real than before. I could see that the captain found it much funnier than Mother did, and his face grew red and tears came to his eyes. As he reached in his pocket for a handkerchief, he gestured with the other hand for Mother to explain to Auntie

Paula and Miss Bronia. Mother then told about how shocked the captain had been at the sight of her eye makeup running in the rain. In the meanwhile the captain was pointing to his own tears and laughing even harder. Auntie Paula was laughing as well now, and I wondered if it was just for the comrade captain's sake.

Captain Vrushin whispered something to Mother again, and Mother translated that he was asking how much more beautiful Auntie Edna was planning to become. The captain was laughing at this as well, and Mother got up and walked into the other room. From where I sat, I could see Auntie Edna sitting on the edge of Fredek's bed, waving a wet cloth in the air to cool it for his forehead.

Because I was close to the archway leading into the inner room, I could hear bits of what Mother was saying quietly to Auntie Edna. There was something about how the captain had been kind to us, both before and now and how he was probably lonely in a foreign city and trying to be friendly. I couldn't tell what Auntie Edna said in return, but Mother's voice got louder, though she was still trying not to let our visitor hear her. "Don't be a fool, Edna. He sent us firewood, and he could help with other things. He could get medicine for Fredek. He's attracted to me because I speak fluent Russian and he feels comfortable. Now put on some makeup and a fresh sweater and come out and be the hostess you were in Warsaw." Then she came out and announced that Auntie Edna would be out in a minute.

"Bronia, why don't you come join us," she said to Miss Bronia, who was doing something at the stove. "You work harder than the rest of us put together." Mother's tone was very sweet now, though no more genuine. Miss Bronia immediately came back to the table and picked up her darning.

Then Mother said something to the captain about what great things Miss Bronia could do with the little food that was available in stores. She asked the captain what town he came from and then translated his answer. It wasn't Moscow, which was the only town I knew in Russia. As Mother went on translating, we learned that his mother was director of a high school, and his father had been killed by the Tsarists. I knew who the Tsar was, but I had no idea who the Tsarists were.

Then Auntie Edna came back into the room. She had put on fresh lipstick and a green cardigan. When Mother introduced her to the captain, he had Mother repeat the story about her eye makeup running in the rain and how it had frightened him. The captain found this almost as funny as he had at the first telling, and his eyes began to tear again. Auntie Edna laughed politely.

Then, in the same sweet tone Mother had used speaking to Miss Bronia, she said, "Sonya, dear, why don't you take Yulek into the other room and read to him."

Sonya closed the book, her finger marking the page, and we stood up. As I had been taught to do when there were guests, I said, "Excuse me," and gave a little bow, before leaving the table.

The captain leaned back in his chair and beckoned me with his finger. Then he had a pocket knife in his hands, and I saw that he was actually cutting a button off the pocket of his tunic.

"What are you doing?" Mother asked, and the alarm in her voice was genuine.

"It's for the boy. I have more." He held the button out to me.

Mother nodded her head, indicating that I should accept it.

The button was shiny brass with an enameled red star. In the center of the star there was a little gold hammer and sickle.

"Take it, dear, and say thank you," Mother said.

The hammer and sickle, I had recently discovered, was the Russian emblem, the way the white eagle was ours.

"Take it and say thank you," Mother repeated, the smile fixed on her face.

I didn't want the Russian button. I should have dropped it on the table—or on the floor and stepped on it. Or thrown it at him like a hero, and he would have had me arrested and shot with a blindfold. But I couldn't do that to Capt. Vrushin. He was a soldier, ordered into Poland by his general, and he was helping us out of his own kindness. Actually, I found that I liked him. I could not insult him like that. I took the button and mumbled, "Thank you." But I did not look him in the eye. I did not want him to see my conflict. I followed Sonya into the inner room.

Sonya was standing a few feet from Fredek's bed. Fredek was telling her that his head hurt a lot.

I remembered the headaches that Kiki would sometimes get when she had to lie on her bed with a wet wash cloth over her eyes and forehead. I would freshen the cloth and wring it out in a dish of water, and walk around on tiptoe. I felt sorry for Fredek now. With Sonya and me not permitted to go near him, there was no one to freshen the cloth for him.

"Do you want me to read to you?" Sonya asked him. "I can do it from across the room."

"No," Fredek whispered, then he reached for his throat letting us know that it hurt to talk. Sonya tiptoed to the corner farthest from Fredek and signaled me to follow her. We settled down on the floor, and Sonya opened her book. Then she put it down again and got up to bring over a table lamp that we had acquired a few days earlier. Finally, she switched off the ceiling light and settled down to read to me in a whisper.

Only I don't think it was the same book that she had been reading to me before, because instead of the boy learning to be a knight, we were now dealing with a painter who didn't have enough money to buy food. I would have been disappointed except that I realized how his situation compared to ours. Only we had money, but no food to buy with it. Then, when a beautiful woman came to the studio to pose for him, my mind came wandering back to the people in the other room.

"He wants us to call him Vasilli," I heard Mother say.

"Paula," I heard Auntie Paula say, and I could visualize her tapping her chest with her fingers.

"Paula," the captain repeated.

"Basia," Mother said. The captain repeated it, but putting the accent on the last a.

Now Mother repeated it the way he had said it. Then she said something in Russian. She spoke more quietly to the captain than she did in Polish to the others. Finally she said, "I said to him that Russian is a much prettier language than Polish."

I didn't like hearing that.

Captain Vrushin said something else in his quiet voice. "He says the two languages are very similar," Mother said. "He can understand a lot of what we say."

"Then we have to be careful what we say," Auntie Paula said. "Tell him that." Mother translated and they all seemed to laugh.

"Edna . . . Bronia," Auntie Paula said. I realized that Miss Bronia and Auntie Edna had not given their own first names.

Captain Vrushin repeated the names, and I now recognized that his pronunciation did give a new softness to the two names. Well, if Russian was softer, Polish was more manly, I decided.

Then Sonya's painter was helping the beautiful woman mount a horse, and, at mention of the horse, my attention immediately switched away from the people in the outer room.

My attention snapped back quickly a few minutes later, when I heard the captain's boots crossing the floor. Through the archway, I could see Mother walk the captain to the door.

When the door closed behind him, everyone was talking at once. The three mothers came into the inner room, and Auntie Paula turned on the overhead light.

"Shshsh, I think Fredek is sleeping," Auntie Edna said, and everyone grew quiet.

Mother and Auntie Paula took off their blouses. Mother brushed her teeth while Auntie Paula washed under her arms at the washbasin. Auntie Edna sat on the edge of Fredek's bed and put her hand over one of his.

"Freshen up, Edna," Mother said, speaking around her toothbrush.

"I'll stay with Fredek," Auntie Edna said.

"Oh, come on. Fredek doesn't need you to watch him, and Vasilli likes you," Mother said.

"I'll just stay here," Auntie Edna said again.

I wanted to like Auntie Edna for the way she cared for Fredek when he was sick. But at other times she was mean to him. I didn't understand her.

"Captain Vrushin isn't going to hurt you," Auntie Paula said. Now she was talking around her toothbrush, and Mother was at the basin washing under her arms. "He's just a big, friendly, shy boy in a strange country," she went on. I found the idea of the tall captain described as a shy boy amusing. But he really was shy, and I had never heard of a shy adult before. "He could be the key to our getting food, as well as some medicine for Fredek. You know, it never hurts to have powerful friends." This I understood.

"And we'll have some fun for a change," Mother said.

"I'll stay with Fredek," Miss Bronia said, coming into the room.

"Fredek's asleep. He doesn't need anyone watching him," Mother said. "We'll all be right in the next room. Look, he's bringing his friend, and Paula and I don't want to be two-on-two with them. Come on, Edna . . . Bronia."

"There's safety in numbers," Auntie Paula added with a little laugh.

Auntie Edna sighed and stood up. She walked to the basin and began brushing her teeth. Mother and Auntie Paula were putting on clean blouses.

When the three mothers had returned to the front room, Miss Bronia took off her sweater and proceeded to wash like the others. We were all well accustomed by then to seeing each other in our underwear, but this was the first time I noticed how much larger and rounder Miss Bronia's breasts were in her pink brassiere than those of the others. It was pleasurable looking at them.

At some point during all this, Sonya had stopped reading, and now she casually followed Miss Bronia into the outer room. I followed Sonya. The mothers had cleared the tea things from the table. Auntie Paula was washing cups and glasses in the basin and setting them out on a towel to dry, and Auntie Edna had laid a yellow dishtowel with blue flowers around the edges, in the center of the taller table. Mother was dripping candle wax onto a dish to make the candle stand up. They were all moving quickly, as though in a hurry.

"You two go to bed," Auntie Paula said when she noticed Sonya and me in the room.

"Yes, Yulek, go to bed," Mother chimed in. "And don't listen."

"He's coming back, isn't he," Sonya said to her mother. "He's bringing other men back with him, and you're going to have a party, aren't you?"

"We're not going to have a party," Auntie Paula said. "He's coming back with some ham for us, and he's bringing the man who's in charge of supplies with him. When you wake up tomorrow, we'll have ham for breakfast."

"I'm old enough to stay."

"Go to bed, Sonya. You have to take care of Yulek."

"Yulek doesn't need me to go to bed. And it's not my bed-time."

"You can lie down and read."

"Whatever you're going to be doing, that you don't want me to see, you can see and hear perfectly well from the other room, you know. There isn't any door."

"We're not going to be doing anything."

"Then there's no reason I can't stay."

"There is a reason, Sonya."

"And what's that?"

"Because I said so."

"That's not a reason."

"That is a reason, and it's all the reason you need."

Sonya turned on her heel and marched into the inner room where I had preceded her and was now peeking out from around the side of the arch.

"Go put on your nightshirt," she ordered me.

Sonya's angry attitude surprised me. It certainly wasn't my fault that her mother wouldn't let her stay with the grownups. Why should she be angry with me? But I obeyed and ducked under the blanket of my pallet to change into my nightshirt.

Auntie Edna came in to check again on Fredek, who was asleep. She felt his neck with the back of her fingers and gave a sigh.

Then there was a knock on the door. Auntie Edna looked back into the outer room, straightened her blouse, then started back. I saw Mother cross to the door, but the door, like the table, was out of my field of vision. I heard Capt. Vrushin's voice, "Basia!" With the access on the last a.

"Ah, Vasilli," Mother said, and then some things were said in Russian too quietly for me to hear. I heard another man's voice and the name Boris. Boris was my own middle name, but Capt. Vrushin again pronounced it with accent on the last syllable.

Then the three of them crossed the part of the room that I could see, for further introductions at the table. The brief glimpse I had of the second man showed me that he wasn't as tall or as thin as Captain Vrushin but he had a very large head with a big forehead and a very small face below it. Like his companion's, Comrade Captain Boris's hair was curly on top and cropped short on the sides and back, except that his was quite blond.

He carried a large covered basket in his left hand, with his right stretched out in greeting, and he seemed almost to be skipping across the room in his eagerness. The handshaking took place outside my line of vision, but his voice was high and rasping, as though he had a sore throat. He sounded as though he was trying to shout, but his voice wasn't loud enough.

Then there were ooh's and aah's, followed by a very appreciative oooooh from the mothers as, I suppose, the basket's contents were revealed. The last oooooh, I speculated, must have been over something particularly good, of which, hopefully, there would be some left in the morning.

I could hear Fredek's and my steamer trunk being dragged over the floor and Captain Boris's—I assumed him to be a captain like his friend—high and raspy laughter.

There was a clink of glasses, in fact several clinks, followed by more laughter. Miss Bronia hadn't made any more tea, so it must have been something that Captain Boris had brought in that basket. The talk was too quiet for me to make anything out, but there was a great amount of laughter.

Sonya was sitting on her pallet, still in her clothes, but she had taken off her shoes and stocks and was cutting her toenails with a pair of nail scissors. "What are you looking at?" she demanded.

"I'm just looking at you cutting your nails," I answered

"Don't look at my feet!" she hissed, making a face at me.

I turned away. I didn't understand Sonya.

Now Comrade Captain Boris had begun to sing. I recognize his high, raspy voice singing some Russian song. When he had finished, there was some clapping, then more clinking of glasses. Mother said something in Russian, and Captain Boris began another song, one I recognized as a song Grandmother would sing sometimes. Then Mother joined in the song. But Mother could not carry a tune, and soon they both stopped, followed by more laughter.

Then someone was playing a harmonica. There was the shuffling of feet and suddenly Mother and Captain Boris danced into my field of vision through the archway. It was a fast tune and Captain Boris looked as if he was trying to push Mother to dance faster. Instead of extending his left arm, as I'd seen others do, he had tucked it in close to his chest, with Mother's hand in his, and, for the short moment that I could see them before they danced out of sight again, he did seem to be actually pushing her around the floor with a very serious expression on his face.

There was more laughter and clapping and then Captain Boris danced into sight again, but this time breathing hard and pushing Miss Bronia. He held her tight in his arms, too, and I could see Miss Bronia's legs trying to keep up, but tripping and her being held up by the comrade captain. I could see that Miss Bronia wasn't enjoying this as much as Mother had appeared to. But her turn was soon over and then Captain Boris pushed Auntie Edna onto my stage and then off again. Auntie Edna was much taller than he was, and the impression I had after my brief glimpse of the two of them was of a fat little boy hugging his mother around the waist.

Miss Bronia came into the inner room now to check on Fredek, who was sound asleep. She told me to turn on my side with my back to the other room and go to sleep. I didn't get to see Auntie Paula dance, but did hear more laughter, more clapping, and more clinking of glasses. Then I must have fallen asleep.

The next morning we had eggs for breakfast. There was also most of a large ham, two very big loaves of bread—one white, one black—a large cheese, some jars of caviar, and broken glass in the pail we used for trash. Auntie Paula stayed on her pallet with a cloth over her eyes like Fredek, though I don't think she had a sore throat. Auntie Edna had a big black-and-blue mark on this side of her shin and limped, Mother had two torn stockings, and Fredek was feeling much better.

Mr. Bronia made scrambled eggs with bits of ham for Fredek and me, and some warm milk. It was the first milk we had had since the farm.

Auntie Edna spoon-fed Fredek his eggs in bed, though he wanted to get up. He wanted more scrambled eggs too, but his mother said eggs weren't good for him and made him a ham sandwich, which he gobbled down very quickly. But he had to stay in bed at least one more day.

"Of course he's not a gentleman," Mother said over her shoulder to Auntie Edna from the mirror where she was putting on her makeup. "His father is a shepherd. I didn't invite him for his charm, but for his food. And don't you like Vasilli?"

"Vasilli may be all right," Auntie Edna agreed, "but he's a Bolshevik." Bolshevik was a word I had heard before. Auntie Edna was moving around Fredek's bed, arranging his sheets and blankets. "And that Boris is like a pig. He has no table manners and he was grunting all the time we were dancing."

"Who was grunting like a pig?" Fredek asked. Nobody answered him.

"Vasilli is more than all right," Mother said. "Don't you understand that he brought Boris only because he saw we needed the food?"

"I bet he and Boris are talking about the three of us . . . and Bronia, right now."

"This isn't Warsaw before the war, you know. Officers don't sit around cafes talking about women." Mother was using a tiny little black toothbrush on her eyelashes. "Boris is probably counting his hams, and poor Vasilli 's out in the rain with his men."

"Poor Vasilli? You like Vasilli, don't you."

"Don't be ridiculous. Vasilli introduced us to Boris, and who knows what else he can do for us."

"You gave him your silver fountain pen."

"I gave him the pen because he had never seen a fountain pen before and it intrigued him. He's an engineer. It was like giving a trinket to a child. It's only a few zlotys, and I need him more than I need a fountain pen right now."

"And what else are we going to be giving them?" It was Auntie Paula, still on her pallet, who asked this. I thought she was asleep. She still had the wet cloth over her eyes and her words were very slow and even.

"What we're going to be giving them is a little oasis of sophistication in this stupid town," Mother said. "Four cultured women they can talk to like human beings, who can laugh with them, have a drink with them, and even dance with them without anybody getting wrong ideas."

"You don't think Boris gets wrong ideas?" Auntie Edna asked.

"I can handle Boris, and so can you. You've handled people worse than him in Warsaw. Remember Stefan Gorovich?"

"You sound like you're opening a salon?" Auntie Paula said.

Mother suddenly turned away from the mirror, the little brush still in her hand. "Look, Paula," she said, "I don't like dancing with that fat little peasant any more than you do, but, thank God, they're not all like him, and this morning we have eggs and ham to eat instead of Bronia standing in line for bread. Do you two want to go on eating carrot soup for supper? Do you want your children to go on getting sick because they have to stand in the rain for firewood . . . or because there isn't any firewood?

"Intelligent people don't stand in line like peasants. My father built a stocking factory in Lodz from nothing . . . nothing. My mother's people were the biggest chocolate manufacturers in Russia. When she was a little girl, Anton Chekhov used to come to dinner and read his plays to the family before they were produced. These weren't people who stood in line . . . and I'm not either."

"You forget what happened on the farm?" Auntie Paula said in her careful voice.

"What happened on the farm?"

"You got us thrown out, that's what happened."

"I didn't get us thrown out. For godsakes, you keep saying that. I told you they were just looking for a chance to throw us out, otherwise they would have had to give us a share of the farm."

"And you gave them that chance."

"And you wish you were still living there with those self-important, opera-bouffe Bolsheviks? They've probably already shot old Mrs. Chernievich and moved into her house . . . along with their pigs and chickens."

"So where are you going?" Auntie Edna asked.

"I'm going out to find some decent dishes and a samovar. And I'm going to see if I can find a Gramophone and some records."

"I think they've already bought up all the Gramophones," Auntie Edna said.

"All the Gramophones in the stores, maybe," Mother said, "but I bet someone has one in their home."

"And you're going to entertain Bolsheviks," Auntie Edna said. "They're Bolsheviks!"

Now I felt I understood what the word Bolshevik meant and that I really did like Auntie Edna. I understood not trying to throw them out of your apartment when they were there one time and had brought you food, but I understood too that inviting them was treasonous.

"I'm going to trade them some culture, which they're desperately short of, in exchange for food and firewood and protection, which we're desperately short of, in case you haven't noticed."

"Protection?"

"Protection. A powerful friend can be very useful in times like this."

A few minutes later Mother had gone out, and the makeup mirror on the wall beside the washbasin was free. Normally, one of the Aunties would have put it to use, but Auntie Paula was just lifting herself to a sitting position and Auntie Edna was seated on the edge of Fredek's bed. Allowed to sit up today, Fredek was drawing a picture on a sheet of paper supported by a large book in his lap.

"She's crazy," Auntie Edna said, and I knew she was talking about my mother. But I also knew she didn't really mean that Mother was crazy. Then Miss Bronia came and told me that she and I were going to go in the other room and I would practice my reading with her.

It was a children's story about a sickly boy who went to a camp of some sort in the summer and became strong and healthy from the fresh air and exercise. But even knowing the story, I found the words difficult. I knew all of the letters of the alphabet but trying to read at a speaking pace, I would see a letter and read it as a different letter and not be able to make sense out of the word.

I envied Fredek for his ability to breeze through sentences, just the way he did through multiplication tables. I had heard Kiki talking with his Miss Frania about the fact that Fredek had special talents. While I, on the other hand, I supposed, had secretly ruined my mind with the birdie business. Even the train Fredek was drawing now actually looked like a train and not the shoeboxes with wheels that I would have drawn.

Eventually Auntie Edna, Auntie Paula, and Sonya went out "shopping." Miss Bronia and I went on reading, with Miss Bronia encouraging me and telling me how much better I was doing. I stumbled on in my effort to please her, assembling each word and so intent on the process that I had no idea of what I was reading. Had Miss Bronia asked me what I had read, I would not have been able to tell her.

The Aunties and Sonya came home with a bag of vegetables and several packs of cigarettes. Then Auntie Edna and Auntie Paula sat close together at one end of the table smoking and whispering to each other.

It was almost dark outside when Mother came back, carrying a very large packing box. She had bought a red-and-white, twelve-piece tea setting with a teapot and everything. She said she had bargained the woman down because four of the cups were missing and several others were chipped, but it wouldn't matter to us because the Russians drank their tea out of glasses. But Auntie Edna and Auntie Paula weren't interested and wouldn't even look, and Miss Bronia told me and Sonya to put on our coats quickly because we were going for a walk.

*   *   *

Mother didn't eat supper with the rest of us. She sat on her pallet smoking and doing her solitaire. The next morning she told me she was taking me to the park.

There was a little area, one city block, that had no buildings—just grass, a few trees, and some benches. It certainly wasn't my idea of a park, without a lake and swans, a sculpture of Chopin, a royal palace, or even peacocks. But I realized that, this being a small town, it would have a small park. Possibly it had even had peacocks at one time, but they may have been killed and eaten.

Mother sat down on one of the benches and told me to go play. In Warsaw, Kiki's sitting down on the bench had become a mantra that turned on an imagination switch. This time, none of that happened.

I walked around the deserted little park trying to make something happen. I saw squirrels scurry across the grass, then corkscrew their way around and up and around a tree trunk. I saw the wind lift leaves off the ground, whorl them around at eye level and then drop them to go elsewhere. But my make-believe world would not stir.

And then, as I passed Mother on her bench for the second or third time, she said to me, "Yulian, come sit next to me for a moment. I want to talk to you."

I sat down immediately.

"Yulian, you're a young man now, you know," Mother began. "You are now master of the house."

Master of the house was something I had never heard of.

"You are my protecting knight," she went on. And then I understood that what master of the house must be was some sort of limited title, conferring adult status on children, but valid only within the confines of their domicile, under emergency conditions. It was as though Poland's great warrior king of an earlier era, King Arthur, were departing for the Crusades with his knights of the round table, and in their absence the boys of the castle were dubbed temporary knights within the castle walls.

Mother was saying something about how Auntie Paula and Auntie Edna were not brave like she and I and were afraid to do what was necessary to save themselves, and I was visualizing myself and other boys of the castle in our miniature suits of armor guarding the ramparts against invaders.

"You have to defend me," Mother was saying, and I was dueling with an invader to protect Miss Bronia, who stood behind me in a flowing blue gown.

"I'm the only mother you'll ever have, and I will never have any other children," Mother said. I wondered whether Fredek was also being elevated to master-of-the-house status by his mother at the same time.

Then Mother said, "But that has to be our secret. You mustn't tell anybody until it happens. Can I count on you to keep our secret?"

That caught my attention, and I realized that I must have missed something after her never having any more children. But I assured Mother that, yes, I knew how to keep the secret, since that was what she obviously wanted to hear, and particularly because I had no idea what her secret was.

Then my mother took me to visit Mr. and Mrs. Rokief. He was the man Mother had pretended to mistake for Judge Starecki and lied to about Uncle Pavew. I wondered if this would be for the purpose of proclaiming my new status to her friends. I didn't like Mr. Rokief and his un-Christian ways, but whatever it was that was about to take place intrigued me.

Mr. and Mrs. Rokief lived in one room in some lady's apartment, and their two daughters, who weren't home, lived in another. Mrs. Rokief was almost as small and thin as Mother—since our first days at the farm, I had begun to see my mother as quite small—only with a slightly older face and totally white hair in soft curls all over her head. She seemed very happy to see us. She quickly apologized for having nothing but tea to offer us and for the fact that her two daughters weren't home to meet me.

"We drink a lot of tea to keep warm," she explained to me with a little make-believe shiver to illustrate her point. I decided that I liked her.

It was cold in the room. Mr. and Mrs. Rokief had on matching ski sweaters, blue with white reindeer. Mr. Rokief was even wearing gloves, but the fingers of the right hand had been cut off. He held the little gold pencil I had seen before and had, apparently, been writing. Mrs. Rokief quickly poured us some tea from a large teapot and invited us to sit down at the little table.

There were also two beds, pushed together, in the room, a bureau, a clothes cupboard, four chairs around the table, a wicker armchair in which Mr. Rokief was sitting, a rug on the floor and a little round stove. The beds were neatly made and, unlike our place, this room was neat and tidy. Only it was full of cigarette smoke.

"Something is wrong, Basia," Mrs. Rokief said. "I can see it in your face."

"Oh, Helenka," mother answered, her voice very sad, "you are so observant and always so caring."

"So what's the trouble? Is it Edna and Paula again?"

"You're so observant, my dear Helenka," Mother said again. But this time it was in that little-girl voice of hers.

Mr. Rokief put his cigarette out in an ashtray on the arm of his wicker chair. "You poor thing," he said. "Have some tea and tell your friends all about it."

I didn't believe that Mr. Rokief really cared as much as his wife did.

"You really are my friends, Roman and Helenka, aren't you," Mother said in that same little-girl voice. "You and Helenka are my dearest friends in the world. It's so sad, isn't it. I used to have so many friends in Warsaw, and now I have only the two of you. But you are wonderful to me."

"So you've been causing trouble for them again?" Mr. Rokief said laughing

"Yes, I have," Mother said. She said it half-proud and half-afraid of what she had done. We had sat down at the table now, except for Mr. Rokief who was still in his wicker armchair.

"We had two Russian officers to our apartment. We drank vodka, we sang, and we danced. And they left us ham, eggs, bread, vodka. . . . And now my two relatives think it was awful, even though they ate, drank, and danced as much as I did. When I went out yesterday morning, Paula was in bed with a hangover.

"But now they're telling me that having Russian officers to our apartment once in a while and asking them to bring food, is bad. They'd rather stand in line for their food and let their children go hungry. Now they won't even talk to me. Only Yulian talks to me. He's my one friend in the whole world, my knight in shining armor." There it came.

"We're your friends, Basia," Mr. and Mrs. Rokief said almost in unison.

"Yes, I know. You are my very dear friends. I know that. That's why I came here today."

"And it's well that you did," Mr. Rokief said.

Mrs. Rokief pulled her chair next to Mother and put her arms around her. "We all do what we have to to survive and to provide for our children," she said

"For the most part, the Bolsheviks aren't bad people," Mr. Rokief said. "And they're not all stupid, either. You can do business with them. And that's exactly what you're trying to do. Your in-laws, or whatever they are, are fools. You are the best hope they have, and they don't appreciate you."

"Oh, I'm so glad that you say that," Mother said. "They make me feel like I'm doing something awful." She was almost crying as she said it.

"You wouldn't do something awful," Mrs. Rokief said. "Remember that, Basia. You have imagination and courage, and they just don't appreciate that."

Then the door opened and two girls, Sonya's age, came in.

"Oh," Mrs. Rokief said. "Yulian, this is Zosia and Renia. You girls know Mrs. Padovich. This is her big son, Yulian. Why don't you take Yulian to your room and show him your picture album. Maybe Zosia can tell him a story."

Zosia's and Renia's room wasn't at all as neat as their parents'. There were clothes on the beds and on the table, and, as we walked in, I saw Zosia, the taller one, kick something under the bed. They cleared a spot on one of the beds for me to sit and then, standing in front of me, Renia asked, "Do you prefer stories or looking at pictures?"

I didn't know what to answer, but I knew I had to. "I don't know," I finally said.

Zosia came to my rescue. "Of course he doesn't know," she said. "What kind of question is that? It depends on the story and the pictures, doesn't it?"

It took me a moment to realize that I was expected to respond. I nodded my head.

"Well, then, we're going to tell you a story." Renia said. "It won't be one of those kiddy stories—I bet you're tired of those, aren't you? You've been a kid how long?"

"Seven years," I said.

"Maybe he would prefer just a children's story," Zosia interrupted.

"Would you?" Renia said. "Would you prefer just a children's story?"

I could tell that she wanted to tell me the grown-up story so I shook my head. I was hoping it wasn't the kind of grown-up story I had heard Lolek tell Kiki once about a curtain blowing open and somebody being seen naked on the beach. Kiki had pretended to laugh and I pretended I didn't hear it.

"All right." Renia said. "Let's do Mrs. Dr. Korevich," she said to her sister.

"Are you sure that's what you'd like to hear?" Zosia asked.

"How can he know that before he's heard it?" Renia said.

"All right," Zosia said. I liked her better than her sister. Now she went over to the other bed, rummaged around in the clothes lying on it, and pulled out a kerchief, which she put on her head. Renia, in the meantime, had put on a beret.

Now they faced each other in the middle of the room. "Good afternoon, Mrs. Sobinski," Renia said to her sister in a deep voice. "How nice to see you today."

"Ah, Dr. Korevich," Zosia answered, "imagine bumping into you on the street like this. And how is Mrs. Dr. Korevich?"

"Well, she had a bit of an accident yesterday," Renia said.

"Oh, I'm so sorry to hear that." And then they went into a conversation that I could not follow with something about a lawyer, and train conductor, and an actor. Then Renia pulled her beret from over her left ear to over her right and became the lawyer or the actor or something and Zosia took off the kerchief and became the doctor's cook. Several times they stopped and I suspected that I was supposed to laugh, but I wasn't sure, so I smiled. Finally, they held hands and bowed to me, so I knew it was over and applauded.

"Do you do anything . . . like sing or dance?" Renia asked.

"I know some poems," I said. I was hoping that they would ask me to recite one.

"That's terrific," Zosia said. "So now you go on the stage and we will be your audience."

We changed places and I recited the poem about not being afraid of anything and even standing up to a tiger. I made all the gestures that Kiki had taught me with my fist in the air at one point and on my hip at another.

When I finished they both applauded. "That's wonderful!" Renia said. "You did that like a real actor, didn't he?"

Zosia agreed.

"For a moment I thought I really was among soldiers, didn't you?" Renia went on. Her sister agreed to this as well.

"You know any other poems?" Renia asked. Now I thought that I liked Renia better. She seemed to be more fun.

Yes, I did know other poems, but I had an idea. I reached my hand into my pocket where my steel washer always rested and palmed the washer.

"Oh, what do you have in your ear?" I said, approaching Renia. I reached my hand to her ear and with a twist of my wrist produced the washer.

"Oh, my gosh! Have I been carrying that around in my ear all this time?" Renia said.

"That was like a real magician!" Zosia said.

"Yes," Renia said. "It was just like that magician we saw in the hotel in Prague."

I waved my hand and the washer disappeared.

"Oh, my gosh!" Renia said. "You really are a magician."

I couldn't think of a happier moment in my life. Unfortunately, I had no other tricks.

"Would you like to see pictures of our house in a Krakow?" Renia asked. "Father says it may not be there anymore. But we'll build an even bigger one when we go back."

We spent some time looking through an album of family photographs, and I pretended to be very interested. Then Mother and Mrs. Rokief came in and we had to say goodbye. "We had such a good time, Mrs. Padovich," Zosia said to my mother. "Could Missus please bring Yulek with her again the next time she comes?"

Walking home, I felt positively five feet tall!

*   *   *

The others had gone out when we got home, and when they got back late in the afternoon, Mother and the Aunties weren't talking to each other again. Fredek, it seemed, had acquired a block of wood cut into the shape of a sedan with windows and tires painted on it, and Sonya was displaying a surprising degree of interest in pushing the thing back and forth between them at the table while we waited for Miss Bronia's stew to the heat up. I wanted a closer look at the new toy, but I was afraid that if I showed an interest, they would move into the other room or something. Instead, I practiced with my washer.

Of course they had been told to play with each other but not with me, and this was because they were angry at Mother. Mr. Rokief had said that Mother was right and that they just didn't appreciate her courage. But I didn't like Mr. Rokief, though I could see how it took courage to dance with Captain Boris. But the others had all danced with him as well. Somehow, Mother had again instigated a problem.

She made me eat supper sitting on her pallet with her while everyone else ate at the table in the other room. I spilled some sauce on her blanket and heard her say, "Oh, my God!" under her breath, but she didn't scold me. Instead she said, "Yulian, you're my knight, aren't you?" As though she weren't as sure of it as before. I gave her pretty much of a noncommittal smile and, fortunately, she didn't press me any further for an answer.

Later that evening Fredek and I had been put to bed, each personally by his own mother. This was not the way it was usually done, but, instead of being directed to go to bed, Fredek was led in by the hand from the outer room by Auntie Edna. She had then stood over him at the washbasin while he brushed his teeth with salt and baking soda, undressed him, put his night-shirt on him, and tucked him into our pallet without acknowledging Mother's and my presence. She had kissed him, and

Fredek had put his arms around his mother and hugged her. Only when she was about to leave had Auntie Edna turned to Mother and me, sitting still on Mother's pallet, and said, "I'm going to turn the light off now." If that's all right with you, was implicit in her tone. Mother said yes, then, when Auntie Edna had gone out, she had stood up and informed me that it was time for me to retire as well. She took my hand for the walk across the room to the washbasin, undressed me, put my nightshirt on, and kissed me. I felt no urge to hug my mother. Then with her deck of cards in her hand, she had tiptoed out into the other room.

"My mother and Auntie Paula hate your mother," Fredek whispered in my ear. "They want to kill her."

I knew this was an exaggeration, but suddenly I felt the urge to tell Fredek about my own angry feelings towards my mother. In my fantasy I could hear myself telling how bad she was and feeling that wonderful sensation of unburdening, except that I could not hear the words that my fantasy self was using. The things she did, like cutting ahead of people in line, lying to Mr. Rokief about mistaking him for Judge Staretski and about Uncle Pavew living in Krakow, or being friendly to Russian soldiers who were our enemies, did not sound anywhere near bad enough in words to justify my anger.

"I'm not supposed to talk to you," Fredek went on.

I didn't know what to answer, but I didn't want him thinking that I wasn't speaking to him. "That's all right," I finally said. "I knew it was like that."

"My mother says . . ." he began, but he was interrupted by a knock on the front door and we both began listing intently. We watched Miss Bronia pass across the archway to answer the door and then the unmistakable gravel voice of the objectionable Capt. Boris. "Basia!" followed by a loud Russian greeting.

Mother, apparently, must have been at that end of the room already, away from the others at the table, because we didn't see her walk across. We heard her greet him, but not with the same enthusiasm. Then there was a shuffling of feet and some talk I couldn't quite hear, some masculine laughter, and finally a run of chords from an accordion. Capt. Boris bounced past the archway to where Auntie Edna and Auntie Paula must have been sitting. He was carrying the same basket from the previous visit.

The accordion, now playing a melody I didn't recognize, drowned out any of the dialogue, but in a moment, Capt. Boris was followed by three other officers. One carried a long sausage, one a paper bag, and the third bottle of vodka. The accordion player, apparently, stayed on the front-door side of the room, because I never saw him.

"They're going to have a party," Fredek whispered, though there was no need to whisper now. "Mother and Auntie Paula didn't want them to come back—they're the enemy. But your mother invited them for the food. She's a traitor and they'll hang her."

That my mother did unpatriotic things, was, of course, something of which I had accused her all along. But to hear Fredek articulate the word, traitor, suddenly upset me. From the tone of Mother's voice, I had formed the impression that she really was as surprised by Capt. Boris's appearance as anyone. But even if she had not actually invited the captain, she had been talking about having Russian officers come to visit. Then, on a sudden inspiration, I whispered to Fredek, "She's not a traitor—she's a spy. She's trying to find out their secrets."

This seemed to give Fredek food for a moment's thought. I turned away from him and closed my eyes. Pretending to be asleep would be the best way to give finality to my statement. I was delighted with my cleverness.

"Who does she pass the information on to?" My pallet mate finally asked. I could not resist answering this one. I turned back to face him. "There is a man who lives on the other side of the church. His name is Rokief. She reports to him, and whom he passes it on to is a military secret."

There was another long pause. "What does he looks like?" The question finally came.

"He's tall with dark hair and a little mustache," I said. "He dresses in a suit like the people in Warsaw."

"If I see him, I'll pretend I don't know anything about him." Fredek seemed to be reassuring me.

"That's a good idea."

Suddenly the light from the other room dimmed and we saw that two men were standing on chairs to hang our flowered tablecloth over the archway. Then the light got dimmer still when someone turned off the overhead light. They had lit flickering candles on the table. The music continued.

"Look, they're dancing again!" Fredek exclaimed. On the flowered tablecloth in front of us there were now silhouettes of couples dancing to a fast tune.

"Yes," I said, displaying, I hoped, total lack of interest.

The next morning there was a smell of stale cigarette smoke and it was Auntie Edna and Auntie Paula who were arguing with each other. Auntie Edna was saying that she believed my mother when she said that she didn't know the Russians were coming over and Auntie Paula didn't actually say she didn't believe that, but she was just being angry.

"Of course," Mother was saying, "they can't just pop in when they feel like it!" She put down the knife, with which she had been slicing the bread a little too hard. It tumbled to the floor.

"Yes, the food is a big help," Auntie Paula said, stooping to pick up the knife that had landed at her feet, "but I don't want to have to dance for it!"

"They really are quite well behaved," Auntie Edna said.

From what I could tell, nobody was disagreeing with anyone, but everyone was angry. On the other hand, our table and the tin box that Miss Bronia had rigged outside the window for refrigeration, were again well-stocked with food.

It was decided that Mother should go see Capt. Vrushin, who was a more cultured man than Capt. Boris, and ask him to explain to his friend that bursting in unannounced with three friends and an accordion player was not cultured behavior.

That evening Mother returned from her mission declaring it a success, and for the next two weeks or so, we saw no sign of Capt. Boris. Our supply of gift food, of course, depleted to a jar of caviar and one of herring that we saved for a social emergency.

Supplies of food in stores seemed to get scarcer as well. The foraging expeditions that the mothers carried on every day managed to put something on the table every morning and evening, but more often than not it wasn't meat. Milk, eggs, butter, and, of course coffee were not available at all, and it seemed that the adults would come home from their search later and later, and more and more exhausted every evening.

The supply of firewood that the soldiers had brought back from the train station for us, was long gone by now. Miss Bronia had discovered a peasant who, one day a week—not the same day unfortunately—could be found driving his wagon around our neighborhood with a load of wood. When she or any of the mothers came across it, they would buy as much wood as could be carried home. Capt. Vrushin had said he would let us know when another wood train came in.

Nights, we were still able to get through in layers of cloth-ing so that the wood could be saved for cooking. But winter was coming, and, if there was a plan for dealing with the cold, I was not aware of it.

Capt. Vrushin came by one evening, by invitation. He came by himself, brought us a large piece of cheese, and had tea out of a glass.

He didn't play his harmonica this time or laugh a lot, but talked quietly with our four adults. Remembering the business of the brass button with a red star he had given me, I kept out of the way so no one would ask me what I had done with it. Fredek, who had been sick that day, was introduced and got a button too, though it was an extra one the captain had brought in his pocket, and he didn't have to cut it off his uniform. When Fredek showed it to me later, I stressed that it came from a Russian army uniform. Fredek told me that his father had a German helmet from the Big War and what was wrong, he asked, with collecting enemy souvenirs. I couldn't come up with an answer.

*   *   *

A few days later, Mrs. Rokief came to our door looking for Mother. Everyone was out except Fredek, me, and Sonya. I was the only one Mrs. Rokief knew or who had any idea who she was. Remembering the kind way in which she had treated me, I introduced her to my friends. I had been schooled in this amenity by Kiki.

Mrs. Rokief asked if she could wait for Mother, and Sonya, equally schooled in amenities, offered to make her tea. Mrs. Rokief accepted.

She sat leaning forward in her chair, her knees and feet tight together, her hands clasped in her lap. To me she looked worried. She wore a black overcoat that was too big for her, a kerchief on her head, and her soft gray eyes were squinted into a frown.

I knew that it was up to me to entertain my mother's visitor. I pulled up a chair facing her and asked how she was feeling. Mrs. Rokief gave me a quick little smile and said she was fine. I next asked about Mr. Rokief and her daughters, and they were fine too. I wondered why she was upset, but had the presence of mind not to do it aloud.

Sonya brought a cup of tea, and I apologized for having no milk to offer, as Mrs. Rokief had done on our visit there. Mrs. Rokief said that that was all right.

I told her what a nice time I had had with Zosia and Renia the other day. Mrs. Rokief said that they had enjoyed my company as well. She picked up her teacup but her hand trembled and she had to steady it with her other one.

I asked if she thought it was going to snow. Mrs. Rokief answered that she hadn't noticed. I asked if her tea was all right, and she said it was fine, and then I racked my brain for another topic to discuss.

I saw Fredek whispering something to Sonya over by the stove. I guessed it was about Mr. Rokief's being a spy and found some pleasure in the way my fabrication had grown. Then, on an inspiration, I asked Mrs. Rokief if she wanted to see a magic trick. She smiled and said, yes, and I proceeded to make my washer appear out of her right ear, then her left, and finally disappear into thin air. I thought it was the best I had ever done it, and Mrs. Rokief smiled and said that was nice. Then she asked when I thought my mother would be back. I said I didn't know, but secretly hoped it would be very soon.

"Would Missus like to hear some poetry?" I asked.

"No thank you, dear," she said and then changed her mind. "Yes, I would love to hear you recite."

I must have filled the next half-hour reciting every poem I knew. I was just considering singing the national anthem when Mother and Miss Bronia finally came in the door. From the shape of their shopping bags, I guessed they had found vegetables.

"Helenka!" Mother said as soon as she saw Mrs. Rokief sitting there. "What's wrong?" She crossed the room quickly. Mrs. Rokief stood up and almost fell into Mother's arms. "Basia, Basia, Yulian has been taking such good care of me," she cried as though that were her complaint.

"What's the matter?" Mother said.

"They've detained Roman."

"Detained?"

"That's what they said."

"Oh my God! What's happened?"

"I don't know. He didn't do anything. They came last night, knocked on the door, and said the commissar had some questions to ask him and they would bring him back in two hours."

"And he's not back yet?" Mother asked.

Mrs. Rokief shook her head. I could see Fredek and Sonya whispering again by the stove.

Suddenly I remembered Fredek talking with Capt. Vrushin that evening. Would Fredek have told the captain my fib about Mr. Rokief's being a spy? No, he wouldn't have.

"I will go see Capt. Vrushin," I heard Mother telling Mrs. Rokief. "If Roman isn't back, I will go see him first thing tomorrow. I'm sure it's a mistake of some kind."

"Oh Basia, why would they do this? Roman hasn't done anything," Mrs. Rokief said.

"It's a mistake. It's simply a mistake. Maybe there's somebody else with your name or who looks like Roman. I don't know. I will straighten it out. Or maybe Roman is home already. Go home now, Helenka, and see if Roman isn't home. I'll bet he is. And tomorrow morning, if Roman still isn't back, you come over here and we'll go see Vasilli together."

When Auntie Paula and Auntie Edna came home later, Mother said, "They've detained Roman Rokief, that lawyer from Krakow that I met."

Auntie Paula and Auntie Edna looked at each other. "Detained?" Auntie Edna said.

"Well, that's what they call it. I don't know exactly what it means."

"What did he do?" Auntie Paula asked.

"I don't think he did anything."

"Then why would they arrest—or detain—him?" Auntie Paula asked.

Chapter Five

The next morning Mrs. Rokief came back, more upset than she had been the day before, and she and Mother went to see Capt. Vrushin.

"He said I should go see the commissar, a Colonel Bawatchov," Mother explained to Auntie Edna and Auntie Paula that evening. "He said he has no idea what it's all about, but the colonel will like it that I speak Russian so well. He said to be sure to tell him I've been to Paris. This sounds like I should go without poor Helenka who's likely to cry. Vasilli said he could get me in to see him tomorrow."

"No," Auntie Paula said suddenly. "You can't go to see the commissar."

"What do you mean I can't go?"

"You want to go," Auntie Paula said, "speak Russian to him, tell him you've been to Paris, and invite him here for vodka and dancing. Then, if Sonya doesn't want to dance with one of his officers or Fredek pretends to shoot him in the head, he has us all arrested and sent to Siberia."

I had heard of Siberia. It was the coldest place on earth and criminals were sent there for punishment.

"This isn't our problem," Auntie Edna said. "We don't even know your Roman Rokief."

"They're my friends. They've been very kind to me." Mother was speaking angrily now.

"They may be your friends," Auntie Edna continued, "but you're involving all of us. You're putting us all in danger."

"How am I putting anyone in danger? I'm just going to talk to him. Vasilli says he's a reasonable man."

"Don't you see, Basia . . . ?" Auntie Edna began again, but Auntie Paula interrupted her. "No, she doesn't see. She doesn't see because she doesn't want to."

"No, you're the ones who don't see. You don't see because you're afraid to see. You're afraid to do anything to help yourselves. You're two old Jewesses afraid to do anything to help yourselves because it means taking a risk. To save my dear friends, or to save my son, I'm not afraid to take a risk."

Suddenly, my mother was sounding like one of the poems Kiki had taught me. Except that the part about the old Jewesses had really surprised me.

The next morning I saw that Mother had taken a diamond brooch of hers out of the jacket lining where she had hidden it that day on the farm. She had on a gray wool suit that I hadn't seen her wear for a while, and she used the diamond brooch to make her décolleté lower so that you could see the line where her breasts came together.

"No, Basia, you can't do that!" Auntie Paula almost shouted. "This is a man far from home with total power in this town. You can't tease him like that."

I expected Mother to make another brave speech about not being afraid, but she let herself be persuaded to take off the brooch and to bring me with her.

"A beautiful woman with a little child would be much more compelling," Auntie Edna said. "Maybe he has a child at home." Auntie Edna and Auntie Paula were sounding as though they didn't want Mother to make any more speeches.

Capt. Vrushin's office was in a palace. I had no idea there was such a place in Durnoval, this town of low, gray, and mostly dirty buildings. The hallway had moldings painted gold, and large dark blue rectangles in the lighter blue walls. The dark rectangles weren't all the same size and I wondered what sort of design scheme that was. Frankly, I didn't find it very attractive. There were designs and angels painted on the ceiling. Only the floor, inlaid with different kinds of wood, was scratched and muddy. I was reminded of the slippers they made you put over your shoes when you went into the Royal Palace in the park in Warsaw.

Capt. Vrushin's office was on the ground floor, and he wasn't there. But a soldier had been instructed to take us upstairs to the commissar's office. As he walked ahead of us, back down the hall toward the stairs, I could actually see the marks that his metal heels were making in the wood floor. They looked like large fingernail clippings. He climbed the stairs two at a time, then waited at the top for Mother and me to catch up.

"If he asks you anything," Mother whispered to me, "pretend you don't understand any Russian."

There was a very large room with pink walls and, again, the large rectangles of a darker pink, in the middle of the lighter pink, under which people in overcoats and heavy jacket sat in chairs lining the walls. A few spoke together in whispers. A soldier sat at a little desk with spindly legs and carved metal corner ornaments, guarding a set of tall double doors. His rifle rested against the side of the desk.

Our guide led us up to the soldier at the door, put his hands on the desk and said something to him quietly. Then our soldier let himself through the doors into the next room. As we waited, I saw my mother bite her lower lip, something Kiki told me only babies did. Then she suddenly stopped, straightened up, and pulled down on the décolleté, which she had originally wanted to hold down with the brooch.

In a few moments the soldier came out again and held the door for us to go into the commissar's office. "Hold my hand," Mother said out of the side of her mouth as we passed through the open door.

It was much warmer in this room. Col. Bawatchov stood up as we came in and held his hand out across his desk. "I've been told you speak beautiful Russian," he said to Mother, in

Russian, of course. Immediately I saw him to be a larger version of the little officer who had offered us sugar cubes in the
hotel lobby on our first day in town. His head was round like a
soccer ball, mostly bald, with small but widely set round eyes,
over a short, fleshy nose. His roundish torso reminded me of a
snowman. Unlike the overcoated people in the waiting room,
he had his jacket off, and a pair of blue suspenders held up his
blue pants. I noticed that there was a fire going in the large
fireplace. A pair of tall boots warmed themselves at a discreet
distance from the fire.

"My little mother is Russian," my mother said, shaking
hands. "She is from Moscow."

An all-red flag stood next to the commissar's large ornate
desk. Directly behind him, a portrait I recognized to be of
Joseph Stalin hung in a much larger rectangle of bright green
paint in the duller green wall. As in the other room, rectangles
of bright paint contrasting with the duller color decorated the
walls. Except for this one of Stalin and the angels on the ceiling, I had seen no pictures anywhere in the palace. One wall
panel, painted white, was framed in a fringe of gray material
looking as though something had been cut out of it.

The commissar motioned us to two chairs. They were white
with antique gold trim, curvy legs, and seats upholstered in a
white-and-pink striped material. They were a lot like the chairs
in our Warsaw apartment and the ones you weren't allowed to
sit on in the Royal Palace in the park. Except that this uphol-
stery had been stained by what I speculated must have been
tea, since this was what Russians liked to drink.

Climbing up onto the chair indicated for me, I immediately
found myself sliding forward again on the slippery material.
Her spike-heeled shoe anchored to the floor and her right knee
crossed over the left, my mother had no such problem. My own
feet dangled inches above the inlaid floor and gravity exerted
its pull to draw me ever closer to the front edge of the padded
seat. In Warsaw, I had had the table to stop my slide, but here

I had to clamp my fingers around the wood underside of the seat and hang on.

Col. Bawatchov said that he understood Mother was there regarding a Roman Rokief, except that he had no record of any Roman Rokief. What that must mean, he said, was that her friend was being detained by the political commissar. He himself, he explained, was the military commissar, but there was also a political commissar who operated independently of him.

A lot of this I understood as he spoke. What I didn't catch, I picked up later as Mother explained it to the Aunties.

Suddenly I heard Col. Bawatchov shout out a name. It may have been the loudest shout I had ever heard. In a moment a door to the commissar's left opened and a young officer came in. I heard the colonel give him instructions to bring him something. I couldn't make out what he said, but when the officer had gone out again, the colonel explained to Mother that he had sent him to the political commissar's office to find out about Mr. Rokief.

Mother thanked him for his kindness, then produced her silver cigarette case and, leaning forward, offered him a cigarette. The colonel quickly stood up and accepted one. Then he picked a box of matches out of his desk drawer and lit Mother's cigarette. His own, he placed in a long, black-and-silver cigarette holder before lighting it. He must have caught Mother looking longingly at the precious matches because he handed them to her and told her to keep them. "I have more," he said.

Mother thanked him and asked what part of Russia he came from. I knew that Russia was the biggest country in the world and in parts of it people looked almost Chinese. He mentioned a place whose name had no meaning to me and went on to say that his father had herded cows. Mother congratulated him on how much he had achieved.

"In the Soviet Union," he said, "a man can become anything he wants to be."

This claim for the ubiquitous Soviet Union snapped my mind to sharp attention. Certainly a man could not become an eagle or an elephant however much he might want to be one. And what if half the men in the Soviet Union decided they all wanted to be king? That, obviously, wasn't workable. And what if a man wanted to be a doctor, but didn't know what medicine cured what sickness—how fair would that be to his patients? Was it possible that magic really did exist and that the Soviet Union . . . ? No, Kiki had told me quite unequivocally that magic existed only in fairy tales. It was quite clear, I decided, that the commissar, just like the announcements over the loudspeakers, was telling us lies.

"I am a language teacher," I heard Mother say in response to some question. "I used to teach French and German in a high school in Warsaw. I was in Paris last summer." I remembered Mother's saying that Capt. Vrushin had told her to be sure and mention that she had been to Paris. And as far as being a language teacher was concerned—well, this Russian deserved to be lied to, I decided.

"Now, with us here, comrade, you could teach at a university, if you are a good enough teacher, and I'm sure you are. And some day you and your son could have your own apartment."

I found it amusing to hear him address Mother as comrade, which Miss Bronia had explained was the way all Russians addressed each other. Mother did not tell the colonel that in Warsaw we already had our own apartment. I understood that they were passing the time while they waited for the young officer to return with information.

Colonel Bawatchov asked Mother what my name was, to which she answered "Yulli," which was what my Russian grandmother sometimes called me.

"Yulli, do you like soldiers?" the colonel asked me.

"Yulli doesn't speak Russian," Mother quickly interjected. She was saying it to the colonel, but looking straight at me.

Technically, of course, she was right. I was finding that I understood a great deal more Russian then I had thought, but I had never actually tried speaking it.

"I don't understand," I said in Polish, looking as blankly as I could from one to the other. I was enjoying this sanctioned mendacity. But I hoped I wouldn't have to act sickly again.

"The colonel asks if you like military things, darling," Mother translated for me.

"Yes," I said, nodding my head.

"Yes, Yulli is a real little soldier," Mother said. "In Warsaw he always wears a sword to the park, and he's great friends with Capt. Vrushin."

This was almost as bad as saying I was sickly. But realizing that we were here to gain the release of Mr. Rokief, for whose arrest I may possibly have been responsible, I began to nod my head. Then, remembering that I wasn't supposed to have understood what Mother had said, I changed the nod to scratching the top of my head and assumed my blank look. But having released my grip on the bottom of the chair seat, I found myself sliding forward again.

I grabbed for the seat again, but even with both hands back under the seat, I could not check my slide. In a moment I was standing once more, the sound of my shoes against the floor echoing through the large room.

"Stop fidgeting, dear," Mother said. Then she smiled at the colonel. She said something to him that I couldn't understand, but I would have bet that it had something to do with my alleged inability to sit still. The colonel smiled at me. It was actually a very kind smile, and I found myself wishing that he wasn't a Russian. Then he opened a drawer in his desk and produced a brass military button with the same red star with the hammer and sickle on it that Capt. Vrushin had given me. This time I had no qualms about stepping forward and accepting it. My mother and I were on a mission, which I did not want to jeopardize.

"Say thank you," Mother prompted, just as I was in the process of doing exactly that.

Now I had my choice of either climbing back up on my chair, knee first, a rather awkward procedure to be carrying out under the gaze of my adult companions, or performing a single, well-executed backwards hop. I chose the latter, but, alas, missed the crown of the slippery seat, which I knew would eventually cause me to slide back down to the floor. I slid down, landing as quietly as I could to try one more, better directed hop.

"Stop that," Mother whispered out of the side of her mouth. But the colonel, I could see, was watching the two of us closely. "He does this to annoy me," Mother said to the commissar.

"He is a boy," Col. Bawatchov said, smiling at me. "I have two boys, one is Yulli's age." Then he signaled me with his finger to step towards the desk again. From the drawer he produced a pocket knife. It wasn't new. Its sides were wood, stained brown and worn with handling. The two blades, one large, one small, had little grooves in them where you hooked your thumbnail in order to open them. I had seen Grandfather's coachman, Adam, do that so he could peel an apple for me.

As I reached across the desk to take the knife from his hand, the colonel surprised me by not releasing his grip. "Nosh," he said, pronouncing the Russian word for knife, as we each held one end.

"Nosh," I repeated.

With his other hand, the colonel pointed to his chest. "Moi nosh," he said.

"The colonel said, my knife," Mother said.

"Moi nosh," I said after him, pointing to my own chest and not acknowledging Mother.

Now the colonel pointed the finger at me. "Tvoi nosh," he said.

"Da, moi nosh," I said quickly, before Mother could interfere, pointing to my own chest again.

The colonel laughed and released the knife. "Haroshy mal-chyk," he said, which I knew meant nice boy or something like that, but didn't let on. Mother looked pleased.

Earlier that very same year I had been permitted my first knife, the little hunting knife that I would wear to the park. I had not been allowed to unsheathe it without Kiki's supervision, and I had had little actual application for the instrument. I certainly would not have been permitted to peel an apple or an orange. But its very presence, hanging there from the button that held my pants to my shirt on my left side, had been my badge of maturity until Lolek had preempted it as he left for the war.

I fully expected the same rules of deployment to be applied to this weapon, but its presence in my pocket—no, the very fact that it had been entrusted to me—was a symbol of my manhood. Taking the knife from Col. Bawatchov, I noticed that most of the third and fourth fingers on his left hand were missing. That was like Adam, who had a piece of a finger missing as well. I wondered whether I was being sent a message.

With the knife secure now in my hand, I stood to attention and said, "Thank you, Colonel," in Polish. Military men, even in opposing armies, I knew, were respectful of one another's rank.

"Haroschi malchik," the Colonel repeated. I, of course knew what it meant, but pretended ignorance. I would have liked to examine the knife, but I thought it more appropriate to pocket it and returned to my seat. This time, my hop landed me at the back of the seat, where the slope was towards the white-and-gold chair back.

I could see the shape of the knife outlined through the material over my left thigh. It was just exactly the length of the spread of my hand, thumb to pinky. I could visualize myself opening the two blades and feeling their sharpness against my thumb, as I had seen Adam do. Then he had stroked it up and down on the side of his boot. My eyes wandered to the colonel's boots by the fireplace and I wondered whether this had been his own, personal knife. I wondered whether I should tell Fredek about it or let him discover its shape in my pocket while I acted as though it were nothing.

Then the young officer came back into the room carrying a file. He handed it to the colonel who put on a pair of rimless glasses and began leafing through it. He pronounced names under his breath. "Aha, Roman Rokief," he finally said. After studying several pages he looked up at Mother. "It's nothing," he said. Then he said some more things that I didn't understand and assured her that Mr. Rokief would be released by the end of the day.

Thanking him warmly, Mother stood up to shake hands. I wiggled forward and then slid to the floor, landing quite silently. But the colonel, using both hands, waved us back to our seats.

"You are a very intelligent woman, Comrade Barbara," he said, "tell me, how do the Poles like us?"

"As you know," Mother said, smiling, "my little mother is Russian. She's from Moscow. I love Russian people."

"But the others. How do they feel about us? I give orders, you know, to be very courteous. We are very kind to children."

"I have seen great courtesy from some of your soldiers, Comrade Colonel. Captain Vrushin has been particularly kind."

I could tell that Mother was trying not to tell the colonel anything that might make him angry. The colonel, too, must have sensed that Mother was holding back. He didn't say anything and there was now a silence.

Mother re-crossed her legs. "I will be honest with you, Comrade Colonel, because I know that is what you would want me to be," she finally said, and she was speaking very carefully. "We liked the Russians much better when we could visit them in Russia instead of seeing them in our streets with rifles."

The colonel didn't get angry at this, but thought about it for a moment before speaking. "Russians and Poles are like brothers—our language is almost the same. But Russia is the bigger, stronger brother, and Poland is the little brother. The Germans attacked you, and we had to come and save you. But the reason Poland is so weak, like the other countries, is that the rich capitalists suck the life out of the people. In the Soviet Union, a factory or a farm isn't owned by one man who gets richer and richer, but by all the people. And now, you know, you are one of the factory owners, too. Have you ever thought of yourself as an owner of a factory, Comrade?"

Now it was my mothers turned to think.

"I have surprised you, haven't I?" the colonel said. "Think about it. You and I are owners of every factory in the Soviet Union that Poland is now a part of. We even own this beautiful palace."

"But if I own this palace and every factory and farm in Poland and the Soviet Union," Mother said, "why don't I have meat or milk to give to my son?"

The colonel shifted his gaze to me. Suddenly he stood up and went to the door through which the young officer had first appeared. He walked silently, and I realized he had no shoes on. He disappeared for about thirty seconds, then returned and resumed his seat.

"That is a temporary problem," he said. "We will soon make your farms and your factories efficient."

"Our farms and factories . . ." Mother began, but then she stopped.

"Yes?" He said

"Oh, nothing, Comrade Colonel," Mother answered.

"You were going to tell me something about your farms and factories. You must not be afraid to tell me what you think. I asked you to tell me. Do you remember?"

Mother took the cigarette case out of her purse again and they both lit up. "This is the Ukraine," Mother finally said. "It's the richest soil in all of Europe. Before you came we had the most beautiful vegetables, milk, cheese, eggs, chickens."

"This is only temporary," the colonel said again. "Soon you'll see. The Soviet Union is a paradise."

"We will all look forward to it, Comrade Colonel," Mother said, standing up and extending her hand again.

Once more the colonel stopped her. We resumed our seats and waited. Then the young officer came back into the room. He carried a package wrapped in a newspaper and tied with string, which he placed on the colonel's desk. "For the boy," the colonel said to my mother, "some bread and ham."

"Thank you very much, Comrade Colonel," Mother said. "You are a very kind man."

Now the colonel reached into his drawer one more time, pulled out a small piece of paper and wrote something on it. "Please come to see me whenever you have a problem," he said. "This will get you in without having to wait." They shook hands. Mother thanked him again and we left. I carried the package under my arm.

As we headed out into the street, Mother stopped. "Let's see if Vasilli is in," she said, and we headed back into the building and down the hall to Capt. Vrushin's office. This time the captain was there, and I sat at an empty desk with a piece of paper to draw on and a pencil that the captain had given me, while Mother and the captain talked quietly at the far corner of the room.

I wasn't interested in the pencil and paper, though this was the first sheet of clean paper I had seen in a long time. I pulled the knife out of my pocket and hiding it behind the desk, proceeded to open it. The big blade felt sharp, as I had known it would be, when I rubbed my thumb across it the way Adam had done. The small blade was very hard to open, which surprised me. When it finally did open, I saw that the point was broken off. At first that was a disappointment, like the time Kiki and I had opened the birthday present from my Uncle Pavew and found a wing broken off the airplane that was really supposed to fly. But I quickly realized that this blade was like the colonel's fingers, the ones with the tips missing.

*　　*　　*

We went to the Rokiefs' before going home. "Oh, Basia, you are so good to us," Mrs. Rokief said. She was wearing the blue-and-white ski sweater she had worn on our last visit, only it seemed much bulkier. I realized that it was Mr. Rokief's sweater that she had put on over her own. It was colder here than it had been before. It seemed even colder than it was outside, and I wondered how that could be.

Renia and Zosia, who had been sitting together on one of the beds, came to the door to greet us. "Zosia," Mrs. Rokief said, "why don't you go to the kitchen and make our guests some tea."

"No, that's all right, Helenka," Mother said. "I just wanted to tell you about my visit to the commissar, and then we have to leave."

"What did he say?" she asked quickly, then interrupted herself. "Sit down, Basia."

"Don't fuss, Helenka," Mother said. But she sat down, and Mrs. Rokief pulled up another chair and sat down opposite her. She took Mother's hands in her own. Zosia and Renia crowded around her.

"As I said," Mother went on, "the commissar is a very nice man and he said Roman should be home today."

All three Rokiefs showed great relief. "You are so good, Basia!" Mrs. Rokief repeated.

"But why did they arrest him?" Renia asked.

"Detained him, dear," her mother corrected.

"Why did they detain him?"

"I don't know," Mother said. "Col. Bawatchov said it was nothing, and I didn't want to press him."

"Yes, that's best," Mrs. Rokief said. "We just want him back. And Yulian, I want to thank you so much for cheering me up so well when I was waiting for your dear mother in your apartment. He did magic tricks for me, you know, and recited some poems. He's so good at it." I was embarrassed by the praise. I slipped my hand in my pocket and fingered my new knife.

"Yulek is very caring," Mother said. Then we left. On the walk home, she said, "You are not to open that knife without a grownup," just as I had anticipated. Actually, I wouldn't have been surprised if she had taken it away from me. "I know I can trust you," she went on, but her tone made it more an admonishment than praise.

*   *   *

"So, did you get to see your commissar?" Auntie Paula asked when she, Auntie Edna, and Sonya came home that evening. "They tell me you have to wait two days to get in to see him."

"Vasilli got me right in," Mother answered. She was sitting at the table sewing up the strap on a black brassiere. "He was actually very nice," she said, "but I don't like what I heard." Both Aunties and Sonya sat down immediately to hear the details.

Mother put down her sewing. I thought she was going to tell them about the funny things he said about owning farms and factories. "As I said, Colonel Bawatchov was very nice," she went on. "He even gave Yulek a pocket knife and some bread and ham to take home. But Roman wasn't arrested—or detained—under his authority. He knew nothing about it. It seems that there are two commissars, a military one and a political one. Vasilli told me afterwards that the political commissar is changed every two weeks so that no one can get friendly with him. His job is to see to it that everything is done strictly according to the party line."

"It's a political police?" Auntie Edna said. "Like the Gestapo?"

"I guess," Mother said.

"What did your friend Roman do?" Auntie Edna asked.

"I don't think he did anything. I don't know. Col. Bawatchov said it was nothing and he'd be released sometime today, but I don't know."

"Maybe they have some questions about Polish law. Didn't you say he was a lawyer?" Auntie Edna asked.

"For three days?" Auntie Paula said. It seemed reasonable to me as well that they wouldn't hold a man for three days and nights just to ask him about the law. "I don't think they much care what Polish law is," Auntie Paula went on.

"I didn't want to mention anything to Helenka about this political commissar business," Mother said, "but I don't like the sound of it."

"We're not political," Auntie Edna said. "I don't intend to go around bad-mouthing Communism. Maybe that's what your friend Rokief did."

"I don't think he'd be that stupid," Mother said.

"Just don't get us involved in political issues," Auntie Paula said. "You didn't say anything political to the commissar, did you?"

I wished I knew what political meant. I noticed Mother wasn't saying anything about what she had said about not liking Russians in our streets.

When Fredek came home with Miss Bronia, it didn't take him long to notice the bulge against my leg. "What did you get?" he asked.

I got up without a word and walked into the other room. Fredek followed. I did that because I didn't want to remind my mother about the knife, in case she wanted to take it away. But the mysterious nature that this lent to the whole business was not lost on me either.

Fredek grabbed the knife from my hand the moment I had it out of my pocket. He snapped the big blade open and felt its edge with his thumb. "Not very sharp," he said. "That's good—you won't cut yourself. Your mother buy it for you?"

I placed myself between Fredek and the other room so no one would see. "No, the commissar gave it to me," I said. I saw Fredek's eyes flick up at me for an instant as he struggled with a smaller blade.

"Ha, it's broken," he said when he finally had the blade open. Fredek snapped both blades shut and handed the knife back with no further interest. "No wonder," he added.

I wasn't quite sure what he meant, but let the matter pass. I put the knife back in my pocket, its value enhanced in my mind.

That evening I sneaked the knife under my pillow and wrapped my fingers around it. The knife had belonged to Col. Bawatchov, whose father had herded cows, and he had worked his way up through the ranks of the army to where he was almost a general. Maybe the knife had been given him when he was still a cowherd's son so he could use it to sharpen sticks and carve things and cut rope. I could see him at my age, walking beside his father, leading a herd of cows through the meadows. "You are old enough now to have your own knife," the father says, handing it to him. "A big boy should have a knife."

Now the boy could do for himself many of the things adults did and had done for him before. He could cut open an orange or carve himself a whistle or sharpen a stick to fight off wolves that threatened the cows. And then, when he went into the army, he used it for opening letters and packages, sharpening pencils, slicing cheese, cutting holes in harness. When he got married and had children, maybe he even used the knife to make a cradle.

Somewhere along the line he had snapped off the tip of the small blade. I could not imagine how he might have done that, but he had taken on some task that proved too much for the knife, saddening him.

But it hadn't destroyed the knife. It had continued serving . . . just like . . . just like the two missing fingers. They had been shot off by a bullet or lost in a sword fight or a wood-chopping accident. The colonel had experienced something like that, suffered like a soldier, then gone on, a stronger man.

And now he had given the knife to me, and it was lying right in my hand, under my pillow. A grown man had given me something that he had lived with and now I owned it.

It did occur to me, of course, that none of that might have been true. It might have been a knife that he had found on the sidewalk on his way to work just that morning. But even then, it would have been part of somebody's life—somebody did break that tip. And the wood sides did show plenty of wear, a lot of handling. Who knew how many people had handled it? And now it was mine.

Chapter Six

The next morning it was snowing. I had visions of building a snowman in front of the house. Fredek fantasized throwing snowballs at people. He had already pelted most of our household with imaginary snowballs accompanied by vocal sound effects, when the decision was made that it was not worth the risk of our catching cold to allow either of us to go outside without the proper winter clothing that had been left in Warsaw. Miss Bronia tore a brown paper bag into sheets and Fredek and I were set to drawing pictures of what we would like to be doing out in the snow. Then we were left in Sonya's charge while the adults went on their daily forage. Firewood was particularly on people's minds this morning.

I finished quickly, quite pleasantly surprised by how realistic my snowman turned out. I could well imagine what Fredek's picture would be like, as I watched him at work, his drawing accented by his continued sound effects.

When I showed my finished work to Sonya, she gave it mild approval, but suggested that I include people building a snowman. Well aware of my limitations when it came to drawing people, I protested that the snowman was already finished. With an air of authority that I found unnecessary, Sonya suggested that I turn the paper over and start again.

Had this suggestion come from Miss Bronia, I would have obeyed without hesitation. The problem, however, was that I had no assurance that I would be able to draw as good a snowman as I had the first time, and so I decided to avoid the risk and draw a car instead. I was well practiced in drawing a car, even with passengers inside.

But I hadn't gotten much beyond the front bumper when there was a knock on our door. As she had been instructed, Sonya opened the door only far enough to see and blocked it with her foot. "Yes?" she said, not recognizing the caller.

"Does Mrs. Padovich live here?" a young woman's voice asked. Sonya, who, it seemed, only knew Mother by her present name, Waisbrem, though she had heard her use Padovich several times, said that she did not. But I identified the voice as that of Renia Rokief.

"That's my mother!" I called to Sonya. "She's looking for my mother. I know this girl."

Sonya opened the door cautiously, and Renia and her sister stepped inside. I introduced our visitors, as I'd been taught. They shook hands with Sonya and Fredek. "They won't let us go out and throw snowballs," Fredek said.

"It's so good to see you, Yulian" Zosia said, and I was filled with pride at being greeted like that in front of Sonya and Fredek. But realizing their purpose was not social, I explained to the sisters that we had no idea when Mother might return.

"Please tell your mother," Renia said, and she said it to me and not Sonya, "that our father has not returned and Mother is sick with worry. She can't get out of bed, and if your mother could go see the commissar again. . . . oh, please."

I assured them that I would deliver the message and offered them tea, though we had no milk. The girls said they had to hurry back to their mother, who was alone.

The pride over my very grown-up assignment prevented me from trying to draw anything recognizable for the rest of the day. I scribbled lines, circles, and crosses and watched the snow fall in the street as I visualized poor, sweet Mrs. Rokief lying on her bed with a wet cloth over her eyes and forehead the way Kiki would do when she had her headaches.

Then I remembered prayer. I had not stopped saying the Our Father and the Hail Mary in bed every night, but, I now realized, I had given little thought to God in recent weeks. Now I walked into the privacy of the inner room, made the sign of the cross, and proceeded to beseech the Lord and the Holy Virgin for the prompt reunion of Mr. and Mrs. Rokief.

Anxious as I was to deliver my urgent message, Mother didn't return till after supper. She had stopped in at the Rokiefs and already knew what I had to tell her.

The next morning, she again dressed to see the commissar. It was a green suit this time, with a fur collar. "I'm bringing Yulek," she said. "Colonel Bawatchov likes him." Then to me she said, "Bring that knife he gave you."

For a moment I was gripped by the fear that she would make me return it. But I soon realized that it would be only to show him how much I appreciated his gift . . . I hoped.

"Edna," Mother said, as I waited by the door in the red and black plaid, grownup's winter jacket that Mother had bought for me the week before and Miss Bronia had shortened the sleeves so I could wear it as an overcoat, "let Fredek exchange coats with Yulek today. I want Bawatchov to see him dressed a little better."

"That's a woman's coat," Fredek complained. "It even buttons the wrong way."

I hadn't been aware of a difference in the way men's and women's coats buttoned, and this was the first time that my coat's true gender had occurred to me. But the logic added up. This was an adult's jacket, and I had never seen a grown man in a plaid one.

"Scots wear plaid jackets all the time," my mother said to Fredek.

"And I can give you a nice wide leather belt like soldiers wear, so you won't even have to button it," Miss Bronia quickly added.

This seemed to convince Fredek, though it wouldn't have convinced me. I knew that Scottish men wore plaid skirts, but I had never seen a picture of one in a plaid jacket. As we were on our way to Col. Bawatchov's office, I was very glad that Auntie Edna approved the exchange. I only hoped that Miss Bronia's wide leather belt, which did to an extent make up for the plaid, would at least stay with the jacket when it was returned to me.

This time we went straight up the stairs to the second floor of the palace. Mother showed the slip of paper to the guard outside the colonel's door, and after a short wait we were in the commissar's office again.

Col. Bawatchov was happy to see Mother. "Shake hands," Mother said to me, which I was already prepared to do as soon as he made the offer. The colonel held his large hand out to me and I shook it firmly.

As I was about to retrolaunch myself again onto the chair, the colonel held up the index fingers of both hands, signaling me to stop. He shouted something to the young officer behind the door to his left and in a moment the man came in carrying a footstool. "For the boy," the colonel said, and the officer placed it in front of my chair.

"Say thank you," Mother started to say, but I had beaten her to it. Using this stool, I mounted the chair as elegantly as a cavalryman.

The colonel asked about Mother's health.

"I and my son are well, Comrade Colonel," Mother answered, "but my friend, Comrade Rokief has not been released."

This surprised the colonel and again he shouted for his aide and sent him once more for the "detainees" file.

"Are you keeping warm, Comrade Barbara?" he asked while we waited.

"Not really, Comrade Colonel," Mother answered. "Wood is very hard to find."

"We brought in a train of firewood just last week, which we gave away free."

"Capt. Vrushin told me about it. But he said it was all logs, which we have no way of either carrying or cutting up."

This surprised the colonel as well. "I must talk to Vrushin," he said.

"We were very grateful for the bread and ham you gave us," Mother said quickly.

The colonel looked at me. "You like ham, Yulli?" And I almost answered him before remembering that I was not supposed to understand Russian.

"Answer him," Mother prompted *sotto voce* in Polish.

"What did he say, Mummy?" I asked innocently.

"The colonel asked if you like ham," she explained, remembering our subterfuge.

"Oh, yes, a lot!"

"He says he likes it and thanks you," Mother translated.

"Do you like herring?" the colonel asked, and Mother translated again.

"Oh, yes!" I said enthusiastically.

Not needing a translation, the colonel said that he had some cases of that and would give us a few jars. Mother expressed her gratitude.

"And the knife? I hope you haven't been cutting up anything you shouldn't."

My eyes went to the lump on top of my left thigh before Mother's translation, and I realized that I may have given away our game. But the colonel seemed to take no notice.

"He hasn't had a chance to use it yet," Mother interjected. "He is not allowed to open it without supervision."

"A boy should have a knife. It teaches him to be a man. He'll cut his fingers a few times, and he'll learn."

Then the young officer returned with the file and handed it to his commander.

"Ah," the colonel said, putting on his glasses. "Alexander Rokief, right?"

"Roman Rokief," Mother corrected. Col. Bawatchov repeated the name and began thumbing through the file. Again he muttered names under his breath.

He went through the entire file and then began again, going more slowly. Then, turning to his left, he called for his aide. This time, however, he got up from the desk and spoke to the officer out of our earshot. The aide marched out again. The lieutenant was tall and thin, with black hair, black eyebrows, a long chin, and a very serious look on his face. As he marched out, I realized that he reminded me of an unsmiling university student I had seen once or twice at my grandparents', who was supposed to be a cousin.

"Comrade Lieutenant Rostov is going to check some more," the colonel said, pushing his glasses up on his forehead. Looking at Mother, I saw her biting her lower lip. "There have been some records misplaced," the colonel said. "We'll have it straightened out shortly."

The colonel's boots were by the fireplace again. Sitting back in his chair with the glasses on his forehead, he reminded me of a pilot.

"Do you have a husband, Comrade?" he asked as we waited.

"He was in the army, fighting the Germans. I don't have any news about him."

"Where was he fighting? Do you know his regiment? Maybe I can find out something."

Mother gave him some regimental name. "He was fighting outside of Warsaw," she said. "His name is Capt. Leon Pad . . . Waisbrem, Capt. Leon Waisbrem."

The colonel was writing it down. "I will see what I can do."

"You are again being very kind, Comrade Colonel."

"Ask Yulli how he likes Russians," the colonel suddenly asked.

"He doesn't know any Russians except you, Comrade Colonel, and his grandmother . . . and, of course, Capt. Vrushin. As for you, you have been more than kind to him."

"Let him speak. I want to hear what he has to say."

Mother translated for me. She gave me a hard look, and I understood that I was supposed to say something nice, though the similarity between the two languages made it inadvisable for her to prompt me.

The fact of the matter was that I had no problem with telling the colonel that I liked Russians, or anything else that might help free Mrs. Rokief's husband. But what was a problem was that I had actually come to like this Russian.

Then it came to me. "I like soldiers," I said. Mother smiled, then translated.

"A clever answer," the colonel answered. Then he offered Mother a cigarette, put one into his cigarette holder, and lit both. Without a word, he handed Mother the box of matches and signaled with his hand that she should keep them. Sitting back in his chair, he pushed the glasses up onto his forehead. "When did you go to Paris, Comrade?" he asked.

I understood that he supposed she had been only once and waited for Mother to tell him she went all the time. "We usually go in the spring for the fashions," Mother said.

I didn't understand what going for the fashions meant, and I didn't think the colonel would either. Instead of being impressed by her travels, as I thought he would be, he said, "In the Soviet Union we have fine language teachers in our own universities. You don't have to go to Paris to learn French."

I remembered Mother telling him that she was a language teacher.

"I didn't go just to learn the language," Mother said. "Paris is beautiful in the spring, and my husband and I used to go just to vacation."

Now there was a frown on the colonel's face, and I felt that Mother wasn't succeeding at pleasing him. "Your husband was in the government?" he asked.

"Oh, no, he manufactured shirts."

"A factory manager?"

"Yes," she said. I noticed she didn't say that he owned the factory. "He had to buy materials and machines, and he always scheduled it for my vacation time."

"In the Soviet Union, we manufacture our own materials and our own machines."

"Poland is a much smaller country."

"Now it's part of the Soviet Union. If your husband comes back from the war, he'll be able to go to Leningrad for his supplies."

Mother agreed that that would be welcome.

"Our machines are made better," he added. Mother nodded in agreement.

"Do you know why our machines are better?" he asked.

"No."

"Because they are designed and built by workers who are happy at their work. Our workers aren't exploited—we got rid of all the factory owners. And when workers are happy, they do better work."

Mother didn't disagree. On our other visit, she had told him about not liking the sight of Russian soldiers in our streets—this time she didn't seem to want to say anything disagreeable.

"You will see, Comrade, the Soviet Union is a paradise."

"We are looking forward to it," Mother said.

Then Lt. Rostov returned with two more files. Mother and I sat silently and the lieutenant stood by as the colonel looked through both files. Finally he looked up and removed his glasses altogether. "There is no record of Roman Rokief," he said.

"Could he have been released this morning or late last night?" Mother asked.

The colonel took a moment before answering. "There is no record of him being released," he finally said. "There is no record of him having been here."

"But you had a record of his being here two days ago. I saw it in your hand, Comrade Colonel. There were several pages clipped together and you said it was nothing."

"Yes," the colonel said, and suddenly I saw his ears turn a bright red. I had heard Kiki talk about someone's face turning red, though I had never seen it. But I had never heard of ears turning red.

"Is there a list of detainees?" Mother asked.

The colonel didn't answer immediately. He was looking through the files again. "There is," he finally said, not looking up. "But he isn't on it."

"Any more."

"Yes, he is not on it . . . now."

"What does that mean?"

"That means that he was never here."

"But we know he was."

"We were mistaken," the colonel said quickly.

"But you had his papers in your hand."

I really wasn't following this conversation. I had seen the papers in the colonel's hand and heard him read Mr. Rokief's name. He couldn't have forgotten that.

The colonel moved his head to the side, signaling the lieutenant to leave. Then he leaned forward and in a quiet voice asked, "What is Comrade Rokief to you?"

"A friend. He and his wife are friends of mine. They've been kind to me . . . as you have."

"Then you should forget about Comrade Rokief. Tell his wife to go to another town . . . quickly."

Mother was sitting very, very straight and still in her chair now. Only her lips were trembling a little. And suddenly I understood that something terrible had happened to Mr. Rokief.

"It is a political matter," the colonel said. "I can do nothing. I will write a travel permit to Lvow for Rokief's wife. She can take a train or a bus, but she must go quickly. What is her name?"

"It's Helen," Mother said. "And she has two daughters."

Suddenly I thought of poor Mrs. Rokief, who maybe would never see her husband again, and it was as though something had shot through me. There was a deep ache inside of me, and I was crying so that I couldn't get my breath. I felt myself shaking. I was swaying from side to side on the chair.

I heard the colonel shout for water. Then he had his arm around me.

"What's the matter with him?" Mother was asking. "He hardly even knows Roman."

The lieutenant was there with a glass of water, and the colonel poured some on a cloth, which he held against my forehead. The he put the glass up to my lips. "Just sip," he said in a commanding tone that surprised me. Then to Mother, "Tell him to take just a little sip."

Mother translated and I sipped the water.

"He did this once before," Mother was saying. Then, to me, in a gentle voice she asked, "Did something frighten you, Yuletchku? Tell us." It was the second time someone had used that very diminutive form of my name.

Nothing had frightened me, but there was that deep ache that was like the one I would have when Kiki took her day off in Warsaw, and I would lie on the floor crying. I had no more understanding of it now than I did then.

But the colonel's arm around me was comforting. His shirt smelled of a very strong soap. "He may be remembering about his own father going to the war," he said.

Then I could smell Mother's perfume, and he was releasing me. I felt Mother's arm around me. "Don't be afraid, Yuletchku," she was saying.

I wanted to tell her that I wasn't afraid. But more than that I wanted her not to let go. Then I felt her other arm encircle me. She wasn't soft, like Miss Bronia, and her jacket was scratchy and smelled of her strong perfume and cigarette smoke, but it felt very good, nevertheless.

*   *   *

Mother and I waited in our apartment until someone came home. "You have to come with me to see Helenka," she said to Auntie Edna when she came back with Sonya soon after lunchtime. They carried armloads of firewood. "I have to tell her that her husband is probably on his way to Siberia and she has to leave Durnoval immediately," she explained when Auntie Edna asked what it was all about.

Auntie Edna stopped in the middle of stirring the embers from last night's fire in the stove. "To Siberia?" she said. "Siberia? No, how do you know?"

"Sonya, please take Yulek into the other room and read to him or something," Mother said.

Sonya cut herself a piece of the sausage we had brought from the commissar along with the three jars of herring and said, "Come on," heading into the other room. I followed.

Sonya sat down cross-legged on her pallet, and I sat down near her. Instead of picking up a book, she leaned toward me. "What happened at the commissar's?" she whispered.

"He said it's a political matter," I whispered back.

"What does that mean?"

"I think political means that it's a big secret."

"That's not what political means," she said angrily. "I know what political means. What does it mean that it's a political matter?"

"The colonel can't find his records. He sent Lieutenant Rostov back to look some more, but they can't find them. But it's not the colonel's fault—somebody else lost it."

"Are you sure he was there in the first place?"

"Yes, because when we were there before, the colonel read his name out of the file."

"Maybe they released him."

"No, because they have a list of people they released and he wasn't on that list either. And the colonel said that Mother should forget about him, and Mrs. Rokief should go away from here. He wasn't nasty about it. He even gave her a permit to travel to Lvow."

"So what does Aunt Barbara think happened?"

"She said that they're taking him to Siberia. I don't know what that's all about."

"It's where the Russians send prisoners. It's so cold there, they can't escape."

"He hasn't done anything," I said.

"Fredek says he's a spy." I had forgotten about this, having convinced myself that it would have been childish to assume that he had passed my fib on to Capt. Vrushin. Now I found myself revisiting my logic.

"Childish nonsense," I said scornfully, availing myself of that powerful phrase for the first time in my life. "How would he know?"

"Sometimes he knows these things."

"All I know about Mr. Rokief is that he comes from Krakow and he's a lawyer," I said with finality. Sonya picked up a file from beside her pallet and began filing her nails. My mind turned back to the colonel's arm around my shoulders.

*   *   *

Auntie Edna came home without Mother. "I don't really even know the woman. What do they expect me to do?" she said to Auntie Paula, who had come home just before her. "I went over with Basia and sat with her while she told the poor woman about her husband, and I thought my heart would break. And she has those two daughters, you know. But I don't know what to say to her. We're not even on a first-name basis."

"I didn't even know they existed until she showed up here the other day," Auntie Paula said. "Basia mentioned once that she had met a lawyer from Krakow, but I had no idea she was seeing them secretly. The man may well be a spy. Why else would they be sending him to Siberia?"

"Basia says he's disappeared from their records. She says his name was there before, but it's not there now. There's no record of sending him to Siberia or anywhere," Auntie Edna said.

"Then maybe they didn't send him to Siberia."

"Basia is afraid they may have shot him."

Auntie Paula didn't say anything. Then, after a moment, Auntie Edna said, "Basia says the colonel told her to forget about ever knowing the man and that his wife should leave Durnoval. He said the matter is totally out of his hands. That sounds like a warning to me—a clear warning to have nothing more to do with those people. The political commissar could have them all arrested as well, and Basia's colonel wouldn't be able to intervene."

"Basia could get us all arrested," Auntie Paula said.

"Where are Fredek and Bronia?" Auntie Edna suddenly asked. "Shouldn't they have returned by now?"

"Don't worry," Auntie Paula said. "There's nothing connecting them to this Rokief man. And I'm not sure he isn't a spy of some sort. We'll just have to sit Barbara down and tell her she can't do this kind of thing anymore. Children are involved. Or she can take Yulek and go live by themselves somewhere."

If Mr. Rokief was a spy, he was on our side, and he must have been spying on the Russians for Poland and that made him a hero. And then I thought of poor, sweet Mrs. Rokief again, and I was beginning to feel that ache, but I wouldn't let myself cry this time. It had taken me totally by surprise before, but I was better prepared now, and I would not let Auntie Edna and Auntie Paula see me cry.

Then Auntie Paula's last statement registered with me, the one about Mother and me going to live by ourselves. That would mean leaving Miss Bronia, and now I could feel that ache getting stronger. But I wasn't going to give into it in front of the Aunties. My mother was being a good friend to Mrs. Rokief, staying with her in her time of pain, and the Aunties were worrying about things that might happen. And I was worrying about things that might happen, which was not the way soldiers behaved. Soldiers didn't worry about things—they acted.

I picked up the little blanket that we would put around our shoulders when we went out into the hall to go to the privy, and let myself quietly out the door. Auntie Paula looked up, hearing the door open, but she had seen me heading for the privy many times before.

Turning the other way in the hall, I was out in the street in a few steps. It was dark out, but I was sure I knew the way to the Rokiefs.

I ran to the corner and stopped to look both ways before crossing. There was no traffic, and I ran on, my heart pounding not from the run, but the urgency. It was the first time I had been on a city street alone. I didn't care if I looked stupid with a blanket wrapped around me.

I looked for the name of the street I had to turn left on. But I couldn't read the sign. There was only one light at each intersection, and this one was diagonally across from the street sign. Its brightness didn't reach the street sign. The stores, all of them shuttered now, looked nothing like the way they did in the daytime when some were open.

Now for the first time, I was aware of how empty and dark streets could be. In Warsaw there had been many street lamps, bright store windows, people, cars, horses, trolleys. Older boys would be darting in and out among pedestrians. Here there was only one lamp at each intersection and the light from apartment windows. A few figures moved through the shadows. Six soldiers marched by down the middle of the street, counting cadence in Russian. A horse and wagon clopped noisily across the next intersection.

A figure came out of a dark doorway and walked quickly toward me. It was a man in a long coat and flat cap. Instinctively I pressed myself against the cold building wall, and he walked past me. I should have asked him what street this was, I realized when it was too late. The next person that came by, I would hold my hand up to stop him or her and say, "Excuse me, is this Mikowanski street?" After all, I had marched up to the general in Warsaw, saluted and asked for his autograph.

I saw two people scurry by on the other side of the street. I should run across and ask them, I knew. But I would have to stop them from behind, and I didn't have a strategy for that. Maybe if I walked one more block, I would recognize something.

I resumed walking, staying close to the wall. If I were to stop someone, I would have to walk in the middle of the street where they could see me. I shouldn't jump at them out of the shadows and scare them. It felt safer near the wall, but I moved out into the middle of the sidewalk.

At the next corner, there was no street sign at all. This could have been the street. I didn't think it was the next one—that would have been too far. It was either this street or the one before or the one before that.

Another man was walking toward me. 'Excuse me, is this Mikowanski street?' I was going to say. I could feel my heart pounding in my chest.

Then I heard my name called from behind. "Yulian!" it was Miss Bronia's voice. "What are you doing out here?" she demanded.

Turning around, I saw Miss Bronia and Fredek hurrying down the street toward me. In one hand, Miss Bronia held a headless chicken by its feet—a sight I had seen before on these streets. "What in heaven's name . . . are you doing . . . out in the street?" She asked again. She was out of breath, and I realized they must have been running to catch up to me.

"My mommy's at Mrs. Rokief's," I explained. "They sent her husband to Siberia. Or maybe they've already shot him."

"They shot Mr. Rokief?" Fredek repeated.

"Hush!" Miss Bronia said. "Here!" She handed the chicken to Fredek. Fredek demurred holding the dead bird. "Take it!" Miss Bronia commanded, transferring the feet to his hand. "Yulian, give me your hand!"

I obeyed. Her hand wasn't as gentle as it usually was. She held me as though I might try to run away. I saw her take a deep breath. "Isn't anyone home?" she finally said.

"Auntie Edna, Auntie Paula, and Sonya."

Miss Bronia took another deep breath and let it out slowly. "How did you get out?"

"I pretended to . . ." I began, but she interrupted me. "It's all right," she said in a calmer voice now. She lowered herself to one knee and put her arms around me. "I know," she said. "I know. Let's go back now, and we'll wait for Mommy to come back. She'll be home soon."

Miss Bronia didn't really understand. "Mrs. Rokief . . ." I began, but didn't know what else to say.

"Mrs. Rokief will be all right."

I must have begun to cry, because I felt Fredek's hand on my shoulder. "She'll be all right," he echoed. "You'll see. We'll go home and wait for Auntie Barbara."

My urge to go to Mrs. Rokief and her daughters wasn't as strong anymore, and I was glad for the encounter as we walked home.

Auntie Edna and Auntie Paula were on the sidewalk in front of our house when we got there. "What did you think you were doing?" Auntie Paula demanded as we got close.

"He's very upset," Miss Bronia said, leading me straight inside. I heard Fredek say, "He'll never do it again."

"Take off your clothes and get straight into bed," Miss Bronia said. "I'm going to make you some tea. Have you had any supper?"

I shook my head.

"I will bring you something. Don't get out of bed. Cover yourself up well."

As I was undressing under my covers, Fredek came over to our pallets. "What were you going to do there?" he wanted to know.

"There," of course, meaning at the Rokiefs, and I had no answer to give him. "I don't know," I admitted.

"So why were you going there?"

"I don't know," I said again, and, actually, I had no idea anymore why I had had such a great urge to be with Mrs. Rokief. I still felt sorry for her—very sorry—but now I could see no way that my presence might have mitigated the tragedy.

"The woman cut the chicken's head off right there on the street," Fredek said. "She had a little log standing on end, and she put his head down and just went chop!"

Then Miss Bronia brought me a cup of tea and told Fredek to leave me alone.

In a few minutes, I could hear her speaking to Auntie Edna and Auntie Paula. She was speaking quietly, but she sounded angry. I had never heard her speaking angrily to the other grownups before.

Sonya bought me some bread and ham. "I'm not supposed to talk to you," she announced. I got the sense that there was something more she was trying to communicate, but it eluded me.

The following morning, Mother still hadn't come home. But nobody seemed concerned. It was only Fredek who asked at breakfast why Auntie Barbara hadn't come home.

"Hush," his mother said. "We're not going to talk about that."

"Just answer his question," Auntie Paula said.

"All right, Auntie Barbara is spending the night with a sick friend."

"Why did they send Mr. Rokief to Siberia or did they shoot him?" Fredek asked.

"That's what we're not going to talk about."

Auntie Paula broke in. "Miss Bronia has heard that the Russians have arrested a few men and we don't know why."

"Was Mr. Rokief a spy?" Fredek asked.

"We don't know. None of us knew Mr. Rokief."

"You said 'knew.' Does that mean they shot him already?"

"We don't know."

Now it was Miss Bronia who broke in. "Because it's too cold and rainy to go out, the boys and I are going to do what we've needed to do for some time." She paused long enough for us to wonder what that was. "We're going to start washing and re-stuffing the pallets."

We had sewn an extra pallet cover over the previous week for someone to sleep on while theirs was washed and hung on the clothesline that Miss Bronia had rigged above the stove. We had been collecting straw for a change of stuffing for some time, and now Fredek and I welcomed the opportunity for the physical activity. The Aunties and Sonya, who had proper weather gear, albeit some of it makeshift, went out on their rounds of foraging.

*   *   *

Mother came home that evening. Her eyes were bloodshot and most of her makeup had been wiped off. She spent the night, she said, convincing Mrs. Rokief to go to Lvow, as Col. Bawatchov had advised—and the day waiting for this morning's train to Lvow to leave the station.

"It's very different in Lvow," Mother said. "I talked to people who have been there. There is food. There are restaurants. There is coffee, and matches."

Mother said we should pack up and go there. She could get Col. Bawatchov to give us travel permits.

Auntie Edna said that it had been announced that children between certain ages all had to be registered for school and she and Auntie Paula had registered Fredek and Sonya. Mother answered her that the teachers weren't going to chase her to Lvow if Fredek failed to show up for class.

For a change, Auntie Paula agreed with my mother. She had also heard that conditions were much better in Lvow, and if Mother could really get us travel permits, and if we could be sure we could find housing, then we should go. Mother said she would go see the colonel the next day.

"Isn't he going to get tired of seeing you so often?" Auntie Edna asked.

"He likes Yulek," Mother said.

"My throat hurts," said Fredek.

*　　　　*　　　　*

As we climbed the stairs to the colonel's office the next morning, I was well aware of my own importance. Col. Bawatchov genuinely liked me. He wasn't like some of my mother's friends who made a big show of being nice to the little boy.

Perhaps we were wrong about calling the Russians our enemies. They had said that they had come to stop the advance of the Germans, whom we weren't strong enough to resist because Poland was a smaller country than Germany, and they did stop them. The food and firewood supply systems had been disrupted, but that couldn't be helped in view of all the extra people who were in town now, and it would, as the colonel said, get all straightened out. I only regretted that we had lied to this kind man about my ability to understand Russian. I started to climb the steps two at a time, but Mother pulled me back.

This time we had to wait a few minutes outside the colonel's office until an elderly couple came out. The woman was crying, and the colonel had, himself, opened the door for them.

"I do what I can," he said to Mother when the door had closed behind us, "but there's only so much one can do."

They shook hands. "You have a very difficult responsibility, Comrade Colonel," Mother said.

I saw the little footstool from last time now under the colonel's desk. Reaching with my foot, I slid it over to my chair

"Ah, Yulli," the colonel said, "you are at home here."

I wasn't sure if that was a greeting or a rebuke, and I was grateful for the opportunity to wait for Mother's interpretation—which, of course, didn't come. Mother had forgotten again. She appeared not to notice my intentionally blank look and answer for me, "He admires you very much, Comrade Colonel." Since I had never discussed the colonel with Mother, this was pure fabrication—even if partially true.

"And I am very grateful to you," Mother went on. She had sat down in her chair and crossed her legs, but the colonel had pulled up a third chair so that he was now sitting on our side of the desk, and Mother turned to face him. "I put my friend and her daughters on the Lvow train yesterday," she continued.

"Yes, I know," he said.

Mother laughed. It was a throaty laugh that I had not heard from her before. "You know everything that goes on in your town, Comrade Colonel." In view of his ignorance of Mr. Rokief's fate, I thought this somewhat of an exaggeration.

"I try to know everything I need to know," he said. "I'm sorry you and your friend had to wait so long. The engineer is sick, and his assistant was . . . ." and the colonel put his thumb to his lips and lifted his head quickly to simulate drinking from a bottle.

"It gave me a chance to speak with some people who have been to Lvow lately," Mother said. "They tell me the conditions there are better than they are here."

"And you would like to move to Lvow."

"Yes, Comrade Colonel."

"I can't give you a permit," the Colonel said.

"But Comrade Colonel . . ."

"I did it for Rokief's wife because she was in danger, but I can't do it for you."

"But Comrade Colonel . . ."

He cut her off again. "I am watched closely, too," he said.

Mother didn't say anything.

"But I can take you to visit Lvow," he said. "It's a beautiful city. It's our regional headquarters, you know. The commissar there is a general, and I have to report to him next Tuesday. My driver drives me and they have a room for me at the George. It's the best hotel in the city. Would you like to come with me?"

Mother looked quickly in my direction. I could tell he had taken her by surprise. She had hoped for a permit to travel and suddenly he was offering transportation. Of course, if it was just going to be an overnight trip, I didn't understand why Mother should be so anxious about me. It didn't matter to me whether or not I went too.

Then the colonel was shouting for Lt. Rostov again. "Take Yulli and get him a glass of tea," he said to the young man.

"Go with the lieutenant," Mother said to me. "Our talk will just bore you."

That was fine with me, though I hoped the lieutenant spoke Polish so I wouldn't have to carry on the charade that I didn't understand what he was saying when I really did.

He led me out through the side door from which he had come. The room on the other side was barely large enough to hold the two desks in it. Nobody sat at one, and I presumed it to be Lt. Rostov's. It was covered with papers. A soldier sat typing at the second desk. "I'm taking this child to get him some tea," the lieutenant said.

"Yes, Comrade," the soldier answered, and only then did I realize that this soldier was actually a woman. I had never heard of women soldiers before. Her hair was short, a little longer, I realized, than a man's, and I could now see that her chest bulged. But her features were hard; her mouth turned down in the corners. While she would have made a possibly handsome man—less handsome than the black-haired, unsmiling lieutenant—she was, I decided, a definitely ugly woman. I would not have enjoyed her hugging me.

"The colonel is blah-blahing his mother," the lieutenant added, using words that I could not even decipher from their context. The woman gave a little laugh as we passed through into a narrow hall.

A few doors down, Lt. Rostov opened a door and led me through it. It was a large bathroom with a tub, a sink, a toilet, a bidet, and an enameled stove. A board lay across the bidet, and on it stood a brass samovar. A wisp of smoke came out of its chimney and around the little ceramic pot in which, I knew, the tea leaves were steeping. My grandmother made tea in a samovar.

The lieutenant took a glass off a shelf and rinsed it under the sink faucet. Into it he poured a little of the concentrated tea from the small pot and then filled it with hot water from the little spigot on the samovar. This he handed to me without a word.

"Thank you," I said in Polish, and he grunted.

The glass was very hot, and I had to pass it from hand to hand. It proved still too hot so I put it down on the floor.

"Gariache," the lieutenant said. It meant hot in Russian.

Realizing he was trying to teach me Russian words, I repeated it after him.

The serious expression on his face softened a little. "Harasho," he said, meaning, good.

"Harasho," I repeated, playing dumb.

"No, I mean . . ." he began, then grew embarrassed and shook his head, holding his hands palms out to indicate the end of the lesson. I answered with my well-practiced blank look.

The lieutenant took a sugar cube out of an open tin can. "Sahar," he said, the Russian for sugar. I continued to look blank.

He pointed at me and in enunciated "Sah-ar." I pointed to my chest and repeated, "Sah-ar."

The young lieutenant's face grew red again. He shook his head and once more raised his open palms. Then he held up one finger, the same way my teacher in Warsaw used to do to call our attention. He pointed to the sugar cube in his other hand. "Sah-ar," he said again. Then he pointed the finger at me. "Yulli," he said.

I nodded my head. "Sah-ar," I said pointing to the sugar. Then I pointed to myself and said, "Yulli." The lieutenant's face brightened. He handed me the sugar cube and pointed to himself. "Gregor," he said.

"Gregor," I repeated. The lieutenant smiled. He took another glass from the shelf and, without bothering to rinse it, filled it with tea. In the meanwhile, I placed the sugar cube between my teeth as I had seen others do and picked my glass up off the floor with both hands. I brought the glass carefully up to my lips, but it grew too hot, and I had to put it down again.

Seeing my problem, the lieutenant handed me a cloth to wrap around the glass. I noticed that he had no trouble holding his glass in one hand.

With the help of a cloth, I got the glass up to my lips, but the sugar cube was in the way. I realized that I had it sticking out too far. In the meantime, the back end of the cube, melting in my mouth, was heavenly. It had been some time since I had had any sweets.

I adjusted the sugar between my teeth and tried again. This time it worked.

Lieutenant Rostov was drinking his the same way. He smiled at me, then pointed to his glass again. "Chai," he said, the Russian for tea.

I put on my most confused look. Pointing to my glass I said the word for hot which he had given me earlier, gariachi.

"Chai," he said again.

"Gariachi," I repeated, innocently. I saw the lieutenant roll his eyes in frustration. It was the first time I had done this to someone intentionally, and I found myself enjoying it. I felt myself smarter than the very serious lieutenant, and I knew the sense of power.

But I also knew it wasn't being nice. "Gariachi chai," I said.

The lieutenant was much relieved. "Gariachi chai," he repeated, then he blew into his glass.

"Gariachi chai," I repeated.

"Haroshi chai," he said rubbing his stomach, using the word for good.

"Haroshi chai," I dutifully repeated.

"Ochin haroshoi," very good, he said.

"Ochin haroshi," I repeated. "Ochin haroshoi chai."

The lieutenant was delighted. He pointed to the brass sconce on the wall, said the word for lamp, and I repeated it.

In similar fashion we covered the ceiling, wall, door, floor, and water. Then another officer came in. He expressed surprise at seeing me, and Lt. Rostov explained that he was taking care of me while the colonel was blah-blahing my mother.

The other officer laughed. Then he unbuttoned his trousers lowered them, and sat down on the toilet.

I was mortified. Before I knew it, I had run out into the hall, and to my utter shame I had begun to cry.

Lt. Rostov came out after me. At first he was laughing, but when he saw me crying, quickly grew serious. I don't know whether it was because of my crying, but soon there were others in the hall. Lt. Rostov was explaining that he was taking care of me for the colonel and making me tea and then the other man had come in to take a blah-blah, and I had started to cry and ran out. And now the colonel was going to have his blah-blah.

This time I had a good idea of what this blah-blah meant. But I also understood that I had just done something very unmanly,

certainly unmilitary. I could hear a combination of voiced concerns mixed with some snickers. Then another woman soldier
was in front of me saying, "Don't be afraid, little boy."

"You didn't see anything she hasn't seen," somebody said,
and there was laughter.

"Take him back to his mother," somebody suggested, and
Lt. Rostov explained that he couldn't because the colonel was
blah-blahing my mother, and there was more laughter.

"Tell the colonel I'm taking him to the blah-blah room," the
woman soldier said, getting to her feet. She took my hand in
hers. It was a hard, callused hand, but she held me gently. We
started down the hall.

"He doesn't speak any Russian," Lt. Rostov said behind us.

"You stay here for when the colonel wants him back," the
woman said. Then she and I turned the corner and went downstairs by a back staircase.

This woman soldier wasn't as ugly as the other one, but
she still wasn't like any of the women I knew. Maybe she was
a little like the peasant women from the farm. Her legs were
thick below her skirt and her skin looked coarse. She wore no
makeup. Her blond hair was wound in braids around her head.
Her eyebrows were so blond that she almost didn't have any.

She took me to an office where another woman soldier sat
behind a desk. "Captain Milenoff dropped his pants in the
bathroom and frightened him," the first one explained. "He
doesn't understand Russian."

Like the first two, this woman soldier was also fatter than
most women I knew. She had very dark hair and puffy cheeks.
"Oh, he's so cute," she said, and I was glad I wasn't supposed
to understand her. "Bring him over here," she said.

Suddenly I felt myself being lifted onto this latest woman's
desk. "Captain Milenoff's blah-blah frightened you, little boy,"
she said. "I should show you what I have."

"Oh, stop that," the first one said. "He's a little boy and
he's frightened."

"I'm not going to hurt him." She smiled at me. "He doesn't understand what I'm saying."

I smiled back, but I hoped she wasn't going to start taking off her clothes.

"Can you imagine what a tiny blah-blah he must have?" she continued. This time I knew exactly what blah-blah meant. She had her hands up, her fingers moving as though anxious to touch me. "The colonel is blah-blahing his mother," the first woman soldier said, and the second one's hands suddenly stopped their twitter.

"What's his name?" the second one said.

"I don't know."

"What . . . is . . . your . . . name?" The second one said to me, speaking slower and louder than before.

I did my blank look, not to tease her this time, but because I hoped it would prevent complications.

The woman pointed to her own large chest. "Mina," she said. Then she pointed to the first woman. "Ania." Finally she put her finger against my chest. I had little choice. "Yulli," I said.

"Yulli," she repeated. "So how big is your blah-blah?"

"Mina!" the first one said.

"He doesn't understand what I'm saying. . . . Do you?"

I almost shook my head.

"Would you like to show your little blah-blah to your Auntie Mina?"

I was sure she was only teasing, in her peculiar way. I knew Ania wasn't going to let her do anything bad to me, but it didn't stop me from wishing this would all end.

"Give him some candy," Ania said.

Mina opened a drawer in the desk on which I was still standing and took out a piece of hard candy wrapped in paper.

I shook my head. "No, thank you," I said in Polish. "No, thank you."

"He doesn't want it," Mina said

"He's afraid of it. See the look on his face? They've been told not to accept candy from us."

Mina raised her thick eyebrows. She unwrapped the candy and put it in her own mouth. "Mmmm," she said, making the appropriate face and massaging her stomach. Then she took a second candy from her desk and held it up for me. In the interest of peace, I put it in my mouth.

"Now let's put you on the floor," she said as though we were about to play a game. She wrapped her arms around my waist and held me tight against her. I could feel my privates pressed against the bulge of her stomach and her fingers reaching for my rear end.

"What are you doing?" Ania demanded.

"I'm just giving him a little hug," Mina said. "He's such a sweet little boy."

Then we heard the door opening, and she set me down quickly. Mother and the colonel were standing in the doorway. The colonel had his boots and his tunic on. "What are you doing?" he demanded.

"We gave the boy some candy, Comrade Colonel," Ania said.

The colonel used a lot of angry words I didn't understand. His voice was wonderfully deep and commanding, quite different from the way he had spoken upstairs. The two women stood stiffly at attention. I understood that they would be reporting to him in the morning.

"Come here, Yulek," Mother said. I walked over to where she was standing and took her hand.

"Did they do anything to you?" the colonel asked me.

"Answer the colonel," Mother said angrily when I didn't answer. "Did they do anything to you?"

"She gave me candy and a hug—that one," I said pointing to Mina.

"What did he say?" the colonel asked.

"He says that one gave him candy and a hug."

The colonel said some other words I didn't understand to the two women. Then he turned to Mother "We're going," he said. "I'll deal with them in the morning."

I thought of how Ania had tried to stop Mina. "She tried to stop her," I said to Mother and waited for her to translate. But she didn't. "Don't keep the colonel waiting," she said. The colonel had already started down the hall. Mother and I followed quickly.

A soldier opened the door of a car standing at the curb in front of the building. The colonel waited while Mother and I got in. I wondered if we were going directly to Lvow. "What is your address, Comrade Barbara?" he asked, getting in beside me. Mother gave our address to the soldier, and we started.

"Tell him that the other woman, the one named Ania tried to stop her from touching me," I urged Mother.

"What does he want?" the colonel asked.

"He's just telling me about some friends of his," Mother said.

"Ask him if he'd like to sit up front with the driver," he said.

"He would love to," Mother answered for me. She was right. Sitting with the driver was like sitting up on the coachman seat with Grandfather's Adam.

With his hands on my waist, the colonel lifted me up. I tucked my legs, and he dropped me on the soft seat next to the driver. Sitting up very straight, I could see over the dashboard; people in the queues in front of stores looked at us as we passed. "I warn you, Comrade Colonel, our apartment is very dirty," Mother was saying in the back seat.

"Oh, my God!" Auntie Edna exclaimed as the three of us walked into our apartment. After Mother had introduced her to the colonel, she said, "Fredek has a fever again. It's his tonsils. They're the size of oranges." Then she excused herself to bring him the tea she had been brewing.

"Edna is an extremely devoted mother," my mother explained. "Her little son is Yulli's age and has bad tonsils."

"In the Soviet Union we cut children's tonsils out."

"We do too. Yulli had his done last year. Edna was waiting with Fredek till next spring."

"Give him aspirin for the fever," the colonel said. The three of us were still standing by the barely warm stove where we had met Auntie Edna. The pallet cover that Miss Bronia must have washed that morning was hanging on a line across the room.

"There is no aspirin," Mother said. "There is almost no firewood. We have tea, but no milk or sugar." Then she gave a little laugh. "Cigarettes, but no matches."

"The children have had no fruit for months. This," she pointed to the wet pallet cover, "is what we sleep on, stuffed with straw. We have one bed for seven people."

Col. Bawatchov walked to the archway into the other room. Auntie Edna looked up from Fredek's bedside. The colonel marched in and laid his fingers against Fredek's neck. "He has high fever," he said. Auntie Edna nodded. "Tell him that I'm afraid he will get another asthma attack," she said. Mother told him.

The colonel walked out of the room and out of our apartment. In a moment he was back. "My driver will bring aspirin," he said. Mother, who, like me, must have wondered whether he was returning, now sat the colonel down at the table and poured tea with the water that continually simmered on the stove. "Will you have tea with us?" she called to Auntie Edna in the other room. Auntie Edna called back that she wouldn't.

Mother poured the tea into glasses for the three of us, then apologized for there being neither sugar nor milk. I watched to see whether the colonel would produce his own lump of sugar from his pocket the way Capt. Vrushin had, but he did not.

Mother told me to get my book quietly from the other room and then to sit at the other end of the table and not to listen. If I had wanted to obey, there would have been no way that I could have concentrated on my book with their conversation going on. Fredek and Sonya could do that, but I couldn't.

"I'm going to show you some things," Mother said to the colonel with great seriousness. Then she went into the other room. I pretended to be very busy with my book. Out of the corner of my eye, I saw the colonel take a sip of his unsweetened tea and put it down again quickly.

In a few minutes Mother was back. In her hands she carried a number of objects, one of which I immediately recognized as my real father's gold pocket watch. She sat down beside the colonel, pulling her chair closer to his. He offered her a cigarette, and they both lit up.

Mother held up the gold watch. "This was Yulli's father's," she said. "I told you that he died when Yulli was just a year old." She snapped the back open, exposing, as I knew, a second cover with medals etched on it. "You see, here it says, 'Exposisions Universelles, Paris 1900, Liege 1905, Bruxelles 1910, Grand Prix.' That means 'Universal Exposition, Paris 1900, Liege 1905, and Brussels 1910, Grand Prize.' Yulli's grandfather bought it in Brussels in 1910. It's a Movado made in Switzerland and it's very expensive and very beautiful."

For a moment I feared that she was going to give him my watch, but she put it down, picked up a photograph, and went on. "This is a photograph of me and Yulli's father in Egypt, in front of the pyramids on our honeymoon. This is a picture of me with my second husband in our living room in Warsaw. You see the furniture? It's Louis Quinze, the same as you have in your office. Our living room was almost as big as your office. Here are my husband and I in Vienna."

"This is your second husband or Yulli's father?" the colonel asked in a very respectful tone. He had put on his glasses and was looking with great interest at the photographs in Mother's hands.

"It's Lolek, my second husband. I was a widow of twenty-one with a baby who needed a father. Friends introduced me to Lolek who seemed kind, and he was rich and fell madly in love with me. My father, you know, was a general. His name was Mikhail, like yours. He was a hero in the Big War. I used to love to look at him in his uniform with his sword." Here Mother was dealing in her sword fantasy again. "When I rode through the streets with my father in his carriage, people would take their hats off to him." My grandfather, of course, had been a sock manufacturer, not a general, and his name wasn't Mikhail, but Moses.

"Do you have a picture of your father in his uniform?" the colonel asked.

"No, I had a beautiful painting of him in my apartment in Warsaw, but the Germans have probably blown it to pieces. It was such a beautiful apartment. We had a cook and two maids and Yulli had a governess."

Mother paused and gestured around the room. "And now look how I live," she said. "Look how we all live, Mikhail Sergeiovitch. And my sister-in-law Edna had an even bigger apartment. We could all die here."

Col. Bawatchov laid one of his large hands on top of Mother's. "Comrade Barbara," he said, "I cannot give you a travel permit. I have sent my driver for aspirin, and I will see about some firewood, and you will not die. But you are a bourgeoisie, and in the Soviet Union we got rid of our bourgeois class. Some we sent for re-education, some we had to shoot. You are an intelligent woman, but you are a bourgeoisie. You are fortunate that I am your friend, but you will have to learn better ways. Yulli is a strong boy who will grow to be a hero of the Red Army some day. Now he will go to school, and I will get you a position teaching French. Some day you may teach at the university. You will be proud of what you do and Yulli will be proud of his mother."

"But, Mikhail Sergeiovitch, we will not survive that long. Look how thin Yulli is. Look at his little arms. Look at his legs. It is cold and damp here."

"I will take care of the cold and damp, Comrade, I told you so. And I have another idea. I will come here every Tuesday afternoon, and you will teach me French. And for that I will pay you with a ham or a chicken or something every time." I could tell by the colonel's voice and the bright expression on his face that he was very pleased with his new idea. I realized that I had never seen an adult who showed his feelings on his face and in his voice as much as the colonel did. "Next Tuesday, of course, we will be going to Lvow, and you can give me my first lesson in the car. And then the following Tuesday I will come here again."

"But my books, Mikhail Sergeiovitch. I don't have any French books."

"I will get you French books. We have grammar books and reading books. We have the great authors from all the world and you can teach me Victor Hugo and Voltaire and Ibsen in their original language."

I already knew that my mother couldn't read or write in French. It had been a disaster when she had tried to give Fredek and me lessons.

Then Miss Bronia came home. "I found cabbage!" she announced before she noticed the colonel at the table.

Mother introduced them quickly. "This is my friend Bronia who also lives here," she said. "She doesn't speak Russian." The colonel stood up to shake hands.

"How is Fredek?" Miss Bronia asked anxiously.

"He has a very high fever," Mother said. "The comrade colonel has sent his driver for aspirin."

Miss Bronia went into the other room to see Fredek.

"Bronia is the only one of us who knows how to cook," Mother said.

"Soon you will learn to cook too," the colonel said. "Even I know how to cook." I had never heard of a man who could cook, and my admiration for Colonel Bawatchov went up another notch.

Auntie Edna came out to report that Fredek was burning up. "Please tell your colonel that he's burning up."

"She says her son is burning up," Mother said in Russian. Then, to Auntie Edna, she said, "He has already sent his driver for aspirin."

Auntie Edna was wringing her hands. "Oh, I hope he comes soon," she said.

"Have her wash down his whole body," the colonel said to Mother. He had stood up again and so had Mother.

"Yes, I understood," Auntie Edna said when Mother started to translate. "Bronia is doing that."

"Tell her to use vodka," the Colonel said.

"Vodka?" Auntie Edna said.

"It evaporates faster and cools more," the Colonel explained.

We had a bottle of vodka that Capt. Boris had brought "Capt. Vrushin brought us some vodka," Mother said to the colonel as Auntie Edna got it from the corner where it was kept on the floor with other supplies. We had used a wooden crate as a cabinet for a while, but had had to break it up for firewood.

Then there was a knock on the door, and it was the colonel's driver. He had brought a few packets of aspirin powder. Mother took them into the other room, then returned.

The Colonel said he had better go back to work. He and Mother made arrangements to pick her up for the trip to Lvow the following Tuesday. He patted me on the head, told Mother she should start teaching me Russian, and then left. Mother went into the other room where Auntie Edna and Miss Bronia were attending to Fredek. I followed partly into the room since I wasn't supposed to be anywhere near Fredek when he was sick.

"He wants me to give him French lessons," Mother was saying. "I told him I was a language teacher in Warsaw. I don't know any French grammar—I don't know Polish grammar. He wants me to teach him Victor Hugo, Voltaire, and Ibsen."

"Ibsen was English," Auntie Edna said.

"Actually, he was Norwegian," Miss Bronia corrected.

"Why don't you tell him that you teach conversational French," Auntie Edna said, "not French grammar or French literature. Tell him that in Poland we have different teachers for that."

"That's a good idea. He also wants me to go to Lvow overnight with him."

"Are you going to go?" Auntie Edna asked.

Mother looked at me. "Yulek, go in the other room," she said.

*   *   *

The following morning, we heard a vehicle pull up in front of our house. "It's an ambulance for Fredek," Sonya said, looking between the café curtains.

"Oh, my God!" Auntie Edna cried. "I don't want them taking him to a Russian hospital!" Fredek's fever was actually down, though his chest was now becoming congested.

But the ambulance wasn't there to pick up Fredek. Two soldiers carried bags of coal across the sidewalk and into our rooms, as passersby stood and watched enviously. Miss Bronia estimated that we had enough coal for the entire winter. Then, early Tuesday morning, the colonel's driver knocked on the door to pick up Mother. She had on one of her nice suits, and she had packed her little suitcase. The driver dropped off a ham, which he said the colonel said was payment for the first French lesson. He carried Mother's little suitcase to the car where the colonel was waiting.

It took some time, but I noticed that our walls were beginning to warm up, and the bags of coal, our great black treasure, stood lined up against the wall.

When Mother came back Wednesday evening, everyone was eager to hear about her trip. Except for Fredek, who had been in bed all day coughing, we all quickly sat down around the table. Auntie Paula, who earlier that day had unraveled a green sweater, was now knitting the yarn into what looked like another sweater. Miss Bronia and Auntie Edna had done some wash that day, and it hung on the lines that crisscrossed the room.

"He was a perfect gentleman," Mother said first, speaking, I presumed, of the colonel and telling me nothing. But I could see that she was very excited.

"Lvow is alive," Mother said. "It's a beautiful city, you know, with wide boulevards, trees, parks. . . . But, listen, there are restaurants that are open and cafes that actually serve coffee, and half of Warsaw is there." She stopped, and I saw her look at Auntie Edna and Auntie Paula, who seemed eager to hear more. "I met the Mitzins, Sasha and Irenka, right in the street. You've never seen Irenka like that. She was wearing a black wool peasant skirt down to her ankles, peasant boots, and a man's fleece-lined jacket tied with an orange scarf. Sasha had found an army coat somewhere, and he had on brown tweed knickerbocker trousers with green socks. But it wasn't just the funny clothes they were wearing—it was the way they laugh at themselves in their crazy clothes. They all dress crazy like that in Lvow because there's no decent clothing left in the stores. But they all laugh at each other and at themselves. They sit in the cafes dressed like for a carnival and they tell stories. They talk about who just arrived from Warsaw with what news. One man, they said, has been to Warsaw and back three times. He knows how to sneak past the Russian and German guards, and he carries messages. He says there is nothing left of Warsaw."

Auntie Edna gave a gasp. "My mother," she said.

"He was talking about the buildings," Mother said. "And, of course, he was exaggerating. It's an expression."

There was a moment's silence. "Did you hear anything about Morris or Artur or Lolek?" Auntie Edna asked anxiously.

"No, I didn't," Mother said. "I did ask, but nobody I talked to had heard anything. They did say, though, that a lot of the men escaped to France where they're forming a Polish army, and, of course, many were taken prisoner. The people I spoke to didn't know any more."

There was another silence, except for the clicking of Auntie Paula's needles.

"But Lvow is alive," Mother said again. "They have movies and there is a night life. Yes, there are shortages of things, but you can also find things if you know the right people. And they laugh at everything. They laugh at what they don't have and at how they make do.

"They laugh at the Russians. When the Russians first came, you know, they bought up all the wristwatches in town. You would see Russian soldiers with watches up their arms. When the stores ran out of real watches, they would buy children's toy watches and wear them too." Mother laughed.

"That must look stupid," Sonya said.

"That's right. The whole town is like a carnival. They tell one story about a soldier who bought a pepper mill and then brought it back the next day because, when he turned the crank, it didn't play. And they also tell about the two officers who both wanted the same Persian rug . . . so they had the storekeeper cut it in half."

"They're so stupid," Sonya said.

"Russia used to be such a cultured country," Auntie Edna said. "Pushkin, Chekhov, Tchaikovsky."

"Yes," Mother said, "and guess who else I saw." She stopped again and looked around, but nobody guessed. "I had a lot of time while Bawatchov was in his meetings, so I went to the autobus station to see what I could find out, and guess who I ran into. Lupicki. Remember Lupicki?"

I remembered him well and fingered the washer inside my pocket.

"Would you like to know what he's doing now?" Mother continued, "he drives . . . an autobus . . . between Durnoval and Lvow." Mother said the last part very slowly and distinctly.

Then she added, "He says he can smuggle us onto his autobus without a travel permit."

"Who is Mr. Lupicki?" Auntie Edna asked.

"The little man we picked up on the road outside Lublin," Auntie Paula told her. With her glasses pushed to the end of her nose, she was counting the stitches on her needle. Her lips moved, but no sound came out.

"Oh, yes, Herman Lupicki," Auntie Edna said. "A disgusting little man with a gun."

"He didn't have a gun," Auntie Paula said. "Fredek only said he had a gun." She added one more stitch, then switched the needles around to start the next row.

"He had a gun."

"All right," Mother said, " he had a gun, he didn't have a gun—it doesn't matter. What matters is that he drives to Lvow every Monday, Wednesday, and Friday, and he says that they check who gets on the autobus in Durnoval, but not who gets off in Lvow. If we wait at a certain crossroads four kilometers out of town, he'll watch for us and pick us up."

"I have to care for Fredek," Auntie Edna said, getting up from the table.

"Edna, this is important," Mother said with annoyance. "You can tend him in a minute."

"I'll go check him," Miss Bronia said.

Auntie Edna ignored them both and walked into the other room.

Mother looked at Auntie Paula.

"Fredek is still congested," Auntie Paula said. "He's still coughing." With her bent wrist she pushed the glasses higher up on her nose.

"But he's better than he was, isn't he? Now that the place is warm," Mother said.

"He's coughing less today," Miss Bronia said.

"Bronia found goat's milk today," Auntie Paula said. "Of course, we had to almost force it down his throat." I didn't know that goats gave milk.

"He'll be able to travel soon," Mother said. "And once Edna sees some of her old friends and doesn't have to stand in queues all day, she'll pull herself together."

"I know someone with a wagon who can take us to the rendezvous point," Miss Bronia said.

"Rendezvous point," Sonya repeated. "How romantic."

"Romantic is right," Auntie Paula said. "How much does your Mr. Lupicki want to be paid for this little service?"

"He didn't mention money. I'm sure that whatever we want to give him . . ."

"And when you and Yulek are standing at the side of the road," Auntie Paula interrupted, "in the snow, four kilometers outside of town, he suddenly mentions money."

Mother gave a sigh. "Paula, why do you always look at the negative side? Look, in Lvow there are also people who will take you over the mountains into Hungary. They are local peasants who know the woods and the mountains like their hand, and they hire out as guides."

Auntie Paula looked at Mother over her glasses. "And you want to go?"

"Yes," Mother said.

"That's insane, Basia."

"What do you mean it's insane?"

"Insane," and Auntie Paula laughed as she said it. "You're going to drag us over the Carpathian Mountains, across an armed border to Hungary? That's pure craziness. If the border guards don't get us, the wolves will."

Miss Bronia had gotten up from the table and begun taking clothes off the lines and folding them. "Hungary doesn't border with Poland," she said.

"It used to be Czechoslovakia before Hitler marched in," Mother explained. "But he gave a piece to Hungary who had a long-standing claim to it."

I knew that if it weren't for Fredek's cough, I would have been sent into the other room. I pretended to be very busy with my book, something about a train full of circus people and animals.

"Why are you laughing?" Mother said to Auntie Paula. "The guides have guns against the wolves, and they know where the guards are. People have done it, you know."

"Who?" Auntie Paula was counting stitches again. I wondered at the way she could speak and keep count at the same time.

"People. I don't know their names."

"Women and children?"

Mother took a pack of cigarettes out of her purse, then stood up and crossed the room to the stove. Lifting the round lid by its handle, she stuck a cigarette tip part way into the hole. In a moment she pulled it out glowing. Mother took a drag and turned to face us again. She spat a flake of tobacco off her tongue.

"All right," she said, "at least there is food in Lvow and civilized people. We could all die here in Durnoval before spring. Bawatchov is our friend now, but he could be transferred any day, he told me. That's the way they work. They're not trusted to stay too long in any one place."

"And what's the punishment for trying to go to Lvow without a travel permit? Do they send you to Siberia, or do they just shoot you?" Auntie Paula had switched needles again and was starting another row.

"They won't know."

"Look, Bawatchov already knows you want to go to Lvow. Now, thanks to you, he'll show up for his French lesson and find us gone. He's not stupid."

"He won't do anything."

"Won't do anything?"

"No."

"Didn't he already tell you that we're bourgeoisie who should consider ourselves lucky we weren't shot like in Russia? You, of course, had to tell him. You had to show him pictures of your apartment and your visit to the pyramids."

"Mikhail isn't like that," Mother said, but her voice was quieter. She didn't sound so sure of herself now. "Under that

Communist propaganda, he's a human being. . . . And I think he loves me."

"Loves you?" Auntie Paula was laughing again. "Barbara, what are you talking about?"

"I think he does," Mother said. Her voice was quieter still.

"Because he told you so?" Auntie Paula was still almost shouting and still laughing.

"I can tell these things."

"Like you could tell with the Village Census Committee on the farm or with that grunting pig Boris with his hands all over you? Who was it that was going to establish a salon for Russian officers?"

"All right. So I was wrong."

"Bawatchov doesn't love you, whatever he may have said."

"It's not that he said anything—I just feel these things."

"You feel these things. He's attracted to you, like every man in Warsaw was. You're 'Beautiful Basia,' and you attract men. But you have absolutely no idea of what goes on inside their heads."

"That's not true."

"Yes, it is. You make up stories about swords and your father the general and you think you're controlling the men somehow, making them do what you want. But it all ends up hitting you in the face. You dream about how you would like things to be, and then you make yourself believe that's the way they're going to turn out. Now you'll go wait for your Mr. Lupicki in the middle of nowhere, and won't you be surprised when he doesn't show up or doesn't stop? Then where will you be?"

"For heaven's sakes!" It was Miss Bronia speaking now. "Two grown women . . . the children!"

Mother and Auntie Paula stopped speaking. Mother took a second cigarette out of the pack and lit it from the first one, which she now dropped into the stove. Then she walked back across the room and sat down next to Auntie Paula. "You're jealous of me," she said. She said it quietly, so that I could barely hear at the other end of the table.

"You've always been jealous of me—my looks, my house, the kind of people who come to my house, my friends. . . . You're jealous that the men don't pay attention to you the way they do to me or to Edna."

"Your friends, Basia?" Auntie Paula answered in the same, quiet voice. "Your friends. Warsaw is wiped out, people are killed, and your friends sit in cafes and laugh at their funny skirts and boots."

"Oh, poor Paula. That's why men never pay attention to you. You have absolutely no sense of humor. You don't understand that these people are laughing because they're alive. They're laughing because even with all their homes and their businesses destroyed, they're still alive."

I didn't like Auntie Paula much, but she did talk more sense than Mother. Laughing when other people were killed and you weren't, was cruel. It was like laughing when somebody fell down and skinned her knee. It was certainly un-Christian.

I tried to visualize Lvow. Mother had said it was like a carnival. I knew about carnivals—Kiki and I had read a whole book about a carnival in America, with pictures. There were tents with stripes on them, but the people weren't dressed funny, except for the performers, and they didn't laugh inappropriately. Mother hadn't mentioned anything about tents.

What Mother's description of the laughing people and Russian soldiers with wristwatches all up their arms did sound like, though, was the pictures Kiki had shown me, in a book of hers, of one of the two Polish cities that God had destroyed and turned the people into pillars of salt because they were wicked.

It was in the days before they wore pants and jackets, and in the pictures men and women, instead of obeying God, were all chasing and grabbing at each other. And some were even laughing at others lying dead on the ground. The women were wearing very red lipstick with heavy rouge on their cheeks and all sorts of makeup around their eyes, sometimes, like those friends of Mother and Lolek's that Kiki and Marta called painted women. I wondered if Lvow was something like that and what God might have in mind for its future.

By the time I was sent to bed, Miss Bronia and Auntie Edna had hung a blanket on a line next to Fredek's bed so that if he coughed during the night, he would not spread his germs over the rest of us. As the next-to-youngest and, supposedly, most vulnerable family member, I was assigned to the corner pallet, diagonally across the room from the sickbed, with Sonya beside me.

"You sleep on your side, facing the wall!" Sonya had commanded me, even though she herself wasn't coming to bed till later. That was fine with me.

When I had settled down and all was quiet in the room, I could hear Fredek's labored breathing. I wondered if it was asthma. Auntie Edna, I presumed, was sitting on the side of his bed, behind the blanket, probably holding his hand. I wondered if Fredek was in danger of dying.

I began to pray for God to spare Fredek, even though he was Jewish. Kiki had told me the trick of praying to Mary and asking Her to talk to God. God was more likely to listen to Her than to me. I realized I was doing something very grownup and very Catholic.

Then, in the middle of my sixth Hail Mary—I kept count on my fingers—it suddenly struck me like a ton. If Mother and I were to go to Lvow and Auntie Paula and Sonya were to stay in Durnoval, then Miss Bronia would certainly stay with them. Suddenly, the bottom had fallen out of my life, and I actually heard myself gasp. I knew that I must not interrupt my communion with the Blessed Mother and bit my lower lip to keep from crying. Apologizing for my gasp, I proceeded to complete the twenty Hail Marys I had declared at the beginning, plus one to replace the interrupted sixth.

Now I was convinced that Lvow was indeed a wicked city, attractive to my mother because of her own vileness. I thought with irony of my naïve intentions to save her immortal soul through conversion. I knew there was nothing I could do to influence events. Mother and I would go, and Miss Bronia, if that was her intention, would stay, no matter what I might do.

On the other hand, I could pray that Mr. Lupicki wouldn't stop for us. There could be a snowstorm so that he couldn't see us standing by the side of the road. Or what if the colonel were to find out? He definitely didn't want her to go. Was there a way I could tell him? Would he believe me?

With those two possibilities, the ache in my heart was mitigated, which was doubly welcome since I was not comfortable with the idea of the Holy Mother seeing that my own distress was more painful to me than Fredek's mortal peril. Thus assuaged, I fell asleep.

In the morning, it took a moment before my grief of last night descended on me again. Then the prospect of parting from Miss Bronia hit me full force again.

On the other hand, Fredek was visibly and audibly much improved. His breathing had returned to normal, and he wanted to sit up, which his mother wouldn't allow.

"It's God's miracle," Auntie Paula said of his dramatic recovery. I knew she was just using an expression, but that was because she wasn't aware of my involvement in the matter. As for me, I was thrilled to see the power that my prayers had had. And then I immediately set about purging my mind of any sense of pride that the Mother of God might perceive.

On the other hand, I had seen proof of Kiki's representation that the Holy Mother was a conduit to God. I wondered how many other people were aware of this device and I knew intuitively that its use had to be limited to issues of appropriate worthiness and decorum.

The idea of applying this protocol to my most urgent issue grew slowly in my mind, like the wick of the lamps we had on the farm that begins with a little glow and grows into a bright, light-spreading flame. Kneeling on my pallet, as though I was cleaning a spot on the wall, I put my problem in Mary's most holy hands, proposing the two solutions I had thought of the night before, namely either Mr. Lupicki missing us in a snowstorm or the colonel discovering Mother's plans. Of the two, I favored the latter since it did not involve making our way back on foot in a snowstorm, but I left it up to the Blessed Mother to present the matter in whatever way She thought most effective. Or it could be up to God Himself to fit it most conveniently into His agenda. On the other hand, if God had a third alternative for thwarting Mother's plans, I was certainly open to it and would be eternally grateful.

While this was undeniably a less selfless request than last night's, I explained, I cited the wickedness prevalent in Lvow and the righteousness of leading us not into temptation. Then I promised forty Hail Marys to be offered that night and another forty upon delivery. I could not help but be aware of the power I now had to influence events.

When, later that same day, I heard Auntie Edna appeal to Mother to overlook her emotionalism and Auntie Paula's nasty words, and to change her mind about putting herself and her little son at risk, I thought that God was already at work on my case. There were tears and hugs and professions of eternal friendship and love, but Mother seemed to remain resolute.

A day or two later, Auntie Paula herself apologized to Mother for saying bad things about her, though they didn't hug or kiss, and this didn't change anything, either. But that same day, Miss Bronia said that she had heard that they were going to institute a system of ration cards so that everyone could buy the food and firewood and clothes that they needed, and living conditions in Durnoval would, surely, become much better. This didn't have any effect on Mother's decision either. It did, however, lead me to speculate that maybe God didn't have any direct or real power over Jews and could only manipulate circumstances to influence them towards a certain course of action. Of course, neither Col. Bawatchov nor Mr. Lupicki were Jewish.

Mother decided that we would leave the following Wednesday. That would be the day after Col. Bawatchov had been here for his French lesson, giving us a full week until he returned and found us gone. Miss Bronia made arrangements with the man with the wagon to drive us to our "rendezvous" point.

Hearing these arrangements was like watching my own scaffold being built. I knew that maintaining faith in God's ability to deliver was an important element of the protocol, and I tried hard to dispel my fears. I had debated repeating my supplications to the Blessed Mother, but decided that that would show a lack of confidence in Her. I did, though, make sure that my regular evening prayers were particularly heartfelt.

On Monday, Fredek was well enough to attend school, and he and Sonya accompanied their mothers the three blocks to the school. The sign, carved in cement, said gimnazium, which meant high school, but, at the moment, it housed all school grades.

All the previous day, Fredek had talked about teaching the other boys to march and shoot guns, while Miss Bronia did her best with needle and thread to allay Sonya's concern that she had nothing to wear. For my part, recalling my previous school year's experience, I was relieved not to be going with them, though I knew this to be only a temporary reprieve.

When Fredek and Sonya came home that afternoon, they brought back books that were all in Russian. They would learn the Russian language, Russian history, and Russian literature, which Sonya had been told in her class was the greatest literature in the world. Their homework was learning some of the Russian alphabet, and Fredek said that he had already memorized half of it. Sonya couldn't understand how the Russians could call themselves part of modern Europe if they didn't even use the same alphabet. Nothing in either of their curricula pertained to anything Polish.

"This is what you want your son to learn?" Mother said to Auntie Edna, pointing to the pictures of Stalin that adorned each of their books.

Auntie Edna didn't answer, but Auntie Paula said, "They'll have plenty for both of you to learn in Siberia."

"I would rather we were both . . ." Mother began, but stopped in mid sentence.

"Yulek, Fredek, come in the other room and help me move Fredek's bed," Miss Bronia said. Though he was now recovered, it had been decided that Fredek would continue sleeping in the bed to prevent his asthma from returning. We didn't move the bed far, only swung it away from the wall a bit, and Miss Bronia could easily have done it without us.

*   *   *

The next day was Tuesday, and Col. Bawatchov would be coming for his second French lesson. I was curious to see how God might deal with this situation—if He, indeed, wanted to honor my preference of solutions. But before his scheduled arrival, Miss Bronia said, "Put your coat on, Yulian. We're going for a walk." From the tone of her voice and her use of my full name, I understood that she meant this to be a kind of goodbye for us. Unaware of my commerce with the Divine, Miss Bronia would, of course, have no idea that heavenly intervention was at work on the situation. I took her hand the moment we were out on the sidewalk.

We came across a queue outside a pork butcher's store, but walked right by it. We continued on to the little park. "Let's sit on this bench for a bit," Miss Bronia said. "If we get cold, we can get up and walk around." I consented to the plan.

"You know, Yulian, tomorrow you and your mother will be setting out on a great, exciting adventure. I'm going to miss you very much, but I'll just be thinking of the excitement you're experiencing, and I'll be happy for you."

It pained me to hear poor Miss Bronia saying these things, when I knew that none of that was going to happen. I wanted to tell her how much more I would have missed her, but she need not worry because the matter was being taken care of. Except that I didn't know whether telling someone about a prayer would automatically cancel it the way it would a wish.

Miss Bronia went on to tell me about how brave my mother was and how much she loved me and how co-operative and supportive and loving I had to be, but I knew she was just trying to prompt me for a trip that wasn't going to take place. Besides which, my mother was a wicked person who wanted to go live in that sinful city and take me away from her, and there was no way that I could love Mother.

Miss Bronia also said something about how she and I would never really be apart as long as we were in each other's thoughts and hearts. This, of course, really made me feel terrible, while I couldn't tell her that there was nothing to worry about.

Of course, when this was over, I could tell Miss Bronia how I had entreated the Holy Mother to speak on Miss Bronia's and my behalf to God, who had arranged things to come out the way they did. And, as a matter of fact, we might see a resolution when we returned right after the colonel's French lesson.

When we did return to the apartment, neither Mother nor the colonel was there, so I didn't know if God was taking that route—unless Col. Bawatchov had arrested Mother. I had been entertaining the fantasy that we would return to find Mother crying because the commissar had learned of her plot and was going, somehow, to prevent her from leaving. This would have enabled me to tell Miss Bronia that we would not be parting after all and to explain how it had all come about.

Neither one of my Aunties seemed to know where Mother had gone, though I didn't dare spill the beans by asking. Actually, nobody seemed surprised by her absence.

Mother came back while I was sleeping, and I awoke to a flurry of packing. The Aunties were helping Mother fit our things into three suitcases, thanking her for the clothes she gave them, and lamenting that most of her things would fit no one except Fredek.

When Miss Bronia's friend pulled up in front of our house with his wagon, we said hasty good-byes on the sidewalk. "Yulek, kiss Auntie Edna and Auntie Paula," Mother said, and, with much experience in that kind of thing, I did. Fredek and I shook hands awkwardly, and I mumbled something unintelligible—even to me—to Sonya.

Miss Bronia hugged me tight, whispering, "Don't forget what I told you," which I acknowledged, though unsure of exactly what she referred to. I felt one of her warm tears on my cheek, and, "Don't worry, it'll be all right," came out of my mouth automatically. I realized that it would be understood as referring to her admonition, rather than the fact that it was beginning to snow.

Miss Bronia's friend with the wagon was a man of indeterminable age with a thick, graying beard. The wagon was similar to the one that had brought us to Durnoval from the farm. There was a bed of straw where our three suitcases bounced gently as we rode over the cobblestone streets. I sat between Mother and Miss Bronia's friend up on the seat, our legs covered by a thick fur blanket. Before we left the house, Miss Bronia had tied her own brown wool scarf over my head and ears.

I was very much aware that in the past I would have objected to the scarf, just as I would have been hoping that Miss Bronia's friend would let me drive the horse. But these were circumstances in which such childish things did not matter. As I watched the snow fall on the rump of the dark brown horse, shaggy in his dull, winter coat, I wondered whether I had actually outgrown such concerns.

The ride must have lasted about an hour, but seemed much, much longer. It didn't take long to get outside town, but then we rode for miles between snow-covered fields. Twice we pulled to the side of the road when we saw army trucks approach. There would have been room for them to pass, but the driver said, "They drive like crazy people." I tried to figure out if the snow was increasing. Where a certain road crossed the Lvow road that we were on, with a post and painted sign identifying the road, our wagon stopped.

"Will you wait with us till the autobus comes?" Mother asked the driver, but he said he had to get back.

"I'll pay you extra," she said, but he shook his head.

"You're going to leave a woman and child out here alone?" she asked. "What if the autobus doesn't come, or it doesn't stop for us?"

This time I was with Mother, but the man shrugged his shoulders.

"Then I won't pay you," Mother said, and I cringed.

The man shrugged his shoulders again and clucked his horse into motion. He turned the wagon around and headed back toward the city. As he passed us, Mother handed him something. Then Mother and I stood at the side of the road with our suitcases watching for a gray autobus with Lvow written on the front.

The wind blew across the white fields, raising clouds of snow that mixed with what fell from the sky. But it didn't yet seem to be enough to make us invisible.

"Stamp your feet to stay warm," Mother said after the wagon had left. I wasn't cold. Mother had on the gray wool dress into which she had sewn all her jewelry over the last few days. The buttons, gems wrapped in layers of cloth, were of irregular size and lumpy. She had a silk scarf over her head. Her mink jacket, too bulky to pack, didn't cover much of her below the waist, and she was probably cold. Her overcoat was in one of the suitcases.

Mother tried to light a cigarette, but the wind wouldn't let her. "Mr. Lupicki will be along any minute," she said.

I watched the snow increasing intensity. It swirled around our feet, and wind was beginning to cut through my clothes. I didn't

relish the walk back with our three suitcases. But I kept in mind
that I'd be walking back to Miss Bronia. I could even picture the
surprise and delight on her face as we walked in the door.

"You remember, Yulian, don't you," Mother was saying
behind me, "that you are my protecting knight. You're a strong,
courageous man, and all you and I have now is each other. We
are partners."

This was talk I had heard before. I remembered thinking at
the time that it meant something important was going to be
different. But it had turned out to be nothing but talk.

"Stop doing that!" Mother was suddenly yelling at me. I
hadn't even been aware that I had hooked my left hand around
the signpost and was going around and around it with my
other arm extended.

"I'm telling you how much we depend on each other now,"
Mother was saying angrily, "and you're playing airplane with
the signpost!"

Now that she had rebuked me that way, I couldn't stop.
Besides, if she and I were, supposedly, partners, I didn't need
to do what she said.

"I said stop playing around that signpost while I'm talking
to you! Do you hear me?"

I heard her, all right. But as her protecting knight, I didn't
have to take orders from anybody.

"Yulian, give me your knife!"

No way was she going to take my knife away from me. I
continued circling the post.

Suddenly, Mother grabbed me from behind by both shoulders. I squirmed to get loose, but she held me tightly. Then she
had one arm diagonally across my chest, and I could feel her
other hand working its way into my pants pocket.

I struggled, but she was stronger than I was. I tried to push
her arm away from my pocket, but couldn't. Then I tried again
to pull away, but couldn't do that either. I swung my arm up
over my head and felt my forearm hit her face.

In a moment she had extracted my knife. She released me, and I saw her slipping it into the pocket of her fur jacket.

"I hate you!" I shouted through my tears. Mother had turned her back. She was rearranging her hair and scarf. "See how much protection you'll get from me without my knife!" I added. But, suddenly, I was aware of a chugging and rattling that I knew in my heart must be the autobus.

I knew that it was the autobus and that Mr. Lupicki would see us and stop for us because, at the last moment, I had blown my whole case—I had told my mother that I hated her. I had broken one of the Ten Commandments that God had given Catholics, the one about honoring your parents under all circumstances. Suddenly, despite the cold, I could feel myself sweating.

Down the road I could now see the gray autobus, like a big whale, enveloped in its own swirl of snowflakes, making its way toward us. Mother stood on tiptoe, waving her red scarf back and forth.

In a moment, the autobus had pulled to a squeaky stop, and what seemed to be a bear leaped down to confront us the moment the folding door opened.

There stood Mr. Lupicki in a fur coat that began just above the ground and ended quite a bit above his head. From within the huge fur collar, the familiar pointed face grinned at us through crooked teeth. A university student's cap, like the one I had always wanted, with its silver braid and shiny bill, was cocked jauntily over one eye. On the front of the cap, Mr. Lupicki had a red enamel star with its hammer and sickle.

"Mrs. Waisbrem," he said, "and Yulian!" I didn't trust the friendliness in his voice anymore.

"And the other ladies?" he asked, and then expressed regret when Mother said they weren't coming. "Life in Lvow is so much better than in Durnoval." From a pocket of the fur coat he produced a silver and gold case and offered a cigarette to Mother. I could see that they were hand-rolled, and Mother politely refused. The paper around hand-rolled cigarettes, I knew, was sealed by the roller's saliva.

Digging through the fur to his pants pocket, Mr. Lupicki next drew out a gold lighter. With his cupped hands he sheltered the flame from the wind and lit his cigarette. "If I had known you would be coming today, I would have brought some chocolates with me," Mr. Lupicki said to me.

"He doesn't deserve chocolates," Mother said. "He's being horrid to me."

Now a second furry creature stepped down from the autobus. A woman, several centimeters taller than Mr. Lupicki, now stood beside him. "This is Vanda," Mr. Lupicki said, "my partner."

Unlike Mr. Lupicki's bulky, floor-length coat, Miss Vanda's looked to me like a stylish lady's mink or something. Under her round fur hat, Miss Vanda looked younger than Mother. Her pale face wore bright red lipstick and heavy splotches of rouge. Her eyes were light blue, and two thick blond braids fell forward over her shoulders.

"This is Mrs. Waisbrem who was kind enough to let me ride in her truck outside of Lublin, and her son, Yulian," Mr. Lupicki explained.

Miss Vanda shook hands eagerly. "You have to sit with me. I have a lap robe," she said. The suggestion of a lap robe in this weather sounded inviting, but the idea of sharing it with this painted lady scared me. Mother, of course, accepted.

"Herman will take care of the suitcases," Miss Vanda went on. Her accent was the same as the farm people's.

As Mother and I settled in the first seat, under the lap robe beside Miss Vanda, with me in the middle, I tried to maintain separation from both my mother and the painted, perfume and cigarette-scented Miss Vanda. Now Miss Vanda had a cigarette case of her own in her hands, a silver and gold one matching her partner's, but smaller, and offered Mother a cigarette. These were manufactured cigarettes, not hand-rolled, and Mother accepted one. Miss Vanda's lighter matched her cigarette case.

The autobus lurched into motion with a loud roar, and Miss Vanda immediately leaned her head over mine and addressed Mother. "Mrs. Waisbrem probably sees that Herman has joined the Communist Party," she said, "but that was only to get the job. He isn't really a Communist. To have an important job like this, a person has to be a party member. But Missus should be assured that neither Herman nor I have any thoughts of revolution. Herman has the best connections among the finest gentry, and we are business people. If Missus wants to sell or buy jewelry or perfume, or if she needs to talk with personages of influence or needs something transported or a message delivered to someone in the German zone, Herman can arrange it. Does Missus have a place to stay?"

Mother said that actually we didn't, but that Mr. Lupicki had told her earlier that he could arrange it.

"And he will. Herman's word is his bond. And for Missus, who has been so kind and generous, he would climb out of his skin. You can stay with us tonight. We have lots of room. Even a bathroom."

Mother said it was very kind of her. I could see on Mother's face how it pleased her to be called kind and generous, even though it wasn't at all true. She had taken both my knife and Miss Bronia away from me so that she could go live with her painted and perfumed friends, sitting in cafes and laughing that other people were killed and they weren't.

I turned around to look at the interior of the autobus behind us. I counted twenty-three other passengers and four empty seats. Empty wooden crates knocked against each other in the last row of seats. Wrapped in big coats or robes of some sort, the people all looked too bulky for the seats.

Miss Vanda was telling Mother about the beautiful suit that Mr. Lupicki wore when they went out in the evening. At the same time, she had taken out her compact, which matched her cigarette case and her lighter, and was applying still more rouge to her cheeks. "This compact," she was saying, "and my cigarette case and lighter, they're a set he gave me for my birthday. Herman has a matching cigarette case too. He got them from some Warsaw Jews for eggs and cheese and things. I thought Jews were supposed to be such sharp businessmen. Herman certainly got the best of that bargain. He used to have his own shoe store in Lublin, you know."

After a while, the autobus stopped and Mr. Lupicki got out. There was nothing there but snow-covered fields. Several of the passengers, men and women, followed him out into the field.

"Do you need to get out, little boy?" Miss Vanda asked me.

I could see no advantage to it. "No, thank you," I said.

"I'll be right back," Miss Vanda said, getting up to join the others.

I watched the people stand around in the snow, as though looking at the horizon, except that you couldn't see it for the falling snow, their feet planted solidly. Then they all climbed back into the autobus, leaving yellow stains in the white snow.

Back in her seat, Miss Vanda opened her compact again and, looking into the mirror, touched up her lipstick. "Do you like the color?" she suddenly asked me. I had to look to make sure she was talking to me. " I have fourteen different lipsticks at home," she went on.

"It's very nice," I said.

"I don't know if I like it or not," she said, her pencilled eyebrows crinkling into a little frown. "But I love the case, don't you?" She handed the blue-enamel case with its spiral of gold to me.

I hated touching her lipstick, but took it and pretended to admire it. "Very nice," I said, handing it back.

"I have a little brother your age, you know," she said. "He's going to be seven next month, and I'm giving him a rocking horse for his birthday."

I knew I should let the matter go, but I could not allow the affront to my honor. "I'm seven-and-a-half," I said. "I'll be eight next month."

The statement had no effect on Miss Vanda. "I gave a pair of good boots for it," she said. "One ear was missing, but Herman made a new one from the end of a belt that was too big for him. He's awfully clever, you know."

Then she leaned across to Mother and raised her voice above the roar and clatter of the autobus. "Like I said, tonight you can stay with us. We have our office in the apartment, so there's lots of room. We have carpets on the floor."

Then I must have fallen asleep because I woke up as the autobus came to another noisy stop. I could see that we weren't in any town yet. There was only a cottage across the road.

Nobody got up this time, except for Miss Vanda, who said she'd be right back and made her way past our feet to the door. I watched her run across the road to the cottage. She wiggled as she ran.

"Do you need to make peepee?" Mother asked.

I shook my head. Actually, I did have to go a little, but I wasn't going to do it at her suggestion.

"Why don't you do it now so you won't have to later," she urged. With the bus quiet now, I was sure people had heard her. I shook my head again.

"Just go over there," she said, pointing to the empty field on the right side of the autobus, "and turn your back. No one will know what you're doing."

That was an outright lie. Of course people would know what I was doing, standing there in the snow. How stupid did she think I was? She was the stupid one to think she was fooling me! Now that I had paid my price for breaking that Commandment, I was free to call her names—to myself, at any rate.

Now I saw a man and a woman come out of the cottage and walk to the rear of the autobus. They opened a door, which immediately sent a cold wind through the autobus, and began unloading the crates from the back seats. Holding a crate in each hand, they walked back to the cottage. In a moment they were out again, this time each holding a crate full of live chickens. After several trips, the back seat was filled with clucking chickens in their wooden crates.

I saw Mother take one look at this procedure at the back of the autobus and then turn to face the front. The other people seemed to take no notice of it at all. When the loading was done, Mr. Lupicki, who had been smoking a cigarette in the driver's seat, stepped down from the autobus and walked around to the back.

In a moment, Miss Vanda came out of the cottage with a covered basket over her arm. She ran back across the road, and I saw her wiggle like before. She seemed, somehow, to run more like a girl than a lady. Maybe that was because I couldn't remember ever having seen a lady run.

Then Miss Vanda was back in her seat beside me, with the basket in her lap.

"We'll be starting in a moment—you'd better go now," Mother said to me. I shook my head. I was sure Miss Vanda had heard her.

Miss Vanda leaned down to me. "Would you like to see some puppies?" she asked.

"Yes," I said eagerly, guessing now that that was what she had in the basket. But Miss Vanda stood up and put the basket down on her seat. She made her way past me and Mother, and then reached back for my hand. I took her hand and followed.

We stepped down from the autobus and, still holding hands, ran across the road. But instead of going into the house, we ran around to the rear. "You can go there," Miss Vanda said. Her voice was low and conspiratorial, even though we were out of anybody's earshot. She was pointing to a privy, like the one we had had on the farm. "When we get back, you can tell your mother you got to hold a puppy."

Well familiar with privies, I used this one gratefully. I found that I was liking Miss Vanda despite her painted face and cigarettes-and-perfume smell. We ran back to the autobus holding hands again.

"Did you like the brown puppy or the black one better?" Miss Vanda asked me aloud when we were back in our seats.

"The brown one," I said. "He has longer ears."

"I liked the black one. He has that white tip on his tail," she said. It was all I could do to keep from laughing out loud at our subterfuge.

Then we were on our way again, the clucking of the chickens drowned in the clatter of the autobus.

"I have some sandwiches here," Miss Vanda said, reaching into her basket. She pulled out a paper-wrapped package and handed it to me. I knew I wasn't supposed to accept anything from her.

"I brought some sandwiches," Mother said.

"These are chicken cutlets," Miss Vanda said. "Missus and the boy will like them."

"It's been months since we've had chicken cutlet," Mother said. "Thank you." I remembered the delicious chicken cutlets Marta used to make.

"Here, let me unwrap it for you, little boy," Miss Vanda said to me. "I had her cut it in four pieces because I didn't know how much you'd eat." For no apparent reason, we both found ourselves laughing as though this, too, were a conspiracy.

"Thank you," I said, as she placed the opened package in my lap. "My name is Yulian."

"Yes, I know," she repeated. "You're the first Yulian I've ever met."

I could think of no appropriate reply to that, so I busied myself with the sandwich, which tasted even better than Marta's. I ate all four pieces. Miss Vanda had also brought pickles, but Mother wouldn't let me have any.

When we had finished eating, Miss Vanda took out her compact and lipstick, and touched up her face. "This is from

Vienna," she said to Mother, indicating her fur coat. "I bought it from a lady who had been to Vienna. The streets, Missus knows, are all water. You go from house to house in a boat." She held her arm towards Mother, across my lap. "Would Missus like to touch it? I love how soft it feels."

Miss Vanda was showing off again. Showing off was a term Kiki and Marta would both use about some of the friends of Mother and Lolek who came to our apartment covered in jewelry and stuff. Mother touched the sleeve that Miss Vanda had proffered and agreed that it was soft, but I could tell that she was just doing it to be polite.

I had begun to like Miss Vanda, particularly after that puppies business. But that, I realized, had just been something to make me like her. The rouge on her cheeks and her talk about all the things she owned, gave away her true character.

I wondered if God really intended to destroy Lvow, as He had those other cities. I wondered if I would be spared, since I didn't laugh at people for being dead or show off, or did cursing my mother this morning doom me as well? Would there be someone in Lvow who could christen me so that I could go to heaven? I should have gotten Miss Bronia to christen me. I should have told her that I was almost a Catholic and that all I needed was to be christened by another Catholic. But I hadn't done anything about it, and now I was riding an autobus into Lvow, which had a good chance of being destroyed, and I wouldn't get to Heaven.

Mother had mentioned escaping from Poland over the mountains. Auntie Paula had mentioned wolves and border guards shooting at us, but that was a risk worth taking to avoid God's wrath. Based on what Kiki had told me of those other cities, our odds were better with the wolves and border guards. If I could only find a Catholic who I could talk into christening me.

Miss Vanda was probably Catholic. But I would, first, have to tell her that I was Jewish, and she didn't sound as though she liked Jews. Of course, once I was christened, I wouldn't be Jewish any more. Miss Vanda was certainly a possibility, and I should maintain a cordial relationship with her. On the other hand, maybe christening by someone like Miss Vanda wouldn't really count. I wondered if there was a technique for finding out what God had in mind. I wondered if the Blessed Virgin could be helpful in that as well.

It was dark when we finally drove into Lvow, and it was like driving back into the past. The streets were wide and well lit, like in Warsaw, and there were people on the sidewalks who didn't look in a hurry to get off the street.

Mr. Lupicki stopped the autobus in front of a house, and Miss Vanda said that this was where we would be getting off. She and Mr. Lupicki unloaded the crates of chickens, along with our suitcases and some other boxes. Then Mr. Lupicki drove the other passengers on to the autobus terminal. Mother and I helped Miss Vanda carry the boxes and chickens into the house.

Miss Vanda's apartment, like ours in Durnoval, was on the ground floor. As we walked along the stone hallway, I could hear a wild barking from the other side of a door, and I dearly hoped the door would turn out to be Miss Vanda's.

"That's Burek," Miss Vanda said. "He guards our apartment."

In a moment we were in the presence of a large German Shepherd, leaping joyfully to lick Miss Vanda's face. "He's very young," she explained between licks, bending down to make his job easier, "but he's a very good guard dog."

I waited, hoping that I might in turn receive a similar greeting. I had never been licked by a dog before. But it was Mother to whom he next turned his attention, sniffing at her legs.

Suddenly I noticed how stiffly Mother was standing. "M . . . Miss Vanda," she murmured through compressed lips, "could Miss please put him in another room."

"He won't hurt Missus. He knows Missus came with me," Miss Vanda said.

"I don't want him near me!" Mother cried suddenly.

Miss Vanda quickly took Burek by the collar and led him inside. I heard an interior door close and the barking begin again, as I watched Mother holding her tense pose—afraid of a friendly dog—even after the dog was gone.

"I'm sorry," she said when Miss Vanda returned, "I'm sure he's very friendly, but I just don't like dogs."

Unlike our Durnoval apartment, this one had several more rooms, radiators, and, as Miss Vanda had said, a bathroom and carpets on the floor. On the living room carpet we discovered what I recognized as a large dog mess. "He gets very upset when we're both away overnight," Miss Vanda said, using a newspaper to clean up.

One door of the bathroom opened onto the hall, the other into her bedroom. Miss Vanda proudly pointed out the richly embroidered canopy over the bed she and Mr. Lupicki slept in, as well as over the bed that comprised the total furnishings of the "guest room" that Mother and I would share. They had come, she said, from the house of a Count. The crates with the chickens went into a smaller room, filled with boxes and crates of various descriptions and a very bad smell.

Mr. Lupicki had introduced Miss Vanda as his "partner," which I had understood to be a business relationship. The idea of business partners sleeping in the same bed was an idea that had never occurred to me before.

What impressed Mother the most was the bathtub in the bathroom. It had a gas hot water heater over it, just like the one in Warsaw, and Mother quickly asked if we could bathe in it. Miss Vanda said that of course we could, but first we might want something to eat—she had some stew in the frigider.

A frigider turned out to be a yellow metal icebox, but without ice, because it kept food cold electrically. I had never seen such a thing, though Mother had. It hummed and had a light inside that Miss Vanda said shut off by itself when you closed the door. I found this hard to believe and watched carefully each time she opened and closed it, but as far as I could tell, she was fibbing. Apparently, the frigider had also belonged to a Count. Whether it was the same count as the one who had slept in the canopy bed or a different one, I couldn't tell, but she was probably fibbing there too.

Mr. Lupicki wasn't home for supper, and Miss Vanda said that he'd be quite late. After we had eaten, Mother gave me my bath, for which Miss Vanda, fortunately, gave us privacy after leaving a stack of towels that she said came from a hotel that had closed. I have to admit that after the sink baths of the farm and the sponge baths of Durnoval, sitting in the warm and soapy water was a pleasure I had never appreciated before. When I was out of the tub and the water had begun to drain, we could see a ring of dirt around the white enamel tub. Mother burst out laughing, and I could not help joining in. Even before the water was all out, Mother was wiping down the tub so that she could refill it.

"A snowman!" Miss Vanda said laughing, when she saw me in the hall, wrapped in the thick white towel, and struggling to keep it from unwinding. "Here, this will make it stay around you," and she handed me a patent leather belt. "But we've got to get your hair drier than that, or you'll catch cold!" she sang out. "Come with me." I followed her into her bedroom. The carpet felt luxurious against my bare feet. Miss Vanda produced another towel from a cupboard and, draping it over my head, began to rub. As she rubbed, she sang a song about an old woman who had a rooster which she put into a boot and then asked how he was doing in that boot. It didn't make any more sense than a lot of songs, but it made me laugh.

"Now let's comb it before it sets that way for the rest of your life," she said after removing the towel. In the mirror over her dressing table, I could see my hair sticking out in all directions and found the idea of it's setting that way for the rest of my life, hilarious. Miss Vanda took a comb from the dressing table and proceeded to comb my hair.

"Hmmm," Miss Vanda said, when she had combed it down on both sides, "that's pretty long, isn't it."

I had to agree that it was. Not given to looking into mirrors over the past months, I had not been aware, until now, of how un-masculine my appearance had actually become.

"Would you like me to trim it a little? I cut my little brother's hair—the one that's a year younger than you."

I nodded my head enthusiastically, delighted at being asked permission. Actually, Miss Vanda was a little nice in some ways.

"Sit here," she said, indicating an upholstered stool in front of her dressing table. "An actress in the theater sat at this makeup table in her dressing room," she said. "Now there are several ways we could to this," she said changing to a tone that I knew was mock serious. "We could part it here," and she parted my still-damp hair in the middle and combed it down both sides. I laughed at the girlish face in the mirror.

"Or we could part it on the side here and . . ." In a few strokes she moved the part to one side, presenting another silly image in the actress's mirror. I wondered what interesting faces that mirror had seen. "Of course, we could always comb it forward like this," and again she had me laughing as I peered at what looked like the back of my head. "What do you think?"

"I think I'd like the part here, please," I answered sheepishly, indicating where my part had always been. I was well aware of how prosaic my response had been in terms of the game we were playing. Miss Vanda complied without comment. I hoped her silence didn't indicate disappointment.

Now she had a long pair of scissors in her hand and had begun cutting. As I followed a snippet of hair to the floor with my eyes, I realized that someone else had had his or her hair cut there recently. Or, maybe, not so recently—a closer look revealed clumps of dust distributed liberally over the carpet.

When she had finished, I could tell that Miss Vanda hadn't done as good a job as my mother's hairdresser used to do on me in Warsaw. But what I was seeing in the mirror was, at the least, a boy again. "I hope your mother doesn't get angry at us," Miss Vanda said conspiratorially, biting her lower lip and shrugging her shoulders.

"I don't care!" I burst out in what I hoped was the appropriate spirit and relieved to still be in her favor. Miss Vanda rewarded me with a laugh.

"Want a chocolate?" she suddenly asked. I nodded my head eagerly. I decided that the restriction on accepting food from strangers could no longer reasonably apply to Miss Vanda, and I followed her down the hall.

When Mother came out of the bathroom, a long time later, wrapped in a towel and quite red from her long soak, she found Miss Vanda and me in the kitchen drinking tea—tea with both sugar and milk. An open box of chocolates, half empty, lay on the table between us. "Ah, Miss cut his hair. Thank you," she said.

"I'd be glad to trim Missus's hair, if she would like," Miss Vanda said.

"Thank Miss very much, but I'm much too tired and too relaxed to sit still that long," Mother said. "Maybe tomorrow, if Miss has the time." Then she told me to say goodnight to Miss Vanda and go to bed.

This was going to be women-talk from now on, I knew, and I might as well go to bed—though there had been no reason to tell me to say goodnight to Miss Vanda.

On the other hand, it did give me a certain opportunity. I slid down from my chair, stood as straight as I could, with my bare heels together, and gave the little bow with my head that Kiki had taught me. "Good night, Miss Vanda," I enunciated. Then, turning my shoulders slightly toward Mother, I repeated the bow. "Goodnight, Mother," I said, adlibbing a military about-face at the end. My bare feet, sticking to the floor, presented an unexpected obstacle and almost an accident.

"Bravo, Yulian!" I heard Miss Vanda exclaim and clap her hands as I marched triumphantly out of the kitchen. Elated, I continued marching down the hall, even though I knew Miss Vanda could no longer see me, the tune of the First Brigade marching song ringing in my head. At the door to the guest room, I halted and executed a left-face before reaching for the door knob.

Under the maroon bedspread, embroidered and fringed to match the canopy, there were no sheets or blankets on the bed. But that didn't matter because the bare, musty-smelling mattress was far more comfortable than my hay-stuffed pallet. I had exchanged the bath towel for my nightshirt, and I was quite warm under the surprisingly heavy bedspread.

Then, as I relived the high points of the evening, I became aware that the painted woman had gotten me to like her. She had gotten me to like her by cutting my hair, by joking with me, and by giving me chocolates. She had made me forget that she was like the painted women in Kiki's picture, and she had made me forget that I might never see Miss Bronia again.

And now the full force of Miss Bronia's passing from my life along with Kiki, hit me, and I again felt the agony that I had known those Sundays in Warsaw. I cried uncontrollably under the bedspread.

I was asleep by the time Mother came to bed, and, the next morning she was up when I woke up. The only sign that she had been there was the scent of bath salts added to the musty smell of the bed. It had been some time since I had smelled bath salts.

Through the door Mother had left open, I could also smell butter frying and visualized eggs for breakfast. Dressing quickly, I hurried to the kitchen where Mother, Miss Vanda, and Mr. Lupicki all sat around the kitchen table smoking cigarettes. Mother and Miss Vanda were in bathrobes. Through a closed door, I could hear Burek pleading to be let in.

"Ah, Yulian, good morning. How do you like your eggs?" Miss Vanda sang out.

"Say good morning," Mother said.

"Good morning, Miss Vanda. Good morning, Mother. Good morning, Mr. Lupicki," I said with all the formality I could muster. I did not want to be charmed by Miss Vanda again.

"Yulian had an excellent governess in Warsaw," Mother said.

"You've grown since I saw you before," Mr. Lupicki said to me across the table.

In my fantasy, I walked up to him and pretended to pull my washer out of his ear, but I didn't have the nerve. "Thank you," I said quickly, heading Mother off. I hoped I would get the chance to show Mr. Lupicki how good I was getting at that trick. "Scrambled please, Miss Vanda," I said.

Mother was looking at something Mr. Lupicki was writing on a piece of paper. "Her husband," he was saying, "was president of the bank, but when the Russians came, he kind of went crazy. She has to keep him locked in the bedroom, and rents out several of the other rooms."

"Missus should tell her that I sent Missus," Miss Vanda said. "She doesn't like Herman very much, but she knows she has to deal with me for supplies. She'll make room for Missus, if she can." Miss Vanda was standing by the stove with an egg in her hand. Mother nodded her head.

Then Mr. Lupicki had to leave for the bus terminal to drive back to Durnoval. Mother, I learned, was going out to find us lodgings, and I would be staying with Miss Vanda—and Burek.

"Are you afraid of Burek?" Miss Vanda asked me after Mother had gone out.

"No," I said emphatically, shaking my head. And in a moment, I was immersed in a wet frenzy of doggie affection. As my hands and face mixed with the fuzzy paws, the soft ears, and the wet nose and tongue, I felt more loved than I could remember ever having felt before.

"He likes you to roll the ball, and he'll bring it back," Miss Vanda said. And as I fed his endless desire for having the wet, rubber ball rolled down the hall and under furniture and for having his ears scratched, which made him immediately roll on his back, I spent the morning as close to heaven as I had ever been.

While Burek and I rolled, hugging and licking, over the floor, Miss Vanda entertained a parade of visitors. Some carried baskets, some came with packages, some left with packages. Out of one corner of my eye, I watched for other painted women, but only one fit the description, and she wore no more makeup than Mother's friends in Warsaw. Even Miss Vanda, who was now in a pink flowered dress, had no makeup on today, other than her lipstick. I wondered if yesterday had been a mistake of some sort. I couldn't imagine what mistake that might have been, but in the possibility, I saw a ray of hope.

Chapter Seven

Mrs. Potkanskova, the woman with the husband locked up in the bedroom, who had a room for us in her apartment, wasn't a painted woman either. She had gray hair pulled back into a bun and glasses with one lens dark, like in sunglasses, and one regular glass. She had a funny way of looking at you, a little sideways.

Our room was the third door on the right when you came in. It was a pretty big room with one wall lined with books and a large, carved-wood desk pushed into one corner. Mrs. Potkanskova spread a white tablecloth over the desk when we arrived, and Mother told me that I shouldn't ever touch it—a statement meant, I thought, as much for Mrs. Potkanskova's benefit as mine. Mrs. Potkanskova, in turn, promised to have the maid bring a table for "the boy" to draw on. There was also an armoire for our clothes, four chairs, and, thankfully, two separate beds, against two walls.

The bathroom was two more doors down the hall, and Mrs. Potkanskova told Mother that "the boy" should be admonished not to loiter, since numerous others, including a professor, had to use it. In the room next to ours, our landlady said, there was a young couple from Lodz with a baby. The baby cried sometimes and you could hear it in the hall, but the walls were thick and we wouldn't hear it in our room. I looked forward to seeing the baby. Then, for some reason, Mother told Mrs. Potkanskova that she must have been very beautiful when she was young, which made the landlady blush. The kitchen, where Mother could cook our meals or make arrangements for the maid to do it, was at the end of the corridor. I wondered behind which door the crazy husband lurked.

Later that day, I did see my second painted woman. She had thin yellow-white hair, a flowered hat that only partially covered a bald spot on top of her head, and skin that hung down well below her thin face. For eyebrows, she had only black, painted lines plus blue eyelids and heavily rouged lips and cheeks against a very white skin. She sat at a table, in a café that we went to, with a younger woman, dressed in a man's brown suit with gray hair cut almost as short as a man's. Neither of them seemed to deserve being turned into pillars of salt.

We did, however, run into a couple that Mother knew from Warsaw, whom she had apparently met here on her previous visit. Mrs. Gnimar wore a long woolen skirt with men's work boots and a man's jacket, fitting Mother's earlier description. She had black hair that I could tell was gathered somehow on top of her head under her cap and billowed out all around. But she had no makeup that I could see, besides some rather ordinary lipstick.

The man, who turned out to be her husband, was thin, mostly bald, and sat very straight in a sheepskin jacket far too large for him. Two other men and a woman sat at their table.

"Basienka!" Mrs. Gnimar cried out, using the diminutive of the diminutive of Mother's name. "And that's Yulek?" The surprise in her tone was one with which I was familiar. It would usually be followed by, He's grown so big!

"He's grown so big!" Mrs. Gnimar said.

"I'll have to start introducing him as my brother," Mother said, at which everyone laughed. Then she explained where we were now living and that we had come alone from Durnoval.

"Yes, Edna is like that," Mrs. Gnimar said, "and Paula, of course, wouldn't move without her."

Mr. Gnimar got two chairs, and I drank tea with milk, but there was no sugar. The grownups talked and did a lot of laughing, though, as far as I could tell, not about anyone being dead.

*   *   *

The following morning, Mrs. Potkanskova's maid Bogda brought us breakfast on a tray. Mother had a soft-boiled egg, but I, Mother said, could not have eggs again because I had had them the day before and would get a rash. I had toast and cheese instead. For my tea, I had a lump of sugar, but there was no milk.

Then, just before lunchtime, Bogda brought a tray with sandwiches, a pot of tea, and three plates and three cups. The extra plate suggested a visitor, and I found myself intrigued by who our lunch guest might be. Having brought no reading or drawing materials from Durnoval, I had spent most of the morning reading book titles off the many volumes that I wasn't to touch on our book-lined wall, under instructions not to leave the room or let anyone in. Mother had spent a good part of her morning in the bath.

"We're going to have a guest for lunch," Mother finally volunteered. Her name was Mlle. de Kessenholtz, and she would be taking care of me for the near future. I was to address her as Mademoiselle. I, of course, knew what this meant in French. Mademoiselle would tutor me in reading, writing, arithmetic, and French, as well as introduce me to some boys of my age whom she knew.

The last item was the most disturbing. While reading, writing, arithmetic, and French were chores to which I didn't look forward, the last boys of my age that I had been introduced to were my classmates back in Warsaw. And that had been an experience I did not care to go through again.

Mademoiselle was of noble French blood, Mother went on to explain, and not just a simple governess like Kiki and Miss

Bronia, but, until very recently, the long-time companion of a Countess Valoska. The elderly Countess's constitution had proven too delicate for the demands of wartime, and she had died from overexposure to the autumn sun in her open carriage on the congested road leading out of Warsaw. A devoted companion, Mademoiselle apparently had not fully recovered from her loss, and I must be on my best behavior.

I now knew a great deal about Mlle de Kessenholtz, but had not the slightest idea what to expect, other than a French accent . . . attached to a German-sounding name. This, regarding the woman who would be successor to Kiki and Miss Bronia, to say nothing of the enigmatic Miss Vanda.

It was only after Mother had checked her wristwatch several times, that there was a knock on our door. Opening the door at Mother's instruction, I felt myself brushed by the folds of a black veil as a very tall lady rushed into our room with, "Oh, Madame, I am so sorry to be late. They have closed off one of the streets, and I had to go several streets out of the way to get here."

I had, of course, been right about the French accent, though it was fainter than I had imagined. To my relief, Mademoiselle spoke Polish almost like a native.

Much taller than Mother, she was also very thin, dressed in a gray coat topped by the kind of black hat and veil that women in mourning wore. I remembered that the Countess she had worked for had died at the beginning of the war.

Removing her coat, she showed a gray wool suit and, turning the veil up over her hat, revealed a narrow, olive-shaped face with a large and thin, somewhat hooked, nose. Her eyes were gray and distorted by the thick lenses of her glasses. The hair, pulled tightly back, was dark, streaked with gray, and she wore no makeup at all. Mademoiselle was not at all pretty.

"It is all so terrible, Madame," she was saying, somewhat breathless from her trip. "These Bolsheviks think they can do anything they want. Yesterday they forced my landlady to take in four Russian women, when we're already three and four to a room. Madame can't imagine."

"This is Yulian," Mother said, changing the subject.

"Yes," Mademoiselle said, turning to me. "Yulian. Is that with an a or an e? My brother is Yulian with an e, the French way, Julien."

"With an a, Mademoiselle," I said.

"Blah, blah, blah?" she asked, and I realized she was addressing me in French. Then she added, "Blah, blah?" in response to my blank stare. "Blah, blah, blah, blah?"

"Answer Mademoiselle," Mother said to me.

"I don't know what she asked me," I said.

"But of course you do, darling," Mother said, smiling. "She is speaking French to you. You spent a whole year at the École."

"Blah, blah, blah, blah," she said to Mademoiselle. This, I was sure, meant either that I was very shy or very stubborn. Then, to me, she said, "Blah, blah, blah, blah?"

I shook my head.

"You mean you didn't learn any French in school?" Mother asked incredulously.

"I learned bonjour and crayon and Padovich dans le coin." The last of these was "Padovich, into the corner," and I saw Mademoiselle laugh behind her hand.

Mother didn't consider it funny. "That's all you learned?"

I smiled weakly.

"That's all?"

I nodded.

"So why did we send you?"

I did know other words, like for notebook and paper, blackboard, boy, and girl, but I enjoyed Mother's frustration. I shrugged my shoulders.

"That's all right," Mademoiselle said, bending a little towards me. "We will speak French this afternoon." Mademoiselle had a funny way of bending. She didn't bend just at the waist, but sort of all over, like a banana.

"Blah, blah, blah, blah, blah," Mother said, shaking her head sadly. Mademoiselle clucked sympathetically.

The two of them spoke French through lunch, and then Mother went out, leaving me with instructions to do everything Mademoiselle told me.

"Alors," she said, once she had removed her black hat and we had put the lunch dishes out into the hall, "we will start from the beginning—Chaise," and she put her hand on the back of one of the chairs. "Repeat after me, chaise."

I repeated. We went on to table, book, shelf, window, floor, and numerous other objects around the room. Then she tested me, walking around the room to suddenly lay her hand on an object, which I would name in French. "Tres bien," she said, which I recognized as meaning very good. In the space of half an hour, my French vocabulary more than doubled.

"Now we will write them," Mademoiselle said. "Go get your notebook."

I explained that I didn't have one. Nor did I have a pencil or pen and ink.

This created a definite problem. She asked if I had any books in French or Polish, and I explained that we hadn't brought any from Durnoval. And the books on the bookshelves, I told her, we were forbidden to touch.

"Alors," Mademoiselle said again, "Madame, voici votre parapluie."

"Madame, voici votre parapluie," I repeated, recognizing all the words except the last.

"Missus, here is your umbrella," Mademoiselle translated. Then she added, "La voiture de Monsieur vous attend devant la porte. The gentleman's automobile is waiting for you in front of the door." This I repeated as well.

"L'opera commence dans une demi heure. The opera begins in half an hour," she continued.

In similar manner, we eventually found ourselves settled in the front row of the Paris opera house waiting for the curtain to go up on something called *The Barber of Seville*, the story of which she was eager to tell me because it was funny. But before she would do that, Mademoiselle felt it necessary to test me on what I had learned to date. It turned out, however, that the automobile, the umbrella, the tickets, the ticket-taker, the carpet, and virtually all of the verbs had failed to take root in my mind.

Mademoiselle's disappointment was unmistakable. "Ah, your mind is tired, poor boy," she finally said. She put her hands together and brought them up to her face in thought. "What shall we do to divert you?"

I shrugged.

"Do you have cards?" she finally asked.

Yes, we did have the cards my mother did her solitaire with. They were well worn. Then, did I know how to play gin rummy? In the next few hours, I learned to play gin rummy.

I had watched my grandmother play gin rummy with Lolek, and I had seen Mother and Lolek play bridge with other couples, and I had always admired the dexterity with which these card players shuffled the cards. But, except for Mr. Lupicki's card tricks, I had never seen cards move as quickly or with as much flourish as they did through the hands of Mademoiselle. Her long, thin fingers seemed magnetic, as they led the nimble cards through their acrobatics.

"Do you miss Warsaw?" Mademoiselle asked, when I no longer needed her guidance to play my hand.

The question was either silly or totally beyond my experience. "Yes," I said, sensing that to be the desired response. I recalled the card players in our Warsaw apartment not looking up from their cards as they mumbled around cigarettes hanging between their lips.

"I miss it very much," Mademoiselle said. "You had a nanny whom you loved very much, your mother told me."

"She was my governess," I corrected her.

"And you had a beautiful apartment and all your little friends."

I acknowledged this to be so, wondering where it was all heading.

"We had a beautiful home too—that is, Mme. la Contesse, whose companion I was, and I. Madame had wonderful, charming friends. And now they're all gone—the house is gone, the friends are gone, and even the poor Countess is gone."

Mademoiselle sniffed, but I detected it to be a sob. I speculated that she had played gin rummy a lot with the Countess and now it made her sad. I wondered if I should show her a trick with my washer, which had cheered up poor Mrs. Rokief when her husband had been detained. But something told me that Mademoiselle would not be so easily cheered up.

"I miss Kiki very much," I finally said. "That was what I called my governess. Her real name was Miss Yanka, but I called her Kiki from when I can remember." It was true, I did miss Kiki, but I said it mostly because I sensed that somehow it would make Mademoiselle feel better.

"You poor boy." Now Mademoiselle had a lace-edged handkerchief up to her eyes. And then I needed a handkerchief as well, though I wasn't sure whether it was over my loss or Mademoiselle's.

We had both recovered our composure by the time Mother returned late in the afternoon and were able to delight her with my recitation of French names for the numerous objects around us. Mademoiselle seemed to take great pleasure in flowing around the room, an expression of mystery on her face, touching objects with quick movements, and I would try to name them as quickly as I could. When I hesitated, Mademoiselle, with her back to Mother, would mouth the words for me.

I saw the gratitude with which Mademoiselle accepted the money that Mother gave her, and I was aware of a tender feeling for the woman that was somehow different from any that I had had for Miss Bronia or Miss Vanda or Kiki, or for anyone. I had the sense that Mademoiselle and I had shared something very special that afternoon. Mademoiselle was not loving like Miss Bronia, fun like Miss Vanda, or engraved in my psyche as Kiki was. But there was a strange quality to the relationship I now had with this adult woman with graying hair, who clearly was not accustomed to relating to children and with whom I had spent only one afternoon. It was a quality I could not name, though I could feel and almost taste it.

*   *   *

"Bonjour, Madame, bonjour, Julien," Mademoiselle said when she came to our room the next morning. She was wearing her black veil again.

"Bonjour, Mademoiselle," I answered. Mother, who was fixing her hair in the little makeup mirror in the lid of her bag, said, "I have to hurry. I'm meeting with your friend, Mr. Botchek." Then she explained that she had arranged for Bogda to bring us lunch at noon, and would Mademoiselle please take me for a walk this morning—making sure that I was warmly dressed.

Out on the sidewalk, I automatically reached for Mademoiselle's gloved hand. I felt it quickly withdraw, when we first touched, then stop and softly grip mine. Through my glove, I could feel a hole in hers. We walked without speaking.

Lvow had a boulevard as wide as the avenues in Warsaw. People were shoveling last night's snow from in front of shops.

"Nous marchons sur le boulevard," Mademoiselle said, breaking the silence. "We are walking on the boulevard."

I automatically repeated the French. Mademoiselle repeated the French sentence again, and I repeated it one more time.

"Nous marchons sur le trotoir. We are walking on the sidewalk."

"Nous marchons sur le trottoir. Nous marchons sur le trot-toir. Nous marchons sur le boulevard. Nous marchons sur le boulevard," I said without further prompting.

"Très bien, Julien."

I knew that this meant very well, and I could tell by her tone that Mademoiselle was pleased. "Nous marchons sous les arbres. We are walking underneath trees," she said.

I repeated this too, along with the previous sentences, delighting Mademoiselle further.

In a similar manner, I learned about walking under clouds, over the snow, and past stores and houses. "Won't we sur-prise your mother when she returns!" Mademoiselle said. For her sake, I practiced silently after she had declared that I had learned as much as I could at one time.

We didn't say anything to each other for awhile after that. I didn't know what to talk about with Mademoiselle, and sus-pected that, unlike the other women in my life, she had the same feeling.

"Oh, do you see that house?" Mademoiselle surprised me after a bit. She didn't point, but said, "That one with the little Doric columns."

I saw a house with pillars holding up a little triangular roof over the doorway. "That's something like Madame's house in Warsaw, except that it had three stories." This one had only two.

I had little interest in the dead Countess's house, which didn't exist any more either, but I felt that it was important to Mademoiselle that I act as if I did. "It must have been very nice," I said.

"The carriage house was in back. Mme. la Contesse had matched chestnuts." The chestnuts I understood to be horses, and would have liked to hear more about them, but knew that I should let Mademoiselle say what she wanted to.

"The Countess did have an automobile as well, but she didn't like riding in it—she said it smelled bad. Although she must have meant on the outside, because it smelled perfectly nice inside, and it was very comfortable. When they came and took it for the army, she was glad to get rid of it. We went everywhere in the carriage. I think she thought it was more elegant."

I could picture this Countess seated in an open carriage with Mademoiselle beside her. She had on a long old-fashioned dress and a large plumed hat. I remembered seeing someone like that riding a carriage in the park. Her dress had been a lavender color with lots of lace, her hair was all white, and there had, in fact, been a younger woman riding with her. Two little dogs sat on the bench across from her.

"Did she have any dogs?" I asked.

"Pardon?" Mademoiselle said. I realized her mind was elsewhere and regretted interrupting.

"I just asked if she had any dogs, the Countess."

"Ah, yes, Madame loved dogs. Whenever we ate dinner, her two little Pekinese would eat from their little bowls in the corner."

"I think I once saw you and the Countess riding in the park," I said.

"Oh yes, that may be." Suddenly Mademoiselle was paying full attention to our conversation. "Yes, that may very well be. Did you walk in the park with your governess?"

"Yes, her name was Kiki."

"And did you love your Kiki very much?"

Ordinarily, that question would have embarrassed me, but somehow, to Mademoiselle, I didn't mind saying, "I guess so."

"And I loved Madame very much. She was like a second mother to me. She died in my arms, you know, on the way here from Warsaw. It was in that same carriage. A heart attack from the heat and trying to run into woods whenever the Stukas came."

I wanted to ask about the dogs and the horses, but knew I shouldn't. I knew that Mademoiselle wanted to tell me more about the Countess.

"There were people all around, but no one to help—no doctors or sisters. All I could do was hold her while she fought to breathe. We were stopped with the road jammed with stopped and overturned wagons and cars. People on foot could move, but we couldn't. They kept walking past the carriage, looking in, and walking on. Then there was like a rattle. There really is a death rattle, you know. And then Madame stopped breathing."

Then Mademoiselle didn't say anything more, and we walked on in silence. I knew I shouldn't say anything, and I was proud of my understanding. I was also well aware that Mademoiselle shouldn't really be telling me all this and that, if Mother found out, Mademoiselle would be in trouble. Maybe she would even be fired, and I didn't want that to happen—not for my sake, because I liked her, and not for her sake, because I knew she was poor.

We were on our way home by now, and I could tell by the changes in the pressure of Mademoiselle's hand that a series of emotional memories must be passing through her mind. Suddenly, Mademoiselle realized that we had walked past our house, and we had a little laugh about that.

"You're a very good friend, Julien," Mademoiselle said as we walked back to the house, and I knew that this meant something more than just a good boy.

As we entered the hall of our apartment, I saw a woman step out of the bathroom carrying a baby. Seeing me stop, when we were about to pass each other, the woman stopped too. "Her name is Nadia," she said, lowering the baby so that I could see her. "You can touch her."

I touched my finger to her little, curly hand and watched her make sucking motions with her mouth. I had never touched a baby before, or even seen one up close.

Our lunch was already on the table when we got to our room. "Oops," Mademoiselle said, laughing, "I think we were out too long. I don't have my watch any more."

"I know where you can get . . ." I began, thinking of Miss Vanda, but stopped, realizing that Mademoiselle had probably had to sell hers.

"Apres le dejeuner, nous allons jouer aux cartes. After lunch we will play cards," she said with an enthusiasm that seemed a little unnatural. I repeated the sentence twice and, as a bonus, added, "Nous marchons sur le boulevard."

"Bravo Julien!" Mademoiselle enthused. That was the same thing Miss Vanda had said two days before, and it felt just as good. The French language, I realized, had real possibilities. I could have recited more, though I couldn't remember the funny word for sidewalk, but something told me that this could also be overdone.

We played gin rummy in silence at first, and I won the first two hands. I had expected more French sentences, but Mademoiselle's mind seemed to be somewhere else, and her hands, which had manipulated the cards with such mastery the day before, now seemed to be shaking.

"If a Russian soldier tries to speak to you," she finally said, "you should just tell him that you don't speak Russian."

"All right," I said, not understanding where this had come from or where it was heading.

"But don't talk to them under any circumstances. Do you understand?"

I said that I did.

"If they try to give you candy or anything, don't accept it."

I didn't want to tell her that I already knew about that and accepted the advice courteously.

"Oh, what they're doing!" she said.

I understood that she meant the Russians.

"I don't know if I should be telling you these things, but I guess you'll know soon enough."

Now I waited anxiously to hear what I wasn't supposed to know.

"They came and arrested poor Mr. Stepkin now, you know. I don't know if your mother knows him." Mademoiselle paused again, and I didn't know whether I was expected to answer her implied question. But she continued. "He didn't do anything except that he was another lawyer."

"Another lawyer?" I said, wondering if Mother had told her about Mr. Rokief.

"Last week it was Mr. Kaftonovich."

"We knew a lawyer in Durnoval who they arrested too," I said. "Mother went to ask about him, but they said he had never been arrested, though the first time we went, they said that he was. Mother says that they either sent him to Siberia or killed him."

From the expression on Mademoiselle's face, I wasn't sure she had really heard me. She was rearranging her cards, and her hands were definitely shaking now.

"Yes," she finally said, "lawyers, judges, army officers, men in government. . . . Oh, do you mind terribly if I smoke? Mrs. Zabalchik, my landlady, says I shouldn't smoke around you, but I do need a cigarette. Do you mind just one—half of one?"

I said that I didn't mind, and Mademoiselle took a pack of lumpy, hand-rolled cigarettes from her purse. "I've even learned to roll my own cigarettes," she said, with an embarrassed smile. "I never thought. . . ." Then I could see the pleasure spread over her face as she inhaled the first puff.

I waited as Mademoiselle filled her lungs three more times. Then she carefully snuffed the cigarette and laid it down on the table, apparently for future use. I remembered Capt. Vrushin and his lump of sugar.

"Alors, where were we?" she finally said, picking up her cards. "Oh, gin! Gin!" and she laid out her hand.

As I shuffled the cards, I formulated my next question. "Why are they arresting lawyers, judges, and army officers?" I asked, when we had begun our next hand.

"We really shouldn't be talking about this," Mademoiselle said, as she arranged her cards with steadier fingers. Anxious to hear more, I had no idea what cards I held.

"Why not?" I asked. It had taken some courage to ask this. It was a question that I was not accustomed to asking.

Mademoiselle let out a loud sigh. "The Russians are really much better than the Germans," she said.

I waited, hoping she would talk about the Germans now. "I hate the Germans," I finally said to fill the silence.

"The Russians haven't bombed us and they don't shoot or club people on the street," she said.

"Shoot or club people on the street?" I said in surprise.

"Mr. Katolski just came from Warsaw, and he says the soldiers will walk down the street, and if they don't like the way you look, they'll just arrest you or shoot you or club you with their rifles. Right there on the sidewalk. Then they'll order people in the street to take the body away."

Mademoiselle was beginning to cry again. She was fumbling for her handkerchief in her purse with her free hand. "Oh, my," she said. "Why am I telling you all this?"

I shrugged.

"I shouldn't be telling you all this and upsetting you, should I?"

"Yes, you should." I knew that I should be more upset about Germans killing people on the streets of Warsaw, the way Mademoiselle was, but it didn't seem real to me. And it was interesting stuff. Mademoiselle's being upset the way she was, was far more disturbing to me. I had a great yearning to make her feel better.

"You're very sweet," she said through her handkerchief. This time I had no idea what she was talking about.

"So tell me how you and your mother got here from Warsaw," Mademoiselle said, evidently wanting to change the subject. I told her about Lolek's truck painted green and Mr. Dembovski wearing an army coat and hat. And about the planes strafing us and the woman whose forearm had been shot off.

Mademoiselle gasped at that part. Then I told her about the man I had seen have a heart attack on the road, and she brought her hand up to her mouth. "Just like Madame," she said.

"Except that he was walking," I pointed out.

"Yes," she agreed. "But what horrors you've seen."

"Yes," I said, for want of a better answer.

"And you don't have nightmares."

"Yes, I do. Except I don't know what they are. Sometimes I wake up crying, but I don't know what I dreamt." It was funny, but telling Mademoiselle that I had been crying didn't embarrass me.

"You can't remember them because they're so horrible. Let me tell you now about The Barber of Seville. It's very funny." Then, Mademoiselle proceeded to tell me a story I couldn't possibly follow about some barber and his friend who kept disguising himself as other people in order to marry some lady. When Mademoiselle laughed, I laughed too.

*   *   *

When Mother came home that evening, I treated her to walking on the boulevard and under clouds and trees.

"Oh, he is so smart, Madame," Mademoiselle said. Mother smiled, but I could tell her mind was on something else too. She seemed to want Mademoiselle to leave quickly.

"Oh, not so much, Madame," Mademoiselle said when Mother paid her, but Mother insisted and almost pushed her out the door.

"Have you said anything to Mademoiselle about being Jewish?" she asked, when Mademoiselle's footsteps had died away.

That was something that I certainly couldn't be accused of, and my body language must have said so.

"You are not to tell anyone that we're Jewish—do you understand?"

I nodded my head.

"Do you understand?" Mother repeated.

"Yes," I said.

"We are Catholic—do you understand that?"

"Yes," I said. I well understood why Jews weren't liked by a lot of people.

"The Germans are killing Jews in Warsaw. Soon the Russians will start. No one is to know we're Jewish. We're not Jewish. We're Catholic, and we've always been Catholic. Here, you have to wear this." And Mother took from her purse a tangle of chain, beads, and crucifixes.

Laying them on the table, she began to separate two rosaries and a silver chain with a medallion of Mary and Jesus. "You must wear this all the time," Mother said, holding the chain by its two ends.

In a daze, I walked over and let her fasten it around my neck. For years I had lusted after such medallions in jewelry stores and on the breasts of the blessed. Now I had one of my own. Only then did I notice a little gold cross, suspended below Mother's throat.

"And this you must carry in your pocket," she said, handing me a white rosary. Then she suddenly changed her mind and handed me the brown one. "Now you must teach me how to use it. I know Miss Yanka taught you."

I knew that Mother had actually learned the words to the Our Father and the Hail Mary that evening on the farm with Father Chernievich, but I made her repeat them after me anyway and then recite them by herself for me. I had to prompt her in a few places.

"That's very good," I finally told her. Then I showed her how to cross herself.

"What's the Holy Ghost?" she asked.

"He's one of the three people of God," I said.

"God has three people?"

"God is three people. The Father, Son, and Holy Ghost."

"God is three people?" There was a note of skepticism in her voice.

I didn't like Mother questioning Catholic doctrine. Jews had no right to do that, particularly when you considered the horrible thing they had done to Jesus. "God is God," I said with annoyance. "He can be anything He wants to be."

"Of course, I don't know as much about this as you do," Mother now said, "so please explain it to me."

That was better.

"Jesus Christ is supposed to be . . . I mean is the son of God, right?" she said.

"Yes," I said, not impressed by her recitation of the obvious.

"But He also is God, is that right?"

"Yes."

"And this Holy Ghost is also God."

"Yes."

"And Mary, the Mother of God, is She God too?"

"Yes, that's the Holy Trinity."

"The four of Them?"

"Yes."

"I see," Mother said. "Miss Yanka taught you all this?"

"Yes."

"Well, thank you for teaching it to me so well."

Well, that was a lot better. I wondered if this meant we would get christened too. "Do you know about heaven?" I asked.

"Yes," she said. But the Polish word for heaven and the word for sky are the same, so I realized that my question had gained me nothing.

"I mean, do you know about the place where God lives?" I asked it cautiously because I realized this was probably a whole new concept for her.

"You tell me about it," Mother said.

Oh, my Lord, what an opportunity this was! "Well," and I remembered now the word paradise, which would finally distinguish heaven from sky. "Paradise is where God and the angels and the saints and the twelve apostles live and where good Catholics go after they die. It's way up in the sky, above the blue, and only good things happen to you there. You can do anything you want, eat anything you want, wear anything you want, and, I think, have anything you want. Wouldn't you like to go there some day?"

"It sounds like a wonderful place. Is your father in Paradise?"

"No. He wasn't Catholic."

"But he was an extremely good man. Doesn't that count?"

"No. You absolutely have to be christened in order to go to paradise. And you also have to believe in the Holy Trinity and be truly sorry for all your sins just before you die."

"And if you don't do all those things, do you go to Hell?"

She had raised a specter now that I tried not to think about—the hot flames, ugly, bad-smelling devils, and unspeakable torture for all eternity that awaited those of us who didn't gain access to paradise. I had no idea Mother even knew about Hell. "Yes," I said.

"And your father, he is in Hell?"

I had asked Kiki that very same question, and she had assured me he wasn't. "No," I said, fearing the question that was to come.

It came. "So where is he?"

"Kiki doesn't know," I said. "That's what's called The Great Mystery. There is a place where good Jews and good Negroes and good Chinamen go after they die, but nobody knows where it is." Here I may have spoken too hastily. Kiki had never actually said that that was what The Great Mystery was. But it did make sense, so probably it was.

"Maybe it's over the rainbow," Mother suggested.

That had never occurred to me. And now I wondered if it had ever occurred to anyone before. Kiki and I had once tried to reach the rainbow, but discovered that it just kept moving further away. But maybe somebody's soul, flying invisibly through the air at who-knows-what speed, could catch it. My mother may have just stumbled on the solution to The Great Mystery. Of course, we would never know for sure until we died.

Suddenly I was seeing Mother in a whole new light. But I was wrong to be so surprised. If I was capable of thinking about and understanding all these grownup things at my age, it made perfect sense that my mother would be extra smart too. Mother thanked me again for teaching her all these things and began to lay out her solitaire. I fingered the new rosary that now occupied the place in my pocket vacated by my pocket knife and felt very good about everything.

*   *   *

The following day, Mademoiselle and I followed the same program as the day before—a walk in the morning, gin rummy in the afternoon, and more French. I learned to buy bananas in French. Neither Mademoiselle nor I had tasted a banana since the beginning of the war, and we agreed to do something about it. So we bought and sold bananas in French. We counted bananas, boxed them, shipped them, peeled them, and fried them. We even resoled my shoes with banana skins. We did similar things with pineapples, oranges, and grapefruit, even though I didn't like grapefruit. I also learned to go to the ball by limousine and invite a young lady to dance with me because she was the most beautiful young lady at the ball. I even learned to play gin rummy in French.

As before, Mademoiselle seemed most impressed with my ability to repeat accurately and to memorize. However, when the statement about the opera starting in half an hour popped into my head from two days before and I pronounced it, she expressed great surprise at my knowing it. Not wanting to imply that she had forgotten teaching it to me, I avoided answering by doing my best to assume a conspiratorial smile. This may have been a mistake, since it immediately resulted in feelings of guilt.

I also learned more about the countess's Warsaw home and life style. I really wasn't much interested in either of these things, but Mademoiselle was, clearly, very anxious to tell me.

Occasionally, I would lightly scratch my chest just below the opening of my collar so that my new medallion would flip out for Mademoiselle to notice. On the other hand, I did not want her asking if it was new. I need not have worried. Mademoiselle gave no sign of noticing it at all.

Before Mademoiselle's arrival that morning, Mother had sat me down to explain that what she herself was doing all this time, was arranging to sell some jewelry and looking for an apartment of our own. She had shown me that she had consolidated all of her jewelry into cloth-covered buttons down the front and the lining of the same blue dress she had worn every day since our arrival in Lvow.

This last, of course, was to be our secret, and I was to tell no one about it.

While I could see precious little opportunity for betraying these confidences, I was also aware that there was probably more to the story than what I had been told. Part of this must have come from Mother's talk with the Aunties about escape, and part simply from the knowledge that whatever I was told generally represented only the already visible tip of the iceberg.

My suspicion was confirmed that very evening. It began when Mother sat me down once more on my bed and explained that we would soon be receiving a visitor. And, contrary to my training, I was not to walk up to him and give a firm handshake, but stay on that very bed and say nothing. Nor was I to listen to the ensuing conversation. But first I was to help Mother to move our table and two chairs to the farthest location from my bed and be ready to jump onto my bed at the first knock on the door. I was also to tell no one about any of this evening's activity because we were partners and this was our secret.

Having moved the table and chairs, I was free to roam the room until I heard the knock, so I stood in the middle of the floor with my hands on my hips wondering how to spend my momentary freedom. Then the knock came, and I leaped for my assigned position.

In a moment, a burly man in a fleece-lined peasant jacket and knee-high boots stood in our room, looking around as though searching for something. Apparently not finding it, he whipped off his cap and mumbled something to Mother. I could make out the now-familiar peasant accent.

"My husband went into the army," Mother said, offering her hand, "and we don't know if he's alive."

Ignoring Mother's hand, the man began inching back toward the door.

"Just sit down and talk with me for a minute. I'll make some tea," Mother said. She had put her hand lightly on his elbow and was urging him towards the table.

The man continued to move towards the door. "No women, no children!" he said, his voice rising in both volume and pitch.

"I am strong like a man," Mother said, her quiet voice contrasting with his. "I was athletic champion in Lodz."

This was news to me, but then grandfather's military career had been too.

"I will pay you extra."

The man was shaking his head. Snow, mountains, border guards, were words that I heard him speak. Finally he gained the door, and in an instant he was gone.

Mother turned to look at me. The expression on her face was of total disappointment and surprise. I had never seen such surprise or such disappointment on her face before. "Ignore what he said," she said in a voice that was totally flat. "He is a crazy peasant. Why is he talking about snow and mountains? Don't pay any attention to him. Don't tell Mademoiselle about any of this."

I said that I wouldn't.

Mother sat down on her own bed. "Come sit next to me," she said.

For the first time in my life, I found that I wanted to sit next to her. I crossed to her bed and sat down beside her. Mother put her arm around my waist and pulled me closer. I didn't resist. I wondered if she was crying. I noticed that one of the cloth-covered buttons on her dress had been replaced by a large black wooden one.

"All right!" she suddenly said. "We will not be sad. We will have some tea and we will be gay." Then she got up, straightened the skirt of her dress, and went to the kitchen.

A few minutes later, she was back with a tray. A man's cane hung from her arm. The tea was sweetened, but there was no milk, she said. The cookie was for me. I wondered about the cane.

Mother leaned the cane against the table as we sat down to tea. "We will not be sad," Mother said again. "Sad people don't win. We will find somebody else. Don't worry."

Then she stood up and picked up the cane. Turning her feet outward, she suddenly began to walk a strange duck-walk up and down the room. She poked the cane left and right in exaggerated movements. She was funny, and I laughed.

Mother laughed too. "Who am I?" she asked.

I had no idea.

"Come on," she said, laughing, and resumed her duck-walk. "Who am I?"

"A duck?" I guessed without conviction.

"Come on—the cane," she said, twirling it around. "And I'm wearing a derby hat," though she really wasn't.

I shrugged my shoulders.

"I'm Charlie Chaplin!" she announced.

"Oh."

"Don't you recognize Charlie Chaplin?"

"Who's Charlie Chaplin?"

"You know, Charlie Chaplin, the funny American movie comic."

I shrugged my shoulders again.

"You don't know who Charlie Chaplin is?"

I shook my head.

"Oh my God! Every child knows who Charlie Chaplin is."

I shrugged my shoulders another time.

"You don't know who Charlie Chaplin is," Mother said still again. But she didn't sound angry as she had the other day about my not learning any French in school, though she was definitely disappointed. "Do you know about Shirley Temple?" Her voice was sad now, as though she were afraid of my negative answer.

I had heard the name and hoped my saying so would cheer her up.

"Have you seen her? Do you know who she is?"

I searched my memory for the ladies who had come to our Warsaw apartment. She may even have been an Auntie. "Is she the one who brought me chocolates?" I guessed wildly.

Mother came over to where I was sitting and put her arm around my shoulders. I saw that now she was crying. I felt terrible for having made her cry. "Was she at my birthday party?" I speculated desperately.

*   *   *

When Mademoiselle came the next morning, she and Mother had a quiet talk in French before Mother went out. On our walk later that morning, Mademoiselle said that she had been told that I didn't know who Charlie Chaplin and Shirley Temple were. She then proceeded to tell me about the baggy-trousered

English comedian and the American child actress, who was about the same age as I was. She also went on to tell me about a magnificent French actress, whom Mademoiselle had once seen on stage, but who was now dead, named Sarah Bernhardt, and a great Polish opera singer named Yan Kiepura, whom she had seen as well, and who was still alive. She also told me about an opera in which a beautiful girl who makes cigars and a man who fights with cows fall in love and everyone dies.

Mother surprised us after lunch by coming home early and taking Mademoiselle and me to a café where, she said, they had cheesecake that day. They didn't advertise it, she said with a little laugh, but if they knew you, and you asked for it, they had it. The café was dimly lit, and the glass display case by the front entrance was empty, except for a small white teddy bear. I supposed that it must have been placed there temporarily by the son or daughter of the café owner, since cafes did not, in my experience, sell teddy bears.

Then I thought I heard my mother ask, "Yulek, would you like that teddy bear?"

I could not have heard right. Such happiness could not be happening to me.

"Oh, Julien," Mademoiselle was saying excitedly, "what a beautiful teddy bear. Wouldn't you like to have it?"

The best I could do was to nod my head, and in a moment the bear was in the crook of my arm, looking up at me through his brown button eyes, the way baby Nadia had looked at me in the hall.

He was about ten inches tall, made of white plush, with arms and legs that turned around wire joints in the shoulders and hips. I did not have to ponder a name, but immediately christened him Meesh, the equivalent of naming an English-speaking bear Teddy.

Seated on my lap, Meesh shared the cheesecake with me, though I would not take the risk of staining him with tea. Teddy bears, I explained to Mother and Mademoiselle, did not like tea.

I had had a bear in Warsaw, a large brown creature, almost as big as I was, who sat among my other toys in the corner by Kiki's bed. I cannot remember his having a name or my ever playing with him. I don't think I would have known how. And dolls, of course, were out of the question. But Meesh was my soulmate the moment my outstretched hands had touched the soft plush of his little body.

I worried about taking him outside without a coat or mittens, but Mademoiselle explained to me that bears not only had fur, but extra layers of fat to insulate them from the cold. While I did not disbelieve her, I did have difficulty internalizing the idea that his little body was not uncomfortable in the December cold. Had I been permitted to unbutton my coat, I would have wrapped him inside along with me, but I had to settle for covering him as well as I could with my arm.

That evening I taught Meesh the Our Father and the Hail Mary. Though he had no knees, by folding his legs back at the hips he could simulate a kneeling position, and I could hold his hands together for him. Unfortunately, there was no way that he could cross himself. Then he slept in my arms, and I remember waking several times, or maybe just dreaming that I did, concerned lest he be crushed by my large presence.

The next morning he accompanied Mademoiselle and me on our walk and we learned to buy sleeping car tickets in French. Mademoiselle waited patiently while Meesh and I both repeated the French, Meesh in a squeaky baby-talk voice that Kiki would not have permitted me to use. On two or three occasions I even had to alert Mademoiselle to the fact that we were ready to go on, since her mind seemed to have wandered in the interim.

For some reason there was no French at all over lunch, as Mademoiselle alternated bites of her bread and cheese with drags on her cigarette and I expounded on table manners to Meesh. It wasn't till she interrupted my explanation of gin rummy with a suggestion that Meesh be put down for a nap, that I realized from her tone that Mademoiselle was annoyed over something.

I promptly complied with her suggestion and turned my attention fully to cards. But instead of resuming the easy conversation of previous days, Mademoiselle surprised me with a most uncomfortable silence as well as the most thorough trouncing I had experience in any card game. Of the two, the silence was the more distressing.

It was after playing three or four hands in virtual silence, and an atmosphere increasingly thicker in smoke, that I decided it was time for Meesh to rejoin us. As Mademoiselle shuffled the cards, I got down from my chair and proceeded toward my bed.

"Where are you going?" Mademoiselle asked.

"Meesh woke up," I explained.

"Sit down."

Mademoiselle's command surprised me, and I resumed my seat.

Mademoiselle laid the deck of cards down on the table with a very deliberate motion. "Julien, you have to realize," she began, "that we are occupied by Communists here in Lvow, while Fascists are occupying the other half of Poland. People are being arrested and people are being killed. Some of us, who are cultured and accustomed to the finer things in life, have suddenly been reduced to living like peasants. You don't know if your own father is alive in a prison camp or dead on a battlefield. This is no time for you be pretending that dolls are alive and talking to them as though they were people." Having said that, Mademoiselle proceeded to light another lumpy cigarette.

I found Mademoiselle's calling Meesh a doll offensive, but could clearly see how upset she was and determined it best for Meesh to extend his nap. When Mademoiselle picked the cards up again, I realized that her hands were as unsteady as they had been a few days before.

"Would Mademoiselle tell me about another one of those funny operas?" I asked, though I had found nothing funny about the cigar girl and the cow fighter.

"Most operas aren't funny," she said. "There is nothing funny about *Carmen*."

This confirmed my own opinion of the piece. Under the impression that all opera was supposed to be funny, I had been harboring a definite doubt as to my own judgement. What was most important, however, was that Mademoiselle was, quite visibly, settling down from being upset. "Most opera is tragic, the way that most life is tragic," Mademoiselle was saying. I realized, it would be best if Meesh maintained a low profile around Mademoiselle.

"As your mother has most certainly learned by now, because everyone knows," Mademoiselle was saying, "last night they arrested more people, some of whom I am sure, she knew."

When Mother came home that evening, she and Mademoiselle again talked in French. I caught words like street and door and chair, and by the gravity of their tone I guessed that they were talking about the arrests of the previous night. But when Mademoiselle finally left, Mother's mood quickly changed as she surprised me with a piece of red cloth which, she explained, was to become a coat for Meesh.

I watched in disbelief as Mother folded the cloth in half and then proceeded to cut it into a shape that, frankly, resembled a dress more than a coat. The finished garment, sewn together with brown thread and fastened by a white button, made my poor Meesh look something like a misshapen red mushroom. But the very idea of my mother's initiative and effort in our behalf, got to my heart and Meesh's as nothing I could remember. I had the desire to wrap my arms around Mother's neck, but I didn't know if she would like it.

Christmas came and went, as did my birthday, three weeks later. I was eight, an age I had waited for decades to achieve, but, somehow, it meant little now. Just before Christmas, Mother gave Mademoiselle some money for us to buy a tree, tabletop size, which we decorated with colored paper cutouts that Mademoiselle proved very clever at making. I understood that there would be no presents, except that Mother gave Mademoiselle a pair of wool gloves, which, Mother explained, weren't a Christmas present. They were used but serviceable, and Mademoiselle was so pleased that her knees bent almost into a curtsey.

I told the Christmas story to Meesh after we had trimmed the tree. Meesh had developed the habit of taking long naps while Mademoiselle was there. Mademoiselle told both of us about Christmas at the Countess's house.

On Christmas Eve, Mother really surprised me by knowing some of the words to some Christmas songs. She didn't know many of the words, but joined Mademoiselle and me when she could. Mother had insisted that Mademoiselle dine with us that evening, and even Mrs. Potkanskova, our landlady, with her one blackened eyeglass, came in with a bottle of vodka and some glasses on a tray and stayed to hear Mademoiselle sing a song in French. I hoped she had remembered to lock her crazy husband's door firmly behind her.

Then it was right on my birthday, January thirteenth, as I turned eight, that Bogda was late and breathless bringing our supper. "Oh, Missus," she said, "I am so sorry for being late with your supper, but I was looking all over for Dr. Kratynovich, and nobody can find him."

When Mother asked why the doctor's services were needed, Bogda told us that baby Nadia was very sick. Besides which, her parents, who already owed Mrs. Potkanskova a lot of rent, didn't have money for doctors or medicine or anything. I immediately reached for Meesh and cradled him in my arms, as Mother asked if that was the reason for all the footsteps we were hearing in the hall. Bogda said that, yes, Mrs. Potkanskova had a thermometer and now was applying wet compresses to the baby's forehead.

"Eat your supper and don't come out," Mother said to me, indicating the plate of cabbage borsch with a boiled potato in the middle. Then she stood up and left the room, followed by Bogda.

It must have been in her excitement that Bogda left the door open. I could hear whispering in the hall, though I could not make out the words. I put a spoonful of the borsch into my mouth, but I could just visualize Fredek in my situation running to the open door the moment that Mother and Bogda were out of the room. It took both my curiosity and a sense that there was something manifestly wrong in my docilely continuing to obey my confining instructions in this instant, to make me follow Fredek's example. In three quiet leaps I was at the door.

Several people stood in a cloud of cigarette smoke in the hall, speaking in whispers, still too quietly for me to understand. One man I recognized from an encounter outside the bathroom. The others, I assumed to be fellow tenants as well. Mother was not among them, and they, I presumed, didn't know about her orders, so I felt safe standing in plain sight in the doorway.

Then, suddenly, Mother came out of the sick room, followed still by Bogda, and catching me full in my guilt. I pressed tightly against the door jamb, holding my breath, but Mother brushed right past me into the room. "I want you to stay with Yulek till I get back," she was saying to Bogda. Then she sat down on the chair and proceeded to pull on her boots.

"You do everything Bogda says," she said to me. She didn't look at me, and I couldn't tell if that was from anger or preoccupation. "I'll be back as soon as I can." Then she was putting on her coat as she marched out the door.

"Missus is going out to find another doctor," Bogda said when Mother had left, but she was looking past me out into the hall.

"Are they Catholic?" I asked her. I had seen Bogda's little gold cross, so I presumed she would understand my concern.

To my surprise, she turned to me with a look of scorn. "Mrs. Potkanskova wouldn't have any Jews living here," she said. Instinctively, my hand went up to scratch my chest, flipping the medallion outside my collar.

"Has she been christened yet?" I asked.

Bogda's eyes opened wide. "Father!" she said. "Somebody has to get Father." With that, Bogda rushed out into the hall and disappeared in the direction of the kitchen.

Left by ourselves, I explained to Meesh that baby Nadia, who lived next door with her parents, was very sick and might die. Mother, I told him, had gone to find a doctor, and Bogda was fetching a priest in the event that Nadia hadn't yet been christened. Christening would get her into heaven, and he and I would be christened as well, as soon as the opportunity arose. Meesh cried about poor Nadia, though he had never actually seen her, and I made him feel better by explaining that it was wartime and a lot of people were being killed. Then I finished my soup, even though it was almost cold, because I was hungry.

In a bit, I could hear the presence of additional people in the hall and even Bogda's voice, but nobody came into our room. With the hall noises of no more interest to me, I closed the door quietly and decided to put Meesh to bed. Having tucked him under my blanket, I took off my shoes and lay down beside him to tell him a story.

As I told him about Hanzel and Gretel, however, I couldn't help remembering the way my mother had pulled on her boots and her coat when the others were just milling around in the hall, and gone out to find a doctor for Nadia. "Missus is going out to find another doctor," Bogda had said, clearly not so much to inform me as in awe. I could visualize Mother walking down the streets of this strange city, looking for doctor signs.

Then I realized that I had been asleep, and people were whispering in our room. Someone had spread a blanket over me.

I had learned the trick of opening my eyes just a slit and looking through my lashes, pretending to be asleep, but my head was facing the wrong way. I gave a sleepy sigh while I turned my head and made a show of resettling my shoulders, as I had watched Fredek do, before lifting my eyelids for a glimpse. Now I saw that Mother was standing right beside my bed.

"A healthy looking boy," I heard a man's voice whisper in Russian.

"His legs are like sticks," Mother whispered back. "Look at his little arm, Doctor." Out of the corner of my eye, I could see a piece of blue army trousers. "In Warsaw we would give him tonic and oil," Mother went on.

"He's doing fine," the doctor reassured her. "His breathing is strong." I was imitating the slow, deep breathing I had heard Kiki do in her sleep.

"Can you give him some kind of tonic?" Mother insisted. Then, in a less urgent tone, she added, "You were so good with the baby. You have such gentle hands for an army doctor."

"At the university, I trained to be a blah-blah."

"Oh, what is that?"

"That's a doctor for the lungs."

Then, a third voice intruded. "We have to go, Dr. Bielsky," a man, whom I couldn't see, said.

"Yes, just a minute," the doctor said. He and Mother stepped away from my bed, and I could see them better now. The doctor was a young man with blond hair, and he was buttoning his tunic while looking at something to his left.

"That's my makeup bag," Mother said. "Would you like to have it?"

"I could carry my instruments in it. But no, it's too valuable. It's too beautiful."

"Well, there is no makeup to buy any more, and your instruments are much more important. It's brown, so it's perfect for a man." I saw Mother open the little leather case and take out the few items she had in it. She handed it to him. The doctor's hands stopped in mid-air, as though he was reluctant to touch the soft leather. Now I could see the other man standing by the door. He was in civilian dress, his black overcoat unbuttoned, a gray fedora on his head. His hands were in his coat pockets.

"Please take it, Comrade Doctor. You saved the baby's life, and we are very grateful," Mother said.

"I hope I saved her life. I will have to see her again."

Mother pressed the case into his hands. "It's from Vienna," she said. "And I have other suitcases to sell in case some of your fellow officers are interested."

"Thank you very much, Comrade." I saw that he was already playing with the brass spring latch.

Then I heard the other man speak from where he stood beside the door. "How many suitcases do you have, Comrade?" he asked.

"Three, Comrade. Would you like to see them?"

"No, but I am curious why you would want to sell them."

"I need the money, Comrade," Mother said. "I am a woman alone with a little boy, and I need money to live on."

"And you like it so much here in Lvow, Comrade, that you don't plan to travel again." This wasn't a question.

"I like it very much in Lvow," Mother said. "If we do travel again, Comrade, I'm afraid we will have to do it with more modest luggage."

"And suitcases are awkward to carry through the woods, aren't they?"

"Through the woods?"

"Through the woods and across the border, Comrade."

"You forget, Comrade," Mother answered, "that I am just a woman with a little son, who isn't very strong. I would not dream of going through the snow on foot."

The doctor cut in. "We should go now, Comrade," he said.

The other man ignored him. "No, the border is quite well sealed now. But spring is beautiful in these parts. Don't do anything foolish, Comrade. When spring comes, we will be patrolling the borders so that not even a squirrel can get through." He seemed to find this funny and gave a little laugh.

"Thank you for your warning, Comrade. But I assure you that we have no plans to escape."

"That's good. But we will be keeping an eye on you just the same, Comrade Waisbrem."

Suddenly, I saw Mother flinch. Then she crossed the room and held out her hand. "And I don't know your name, Comrade," she said.

The man didn't take his hands from his pockets. "Come," he said to the doctor. He turned and reached for the doorknob and opened the door. "Come," he said again, stepping into the hall.

The doctor put Mother's bag under his arm and picked up his own canvas bag by the handle. With his other hand, he picked up his hat. "Goodbye, Comrade," he said, "and thank you." Then he followed the other into the hall.

Mother walked to the table and sat down. I saw her put her elbow on the table and rest her chin in her hand. I understood how rude the man had been to not shake her hand or even tell her his name.

Now there was a quiet knock on the door. For a moment, Mother didn't move, and I almost spoke out to tell her. Then she got up and walked slowly to the door. She opened it, holding one finger to her lips for quiet.

It was Nadia's young father who stood in the doorway. I couldn't hear what he was saying, but I could tell by his face and the way he tilted his head left and right that he was thanking Mother. She whispered something back and then patted his hand. He bent over her hands and kissed them both. He looked like he was crying. Mother touched his cheek with her hand, said something, and then closed the door gently.

I realized that I felt proud of my mother now. When everyone else was standing around in the hall, she had gone out and found a doctor somehow and saved the baby's life. But Mother didn't look happy about it.

And then, all of a sudden, it all became clear. Now I suddenly understood what that other strange visitor of a few weeks ago had been all about—the peasant who also wouldn't shake her hand. Mother must have wanted him to lead us through the forest and across the border to Hungary, and he said a woman couldn't do it on foot in the snow. She was trying to tell him how strong she was with her story about being a champion athlete, and he didn't believe her.

Auntie Paula, too, had laughed at Mother's idea of escaping and, of course, if it were possible, everyone else would be doing it. But Mother, I now realized, must have kept wanting to do it anyway until this nasty man, tonight, had guessed what she wanted to do because of the suitcases and told her that they would be watching her from now on.

I couldn't help feeling sorry for Mother's disappointment. She had sat down at the table again, and she was still sitting there when I fell asleep.

*   *   *

I must have had one of those dreams again that night, because I woke up with Mother holding me. I was drenched in sweat and as before I had no idea what I had dreamt, but my face was wet.

"It's only a dream," Mother was saying. "We'll just blow it away." She blew across my forehead. "Come on, blow with me. Help me blow it away."

I blew to humor her.

"There, it's going away. I see it going out the window."

"The window is closed," I said, laughing.

"Dreams can go through closed windows. How do you think it got here?"

I couldn't help laughing again. I was laughing at Mother's joke, and I was laughing because being held felt so good.

"Do you remember what you dreamt about?" Mother asked gently.

"No," I said, shaking my head.

"Do you remember a little piece of the dream—where you were or who else was there?"

I tried to remember, but couldn't. I saw that one lamp was still on in the room. Mother had draped a towel over the shade to give a dim light. Mother herself was still dressed—she hadn't been to bed.

Now she laid me back down on my pillow. "Would you like me to turn the light off?" she asked.

"No, that's all right," I said. "I'll just turn to the wall." I put my arm over Meesh. He had had a bad dream too and was asking me to tell him a story. I realized that the only story I knew that sounded appropriate for someone who had just had a bad dream, was the one Miss Bronia had told about another toy bear named Pooh. I wouldn't tell the part about getting his head stuck in the jar of honey, which Fredek and I had found funny, out of concern for Meesh's feelings.

Meesh had very keen hearing and could hear if I only mouthed the words. At some point in the story, we both fell asleep.

Chapter Eight

I am sitting on my suitcase on the great stone floor of the Warsaw train station, watching Kiki's suitcase, and our train is about to leave. But Kiki hasn't returned from the ladies' room. We have never missed a train before, and that makes the prospect of still being here at the station, when we're supposed to be on our way to Grandmother's, that much more frightening. People will no longer walk around me, but angrily kick our suitcases over because I am not supposed to be here anymore. What is keeping Kiki so long? Will she ever come back? What should I do?

Then I realized that Mother was trying to wake me up. "We have to catch a train," she was saying, and my first thought was about the coincidence of my dreaming about missing a train when, in reality, we did have to catch one.

I didn't want to wake up. The lights in our room were on and hurting my eyes while outside it was deep dark, and it wasn't morning. On the other hand, I didn't want to go back to that dream.

"You have to dress quickly and quietly," Mother was saying.

I racked my brain to remember where we were supposed to be going. It was February now, three weeks after my birthday and baby Nadia's sickness. Nadia was well now, and Mademoiselle and I had done our daily walking and French lessons. Except that we were now walking both mornings and afternoons. We walked all over town with no particular goal except the exercise itself. "Shall we turn to the right here or the left?" Mademoiselle would ask me in French, and I would answer in that same language that had grown considerably less foreign. "This is a new street," I might say or, "Let's go see that brown cat in the window."

Sometimes Mademoiselle would suddenly say, "Let's cross the street now," and quickly lead me by the hand to the other sidewalk. It did not take me long to realize that this was when we saw Russian soldiers approaching us on the sidewalk, and then, if I spotted them first, I would say it and lead her across. I thought this was funny, but Mademoiselle didn't.

The afternoon walks had been difficult at first—difficult for me, that is, not for Mademoiselle, whose spindly legs seemed to know no fatigue. "Madame and I walked all over Paris, Vienna, London, Berlin, Budapest. . . ." she had told me more than once. But by now I had no trouble keeping up with her long stride, and would sometimes even race ahead to the corner. Meesh I would bring only in the morning because he needed an afternoon nap to recover from the morning's outing. The decision had been mine, but Mademoiselle had agreed heartily, as I had known that she would. Our gin rummy games had to be shortened to only a few hands just before Mother came home, but that didn't really bother me.

But now I could not remember either Mother or Mademoiselle mentioning a trip of any sort.

"Go down the hall quietly because people are asleep," Mother instructed me. "Do both number one and number two, wash your hands and face, brush your teeth, comb your hair, and come back as quickly as you can."

It was only now that I became aware of the strange way that Mother was dressed. She had on the blue wool dress that she now always wore, but over it she had put a black skirt almost to her ankles and a gray knit cardigan that was so big that she had it wrapped almost twice around her. On her head was a kerchief tied peasant-style under her chin, and her face was pale and bare of any makeup. Her black eyelashes and brows were now a translucent brown and her lips a light pink. I had never seen Mother look so soft or, I decided, so beautiful.

"You must hurry now," she said, and in a moment I was making my unsteady way down the hall to the bathroom.

When I returned, Mother wasn't in the room, but she had laid some clothes out on my bed. Ordinarily I would have understood them as clothes I was supposed to put on, except that this time she had given me a choice of my gray or my brown pants, three different shirts, and two pairs of knee socks. I didn't normally get to select what to put on, and why she should have given me such a choice now, I did not understand.

A week or two earlier, Mother had brought home for me a pair of brown lace-up boots that came up over my ankles. At first, I had been excited by their military look, but I soon found that their top edges chafed my lower legs when Mademoiselle and I walked. Mother had insisted that I wear them every day till they no longer chafed. Now they were standing in front of my bed, and I saw that Mother had scuffed them so that they no longer looked new. From that and my mother's get-up, I deduced that we were disguising ourselves as peasants, though how giving me a choice of clothes went with that, was still a mystery.

I remembered having been criticized before for creating an unacceptable color combination, so I picked the brown pants and the blue shirt because they were both fairly dark and thus seemed the closest in color. Of the knee socks, the red ones were darker than the tan, so I selected them as well.

I was just beginning the laborious process of lacing up my first boot, when Mother came quietly back into the room. She carried a brown paper bag, filled, I guessed, with food for our trip.

"Oh no, Yulek, you must put them all on," she said.

"All?"

"Yes, and you must put the gray pants on first because I sewed something into the back pocket."

Now I had two big questions to ask, and the mysterious contents of my pocket won out over the two pairs of pants. "What did you sew into the pocket?" I asked.

"Your father's watch."

For a moment I thought that she had somehow retrieved the waterproof shock-resistant, and anti-magnetic wristwatch that Lolek had taken from me in Warsaw, but then I remembered the gold pocket watch that had been my real father's and which had hung under a little glass dome in my Warsaw bedroom. Some day when I was an adult, I had been told numerous times, I would be old enough to wear it in my own vest pocket. But, except for the time Mother had shown it to Col. Bawatchov, I hadn't given any thought to the watch since leaving Warsaw.

Mother held up the gray pants and showed me the little lump in the back pocket. There must have been surprise on my face, because her own face grew very serious as she said, "I think you're old enough to wear it now."

I tried to compose my face into an equally appropriate expression and proceeded to put on the various layers of clothes.

A little later, as I sat on my bed munching my breakfast of bread and cheese, Mother sat down at the table in her long skirt and babushka scarf and began writing. "I'm writing a note to Mademoiselle," she said. "She doesn't know that we're leaving today. Do you want me to add anything from you?"

The idea of Mademoiselle coming later that morning to find us gone, saddened me. And suddenly I realized that I was never going to see Mademoiselle again. This wasn't like taking the train to visit Grandmother and then coming back a week later to the same people you had left. Neither Mademoiselle nor Miss Vanda nor Miss Bronia or Kiki or Fredek or Mr. Lupicki or the Aunties or Sonya or Col. Bawatchov or anyone else I had ever known, would I ever see again. It was as though they all came into my life through one door and out through another. That, I knew, was the nature of wartime. And the crazy thing was that the one I would miss the most would not be Kiki or Miss Bronia, but Mademoiselle.

I instantly felt disloyal to Kiki—Kiki who had lived with me day and night ever since I could remember, who had been almost my entire world and was so good and so religious. But Mademoiselle, with her funny talk of operas that weren't funny at all and dress-up balls that had no interest for me and her fear of the Russians and the Germans and her silly jealousy of the attention I paid to Meesh, had somehow worked her way the deepest into my heart.

"Write Julien dit au revoir," I said. I would also have added, I love you, but I couldn't say it in front of Mother.

"How do you spell that?" Mother asked. I said that I didn't know.

"Here's a handkerchief to blow your nose in," Mother said a few minutes later, stuffing one into my pants pocket. "And don't forget your rosary," holding that out to me. I put it in my pocket reverently.

I also picked the metal washer, that I had grown so adept at making appear and disappear, off the table.

"What do you want that for?" Mother asked.

I hesitated. Finally I ventured, "I like it," for want of a better reason to give.

"All right," Mother said, "and here is your knife." Mother held up the pocket knife she had taken from me while waiting for Mr. Lupicki's bus. She held it up by one end the way my schoolteacher used to hold up a piece of chalk or a pencil when she wanted our attention.

I tried to maintain a perfectly straight face as I took it from her hand and slipped it into my pocket as well. However, I had to admit to a certain quickening of my heartbeat and a sense of growing a few centimeters taller.

There seemed to be one entirely new article of clothing to go over my three shirts and two pairs of pants. This was a strange, bulky coat with a shiny, dark finish, that Mother now held up for me to put on. Only when I went to put my arms in the sleeves, did I recognize it as Mother's mink jacket turned inside out.

Those few centimeters of stature that I had just gained, quickly dissipated when I sniffed the scent of Mother's perfume on my new garment. I must have telegraphed my concern because Mother quickly said, "That scent will go away as soon as we step outside." Then she tied a piece of clothesline around my waist, which helped some to disguise the feminine nature of the garment. With the final addition of a canvas backpack, like solders' knap-sacks, Mother now produced for me to put on, I felt the jacket's offensive gender thoroughly neutralized.

With gloves, a knit cap on my head, and Meesh tucked into the crook of my well-padded arm, I was ready to go. "Do we look like two peasants?" Mother asked laughing, as she slipped on her karakul coat, turned inside out as well, and tied it with clothesline. In her hand she held a partially filled burlap bag. Taking my hand, she led me to the mirror on our wall.

I pulled my hand free and hooked it, instead, around her arm the way grownups do. "Three peasants," I corrected her, lifting Meesh to my shoulder level.

"Three peasants," Mother agreed. In the mirror, I could see Mother's belongings scattered about the room—her suits and dresses, her shoes, her makeup bottles, the notorious leather suitcases.

"Most of the clothes won't fit Mademoiselle," she said, "but she'll be able to sell them."

Then, in the mirror, I saw Mother put her hand over the hand with which I was holding her arm. "Yulian," she said, "we are starting out on a great adventure. We are going to do something the Russians say we are not supposed to do. Today is the first step in that adventure, and we are going disguised as peasants. Now, you know that peasants don't speak the same way we do, so you should not say anything so that you don't give us away. Do you understand?"

I nodded my head solemnly, and I could see Mother's approval in the mirror. Then she added, "You and I are partners in this adventure, you know, and we must take care of each other."

We had been there before. I remembered how Mother had declared us partners just before taking my knife away from me while we waiting for Mr. Lupicki's bus, and I felt my sense of excitement cool considerably.

Then I saw Mother do something that threw the whole matter into confusion again. With a quick, uncertain motion, but wide enough to include us both, Mother made the sign of the cross. "Come quickly," she said, pulling me out into the hall. "Don't look back."

*   *   *

The street on the way to the station had been strangely light under the black sky. A gentle snow of large, widely spaced flakes had reflected the occasional lights to give an almost dusky sense as we hurried along. As we turned the corner into a commercial street, I was surprised to see queues of people already forming in front of certain still dark shops.

"Remember, you are not to talk to anyone," Mother had said as we entered the train station. While I appreciated the importance of this plan, I found the admonition grating a little against my status as partner.

For the Polish-speaking soldier, Mother had produced a travel pass and asked him in Russian what part of the Soviet Union he came from, explaining that her own mother was from Moscow.

We had settled ourselves in the still-empty compartment of one train, Mother's sack on the seat beside me, when a woman wearing a red star on her hat with the gold hammer and sickle like Mr. Lupicki's, had walked along the platform announcing that the train's destination had just been changed and that the one we all wanted was about to leave on another track.

"Merde! Come on, we have to hurry," Mother said, taking me by the hand again and picking up her bag. People poured from the train, funneling into the passageway toward the track indicated. As we ran with the others, Mother's head turned left and right as though looking for something.

Suddenly we found our way barred by a tall, gray-haired woman in an official-looking cap, who informed us in a loud voice that the train for which we were now running lacked an engine and could not move anywhere . . . at which point the train gave a jerk and pulled out of the station.

"They told me it didn't have an engine," the woman whined.

"You could see right from here that it had an engine, you stupid!" somebody shouted.

"She's blind!" somebody else yelled.

"She's not blind. She just closes her eyes and opens her mouth and swallows everything they give her!"

"There was nobody on that train. Where is it going empty like that?"

"That was the last train until tomorrow!"

"That wasn't our train." This last wasn't a shout, but the quiet voice of a man standing behind Mother.

"Oh, Max," I heard Mother say. "Thank God you're here. I was afraid you weren't coming."

"I was in the station master's office. I expected something like this," the man said. He had a wide face and horn-rimmed glasses. A fur hat seemed to sit on top of his broad head with black hair showing on either side. "Our train is back there," he whispered now, "but they have no idea when the track will clear for it to leave." I saw the man take Mother's elbow, and we began to back out of the crowd. I saw he too seemed to be dressed as a peasant in a sheepskin jacket fastened by a wide leather belt.

Free of the crowd, we walked quickly toward another train. Actually, I had to run to keep up with the adults' long strides.

Soon we were all seated in an empty compartment of the new train. "He says the Bolsheviks have screwed up the rail switching system and they can't keep track of what train is where," the man was saying. "They're worse than idiots."

"Max," Mother said, "this is my son Yulian, who is a very grown up young man. Yul, this is Mr. Koppleman. He is going with us."

Seated across from us and leaning forward with his elbows on his knees, Mr. Koppleman nodded at me. "They've arrested everybody who knows how to run anything," he continued, "and their own systems are all different." He had unbuttoned his sheepskin jacket, and underneath he had on a white dress shirt without its collar. I noticed that he hadn't shaved. His pants, tucked into peasant boots, were neatly creased. When he took off his fur hat, I saw that his black hair was parted in the middle and held in place by hair dressing. He took out a pocket comb and combed it back.

While Mr. Koppleman's unexpected appearance in our lives was no longer a surprise to me, I did feel it to be an intrusion. I wondered if this, once more, meant the end of our "partner-ship." I watched him take a packet of cigarette papers out of his jacket pocket, separate one square, shape it into a trough with one hand, and proceed to pour tobacco into it from a little cloth drawstring pouch.

"They've got me rolling my own cigarettes like a peasant," he was saying to Mother. He licked the end of the paper and sealed it. "Look how good I've gotten," he said holding up the cigarette. But the statement did not imply pride, but more like disgust. He offered the perfectly-rolled cigarette to Mother.

"I'll take the next one and let me lick it myself," Mother said.

Mr. Koppleman suddenly looked flustered. "Of course, of course, Basia. I'm sorry. I wasn't thinking." Then he put the first cigarette between his lips and began to roll a second one. But the smooth action of his fingers was no longer there, and I could see that this second cigarette wasn't going to be as perfect as the first. "I'm sorry, Basia," he said again, "I'll start over."

"No, that's all right," Mother said, taking the unfinished cigarette from his hand just as he was about to pour the tobacco back into his pouch. She licked it with the tip of her tongue and sealed it. I saw Mr. Koppleman pull his jaw to one side and run his fingers over the stubble on his fleshy cheek. Then he lit both their cigarettes with a silver cigarette lighter.

"A Bolshevik officer offered me two hundred rubles for it," he said, indicating the lighter. "Not that I couldn't have used the money, but my mother—may she rest in peace—gave it to me on my birthday this last summer, and they'd have to get it off my dead body."

Then the compartment door slid open and a man in a long coat and fedora started to enter.

"You can't come in," Mr. Koppleman said, waving his hand. "The child is sick. It's contagious."

The man backed out of the compartment, sliding the door shut quickly. Mother laughed. I noticed that Mr. Koppleman had made no effort to speak like a peasant.

"You have to be firm with them," Mr. Koppleman said, very seriously. I wondered whom he meant by them, since the other man didn't look like a Russian.

Mr. Koppleman was now pacing back and forth in the little space of our compartment. "The first thing I'm going to do," he said, "is have a long hot bath in the privacy of my own bathroom, then I'll find the best English tailor in Budapest and order some suits and silk shirts." He nodded toward me. "Does he know?" he asked under his breath.

Mother clenched her lips and gave her head a barely discernable shake.

"After the war, that is," Mr. Koppleman said aloud, and I could tell from his tone that this was for my benefit. "After the war I'm going to take a train to Budapest, which is in Hungary, where they have very good tailors."

I knew that Budapest was in Hungary—it was the capital, for heaven's sakes. And now I also knew what our destination in this adventure was, though we wouldn't be going all the way there by train.

"Mr. Koppleman was a friend of your father's," Mother said quickly. "We ran into each other by accident in Lvow, and we've talked a lot about what we want to do when the war is over, and we were just . . ."

Suddenly she stopped. "I think we should tell him, Max," she said.

I saw Mr. Koppleman's round face tense. "All right, all right," he said. "Let me tell him. Yulian, your mother and I are going—and you too, of course—we're all going to a little village in the mountains where it's easier to get food than in the city, and the air is healthier, and you can play in the snow. Have you ever built a snowman? I build the best snowmen in the world, and I'll show you how. Would you like that?"

I nodded my head, thinking it the best thing to do, though I knew he was lying through his teeth. For a moment I worried that this Mr. Koppleman was supposed to be our guide over the mountains, but that concern was quickly quieted when I remembered that a guide had to be a real peasant who lived in the area.

"There, now you know," Mr. Koppleman said. "We're not keeping any more secrets from you." I looked at my mother. She was looking down at her hands. Mr. Koppleman ran his fingers over his stubbly cheek again.

Two more people tried to enter our compartment and were waved off by Mr. Koppleman. Then a gray-haired woman, a wicker basket over her arm, pushed her way in, felt my forehead, and plopped herself down on the seat beside me. Mr. Koppleman shrugged his shoulders, waved his arms, and sat down on the other side of Mother. With the stub of a cigarette still between his lips, he began rolling another one.

"You shouldn't be smoking those cigarettes in front of a sick child," the woman said. Mr. Koppleman rolled his eyes and poured the tobacco back into its pouch. He began running his fingers over his cheek again. I saw a little smile on Mother's face.

Then, just before the train began to move at around midday, two Russian soldiers joined our group. They sat down across from us, their rifles between their knees.

"What part of the Soviet Union are you from, Comrades?" Mother asked as soon as the train was moving. I held Meesh up so he could look out of the window at the passing panorama. In our silent language, I explained that the fields and houses weren't really moving, but just seemed to be, because we were.

Meesh wanted to know where we were going, and I told him without hesitation that we were going to Budapest in Hungary, though we were first going to a little village where we would build a snowman.

*   *   *

It was almost dark and snowing as we stood on the platform that seemed like just a bump in the thick blanket of snow that covered everything I could see in the dim light. We three were the only people who had gotten off, and our footprints were the only recent ones, except for those of a dog who must have walked the length of the platform shortly before we arrived.

For a moment we had stood between two strings of lights, until the one behind us began to move as the train pulled out of the station. Its departure had made me think of watching Auntie Paula or Kiki rip a row of stitches out of her knitting. And now we were left with only the single strand, the kerosene lamp glow of windows in the low houses. The street that separated the tracks from the houses with their thick, steep-pitched snow-covered roofs, was pressed into the snow by a succession of sleigh runners. A dark mound, steaming in the slick street, indicated the recent passage of a horse. In the distance, I could see the silhouette of mountains.

"Where is everybody?" Mother asked.

"They're sitting home by the fire," Mr. Koppleman answered. But his answer didn't quell the anxiety I had heard in Mother's voice and felt in my own chest. I recalled the set on the stage of Warsaw's marionette theater after the curtain went up but before the children and the witch appear, while you prepare to enter another reality. I gripped Mother's hand as I had Kiki's. I knew that her other hand was holding Mr. Koppleman's arm. I looked in both directions along the street for the sleigh that would take us to our hotel.

"Let's go—I'm freezing," Mother said. I could hear a bit of her little-girl whine coming into Mother's tone.

"I'll go with you till you're inside," Mr. Koppleman said, as we stepped down into the street. The idea of entering one of these houses made me apprehensive. I found myself longing for the coziness of the room we had left in Lvow.

"You're not staying with us?" Mother asked.

"They only have one bed. I'm two houses further."

"I wish you were staying with us," Mother said. "You could sleep on the floor."

Mr. Koppleman laughed. "I don't think so," he said. That was a relief.

We were walking down the middle of the empty street now, the way Fredek and I had used to walk on the farm.

"I don't like it being so dark," Mother said.

"No electricity," Mr. Koppleman said with a little laugh.

"We didn't have electricity on the farm, but I don't remember it being this dark."

"You're just nervous."

"I'd better say something to Yulian," Mother said.

"How much does he know?"

Mother didn't answer him. "Yulek," she said to me. I could only see her in silhouette now. "I don't want you to be frightened by anything you see here. These are very simple country people, and they're very old."

"Tell him the man is a rabbi," Mr. Koppleman said.

"I don't think he knows what a rabbi is. Yulek, do you know what a rabbi is?"

I said that I didn't.

"He's like a Jewish priest," Mother said.

"Where does he know about priests from?" Mr. Koppleman asked.

"He had a Catholic governess in Warsaw. She used to take him to Mass."

The idea of a Jewish priest surprised and frightened me, though I did know that Jews had a kind of church that they went to once or twice a year, because that's what Lolek used to do. Now, remembering the Jews from the Warsaw trolleys, I envisioned a bearded figure in black gabardine vestments coming at me out of a forest of candelabras, with a wafer and a chalice. Suddenly I found myself squatted down on the packed snow. "No, I don't want to!" I cried. I didn't want to go into that house.

"What does he want?" Mr. Koppleman asked.

"I don't know," Mother said. "Yulian, what are you doing?"

That was a question I might have asked myself. I realized how stupid I must look. I also realized that I had no choice over the matter. On the other hand, there was nothing really bad that was going to happen to me.

I stood up, embarrassed. "I had a stone in my shoe," I said, though I knew that I was fooling no one. But the soldier-like thing to do, I knew, was to face whatever was there inside the house. I started to say a silent Our Father, but realized immediately that I would feel more comfortable in the hands of the Holy Mother and switched to a Hail Mary. Then, as we stood at the door, waiting for someone to answer Mr. Koppleman's loud knock, I completed the unfinished Our Father.

"You can speak here," Mother said to me, I think in an effort to reassure me. "They know we're not really peasants." I was not greatly reassured.

It was a long and, for me, anxious wait. I told myself that the rabbi would certainly not be answering the door in a vestment, since Catholic priests didn't wear them except for Mass. He would probably just be wearing a long black robe with a white turned-around collar.

Of course, there was another scenario, one that I knew could not possibly be true, but which I could not keep out of my mind. That was one in which Mother and Mr. Koppleman meant to leave me to the rabbi as payment for assistance in their escape over the mountains. I knew that Mother would not do that and that this Jewish priest probably had no need for little boys. But the fantasy continued. Knowing that it couldn't be true gave it a bittersweet taste that I found surprisingly enjoyable.

Nevertheless, I was much relieved when the door was finally opened by a round-faced peasant woman in kerchief and apron, the sort of person I had seen many times before. "Come in quickly," she said in her peasant-accented Polish. In her hand she held a candle in a metal candleholder with a polished reflector.

Mother pushed me inside ahead of her.

"I will see you in the morning," Mr. Koppleman said, but the door was closed before he could finish. I took my hat off inside the house as I had always been taught. "Put your hat back on," Mother whispered.

"Blah, blah, blah," I heard a shrill voice cry from somewhere behind the peasant woman. The peasant woman stepped to the side quickly, giving us a view of a tiny woman wrapped in a gray shawl, making her slow way toward us with the help of a length of stick in her hand.

"I'm sorry, Rebbetzin," Mother said. "We don't speak Yiddish."

"You are crazy!" the woman said in the Jewish accent I had heard on the trolleys. "I say you are crazy in the snow with the baby."

The woman shuffled across the floor, her feet, in wool socks, thrust into back-less slippers. Behind her, someone was coughing.

"We are going now because it will not be possible in the spring," Mother answered in a surprisingly firm tone. "I have a young son, and I don't want him growing up a Soviet."

The woman stopped directly in front of us, holding glasses on a silver stick up to her eyes. By the candlelight, the white skin on her hands and face looked almost transparent except for its variously shaped brown spots. A wrinkled fold hung down on either side of her chin. But in place of the white hair I would have expected, she had a full head of orange-colored waves and curls. Though she stood perfectly straight, she was no taller than I was. She examined us both through her hand-held glasses. The peasant woman brought the candle a little closer to our faces.

"Why you don't speak Yiddish?" the old woman asked.

"I'm sorry, Rebbetzen," Mother said. "My mother is Russian, and we spoke Russian and Polish at home, not Yiddish."

The woman gave a grunt that showed her displeasure. "Go eat," she said, waving her stick toward the back of the room. Following the stick, I could see a table near a stove, dimly lit by a lamp hanging from a beam on the other side of the stove. Two wooden armchairs stood at right angles to each other near the light, and for the first time I noticed a bundled figure occupying one of the chairs. It was a man with a long white beard and wearing a black coat, a wide-brimmed hat, and gloves with the finger-tips cut off. His steel-rimmed glasses were perched halfway down his nose. A cigarette dangled from one corner of his mouth. I saw him lick his bony fingers before turning a page in the book he was reading. He seemed oblivious of our presence.

The old woman indicated that we should sit at the table.

"Take off your coat," Mother said to me, "but keep your hat on." I did not understand the hat business, but it was hot here near the stove. A strong meat and vegetable smell came from the stove, and I suddenly realized that I was very hungry.

We sat down across from each other, and the younger woman brought us blue bowls of steaming stew and wooden spoons. This was accompanied by a thick slice of unbuttered black bread for each.

"Blow, it's hot," Mother said to me. The pieces of meat and vegetables had a very strong smell. I blew on a spoonful of the liquid and sipped it carefully. I didn't like the taste.

"It's delicious," Mother said over her shoulder. "What is it?"

"Blah," the old woman said.

"Goat," the round-faced woman translated.

I actually heard myself gulp. There had been goats on the farm, smelly, aggressive animals that ate garbage and had horns and beards like Satan. That strong flavor now curdled on my tongue, and I began to gag.

I saw Mother look up at me from under her brows and fought to control the feeling.

"Eat," the old woman encouraged. The sudden friendliness in her tone disturbed me further.

"Try it, Yulek. It's very good," Mother urged quietly. There was no way that any of this was going to get through my throat, even if I wanted it to.

"You have to eat," Mother said with more firmness. "We have a long trip tomorrow."

I shook my head.

"Eat just the vegetables and the bread," Mother said. She dipped a piece of her dry bread in the juice.

I shook my head again. I tried eating the bread, but without butter it wouldn't go down my throat either.

"You can't have butter right now," Mother whispered. Then she turned to the two women. "He can't eat the stew. Is there something you can put on his bread?" she asked. The women exchanged some words in Yiddish.

I heard some shuffling behind me, and in a moment the younger woman had placed another slice of black bread in front of me, this one covered with a white jelly-like substance.

I bit into it hungrily. It was greasy and tasted like nothing I had experienced before.

The old woman must have noticed my reaction. "Schmaltz," she said.

"It's goose lard, and it's delicious," Mother said.

I put the bread down and shook my head again.

"You have to eat something," Mother said. The taste of grease was still in my mouth, and I shook my head again. From the man in the chair, there now came a series of dry coughs.

"He isn't used to this kind of food," Mother said to the women. "He needs to eat something—we have a very hard journey tomorrow. Can't you give him some butter or cheese? He hasn't touched the meat."

The old woman sticked her way over to where the man was sitting. They exchanged some words that I couldn't hear, and he coughed some more. Then she hobbled back and spoke to the younger one. The peasant woman busied herself at the cupboard. Finally she returned with a plate holding another slice of bread. On top of the bread was a thick slice of white cheese. I hoped for a layer of butter under the cheese. In her other hand she carried a cup. But instead of setting them down, she indicated with her head that I was to follow her. Mother nodded her consent.

The cheese beckoned, and I picked up Meesh and followed.

The woman led me to the empty chair near where the old man was sitting in the light of the lamp and indicated that I should sit. I had the feeling that I was trespassing in a private space I had no desire to occupy. The old man gave a cough and went on with his reading and smoking, ignoring my presence.

I sat down, squeezing myself against the side of the chair furthest from his, with Meesh between us. I pretended not to be looking at him, while the woman handed me the plate and the cup.

Resting the cup on the arm of the chair and the plate in my lap, I bit into the cheese cautiously. It had a tangy flavor and a creamy texture that I did like. The milk in the cup was thicker than what I knew and had a taste similar to the cheese. I ate eagerly.

At the same time I put my face down so that I could watch the old man through my lowered eyelashes. I had never been this close to anyone so old before. I saw his legs and feet bundled up in a blanket in addition to the coat and hat that he wore despite the heat from the stove. I wondered if he could walk. I watched him moisten his yellow-stained fingertips to turn a page and then brush the cigarette ash out of his beard without, it seemed, interrupting his reading. Then he would cough again out of one side of his mouth, while he held the cigarette firmly in the other.

I presumed that this was the Jewish priest who had grown too old to work. I wondered how he felt about his approaching death without the possibility of going to Heaven. I wondered if he knew about Heaven. It would be even worse if he knew about Heaven and knew he couldn't go there. Here, sitting in the chair right next to mine, I realized, was a man who knew that he would soon be dying. It might happen next month or next week, or even tonight. When my grandfather died, he hadn't been as old as this man and had had no idea he was about to die. But this man was just calmly sitting there waiting for it to happen.

He was even reading. Reading to put new things into his brain even though tomorrow that brain might no longer remember anything. I recalled how I had felt when Kiki and

I would build sand castles on the beach that I knew the sea would come and wash away soon. I didn't feel bad for myself, because I could always build another sand castle, but I felt bad for the castle, which didn't even know that its existence would be snuffed out by the next tide. But here was a man who knew and just sat there reading and waiting for it. It was so very sad—sad and so terribly fascinating. I could not take my eyes from the poor doomed man.

Then the old man caught me. As I turned my eyes up from my bread, I found myself looking right into the eye on my side of his face. He hadn't turned his head, but the eye bypassed the steel-rimmed glasses in the middle of his nose and was staring right at me. The brown pupil was set in a yellowish eyeball with red veins running in all directions, and it stared directly into my left eye.

I looked away instinctively. I would not look up again. But I knew that he knew that I had been watching him. I tried to turn my attention to Meesh, but could not wipe out the sight of that eye looking at me and knowing that I had been watching him. I wondered who else knew that I had been watching him. I kept my eyes on Meesh, on my lap, on my shoes, and on the floor in front of me until the younger woman took Mother and me to where we would be sleeping.

Three walls of our room were of stone, and the one window was a narrow slit just below the ceiling. I realized we were actually below ground level. A kerosene lamp that the peasant woman had lit for us, glowed on the table. Away from the stove it was very cold in this house. "We'll keep our clothes on tonight," Mother said. I had no problem with that.

"Come here and sit down with me," Mother said, seating herself on the bed. The mattress did not seem to give under her. "I want to tell you something." In view of the day's activities, this was not unexpected. I sat down beside her on the bed. The mattress was actually soft, but resting on something that did not give.

"I told you, Yulek, that this is the home of a rabbi," Mother began. "These people are very pious Jews. Do you know what that means?"

"That they pray a lot," I speculated.

"That's right, they pray a lot. And they also obey very closely the laws that God gave them."

This was getting interesting. "What kind of laws did God give them?" I asked.

"Well, one of them is not to eat meat and milk or things made from milk, like butter, at the same time. That's why you couldn't have butter on your bread while the stew was on the table."

This seemed like a very strange issue for God to concern Himself with. "What other laws are there?" I asked.

"Well, I'm not sure what the exact law is, but Jewish men and boys have to keep something on their heads all the time and never cut the hair in front of their ears."

God, I realized, must have been making fun of Jews. I didn't say that aloud, though. Instead, I said, "That's very different from the laws God gave Catholics."

"Oh, what laws are those?"

"Well, they're laws about being good. One is not to kill people and another is not to steal anything."

My mother surprised me by laughing at this. "Those are the Ten Commandments."

"Yes, there are ten altogether, about lying and going to church on Sundays."

"Yulek, God gave the Ten Commandments to the Jews. Don't you know that?"

Now I was confused. "Then how did Catholics get them?" This was more of a rhetorical question since Kiki had shown me a gray card with all ten printed on it.

"My poor Yulechek," Mother laughed. "What has Miss Yanka been teaching you? Don't you know that the first Christians were Jews?"

Mother was talking nonsense now.

"Jesus," Mother went on, "was a Jew."

This was outrageous! "What do you know about Jesus?" I demanded.

"A few things."

"All right, where was He born?"

"In Bethlehem," she answered. "His mother's name was Mary, and his father was a carpenter named Joseph."

She was right. She did know all about Jesus.

"Bethlehem was in Judea, which is Palestine now," she continued. "That's where Jews used to live."

I knew that my grandfather on my father's side lived in Palestine right now. "Well, if He was a Jew," I asked, knowing that I had her now, "how come He's in Heaven?"

"Because God loves Him," Mother said.

"God loves Jews?" This question was rhetorical as well.

My mother closed her eyes and leaned her head back against the wall behind her. "God loves everyone," she said. "Didn't Miss Yanka teach you that? He loves Jews and Catholics and Arabs—who call him Allah—and Chinese people who don't even worship Him."

"How about Negroes in Africa and Indians in America?"

"Even them. Even people who don't believe He exists."

This seemed like a God that was much easier to live with.

"So does that mean that the rabbi will be going to Heaven?" I asked. "Even though he isn't Catholic? I mean when he dies?"

"Of course. What kind of God wouldn't let people into heaven just because they were born Jewish or Chinese? Would that be a loving God?"

She really had me there. It would be a cruel God who sent people to hell forever, just because they hadn't been born to Catholic parents.

"Of course the rabbi is going to Heaven when he dies," Mother said. "He is a very good man. If the Russians knew that they helped people like us to escape, he and his wife would be arrested. Maybe even shot. They're not only very good, but very brave people."

Suddenly I had developed goose bumps. These funny people were real heroes, like the ones Kiki used to tell about, people who risked their lives to help Poland or to stand up for what was right, even if they were Jews. And here I was, right in their house.

"You're very kind to be concerned about the rabbi's getting into Heaven," Mother continued. "It means that you're a very good person as well. But I've known that for a long time."

Of course what that meant was that I'd be getting into Heaven too, whether I was christened or not. And suddenly, there I was, hugging my mother in my joy.

I could tell that it surprised her as well and, as she hugged me back, I could hear the little sniffs that meant she was crying. And it all felt so surprisingly good. Mother, still in her babushka kerchief, her eyes and her lips soft and vulnerable without their makeup and now crying, suddenly wasn't a "grownup" anymore, but somebody that was somehow almost a part of me and of whom I was somehow almost a part, the way Kiki and I had been.

We held on to each other for a while and finally Mother pulled away gently. "It's so funny," she said with a little laugh followed by another sniff, "through all these layers of clothing. We feel so fat." I laughed too, and it felt so good laughing together.

Now, with a little wiggle, Mother slid a few inches away from me. "Yulian," she said, as she resettled herself, "I'm going to tell you everything now. Max, Mr. Koppleman, didn't want to frighten you, but I think you deserve to know the truth." She sniffed one more time, wiped her nose with the back of her wrist, and gave a little, self-conscious laugh. "As I've told you," she said, "we're going on a very big adventure. Tonight we're going to get a good night's sleep here, and tomorrow morning a man is going to pick us and Max up in a sleigh."

At the thought of the horse-drawn sleigh, my happiness gained another level. I had never ridden in one.

"The man," Mother went on, "is a guide. He lives in another town not far from here, and he guides people over the mountains and through the woods into Hungary. There are a few guides like him who get paid a lot of money for doing this because it's hard and dangerous. They come into Lvow and meet secretly with people who want to escape. Do you understand what I'm saying?"

"Yes, if the Russians catch them, they'll be shot or sent to Siberia," I said.

"That's right. But it's not dangerous for us, you understand, because the Russians don't expect women and children to be going in all this snow. And what I've been doing all this time in Lvow is trying to find one of these guides and convince him to take us. You see, they don't want to take a woman and a child. They don't think we're strong enough to climb the mountains, but they don't know how strong you and I are and how far we can walk. Isn't that right?"

I nodded my head to show that I was still listening. "Mademoiselle and I walked from one end of Lvow to the other," I said.

"That's right, but these guides don't know that. Well, I finally found the best and the bravest guide of all the guides, and I offered him extra money if he'd take us. I had run into Max Koppleman, who was a friend of your father, and he wanted to go too, so we both had money to pay the guide, and he agreed to take us. The guide will carry you in the deep snow, and Max says he'll help too."

Now Mother stopped and I saw her looking intently at me. I knew that she wanted to see if I was frightened, but now that I knew I was going to Heaven, Russian border guards held little terror for me. Wolves, on the other hand, were a different story. Wolves lived in the forest and ate people. They even chased sleighs to eat people that fell out. One wolf, I remembered, had even eaten a sleigh horse, eating his way into the harness until he was pulling the sleigh. "What about wolves?" I asked.

"There are no more wolves in these woods. The hunters have killed them all. There are only wolves in zoos."

This reassured me. I understood that the stories Kiki read to me were intended for little gullible kids, whom you could tell anything, and that grownups all knew that they weren't true. What Mother and I were about to do, was a grownup thing, and I would now have to start thinking like a grownup.

"Now, this is the plan," Mother went on. "Tomorrow morning the guide and his nephew are going to pick us and Max up in their sleigh and take us on a road that runs along the base of a small mountain. The border is at the top of the mountain, and when the guards aren't looking, we'll jump out of the sleigh and climb the mountain to the border. Once we're on top, we'll be safe from the Russians."

"What about the horse and the sleigh?" I asked, concerned.

"The guide's nephew will stay in the sleigh and continue driving to the village. Now, if the Russians stop us before we get a chance to jump out, the guide is going to tell them that he and I are getting married and he's bringing us to his village for the wedding. Max, he's going to say, is my brother, coming to the wedding too."

This was going to be a real adventure. "We'll fool the Russians, won't we," I said. "I can pretend I'm sick, and they'll be sorry for me and not suspect anything."

"That's a good idea. But don't say anything. Remember that we're supposed to be peasants."

Mother went on talking, but I realized that I shouldn't act too sick because if I really were, Mother wouldn't be taking me out in the cold weather. Maybe I could pretend to cry a little as though my stomach hurt and I wasn't brave. That would certainly allay any suspicions the Russians might have about our trying to escape. Nobody would try to make a kid with a stomachache climb a mountain.

"You know, when I was your age—well, maybe a little older," Mother said and brought me back to the present, "I used to love adventures. My brother, Pavew, was a year older, but everyone said I should have been the boy and he the girl. Pavew liked to read and play the violin, and I liked to climb trees, swim in the lake, go hiking. . . . Once we were flying a kite with your grandfather, and it got caught in a tree, and Grandfather said for Pavew to climb up and get it, but he wouldn't. So I climbed up and got it, and when I got down, Pavew said, 'She's just too stupid to know that you can fall down.'"

Mother laughed as she finished this story, and I did too. It really wasn't all that funny, but it felt so good to laugh together.

"Then there was one time Pavew and I were spending the summer on a farm with Grandmother, and I discovered that I could climb up high in the barn and jump down into this big stack of hay. Pavew wouldn't do that either."

"Fredek and I did that on the farm too," I interjected eagerly.

"You did?" Mother said in surprise.

"Yes," I admitted, wondering what Mother's reaction would be now.

"And did you have the feeling for just a second that you were flying?" she asked.

"I did," I said, nodding my head enthusiastically. "I spread my arms like this," I said demonstrating, "and I felt like an airplane."

We both laughed again. Mother put her arms out like mine. "When I was little we didn't know about airplanes," she said. And for a reason I couldn't understand, we both found this absolutely hilarious—hilarious and delicious.

When, minutes later, I finally saw Mother's face sober up, I knew just what she was going to say. "You'd better get some sleep now," she said. I wanted our talk to go on, but I knew that arguing would spoil the mood. "Come on, Meesh," I said.

There was a chamber pot for me to use under the bed and a pitcher of water and a basin on a little stand. But the water was too cold to wash anything but my hands. Then I took my shoes off and lay down on the bed with Meesh between me and the wall. Mother laid my coat over me on top of the blankets.

"Don't worry about anything," she said tucking me in. "The guards don't expect a woman and a boy to be trying to escape in this weather. They won't be suspicious of us."

I reached my arms up, and Mother pressed her soft face against mine. "Kiss Meesh," I said. Mother leaned across me and gave my bear a kiss. "Good night, Meesh," she said. "Take good care of your master tonight."

"He's my son," I corrected her.

"I'm sorry. Take good care of your father."

I hugged Meesh very tight and must have fallen asleep almost immediately.

*   *   *

They were whispering when I woke up. The kerosene lamp was glowing dimly, and I could see Mother and Mr. Koppleman sitting at the table.

"They were dressed as women," Mr. Koppleman was saying in a very agitated voice.

"Maybe they weren't very convincing," Mother answered, the calmness of her voice contrasting to his. "Maybe they hadn't shaved recently—how do I know. You discover two men in a sleigh dressed as women and what else are you going to think?"

"Well, they're all going to be on the alert now," he said. Instinct told me to pretend sleep.

"They can check and see that I'm a woman," Mother said. She was sounding angry now.

"That's not going to save you when they see you jump out of the sleigh. No, Basia, it's much too dangerous for us now. I'm not going."

"You're not going? Max, please. I need you to help with Yulian."

"Don't be ridiculous. I'm not going, and you're not going. The snow is a meter deep, and you wouldn't make it even without the boy."

"I don't care how deep it is. We're going. Max, please. Be a man—I need you."

"You're not going. I won't allow it. I forbid you!"

"You forbid me? You're being ridiculous. You're afraid. Max, you're not a man."

"Yes, I am afraid. I'm afraid for you and the boy. I was Nahtek's friend. What would he have said?" Nahtek had been my father, Nathan.

"Nahtek is dead. Nahtek shot himself when things got too tough for him. He's got nothing to say here. I'm taking his son out of this hell so he can grow up a stronger man than his father. Nahtek was a very good man—Nahtek was a saint, but he wasn't strong enough. If we get through this, Yulek will have today to look back on for the rest of his life and know that he did something heroic. It's the most I can give him."

"I am thinking of Yulek," Mr. Koppleman said, but without much conviction.

"You're not a man," Mother said again. "Go back to Lvow. Go on. I don't want to look at you anymore!"

"Basia, you don't know what you're doing. It's suicide. I'm begging you." Now he sounded as though he really were begging.

"Go on, get out of here!" Mother hissed. I had never heard her so angry. "I don't want to look at your fat face."

"You're crazy, Barbara. You're a crazy blah, blah."

Mother didn't answer. I saw her begin to lay out her solitaire.

"It was your crazy demands that drove Nahtek to his death," Mr. Koppleman said. "All of Lodz knows that."

Suddenly I saw Mother scoop up her cards and fling them at the man's face. Mr. Koppleman rocked back in his chair and almost fell over. "Nahtek killed himself," Mother said, "because he couldn't face what he thought he had done to his father's business. His note said he didn't want to lead a gray life. . . . If he had waited two more days. . . ."

Mr. Koppleman stood up, and I thought he was going to hit Mother. I think she did too, because she stopped speaking and stood up with him. "Get out, Max," she said again, but in a very even voice this time.

Mr. Koppleman turned around and marched out of the room. I saw Mother bend over and begin picking up the cards.

*   *   *

Then Mother was waking me up again. "Get washed, Yulek," she said. "Breakfast is almost ready."

I made a face, remembering how cold the water had been last night. Mother laughed. "I poured you some warm water," she said. For the first time in my life, I realized, I was getting up without having to dress. It was also the day we'd be riding in a sleigh and climbing a mountain.

Then Mother sat down at her solitaire, and I remembered the scene with Mr. Koppleman that Mother didn't know I had seen in the middle of the night. I wondered if anything had changed after I had gone back to sleep. Had Mr. Koppleman come back to say he had changed his mind and was going with us? Or had Mother changed her mind and decided not to go without him? Or had I dreamt the whole thing? Mother seemed deeply absorbed in her solitaire.

"Alicia is making scrambled eggs for you," Mother said. Scrambled eggs were my very favorite food, but I was allowed them rarely, and then only in the singular, since they weren't good for me. "Yanek will be here soon," Mother said. Yanek, I presumed, was the name of our guide, which meant that we were still going.

I didn't think much of Alicia's scrambled eggs. She had put something in them that gave them a tang that I didn't like in my eggs. But remembering the difficulties of last night's dinner, I ate them quietly.

The rabbi's wife was in her chair, the one I had eaten in last night, mending a sock. The other chair was empty. I wondered if the rabbi had died during the night. That would mean that he was probably in Heaven by now. He wouldn't have to wear his overcoat and gloves up there any more or have his legs wrapped up in a blanket.

After breakfast we went back to our room to wait for Yanek. Mother did her solitaire, but I had nothing to do. I tried passing the time by telling Meesh about the sleigh ride and the climb that was coming, but I found I didn't want to talk about it. Instead, I found myself thinking about the rabbi up in Heaven where, I knew, he would be young again and reunited with his parents and grandparents, assuming that they had been good.

Of course he would also be introduced to his great-grand-parents, who had probably died before he was born, and of whom there would be eight. And then his great-great-grand-parents of whom there were even more, and he would have to try to remember who was who.

"He should have been here hours ago," Mother said at one point, speaking, I think, more to herself than to me. A little later she said angrily, "You don't keep people waiting three hours."

Then Mother turned to me. "You'd better put Meesh in your backpack," she said.

"In my backpack?" The suggestion was outrageous. He wouldn't be able to see anything. He'd be frightened not know-ing what was happening.

"You will need both hands free," Mother said. "Put him in the backpack or leave him here."

I felt a surge of anger at Mother, but I knew she was right.

I got down off the bed and undid the flap on my backpack. I felt around the bed for Meesh so that I would not have to look at him and plunged him head first into the knapsack. But I knew I had done something grown up. I realized also that a package of some sort had been added to the knapsack.

There was a knock on our door. Mother went to open it, and I saw a young man's face above a thick sheepskin jacket. He wore no hat, and his black hair fell a little over one of his dark eyes.

He looked around the room quickly. "Where is Koppleman?" he asked. "They said he's gone back to Lvow?"

"He has," Mother said. "He changed his mind."

"I don't give back money," the young man said. His accent was different from the peasant accent I had become accustomed to.

"He doesn't ask for his money," Mother said. She was packing her cards in the sack she had carried from Lvow. "This is my son, Yulian. We're ready to go."

The young man turned on his heel and led the way out of the house. Mother detoured to say goodbye to the rabbi's wife. The woman and the younger one were at the table peeling vegetables. "Thank you for your hospitality," Mother said, handing something to the older woman, who quickly stuffed it into a pocket of her sweater.

"Blah, blah," the woman said, and Mother bowed her head respectfully. Then Mother handed something to the younger woman who had stood up. The woman curtsied.

"Goodbye, Rabbi," Mother said turning toward the two armchairs, and I realized that the old man was back in his chair now.

"He doesn't hear," the old woman said.

Mother crossed to where the old man was sitting. I saw him look up at her. He began to say something, but began to cough instead. Mother leaned over and patted one of his gloved hands. The book dropped onto the blanket in his lap, then slipped to the floor. Immediately his hands began searching for it in the empty lap with quick, nervous movements while he continued looking at Mother. Mother squatted down and picked his book off the floor. She handed it into the fluttering fingers, which wrapped around it hungrily. Then Mother followed Yanek outside, and I followed her.

"It's snowing!" Mother said in surprise. Large flakes were floating lazily to the ground.

"They don't see so good in the snow," Yanek answered.

And there, in front of the house, stood a horse and a sleigh. The horse was brown with a black mane and tail. His muzzle was plunged into a leather feedbag, and when he turned his head to look at us, I saw that he had a white star on his forehead. The sleigh was green with black trim, though the paint was peeling. A blanket of fur lay across the interior, and, at the front of the sleigh, a boy not much older than I, his face covered with pimples, causally leaned against the reins hanging over the dashboard. A tall black whip stood in its holder beside him. Suddenly I was filled with the greatest envy, and would have changed places with him in an instant, pimples and all.

Yanek pulled back a corner of the fur robe and awkwardly extended a hand to help Mother climb into the sleigh. I followed, eschewing assistance.

"That's all. The other isn't coming," Yanek said to the boy. Then he walked to the front to unstrap the feedbag from the horse's head. I laughed as the horse, reluctant to surrender the rest of his lunch, followed the bag with his nose as far as he could. The boy made a clucking sound, and the horse stepped forward. Yanek stepped on the runner as the sleigh moved by him and casually swung himself into the sleigh beside me.

Nobody said anything as the sleigh picked up speed. The little village was quickly left behind. The road of packed snow stretched ahead of us in a straight line as far as I could see through the falling snow.

I had never had the cold wind blow in my face that way before. Every once in a while, I could catch a delicious whiff of the horse. I opened my mouth to catch snowflakes. When my face grew too cold, I would duck down into the fur robe with its own animal smell.

Mother kept looking straight ahead toward the mountains. She held a corner of the robe up in front of her face to break the wind, but not close enough to be able to smell it.

"So Missus lived in a big house in Warsaw?" Yanek said after a while.

"An apartment," Mother answered, not taking her eyes off the mountains.

"Missus travels much?" he asked. I had the impression that he was trying to start a conversation.

"No," Mother told him. It wasn't true, so I understood that she didn't want to talk.

After another while, the man said, "When we talk to the border guards, I will have to say, you, to Missus, like I would to my sweetheart."

"That's all right," Mother said. "Mister can call me you now if he wants."

"Maybe I will to get in practice," he said with a little laugh. "How do you like the sleigh ride?"

"I like riding in your sleigh very much." I could tell that Mother was trying to be polite, but her mind was somewhere else.

"Our village is behind that mountain," Yanek said, pointing to our left. "When we reach that little mountain over there," he went on, pointing straight ahead this time, "the road will stop and another road will go left and right along the foot of the mountain. First there will be a guardhouse, and that is where I will tell that Missus—I mean you," and he laughed at his mistake, "are coming to marry me in my village. Then we turn left toward my village, and there will be guards walking back and forth along the road every two hundred meters approximately.

"When they can't see us anymore from the guardhouse, Antek will stop and feed the horse. Then, when I see the guard in front and guard in back both walking away from us, we will jump out of the sleigh and walk as fast as we can to the top of the mountain. I will carry Missus's son on my back. Once we are on top of the mountain we are safe across the border. Then we walk to the next village."

"I understand," Mother said. Nobody said anything else till we reached the guardhouse just before the mountain.

Two soldiers in their long coats and green pointed hats came out of the guardhouse as we approached, rifles slung over their shoulders. Antek reined the horse to a stop and Yanek surprised me by addressing them in neither Polish nor Russian. I recognized it as Ukrainian, which is similar to both, but not a language I understood except for the odd Polish or Russian-sounding phrase. I knew that he was explaining that he was bringing Mother home to marry her. His tone was very jolly, and the two soldiers laughed. Yanek handed one of the soldiers some folded papers, at which the man only glanced before handing them back.

The soldier now walked around to Mother's side of the sleigh and reached for her wool hat. He pushed some of it back from Mother's face. Mother lowered her eyes shyly, which I knew had to be make-believe and would have made me laugh under different circumstances. The soldiers said something to Yanek, and they all laughed. I saw the boy Antek blushing.

The second soldier had lifted a corner of the fur robe to look underneath. The absence of contraband seemed to satisfy his curiosity. The guard said something else to Yanek that I could tell by his body language meant for us to go.

At that point, Yanek produced a bottle of red wine from a pocket deep inside his jacket. He held its neck in his large fist and raised it over his head for a moment, then tossed it across the sleigh to one of the guards. Catching it deftly, the soldier raised it the same way over his own head. He said something to Mother, who again lowered her eyes in that funny way. Then Yanek said something to Antek, who slapped the reins on the rump of the surprised horse, and we were on our way again.

"They will drink to our health," our guide said to Mother with a wink.

Looking ahead for the first time, I now saw the "little mountain" not a hundred yards in front of us. It was a long, fairly straight ridge with trees on top, but nothing but snow on the slope facing us. It really didn't look vary high.

"That's the border, up there where the trees begin," Yanek explained.

"They cleared all the trees between here and the border. But don't worry. If we don't show ourselves to the guard, he won't see us," he said with another wink, a statement that seemed too obvious to make sense. "We climb to the top as fast as we can before they change the guard, then follow the stream to the village."

I could not help looking at Yanek with admiration and looked forward to my ride up the hill on his back.

We came to the end of our road and the horse turned left on his own. The road was only mostly-covered sleigh tracks. Ahead, I saw another soldier in the road, walking in the same direction as we were heading. It wasn't till our horse drew even with him, that the soldier noticed our presence. Turning quickly, he seemed to recognize Yanek, and his face broke into a grin. Yanek shouted something to him and threw him a bottle of wine. The soldier fumbled as the bottle fell through his hands into the snow. He bent over to pick it up, then raised it to shoulder level to show that he had recovered it as we moved on.

Soon we passed another soldier, who recognized Yanek as well. Yanek threw him a bottle too. This one was caught.

"They all know Mister, don't they," Mother said.

"I make sure they like me," Yanek answered. Then Antek pulled the horse to a stop. Far ahead I could see a speck that must have been the next border guard.

Antek got out of the sleigh with the leather feedbag, and I knew that this was where we would be jumping into the snow. My heart began to race.

"Put your knapsack on your back," Mother said to me. I obeyed.

Yanek stood up and turned to look back at the road we had just passed. Mother and I both turned with him. The guard behind us raised his wine bottle as though in greeting and immediately turned around to walk the other way.

"All right, quickly," Yanek whispered. I wondered why he was whispering. "Now jump!"

Mother scrambled out of the sled and into the snow beside the road. She sank almost to her knees. A little cloud of snow rose up around her legs.

"It's light snow," Yanek said behind me as I followed Mother.

There was something slippery under the snow, and I found myself sitting down. The snow was up to my shoulders.

"Oh, Yulek!" Mother said. "Get up quickly." She began fumbling for my hand. "Are you all right?"

"I'm all right," I assured her. Getting to my feet with the backpack wasn't easy. Mother pulled me up. I was standing almost to my hips in snow.

"Oh, my God!" Mother suddenly cried. "Oh, my God!"

I turned in the direction that she was looking. I saw our sleigh pulling away—fast. Holding the reins, slapping them sharply along the horse's, back was our guide, Yanek.

"He's left us!" Mother said. "That blah, blah, blah, blah, blah has left us!" she yelled, and I was afraid the guard would hear her. "He took my money and then he left us! He was supposed to carry you!"

Suddenly, Mother was waddling through the snow after the sleigh. I looked back at the guard who, miraculously, hadn't heard us. I ran after Mother. The snow was surprisingly light, and offered little resistance.

"It's only to the top of the hill," I said. "I can climb that by myself. Then we just follow the stream to the village."

Mother stopped and turned to face me. I could see her forcing a smile over her face. "My little soldier," she said.

"We have to hurry before the guard sees us," I said.

"Yes, yes," she agreed. "We can't stay here."

I started up the hill, hoping she would follow.

In a moment, Mother had passed me. "Get behind me," she commanded, "and walk in my tracks."

"No, no," I insisted. "I can walk by myself."

"Walk behind me," Mother repeated. Then she added, "We can take turns breaking the snow."

That, I could go along with. I moved into Mother's tracks where the going was easier. But we were on the slope now, and the footing was slippery. We were making little headway.

Mother seemed to be having much more trouble than I was. Instead of pushing her legs through the light snow, she kept trying to lift her feet up over it and then slamming them down. I saw her stagger a few times as she slipped on the icy footing. Finally she lost her footing altogether and sat down hard in a cloud of snow. I realized she no longer had her bag.

"Do you want me to go back to get your bag?" I asked. I didn't get an answer.

"I'll hurry," I assured her.

"I said, no!" Mother shouted.

Instinctively I looked back at the guard again. He was still walking away from us, and I saw he must have opened the wine bottle because he now had it raised to his lips.

"We have to go on," Mother said, to my relief. Now she got to her hands and knees and began crawling up the hill on all fours.

I didn't have to do that. I remembered climbing snowy hills with Kiki last winter and turned my toes out to grip with the sides of my feet. But Mother was making better headway than I was, so I had little choice but to drop to my knees and follow her example. There were tree stumps under the snow, making the footing more difficult.

We kept crawling up the slope. I understood that if we reached a certain height before the guard turned around, he wouldn't be as likely to see us.

Mother wasn't crawling as fast as I could have. I could hear her labored breathing. I kept looking over my shoulder at the guard, still with his back to us.

Then suddenly my right arm sank into a bottomless hole, stopping only when my face pressed against the packed snow. I tried to pull it out, but something, there under the snow, held it. Terror gripped me.

"What is it?" Mother asked in alarm, turning back towards me. I realized that I had begun to cry.

"I can't get my arm out!" I said, my face buried in snow. "Something's grabbed me!"

"Shshsh," Mother said, "I'm coming."

"Hurry!" I was suddenly covered in sweat. "It's pulling me down."

"It's not pulling you down. Be quiet."

I clenched my teeth. Mother reached down into the snow and pulled up on my sleeve. I felt my arm release. As the fear dissipated, I felt the space filling with shame.

"There's a crust under the snow here, and your hand broke through," Mother explained unnecessarily. "Just put your elbows down so that your weight is on your whole forearm, and come on." She turned and started up the hill again. Deeply humiliated, I followed.

Crawling with her elbows on the snow, Mother's behind, in its big black skirt, stuck up in the air, wiggling back and forth as she crawled. It looked, I decided, like a giant ball of Kiki's yarn. I spread my own knees apart so as not to offer a similar silhouette.

I looked down at the road to see if the guard had heard us. I saw him turn and begin walking back towards us. "The soldier is walking back towards us," I said, making sure there was no alarm in my tone.

"Don't worry about him," Mother shot back. "Just climb."

I wondered why we shouldn't worry. Would the wine make him so drunk that he wouldn't be able to see us or shoot at us? Was it poisoned wine, maybe? We were only about a quarter of the way up the mountain. Looking down at the guard again, I could see him walking his post still apparently oblivious of our presence.

After a while Mother stopped. "We have to . . . rest," she said, out of breath. She lay down in the snow. "Lie down. It'll . . . make it harder . . . for anyone to see us."

I lay down, though I didn't need to rest. I could feel my heart beating a little faster, but I was certainly not out of breath like my mother. I had been walking all over Lvow with Mademoiselle while Mother had been sitting around cafes, smoking cigarettes.

Now below us I could see a long sleigh, like a farm wagon on runners, pulled by two horses, following along the route our sleigh had traveled. It was filled with soldiers.

"Look, there are more soldiers coming" I said. "I think they're going to change the guard."

"Damn!" Mother said. "Keep your head down," she ordered sharply. "Don't move."

I didn't need to be told that. I made myself as flat as possible, the side of my face against the snow, the way Kiki's brother had done on the battlefield in the last war. I could no longer see the sleigh and hoped that it meant that the soldiers couldn't see me either.

"Damn, they're changing the guard," Mother whispered, which was just what I had said. Of course, it also meant that she wasn't really keeping her head down the way she had told me to.

"All right, we have to be very careful now. There's a new guard—don't let him see you," Mother said after some time. "We have to crawl the rest of the way on our stomachs. And don't make any noise."

I had practiced this in our Warsaw apartment, crawling along the floor between chair legs, the way Kiki's brother had crawled from trench to trench under the barbed wire. I kept the side of my face down almost to the snow, turned my feet out so that my heels wouldn't stick up, and followed Mother.

But she didn't seem to know about turning your feet out, and the heels of her boots bobbed up and down in front of me.

"Put your heels down," I said in a loud whisper.

"Shshsh, be quiet," Mother whispered back. She hadn't put her face down sideways either, and I could see the top of her head in its wool hat.

"Turn your toes out so your feet lie flat and put your face down on its side," I said, speaking with the authority of experience.

"Hush!" Mother said.

I let it go—we were nearing the top anyway.

The ground wasn't as steep anymore. "Yulek," Mother said, "when I give the signal, we're going to stand up and run as fast as we can into the woods. I know how fast you can run."

This was undoubtedly an untruth—Mother had never seen me run. And it was very unlikely that Kiki had reported the results of the races we had had on the beach when I had beaten her. What was more likely was that Mother was just trying to make me want to demonstrate my speed and run faster—which, of course, was totally unnecessary in view of the circumstances. Besides which, she hadn't even said what the signal to run was actually going to be.

For a few minutes Mother lay very still, breathing hard. I knew what she was doing—she was resting up for the sprint to the top. I could have done it without resting. Finally I saw Mother rise to all fours. "Now!" she whispered, straightening to a crouched position and running up the hill. I followed and beat her to the top. In a moment Mother was hugging a tree for support at the top of the hill, trying to catch her breath again. I stood clear of any tree, my hands on my hips. Actually, I did have to take some deep breaths, but I managed to do it through my nose so you couldn't notice.

I heard strange gasps from Mother and realized she was trying to laugh while she gulped air. She slid down the tree trunk, sinking slowly to her knees, and finally sat down. "Yulek," she said, "we're out of Poland. Do you realize that? We've escaped the damned Bolsheviks!"

Mother was looking down at the guard now, the new guard, who hadn't had any wine to drink, who was looking up at us. He had probably noticed us when we had made that last dash, and was now standing in the snow, a few feet from the road with his hands on his hips. Mother got to her feet again and, putting her thumb between her index and middle finger, gave him what we called a "fig," a gesture of derision that I was never allowed to make. The soldier didn't respond, but at that distance he probably could not distinguish the gesture. Mother sank to her knees again, laughing.

I pressed my heels together and, standing at attention, put two fingers up to the imaginary visor of my hat in the Polish military salute to the enemy soldier whom we had beaten.

"What are you doing?" Mother demanded. "Are you saluting that Bolshevik swine?"

I didn't understand Mother's anger. These were not Germans, whom we all hated. Mother had liked Col. Bawatchov and Capt. Vrushin, and she had even talked nicely to the soldiers on the train. For all we knew, the soldier down below was one of the ones who had been on the train with us. "I was saluting Poland," I said, not wanting to create problems.

"Poland," Mother repeated. I detected a little sneer in her voice. "That Polish peasant betrayed us. He took my money and promised to carry you. Then he dumps us into the snow and leaves us there to die."

"I was perfectly able to climb the hill by myself." I did not want to continue that subject.

"We're not there yet. There's a long walk ahead of us. And where is that coward Max? Where is Max right now, please tell me?"

I was thinking now of the way Mother had been last night, telling me about when she had been a little girl and about God.

"He's back in a café in Lvow," she said, I suppose answering her own question. Then she began to laugh. But it wasn't a fun laugh. "He's sitting there at Molenski's telling everyone that we've either been shot or arrested. And they're all saying, 'That crazy Barbara. Serves her right.'"

For some reason, the idea of Mr. Koppleman sitting in a café and telling everyone that we had been shot or arrested, didn't make me laugh as much as it made me aware of the serious nature of what we were doing—this wasn't looking for spies with Fredek.

"All right," Mother said, a bit of the laugh still in her voice, "now we have to go find that stream. When we do, we'll have some lunch and a drink of cold, clear mountain water."

Lunch sounded good. "How are we going to find the stream?" I asked, seeing no indication of where even to look.

"Yulian, where does water always flow?"

I couldn't tell whether this was an admonition over something I should have learned and racked my brains for an answer.

"Hmmm? Which direction does water always flow in? You know." By the tone of her voice, I now knew this was a friendly question, but I still had no clue. Then I had the answer. "Downhill!" I said. "Water always flows downhill. So it must be down there somewhere, doesn't it!" I pointed down the wooded slope.

"That's exactly right! So now we get to go downhill. And when we get to Budapest, we will have a hot bath and a soft warm bed, and eat anything you want."

"Will we be in Budapest tonight?"

"Probably not tonight. We have to find the village first."

"Right, follow the stream to the village."

"Follow the stream to the village! Come on."

As we started into the woods, I saw that Mother was crying.

*   *   *

Going down was only a little less steep than it had been coming up, except that we did have the trees to hold on to. Mother ran with mincing steps, stopping herself against each tree. I found that locking my knees I could slide from tree to tree. At one point I missed my tree and found myself gathering speed. I passed Mother and was heading straight for a log lying across my path.

Instinctively I sat down. I continued sliding, but at a more controlled pace. I raised both feet and was able to cushion my stop against the log.

"That's a good idea," Mother said behind me, holding on to a tree. She sat down too and, holding her skirt around her legs, soon joined me against the log. She laughed. "This is fun," she said. I knew that Mother would much rather have been sitting in a café with a cigarette, but I recognized her good intentions.

I peered into the twilight under the trees for the bottom of the hill and our stream, but could see neither. What if Yanek had lied about the stream as well?

Mother got to her knees, crawled over the log, and sat down on the other side. "Here we go!" she said gaily. Wiggling a little in the snow, she began to move downhill again. Not wanting to wiggle my rear the way she did, I pushed myself off against the log. Bumping our way from tree to tree, we continued down the hill.

Then I saw Mother raise her arm over her head and point somewhere to our left. Looking where she pointed, I could now see jagged sheets of ice and crusted snow that I realized must mark our stream. Coming from somewhere above us on our left, it paralleled our track on a slightly convergent course. On the other side of the stream, the ground rose again, and I had the feeling that we were sliding into the vortex of a giant funnel.

Suddenly, Mother's downward progress stopped with a jolt and a cry of pain in front of me. I lay down on my side, perpendicular to our path, to avoid crashing into her with my boots. I began to roll, slid on my back, head down, and finally came to rest grabbing a low-hanging tree limb.

Mother was a few yards above me now, her left foot sticking out from under the branch of a fallen tree.

"My leg is stuck under this damned log," she said.

I worked my way back to where she was. "Can't you pull it out?" I asked.

"No, I can't," she said, angrily.

"What if I help pull?"

"No!"

"Does it hurt?"

"Yes, it does. See if you can lift the log."

"Did you break your bone?"

"I don't know. Try and lift it off my leg."

I straddled the branch and reached down to lift it. But it would not budge.

"Maybe we can lift it together," Mother said. But I could see that she couldn't get enough of an angle to be of much help.

"What are we going to do now?" I asked.

Mother kicked at the log with her other foot. "Ow!" she cried. "Find a pole of some sort and pry it off," she said. "Go find a stick about this big around," indicating a two-inch diameter with her fingers, "and as tall as you are."

I immediately tried breaking off another branch of the same tree that she was pinned under, but it wouldn't break. I looked around us, but saw nothing else that would do. "I don't see anything," I said.

"Walk around and look," Mother said impatiently. "There's got to be something."

I could see right from where I was standing that nothing like that showed above the snow, but I began to crawl on all fours to our right.

"Take your knapsack off first," Mother said. I pulled my arms out of the straps and immediately felt the relief.

Now I could see a large boulder up ahead of me. In shape and size, I realized, it looked a lot like a tank pointed downhill, except without the gun barrel. There was a fairly cylindrical turret and even the top of a man's head sticking out of the hatch. I thought of Fredek and unconsciously raised an imaginary rifle to aim at the protruding head.

"Yulek, are you looking?" I heard behind me.

"Yes, yes!" I yelled back, "but I really don't see anything!"

"Try on the other side, by the stream!"

I turned around and headed back. Suddenly, I was aware of the coincidence of Mother's predicament and my earlier imprisonment on the other slope. I wondered if there was a divine hand involved. What might be God's reason? Was Mother being punished now for her impatience with me?

"Hurry," Mother said, as I crossed in front of her.

Now I could hear the water splashing and gurgling in front of me, though I couldn't see it. The stream was well below the level of the snow. There were twigs coated with clear ice from, I deduced, water splashing on them. There were sheets of ice, some two feet or more across, that must have been pushed up onto the bank by the current. They stuck up in the air, reminding me of the wafer they stuck into your ice cream in cafes. I wondered why they did that. Kiki had told me that in America somebody had once rolled a wafer into a cone and now everybody there ate their ice cream that way.

One wafer was in the shape of a very big leaf. Another was like a sailboat. A third was like the face of an old woman looking out from behind a rock.

"Do you see anything?!" I heard from Mother, and my thoughts came back to the matter at hand. "Can you hear me?"

"Yes, yes, I'm looking!" I knew I had done wrong letting my mind wander over the ice instead of looking for a stick to get Mother's leg free. I determined to pay attention.

But now, perhaps in reward for my admission, there was something that might do the trick, stuck right in the middle of the water, a few yards downstream. It was planted in the streambed as though it were growing there, except with the thick end up, and vibrating in the air.

I didn't know if I could reach it. Lying flat on my stomach, I stretched my arm out for the branch. The tip of the middle finger of my glove touched it, but I couldn't encircle the stick. I was out over the bank with water running under my face.

I wiggled further out over the water. I heard the crust crack under my weight and experienced an instant of panic as I felt myself go down. But I only dropped a little, and now I had hold of the stick and it helped support me.

"Yulek!" Mother called. "What are you doing!"

"I've found something!" I yelled back.

Suddenly, there was a shadow on the opposite bank. There had been no shadows at all until now, but here was the shadow of a head and shoulders. In an instant I realized that it was my own shadow. But now I was reminded of the witches and horrible hermits that inhabited forests. And that ice wafer that looked like an old woman looking at me from behind a rock, could well have been a witch!

Kiki had assured me that there was no such thing as witches, but she could have been mistaken, since she was brought up in the city. Or she could even have told me that so I wouldn't be afraid to be left in my room alone at night when she went to talk with Marta in the kitchen. Maybe a good fairy or wizard had frozen the witch—or a number of witches—in the ice, and my breaking the ice would release them!

Before I knew it, I was half-crawling, half-running back to Mother. But I had the thick end of the pole in my hand.

"You found one!" Mother said.

Suddenly the sight of my mother sitting there in the snow with her leg trapped under a log was a shock. It was as though

I were seeing her that way for the first time. It was as though I had not really believed her helplessness before.

Filled suddenly with guilt, I jammed the thin end of the pole under the log and pushed. It broke.

"Use the other end," Mother said. I was already turning the stick around.

"Ow! Ow!" Mother cried when I must have made the log move a little.

"I'm sorry," I said. I really was sorry—I had caused Mother more pain. I didn't say anything about either the witch or the shadow. Now, back with Mother, I realized that it had been a childish fantasy.

"It's all right," Mother said very calmly now. "Put the stick in a little further and push straight up. I'll help you." Mother lay back on the snow so that she could put a hand under the stick. Then she put her free foot against the log. Together we pushed up on the pole and suddenly, with another cry of pain, Mother's leg was free.

I saw the big hole in her black woolen stocking and the clotted blood all over her shin. I felt a shiver go through me, as I usually did at the sight of blood. "Is it . . . is it broken?" I asked.

"Just a minute," Mother said. I was sure there was annoyance in her tone. Then she carefully turned her foot left and right. I saw her wince with pain and felt the horrible guilt over playing with the tank and thinking about ice cream wafers while she had sat there hurting.

"Help me stand," Mother said. I helped her to her feet. "Let me lean on you." She put her hand on my shoulder. I braced against her weight. Then I felt her weight shift slowly off my shoulder as she tested her hurt leg.

"Is it all right?" I asked anxiously, before I realized I was rushing her again.

"Yes, I think it is. It just hurts. Let me have that stick."

I wiggled the pole out from under the log and handed it to her. Mother took it, then looked at me very seriously. She looked angry, but she didn't say anything.

There wasn't anything I could think of to say, so I shouldered my backpack again and slid my way down to the next tree and stretched my hand out for her. Mother bit her lip and reached out for my hand. Then, leaning heavily on my hand, she carefully slid down to my tree.

I moved to the next tree and held my hand out again. But I only held it out partway, indicating, I hoped, that I wasn't rushing her, but just there for whenever she was ready.

In a moment, Mother reached out for my hand, and now I stretched it as far as I could toward her. She slid on her good leg and I soon felt her weight against my hand again. Again, I eased her carefully down to my tree and immediately slid down to await her at the next one.

"Just a minute," Mother said, as I had feared she would. She was feeling rushed again.

I waited at the tree while she took some deep breaths, then, slowly as I could, to show that I wasn't hurrying, I slid down to the next tree. This time, though, instead of holding out my hand, I waited till I saw Mother begin to ease herself away from the tree. Then I reached out my hand and caught hers.

In this manner we worked our way down, edging a little to the right to avoid running into the stream. When we reached the bottom, my arm and shoulder ached from the effort.

I could see that there seemed to be a trail beside the stream. The snow covered any marks on the ground, but it was hard to miss the alley where branches had been broken off by some sort of traffic. This indication of others following this same route was, to me, an encouraging sign.

I waited to see if Mother wanted to rest, but found she didn't, so I set out breaking a trail in the four or five inches of loose snow. Mother shuffled along behind me with the aid of her stick.

I walked at a slow pace, and every few minutes I looked over my shoulder to make sure I wasn't going too fast. I would have welcomed a word or even just a smile of approval, but Mother's face was grim.

We were on a very gentle downhill slope now, making the going pretty easy for me. With relief I realized that as long as we followed the stream, we could at least count on not having any more hills to climb. Occasionally there was a log to step over or a rock to walk around, and each time I waited for Mother to negotiate the obstacle.

The slope on the other side of the stream was flattening out, while the one we had descended, on our right, seemed to be getting steeper. Then the other side of the stream flattened out altogether, and the light got brighter. I saw our stream turning to the left. We followed it around.

"I have to stop for a minute," Mother said behind me. We were just approaching a fallen tree on which we could sit.

"Let me have your knapsack, and we'll have a sandwich," Mother said. She spoke through clenched teeth, the way some of the boys in my school in Warsaw spoke when they had something particularly nasty to say to me. I slipped my arms out of the straps and waited.

"Goddamn! Goddamn!" I heard Mother utter behind me.

I turned instinctively. Mother was holding a sandwich that was all covered with frost. "They're hard as rocks," she said. "It didn't occur to me they would freeze."

"That's all right—I'm not hungry," I said quickly. Actually I had been hungry until just that minute.

"How stupid of me!" Mother said furiously.

"It's all right," I repeated. "I'm not hungry at all."

"Here, go down to the stream and get some water," she said, thrusting a tin cup at me.

I walked the few steps to the stream. Then I lay down and reached down to the water. Like earlier, there were wafers of ice and crusted snow broken into a variety of shapes, but I fixed my eyes on the metal cup and would not let my mind engage in fantasies.

As I brought the water back to Mother, I saw her sitting with her hurt leg straight out in front of her. I realized that I was holding the cup at full arm's length so as not to approach too close. She was barely looking at me. "Did you have some?" she asked.

I shook my head.

"Drink some," she said.

"It's all right—I'll go back for more," I assured her.

Mother took the cup in both hands and drank, seemingly hunching her shoulders around it. Her eyes were staring at the snow several feet beyond her outstretched leg.

"You're hot, aren't you," she said. I hadn't been aware that I was, but now I realized that she was right. "Why don't you undo your jacket," she suggested. I untied the piece of clothesline around my waist. "Let me have it," she said. "You may need it later."

When she handed the cup back to me, I asked if she wanted more. "Get some for yourself," she said. "You have to have water."

I nodded and returned to the stream. The water tasted very different from the boiled water I had always been given to drink in the past.

Now I was feeling hungry again, but I knew there was nothing to be done about that. I wondered how much further it was to the village.

"Sit down for a minute and rest," Mother said, when I returned to where she was sitting.

If she was ready to go, I would just as soon have been on our way. "I'm not tired," I said. I wasn't—our pace was much slower than the one Mademoiselle had set around Lvow.

"You can leave that here now," Mother said, as I put my arms through the straps of the backpack.

Meesh was in the backpack. But I didn't want to bring up childish fantasies at this time. I grunted and shook my head, hoping Mother wouldn't ask. She didn't.

"All right, we should get going," Mother said, struggling to her feet. "It's beginning to get dark."

I hadn't noticed it, but now I saw that she was right.

We were on our way again. But I hadn't counted on its getting dark. At night, there were wolves in the forest—I wasn't sure where they were in the daytime. Their eyes shone like little flashlights, and they chased people in sleighs, eating the ones that fell out.

Then I remembered Mother's telling me that hunters had killed all the wolves except the ones in zoos. Of course, what if a zoo had been bombed, and the wolves had escaped? Wouldn't they come back here to the woods where there were smaller animals to eat?

But I had to be a grownup now, didn't I? Mother wasn't afraid of wolves, so I had to rid myself of my childish fear as well. Besides, if you have faith, Kiki had said, God will protect you. Now I wondered whether that was really true or another of the stories meant for kids.

But if you wondered about it, then it couldn't work, could it? It was true—it was absolutely true. God would protect us because He was all-loving and all-powerful and all-seeing and hearing and knowing, and I believed that down to the very bottom of my heart, yes I did.

The stream, I noticed, was growing bigger. I wondered where the extra water came from, though this was not the time to wonder about things like that. Our Father, who art in Heaven, hallowed be Thy name.

But what about Mother's faith? My faith, I realized, would have to be strong enough to protect us both. Yes, I had to believe that it would—yes, it would. "Would you like to lean on my shoulder?" I asked.

Mother smiled for the first time. "No, thank you, Yulian. You know, my leg doesn't hurt as much any more."

I could see that she was walking a little more easily now, and the grim expression was gone from her face. It must have been the pain, I now realized, not anger at me, that I had seen on Mother's face. And only when I felt her squeeze back, did I realize that I had taken Mother's free hand in my own.

"What a pair of adventurers we are," Mother said. All I could do was nod, trying not to show the pleasure I was suddenly feeling. Then I let my mother's hand go and resumed breaking the trail for her.

"No," Mother said, taking hold of my hand again. "I'd rather hold your hand now." We began walking side by side. It was getting dark, though. The trees around us no longer had definition, but were simply black lines across a gray background. Somewhere there must have been a moon, because there was enough light reflecting from the clouds overhead and the snow underfoot to keep it from being pitch black. The ice and snow wafers on the banks of the stream picked up glimmers of light that told me where the stream was. At times, I could hear it.

It had grown chilly, and I had re-tied the piece of clothesline around my jacket. I was tired too, and aware again of my hunger. I had found a stick like Mother's which made the walking somewhat easier. But I soon walked into a low-hanging branch that hit me across the forehead, and the stick now had to become a shield protecting my face.

Now Mother was getting ahead of me. "Walk behind me. It'll be easier," she said. I had taken my turn, a long one, breaking the trail, so it was all right to walk behind Mother now. Mother had picked up a third stick, a long, thin one, of which we now each held one end in our free hand so as not to become separated.

"Yulian!" Mother suddenly said, "I'm sure we're walking uphill."

I hadn't noticed, so it certainly couldn't have been much of an incline.

"Where's the stream?" she asked with alarm.

Now I understood her concern—water didn't flow uphill.

We stopped. Peering to our left, where the stream had been all along, I could see no sign of it. "I don't see it," I said.

"We haven't lost it, you know," Mother was saying. "It has to be somewhere over in that direction and not far away. We'll find it."

We turned to our left and began pushing our way through the underbrush. "Let me go first," Mother said, as she began poking the snow ahead of her with her pole. "We wouldn't want to fall into it." For some reason, I found this idea extremely funny, though I didn't have the energy to laugh.

Then I heard Mother cry, "Aaaaah!" and saw her trip over something under the snow. There was a second cry when she landed, and I realized that she must have fallen on her hurt leg. I knew what a hurt on top of a hurt felt like.

I reached down to help Mother stand up, but instead of trying, she was pounding the snow with her fist and forearm, and yelling words I didn't know. There were tears running down her face at the same time.

I grew afraid. I remembered how she had been that last day in Warsaw when Marta had had to hold her to restrain her from rushing out onto the balcony in the middle of an air raid. But Mother quickly stopped herself.

I tried again to help her stand up, but she waved me off. That grim expression was on her face again, but I knew now that it had nothing to do with me. When she started to walk, I saw that she was in as much pain as she had been earlier.

We found the stream with the path beside it in a few more strides and resumed following it.

We came to a large log, like the one on which we had sat down earlier to eat our lunch. "Can we sit down and rest?" I asked. "I'm a little tired." Actually I was more than a little tired.

Mother surprised me by saying no. "If we sit down, we will freeze," she explained. "Would you like to hear a story?"

I could tell that she was speaking through clenched teeth. It must have been because of the pain. "No, thank you," I said. Besides, I remembered how she had butchered "Three Little Pigs," that afternoon in Warsaw, and I didn't want to see her embarrass herself now. But my legs were growing heavy.

Then the woods opened up. There was a clearing in front of us—a flat expanse of snow made to sparkle by a moon that I could now see.

"Stop!" Mother suddenly said, as I was about to step onto the clearing. "That's a pond, and I don't know how strong the ice is."

I had heard numerous tales about boys skating on ponds that they weren't supposed to be on and falling through the ice.

"We have to walk carefully around the edge to see where the stream comes out," Mother said. I could see our stream disappear under the snow.

We set out to circle the pond. It was slow going, with Mother leading the way, poking the snow with her stick to make sure we stayed on solid land. The moon went behind a cloud, making the going more difficult for a while.

"There it is!" Mother said. "There's the stream." Now I could see a trench in the ground with the ice wafers as before.

"Oh, no," Mother said, stopping at the edge of the stream. Standing beside her now, I could see it too. It was our footprints on the other side of the stream and turning to circle the pond. "We've gone all the way around the pond," I said.

"How stupid of me!" Mother said angrily. "I should have known. Streams go into ponds—they don't come out."

"Does that mean we're lost?" I asked.

Mother didn't answer. In the moonlight, I could see her biting her lower lip.

"We're lost, aren't we?" And suddenly, my use of that "l" word opened the lock on a torrent of emotions born of a lifetime of "Hanzel and Gretel" and "Little Red Riding Hood," and, just as suddenly, my self-control left me. "We're lost," I wailed, and now stark terror overcame me, and I began to cry.

I felt Mother wrap her arms around me. She was saying something in a soothing tone, and I wasn't listening to the words, but burying my face in the softness of her coat, where I felt much safer.

Then I realized that Mother wasn't saying not to cry. "Go ahead cry, cry," she was saying. "You've been brave all day, my little soldier. Now you need to cry." Mother was urging me to cry, and I was obliging her with great, palpable sobs.

We stood that way for, I have no idea how long. And then we were walking again, my mother's arm around my shoulders, and me feeling the unnatural weight shift as Mother managed her hurt leg through the snow. "We're going to go this way. I have a feeling that this is the way to the village," Mother said in a reassuring tone. "You know, mothers have a special sense of direction, and it tells me that it's this way." I followed the pressure of her arm without question.

But it was difficult to lift my feet now, and I was beginning to stumble. "Couldn't we rest a bit when we find a place to sit?" I pleaded.

Mother didn't answer me as we kept walking. Now it was my legs that were turning to lead. "I have to stop," I said.

Mother again didn't answer. We kept walking.

"Can't we sit down for a minute," I pleaded. "Then we'll have more energy to go on."

"If we sit down, we could freeze. We have to keep going."

"I can't keep going. I can't walk any farther," I pleaded.

"Do you know what soldiers do when they can't march any further?"

"No."

"Of course you do—they sing. Let's sing a marching song. Start a marching song."

I, of course knew a number of marching songs, but none of them came to my mind, and I didn't feel like singing anyway.

Now Mother began to sing a soldiers' song that Kiki and I knew. Except that she couldn't keep the tune, and in place of some words, she just sang la, la, la, which I didn't consider appropriate for a soldiers' marching song and was now compelled to correct.

We sang that song through twice, which did take my mind off my legs, and then every other marching song I knew, I don't know how many times. We sang songs that weren't meant for marching and songs that Mother knew and I learned and I suddenly found us shuffling our way along a packed-snow road with a group of thatch-roofed cottages clearly outlined against the night sky in front of us. Mother's arm was across my back, and she was pushing me forward.

I was bewildered. It was as though I had been asleep, except that everyone knows that you can't be asleep at the same time that you're walking. I wondered if some spell hadn't been involved.

The cottages were arranged in rows on both sides of the road. There were no lights in any of the windows, but smoke was rising from all their chimneys.

We shuffled to the door of the first cottage we came to. Mother knocked. She didn't knock politely with her knuckles, but pounded with the side of her fist.

We waited a while before someone came to the door. A man with a quilt wrapped around his shoulders and bare feet, opened the door a crack and looked quizzically at us.

"We've just come from Poland," Mother said.

I couldn't understand the question he asked in response. It wasn't Polish, Ukrainian, or Russian.

"Poland," Mother enunciated in Polish, then in Russian. She was leaning with her hand against the door.

Now there was a woman in a quilt standing behind the man, saying something I couldn't understand. Then the door opened wider. Mother would have fallen, except that the man caught her. Then the woman was supporting Mother staggering across the room while the man picked me up off my feet. With my weight off them, my feet suddenly began to ache terribly.

Then I was sitting on something very warm, about three feet off the floor, and drinking a warm cup of that same cheesy-tasting milk I had had the night before—was it only the night before?—and the woman in the quilt was washing Mother's hurt leg, accompanying it with a stream of words, as Mother sat in a chair across the room. Then I woke up again and it was daylight, and Meesh was in my arms.

Chapter Nine

There were two men standing just inside the front door, talking to Mother. One was a policeman in a dark blue uniform with a big black gun holster in his belt. He had a large round head and his hair was cut close to his scalp. Policemen in Hungary, I deduced, didn't look much different from policemen in Poland.

The other was a civilian. He was much shorter than the policeman and somewhat older, with gray hair and a round face. Over his suit, he had on something I had never seen before, a shiny, all-leather overcoat. And on his head there was a funny green hat with what looked like a little shaving brush stuck in the hatband. He had on brown leather gloves, and under his hat, his left ear stuck straight out from his head.

He spoke quietly with Mother for some minutes, then he tipped his hat and they left.

"Ah, you're awake, my sleepy hero," Mother said, turning to me.

What I had been sleeping on seemed to actually be a part of the great iron stove, of which the other end now held a fire with a steaming kettle on top of it. There was warmth coming up through my bedding. The outer layers of the clothes that I had been wearing hung over two chairs in front of that stove. Mother had on what she had worn yesterday, except that the tear in her stocking had been sewn up in large stitches with a coarse thread.

She limped over to where I was sitting and immediately felt my forehead. "How do you feel?" she asked.

I felt fine and told her so. Mother made a face and felt my forehead again. "You feel warm," she said.

The woman who had tended to Mother's leg last night came over and pressed the back of her hand against the side of my neck. She was smaller than Mother, but looked older, and had small dark eyes. She said something in her language, then pulled down the corners of her mouth and shook her head.

"Does he feel hot?" Mother asked.

"No hot," the woman said in Polish, shaking her head again. Then she added some more words in her language and stepped to the far end of the stove. She slid a black pot from the middle of the stove to the hot end and stirred the contents.

"The police knew right away that we were here," Mother said. I assumed she was speaking to the woman.

"Police," the woman said, nodding her head. "Hungary police."

"Mr. Vostokos speaks excellent Polish. He must have lived in Poland at some time."

The woman said something in her language.

Mother asked in Russian if the woman spoke that language.

"No Ruski—Hungarian police," the woman said.

Mother asked if she spoke German.

"No German," the woman said emphatically.

"Thank you." I could tell that Mother had given up on verbal communication and now turned her attention back to me. "You slept well," she said in a jolly tone, and she seemed especially eager to talk. "There is a train station here," she said with some excitement. "Very soon we will be in Budapest, and there we'll stay at a big hotel where it's warm and one can order anything one wants to eat. Here, put these on." She had taken a change of underwear from my backpack, along with a toothbrush. "We just have to stop at the police station to register, and Mr. Vostokos couldn't believe that we escaped from the Bolsheviks the way we did."

I saw the woman bring the wooden spoon to her mouth and taste what was in the pot. I hoped that was breakfast because I was suddenly starving. I ducked under my quilt to change clothes. Meesh was under the quilt with me, and I told him that I would explain to him all about where we were and what we were doing after breakfast. I really didn't feel like talking to him at the moment, and felt a little guilty about it. But I wanted my breakfast and to get on to Budapest.

Dressed again, I dangled my legs off the end of the stove and dropped to the floor. This had been a mistake, I realized, as a sharp pain hit both my feet as well as my ankles on impact, and I fell to my knees with a cry.

Mother and the woman rushed to my side, the woman arriving first and directing a stream of foreign language at me. Then she and Mother raised me by my elbows, while I carefully tried putting my weight on my feet. Done very gradually while they held me up, it worked with only a tingling. I walked carefully to the table, where a steaming bowl awaited me.

My breakfast turned out to be a highly sweetened lumpy oatmeal of some sort with more of the cheesy milk to drink. I ate two bowls of the oatmeal, accompanied by another stream of the new language from our pleased hostess.

Then we gathered up our belongings, stuffing my extra layers of clothes into the backpack, and prepared to leave for the police station. As our hostess wiped her hands on her apron, I saw Mother put some money into one of her hands. The woman pocketed it without interrupting the flow of advice or whatever it was that she was giving us.

Suddenly, Mother put her arms around the woman. "It's thanks to you and your husband that we are alive," she said. "You have saved our lives." The little woman allowed herself to be hugged, but not interrupted. The verbal flow continued as she stroked my cheek. She was still speaking in the doorway as we waved from the middle of the street.

"I know she didn't understand a word I said," Mother said, laughing, as we walked down the middle of the snow-covered street, Meesh once more in the crook of my arm. "But you know how, sometimes, you just need to talk to someone." I noticed that Mother was walking with less of a limp today. My own feet felt pretty good by then. "Would you believe that after all that, I couldn't get to sleep last night?" she said.

I was very much aware that Mother was speaking differently to me now than she or anyone had talked to me before. She was actually speaking more to herself than to me, the way I had sometimes heard adults talking among themselves.

"And you know what I'm going to do when we get to America? I'm going to write a book. I thought of it as I was lying there trying to sleep, and of course there was no chance of my sleeping after that."

This was the first mention I had heard of our going to America. America was where they made Mickey Mouse cartoons and Snow White and the Seven Dwarfs. It was a place where you could buy watches at a pharmacy for a dollar—a friend of Mother's had one—its capital was New York with skyscrapers, and they gave out prizes for having the most freckles. This was exciting news.

As we made our way along the snowy street, a piece of song came into my mind. It was a song I could not remember ever having heard before, and certainly not one Kiki or Miss Bronia would have sung. But there it was, in my mind, and I wondered where I had heard it. It was something about grabbing yourself a woman and God blessing you for it.

The police station was a little white frame house on a street that crossed the one we had been on. Among the big-roofed clay and sod cottages that were like rows of giant mushrooms growing beside the road, it looked like something from a bigger town recently dropped into the village. Electrical wires ran overhead as far as the little house and terminated there.

Mother stopped outside the door and with her fingers smoothed the hair that showed under her kerchief. Seeing me look at her, she laughed. "I know, I look terrible."

She was right. Without her makeup, Mother had dark rings under her eyes that I had never seen before. Her skin was pale, with freckles that I had never known she had, and her eyelashes were so light they were hard to see at all. "No, no, you look very good," I said. Mother gave her neckline a little tug, as she had done going into the commissar's office. Realizing what she was doing, she laughed at herself again. "Yulek, we're going to be famous!" she said "Both of us!" Then she reached for the door handle.

The police station seemed to be mostly one large room. A low platform against the middle of the far wall held a large desk, behind which sat the policeman I had seen before. He reminded me of my schoolteacher and her platform desk. In the far corner to our left, at a much smaller desk on floor level, but behind a little railing, sat Mr. Vostokos. He stood up when we came in and immediately began to button his jacket with little chubby fingers. The leather coat was now on a coat hanger on the wall behind him. "I thank Missus for coming," he said in excellent, though accented, Polish. He came out from behind his desk and held open a little gate in the railing.

His suit was a well-pressed double-breasted dark blue pin-stripe with a white shirt and a green tie. His gray hair was parted in the middle and held in place with pomade. I saw that on the pinkie of his right hand there was a gold ring with a large black stone.

"Sit there," Mother said to me, indicating one of the several chairs by the entrance door. There were chairs around three walls of the room. Then she stepped through the little gate, which swung closed on a spring behind her. "I am so happy to be back in Hungary," she said to Mr. Vostokos, who now held the chair for her. "I have visited your beautiful Budapest a hundred times with my husband."

I saw Mother's fingers instinctively pluck at her skirt to uncover her knee, before encountering the heavy wool of the ankle-length garment. "I don't have a visa, but my passport is in order and if you call the Polish consul in Budapest, he can arrange for one. He is an old friend of mine, you know, as is the ambassador."

"That will not be necessary," he said with a dismissive motion of his hand. Then he went on. "We are all truly amazed at Missus's accomplishment. Missus must be very tired. The constable can make Turkish coffee."

I saw Mother's eyebrows flick up at the mention of the coffee. The man said something in Hungarian, and the policeman stepped down from his platform and disappeared through a door in back.

"The amazing thing is that I am not one bit tired," Mother said. "I am sure it's the excitement, and I will soon collapse," she laughed. "But now I'm just grateful for the chance to talk to an intelligent person. We've been through so much, and that poor peasant woman speaks nothing but . . . well, I'm not sure what language she spoke. It didn't really sound like the Hungarian one hears in Budapest."

"Yes, one often has a great need to talk after an experience like the one Missus has just had," Mr. Vostokos said, pulling a silver cigarette case out of an inside jacket pocket. "This region was made a part of the new Czechoslovakia after the Big War," he said, "but now it's Hungarian again."

Mother arched her back and leaned forward as the man held his lighter to her cigarette. "Two weeks ago, we had three men come across the border," he continued, "but never a woman. The guides, you know, all bring them within sight of the village, then they disappear back into the woods. That undoubtedly is Missus's experience."

"Not exactly. Our guide never even got out of the sleigh."

"The sleigh?"

"He brought us by sleigh within sight of the border. He had bribed the guards, you know, and then he was supposed to carry my son, but he just drove off and left us there."

"Unbelievable. There in the snow?"

"Right there in the snow."

"And Missus and her son came all this way by themselves? Incredible!"

Mother nodded her head.

"A woman and a child . . ." the man said.

Mother tilted her head back and blew a long train of smoke at the ceiling.

"How did Missus ever find her way?"

"The guide had told us to follow the stream."

"But there is no stream here."

"We followed a stream as far as we could. It ended in a frozen pond. Then we just stumbled around blind. If we hadn't stumbled on this village, purely by chance, we would still be walking—or, more likely, frozen in the snow. God must have been looking out for us. When we got to this village, I didn't know whether we weren't back in Poland."

"Amazing. Just where did Missus cross the border?"

Mother named the village where we had spent the night before. "Somewhere near there," she said. I saw Mr. Vostokos write something down.

Now Mother took the scarf off her head. "I must look awful," she said laughing and patting her hair with her hand.

"Missus has been through an ordeal."

"I thank Mr. Inspector—or is it Mr. Colonel, perhaps?— for his understanding and congratulate him on his excellent Polish," she said. "He must have lived some years among us."

"I attended university in Warsaw," he said.

"Ah, our beautiful Warsaw—our once beautiful Warsaw."

"Ah yes, what sadness. And I'm afraid it's only Mister. I am just a poor civil servant in the service of his country."

"Mister is being modest. He wears his rank like an impeccably tailored English suit."

"Missus is too kind. But the guide who abandoned Missus so shamefully in the snow after taking her money should be punished—does Missus happen to remember his name?"

"I believe it was Michael," Mother said. She lied.

"In case we see him here, I will personally see to his punishment. Does Missus remember his last name?"

"They don't use last names."

"Yes, of course."

I wondered why Mother had lied about Yanek's name. He certainly deserved punishing.

"Does Mr. Minister? . . ." Mother began. "I mean Mister—does Mister happen to be related to General Sir Aubrey Hague?"

"General Hague? I'm afraid I do not know of him. English?"

"Yes, English. And Mister reminds me very much of the general—younger, of course. I met the general at a reception in the Polish embassy in London last summer. He is not a tall man, but there is no question that he is in command."

"Perhaps I have some English relations that I did not know about." He laughed.

I now envisioned Mr. Vostokos in a chubby little braided uniform, a cocktail in his hand, and his left ear sticking out the side of his head.

"Mister Min. . . . Mister has such an air of command," Mother said.

"I did serve in the cavalry in the last war," Mr. Vostokos admitted.

"I knew it would be the cavalry. I love the Hungarian cavalry uniforms."

"I was a little thinner then."

"And Mister has such beautiful children."

Mr. Vostokos glanced at the photograph on his desk. "My wife is Austrian."

"She is beautiful."

"She is a skiing champion. She was on the Austrian national ski team."

"Really?"

"Does Missus, or is it Mrs. Baroness, perhaps. . . ?" I heard him saying.

Mother laughed. "Just Missus."

"Well, Missus . . ." he began, but was interrupted by the policeman carrying a copper tray. "Ah, the coffee."

On the tray were two cups, a plate of sugar cubes, and a little brass kettle with a straight wooden handle sticking, horizontally, out from the left side, just like the man's ear. In a moment, I could smell the rich coffee aroma across the room.

Then the policeman presented me with a little tray as well. There was a cup of tea, sugar cubes, milk, and even the option of a lemon slice.

The tea was too hot for me to drink, but I realized that I had been ignoring Meesh, and I now proceeded to explain to him that Hungary was a different country from Poland, which meant that they spoke a different language. I also explained that there were no Russians in Hungary, so there was no shortage of food, as there had been in Lvow. From now on we would have plenty to eat. Austria, where the man said his wife came from, I explained, was on the other side of the world where it was summer when we had winter.

"We traveled three days and nights closed up in the back of my husband's truck," I heard Mother saying. "My son, my sister-in-law and her little son, and her sister-in-law with her daughter—three pampered society ladies and three small children without their governesses." She didn't even mention Miss Bronia. I recalled Mother's stories about Grandfather being a general and my father a senator.

"Now I must tell Missus . . ." Mr. Vostokos began, but Mother was going on. "None of us knew how to cook or even to give her child a proper bath. And, of course, how was anyone to know what clothes to pack?"

"And to think that Missus would have to go through an ordeal like this," Mr. Vostokos said. "How did Missus ever find such a guide?"

"Oh, Mister knows, one meets someone at a café or, standing in a queue perhaps, who knows someone who knows someone."

Then my eye was caught by a movement outside the window to my right. I saw that a sleigh, much like the one we had ridden in yesterday, had pulled into the yard under the window. It had stopped alongside a wagon sleigh with straw in it but without a horse, that had been there since our arrival. A bearded old man in peasant clothes covered the horse with a blanket, then saw me looking at him through he window. He came close to the window and suddenly broke into a big smile that displayed even more teeth missing than the woman this morning.

I heard him stomp his feet outside the door, and he came in. Passing my chair, by the door, he suddenly reached down and snatched Meesh from my lap and continued with long strides to the back of the room.

"Hey!" I cried in surprise.

The old man turned. I saw the mischievous look on his face and realized he was playing with me. Appreciating the attention, I mimed mock surprise. Mother and Mr. Vostokos both looked at me. I laughed to show that everything was all right. Mr. Vostokos said something nasty-sounding to the old man, who immediately returned Meesh to me. As he handed me my bear, he gave a big wink. I wished that I was able to wink back, but it was a skill, along with whistling, that I hadn't yet acquired.

"They were like a comic opera," Mother was saying. "Soviet helmets over their hats and red armbands. And, of course, guns. Their leader was even wearing a sword." They both laughed at this.

"Does Mister still have his cavalry sword?"

"I do, indeed. Someday it will be my son's. Of course, they won't be wearing swords when he's in the army."

"Of course," Mother said. "I am interested because when we arrive in America, I will write a book about all this, the

Bolsheviks and the Nazis. I have stories about both the Bolshevik and the Nazi zones that the world needs to know about. And Mister will certainly be in it for his kindness."

"Indeed," the man said.

The old man sat down on one of the chairs against the side wall, two chairs from mine on my right, crossed his arms over his chest, and closed his eyes. I started to sip some of my tea.

"We had nothing to give the children to eat except carrots," I heard Mother saying. "It was heartbreaking to look at their poor hungry faces."

Then I felt myself being watched. Looking up from under my eyebrows, I could see that the old man had turned his face partly to me and had opened just his left eye. The mischievous look was on his face again. I grinned back at him. Unable to close just one eye, I covered my left eye with my hand.

The old man now closed his left eye and opened the right. I covered my right eye and looked at him with the left. Now the man opened both eyes and placed his left index finger on his left eyebrow and his thumb on his cheekbone. Bringing the fingers closer together, he now forced the eye shut. I copied him and found that I could now actually close one eye. And when I took my hand away, I could actually keep the one eye closed, though with considerable effort. The man's gap-toothed face registered mock surprise.

I heard Mother and Mr. Vostokos laugh, and I first thought they were laughing at us, but I saw that they weren't looking in our direction. I held Meesh up for the old man to see and covered one of his eyes with his own hand. The old man must have mistaken it for a salute, because he saluted back. I returned the salute.

"Mister must surely be joking!" Mother suddenly said.

"I deeply wish that I were," the man answered, "but our government has an agreement with the Soviet government to return all. . . ."

"The Soviet government?"

"Both the Soviet and the German governments."

"But they are invaders. They are not legitimate authorities. Surely the Hungarian government and the rest of Europe are aware . . ."

"I am truly sorry, Missus, but . . ."

"I demand to see the Polish consul! I know both him and the ambassador."

"Ah, Missus, I regret that I cannot accommodate that request either. There is a train to Lvow at five twenty-three that Missus and her son will be on. It is quite a comfortable train, and we have no accommodations here for. . . ."

"But we will be shot," Mother said. "The Soviets will take us off the train and shoot us."

"Ah, no, Missus. The Soviet authorities. . . ."

Mother stood up. "My son and I did not walk eleven hours to exhaustion through the snow to be put on a train back into Soviet hands!"

"There is nothing I can do. We have our orders."

Now Mother was shouting. "Mister has been giving me cigarettes here and coffee and pumping me for information, knowing all along that he was sending us to our death!"

"It is only a routine report that I have to file . . ."

"Routine report? My son and I are not one of your routine border incidents. We have walked eleven hours through the snow, risking bullets, risking wolves . . ."

"There are no more wolves in these woods—the peasants have. . . ."

"Can Mister even look at me when I speak to him?"

Mr. Vostokos was looking down at something he was writing on his desk. He looked up at Mother now. "I am sorry— there is nothing that I can do. Missus must not be hysterical. The Soviet government does not shoot civilians."

"Not be hysterical? I have lived five months with the Bolsheviks and . . ."

"I must ask Missus to sit down now."

"Mister is not inhuman," Mother said in a suddenly quieter tone. "He has beautiful children of his own . . ."

"I am sorry, but I must ask Missus to sit down."

"I have money . . ."

Mr. Vostokos held up his hand to stop her. "If Missus does not sit down, I will have the constable put her in the cell," he said, looking down at the papers again.

Suddenly Mother reached her two hands under the papers on his desk and flung them into the air.

The policeman jumped down from his platform and grabbed Mother's arm.

"The cell has no stove," Mr. Vostokos said.

Mother sat down. She was breathing hard.

"Missus must go sit with her son now," Mr. Vostokos said. He was gathering his papers, and he pointed blindly in my direction.

The policeman put his hand on Mother's arm again. She stood up and let him lead her to the chair next to mine. Suddenly she looked very tired and much older. As she sat down next to me, I saw tears flowing down her face.

Instinctively, I put my arms around her. "It's all right," I assured her. "Don't cry. Everything will be all right."

"He's secret police," Mother said under her breath.

"What?"

"He's trying to make me tell him things. I have nothing to tell him. Do your rosary."

"My rosary?"

"Your rosary—hurry, do your rosary."

"Are the Russians going to shoot us?" I asked. Until a moment ago, I would have been sure the answer would have to be no. Soldiers and spies were stood up in front of brick walls with a blindfold and a cigarette—Fredek had even made me stand with him in front of a brick wall on the farm, close our eyes and hold our hands behind our backs while he spat defiant words at the Nazi firing squad—but none of this was any part of my mother's and my reality. Except that her mention of the secret police had just crashed into that reality.

"Of course not. Now do your rosary," Mother said.

I could tell now from Mother's tone that piety was not the motive behind her order. Mother had a plan. On the other hand, Mother's plans did not fill me with confidence. I pulled the rosary out of my pocket and began with the crucifix. Mother had her rosary in her hands as well. She was mumbling the Hail Mary where it should have been the Our Father and with a few la-la's in the middle. I raised the volume of my praying, prompting Mother with the correct words, but seemed to have no corrective effect. In fact there were la-la's now where the right words had been earlier. Mother's mind, I understood, was elsewhere.

I looked at the old man. He seemed to be asleep, his arms folded over his chest. I watched the policeman step to the stove to put in more wood. The round stove with its door open looked like Mr. Vostokos with his ear.

After a while Mr. Vostokos stood up. "I am going home to dinner now," he said. "I will be back. Yoosef will bring Missus some dinner. We have a toilet through here." He indicated a door in the back wall, then put on his leather coat and green hat. The old man stood up as well.

Suddenly Mother had stood up too and crossed to meet him just outside his railing. She said something that I couldn't hear.

"Missus will sit down with her son or she will wait in the cell!" he said angrily.

Mother sat down again.

I saw the old man purse his lips and shake his head in imitation of Mr. Vostokos, following him to the door. I suppressed my laugh.

"Pederast," Mother said after they had left the building.

"What did you say?" I asked.

"Nothing."

I had heard her all right. It was just that I had not heard that word before. Now I understood it to be an expletive I should commit to memory.

Through the window I saw the two men get into the sleigh and, with the old man at the reins and Mr. Vostokos in back with the robe over his lap, drive away.

Mother leaned her head back against the wall and closed her eyes, the rosary limp in her hands. I understood it to be no longer necessary to continue saying mine. With all that was going on, my heart had not been in it anyway. At the big desk, the policeman continued writing, but I noticed that, with Mr. Vostokos gone, he had unbuttoned the top two buttons of his tunic. He had on a green flannel undershirt underneath.

"Does Mr. Policeman speak Polish?" Mother asked across the room. Her voice was very friendly now. The policeman shook his head. Like Mr. Vostokos, he kept his eyes down on the paper. Mother tried Russian, German, and French with the same results. "Oh come, this close to the border, Mister must certainly understand a little Polish," she coaxed. The policeman wiggled his hand indicating that he understood a little.

"Is Mister from this village?"

The policeman nodded his head.

"Is Mister married?"

He nodded again.

"Does Mister have children?"

He held up three fingers. Then he put his index finger to his lips signifying silence. I wondered why his children should be kept secret, then realized he was telling Mother to be quiet.

"But why?" Mother asked. "Nobody will know if we speak. And I'm only asking about your children."

The policeman reached back and tapped the wall behind him where the cell must have been. Mother closed her eyes again.

I wondered if I could manage to close one eye now without using my hand. I squeezed my left cheek up against my eye and closed it. I found that the other eye closed as well. But I could then force my right eye open a little, while still keeping the left eye squeezed shut with the help of the rest of the left side of my face. I realized how twisted my face must be, but it was a wink, and when the old man came back, I would surprise him.

It wasn't long before I saw the old man drive his sleigh back into the space outside the window. He was alone now. He covered the horse again and hung a feed bag over his nose. Then he lifted an iron pot out of the sleigh. As he passed my window, he looked in and winked at me.

I began to wink back, but he was already past the window before I got my eye closed. But that was all right—I would wait till he was inside and sitting down.

The man stamped his feet outside and brought the pot into the police station. He walked to the other end of the room and through the door into the back room. The policeman followed him.

"We could run away now," I whispered to Mother. I said it out of a sense of loyalty, but certain that this was not a practical plan.

"Hush," Mother said. I decided to practice my wink one more time.

Then the old man came back in, carrying a tray with two steaming bowls and some sliced bread. I realized that if I showed him my wink now, he would be unable to respond the same way that he could later, when he wasn't doing anything. Of course if he did not sit down near me again . . .

"Do you speak Polish?" I heard Mother ask the old man, as he handed her a bowl. He smiled and nodded his head.

"Do you live in this village?"

He nodded again, handing the other bowl to me. He put the tray with the bread on the chair next to mine and returned to the policeman's desk. The policeman had set two bowls on the desk.

"The old fool doesn't understand a word I said," Mother said.

Our lunch was a meat stew, and it was delicious. Mother didn't want hers and offered it to me, but I was too full. The two men talked in low tones as they ate, seated at the big desk across the room. Mother leaned her head back against the wall. I thought she might be asleep, but then I saw that her eyes were open and staring at the ceiling.

Now I began to explain to Meesh that I had taught myself to wink and would surprise the old man with it at the first opportunity, but I must have fallen asleep because the next thing I knew, Mr. Vostokos was walking across the room to his desk in his leather overcoat. He had a newspaper under his arm.

"I trust Missus's dinner was satisfactory," he said with his back to us as he hung his coat on its coat hanger.

At first, Mother didn't answer him. "It was very good, thank you," she finally said, even though her bowl was still on the chair next to mine, untouched.

"The constable's wife is an excellent cook," Mr. Vostokos said. He was seated sideways at his desk now and he leaned down. I realized he was brushing his shoes.

Through the window, I could see the old man unhitching the horse from the sleigh and then leading him somewhere out of my line of sight. I hoped he was coming back into the building. I also hoped that when he did come, he would again sit near me. Mr. Vostokos was now sitting back up in his chair, reading the newspaper he had brought. "I would give Missus a newspaper to read," he said across the room, "but they're in Hungarian." Mother didn't answer him.

Then the old man came back past my window and winked at me again. This time, I didn't even try to wink back, waiting for a more opportune time and crossing my fingers in hope.

Coming back into the building, the old man sat down where he had sat before and, like before, he crossed his arms, yawned, and then closed his eyes. I waited for him to open the one eye and look at me. But he didn't. Time went by, and the old man seemed to be asleep. I wondered if he really was or whether he was teasing me.

Then, suddenly, the eye popped open. This, I knew was an opportunity I could not let slip—there might not be another. As he watched me, I forced my left cheek up, closing both eyes, then carefully let the right eye open as far as possible without opening the left. The old man opened his mouth wide and put his hands to his face in exaggerated surprise. I mimed a laugh, opening my mouth wide and wagging my head left and right. I didn't know whether we really needed to hide our game from Mr. Vostokos, but, somehow, it made it more fun.

Then I remembered the steel washer in my pocket. I drew it out, held it up for the old man to see, then pretending to throw it at him, I palmed it instead. The old man first raised his hands in pretend fear, then rolled onto his side away from me, covering his head with his arms. Then he turned to look at me over his shoulder. I made the washer reappear out of my ear. The old man gripped his head in make-believe amazement.

I repeated the trick several more times, pretending to throw and then pulling the washer out of my hair, my mouth, my nose. . . . Though he did not roll over to dodge my throw any more, the old man's astonishment at each reappearance was undiminished. After I had pulled the washer out of my nose twice and three times out of my ear, the old man raised a finger to stop me. I opened my eyes wide expressing my eager anticipation of what he would do next and saw him look at that raised finger with equal curiosity—as though he, too, was waiting to see what the finger might be planning to do.

Finally, the finger began to move slowly towards his face. I saw his eyes follow it and begin to cross as the finger approached his nose. Reaching the tip of his nose, the finger pushed it in. Immediately, his tongue propped out of his mouth and his eyebrows shot up in surprise.

Now the finger moved slowly toward his right ear, followed by the eyes. As the finger pressed the ear, the protruding tongue shot to that corner of the mouth, and the man's whole head jerked back in surprise. Then the finger began to move across the face toward the other ear.

Suddenly, Mr. Vostokos's voice startled us both as he barked something in Hungarian, and the old man straightened up in his chair with his hands folded in his lap. I, too, sat up as I would have in response to the teacher's command in school. Mother seemed to be sleeping, but I could see her eyes behind her eyelashes move from Mr. Vostokos to the old man and then to me.

I thought it best to devote some time to Meesh, whom I had ignored, and began to explain that Mr. Vostokos was angry at the old man and me for playing and that Mother was pretending to be asleep, but was really watching and listening and had a plan. What I did not communicate to Meesh was my skepticism regarding any plan of Mother's. And suddenly it began to dawn on me that we were, indeed, going back to Poland and the Russians. I was not so much concerned about being shot as about not getting to that hotel room in Budapest with a comfortable bed, our own modern bathroom, and a restaurant where you could order anything on the menu, which had by now become my reality.

The policeman stepped down from his platform to switch on an overhead light, and I realized it was growing dark. He nodded to the old man, who got up and went outside. I watched him pass my window without looking at me, and disappear.

A few minutes later, he was back outside the window, pushing a wheelbarrow. He stopped at the wagon sleigh and began shoveling something from the wheelbarrow into the sleigh. Steam was rising from it, and it took a minute or two for me to realize that it was horse manure. He shoveled it all into a pile in the middle of the sleigh on top of the straw. The he put the shovel back into the barrow and wheeled it back to wherever he had brought it from.

A few minutes later he was back again, leading the horse. He led him to where the two sleighs stood, turned him around, and backed him between the traces of the wagon sleigh. I could barely see in the fast-growing darkness as he fastened the harness. Then the old man climbed into the iron, one-person driver's seat and drove it forward out of my sight.

In a few minutes, the old man was back inside. He reported something to the policeman, who then went to speak to Mr. Vostokos. I could tell that whatever he said didn't please the man. Mr. Vostokos said something angry across the room to the old man. The old man shrugged his shoulders. The policeman said something else to Mr. Vostokos. The old man pursed his lips and shook his head in imitation of Mr. Vostokos, as he had done earlier.

"It is time to go to the train station," Mr. Vostokos announced. "I hope Missus will come quietly."

Mother stood up and walked to the railing again. "I will come quietly, Mr. Minister," she said in a calm and quiet voice that I could barely hear. "I will also get on that train, but I implore Mister that he send my son to the Polish consul in Budapest."

Suddenly I felt the blood drain from my face. The idea of separating from Mother terrified me.

"No, no!" the words were out before they were in my mind. I was crying. I rushed to where Mother was standing and grabbed her around the waist.

"Yulian, you must be a soldier," Mother scolded. "You must grow up and come back to fight for Poland." Then she turned to Mr. Vostokos again. "I implore you as one parent to another. You have two beautiful children. Think of them."

Much to my relief, Mr. Vostokos was shaking his head. "I cannot help Missus," he said. "I am not a monster. I would like to help, but I can't. I must file my report."

He stood up and began putting on his coat. He nodded to the policeman, who put his hand gently on Mother's elbow.

"Put your coat on, Yulian," Mother said to me. I went back for my coat, my knapsack, and Meesh. In a moment we were all standing in front of the building by the sleigh. I could smell the manure.

"I have some good new for Missus, at least," Mr. Vostokos said. "She will not have to bear the aggravation of my company any longer. The constable informs me that the harness on the passenger sleigh is broken and he must take this farm sleigh. The sleigh is not clean, and I am not dressed for such travel at the moment. I will have to walk home." Then he tipped his green hat and began picking his way carefully through the snow.

The policeman helped Mother into the sleigh. The old man was already in the sleigh, and I saw him fixing a spot in the straw for us to sit at the back.

"It is only in the middle," I said to Mother. The only word I could think of for manure wasn't one I could use with Mother. "There isn't any at the way back—we can sit there."

I climbed in after Mother and moved to the back, but saw her move to the front as the policeman settled himself in the single driver's seat.

"Mr. Policeman," Mother said, kneeling behind him in the straw. "Will you take my son to your home—to your wife? I have money and jewels that will make you and your family rich."

I again felt that terror at the thought of separation. I could see myself being led by the policeman into a strange house with strange people.

Now I saw Mother tear a button off her jacket and unwrap something, which I knew to be jewelry, and hold it out to he policeman in the palm of her hand.

The policeman didn't respond. But he didn't say no, as the other man had, to relieve my fear. He had a sheepskin jacket on over his uniform, and he hunched over the reins and clucked the horse into motion.

The sky was clear with a large moon and many stars as we drove through the dark village with barely glowing windows.

We moved at a walking pace, but even that small wind effect made me shiver with the cold. I didn't have on the layers of clothes that I had worn yesterday. Mother continued talking to the policeman, though I couldn't hear her words any more. The man remained hunched over the reins in his two hands and seemed to make no response to her. The old man sat with his back against the driver seat and grinned at me. I was in no mood to play games now. I clutched Meesh tightly to my chest, mostly for warmth.

Our trip was not long. The railroad platform with its roof and electric light soon appeared before us.

The policeman stopped the horse beside the platform. I wondered how long we would have to wait in the cold for the train. The policeman indicated with his head that we should descend. Mother and I climbed down.

As we stood beside the sleigh, Mother still held her hand out to the policeman. The two men didn't move.

Then the policeman pointed his whip straight over the horse's head. "Lvow," he said. It was the first word I had heard him speak. He turned to face the rear of the sleigh, and pointed the whip again. "Budapest, seventh hour," he said in broken Polish. Then he made a clucking sound, and the horse moved forward. We watched the sleigh turn and head back toward the village. Suddenly Mother and I were standing alone beside the empty platform.

The train to Lvow came a few minutes later. It stopped, but no one got on or off. We shivered deliciously till the Budapest train roared in with a cloud of steam and a splendid rumble and hiss.

It was warm inside the train. Mother and I sat facing each other on the soft plush seats beside the window. I watched the Hungarian countryside fly past us, the moonlight glistening on the crusty snow.

Then I felt Mother take my two hands and turned to look at her. I found myself looking directly into her large brown eyes. Mother and I were the only two people in the whole world.

Epilogue

A ragged and dirty peasant woman hobbles into the lobby of the Hotel Bristol in Pesht, the modern section of the Hungarian capital. She limps badly, and leans heavily on the shoulder of her small son. He is having difficulty concealing his excitement. He holds a small white teddy bear in the crook of his arm. Speaking French, the woman requests a room.

"We have no vacancies," says the desk clerk, in his cutaway coat and striped trousers. He gives an eye signal to one of the bellhops to stand by. The peasant boy sucks on his lower lip to control his face.

"Nonsense," the woman replies, "the Bristol is never out of rooms."

"Madame has stayed with us before?" the clerk asks, unable to resist the temptation for sarcasm.

"Of course, many times," she says in the haughtiest tone she can muster. She is enjoying this. Her son has to cover his mouth to keep from laughing out loud.

"And when might that have been, Madame?" the clerk asks archly, falling into her trap.

She names a date last summer. Her lips are drawn tight to repress a smile

"Ah, yes," he says, repeating the date and opening the register with a flourish. "And the name, Madame?" he asks.

"Waisbrem," she says. "Monsieur and Madame Waisbrem."

It takes a beat and a half for the clerk to look up from his register. He removes his glasses to inspect her more closely. He gasps audibly. "Oh Madame, Madame, what has happened?" He is beginning to cry. She is laughing. They hug across the counter.

Mother and I arrived in New York in the spring of 1941 where, with the help of a translator—Mother spoke little English—she wrote her account of this story. The first of the "escape" books to come out of World War II, *Flight to Freedom*, by Barbara Padowicz got considerable media coverage and sold briskly. Of course in her book I'm only six, which made her younger as well, and our relationship is as smooth as glass. But, hey, it's her book.

Mother would never use the name Waisbrem again because of its Jewish sound. Nor would she ever admit to being anything but Catholic for the rest of her life.

Of the families and friends left behind in Poland, I have heard little more than rumors. Kiki, I have heard, did not survive the war, but the family left in Durnoval did, though I understand that they were deported into the interior of the Soviet Union until war's end. Sometime in the fifties, Mother received a letter from an acquaintance who announced that Mr. Herman Lupicki had been elected to government office.

My grandmother survived as well, by hitchhiking from Lodz to Warsaw where no one knew her, so that she could not be denounced as a Jew. When the war ended, my mother brought her to America, but, her health broken, Grandmother lived only a few more years.

My stepfather, Leon, was taken prisoner of war and escaped to join the Polish army in England. Mother, however, soon divorced him, and I had only sporadic contact with him until his recent death at the age of ninety-three.

Not long after arriving in America, Mother found herself sought in marriage by two men, an elderly English millionaire and a penniless handsome Free French hero of the battle of Bir-Hakim in the North African campaign. The choice was not an easy one for Mother, and I was summoned from boarding school to make the final decision. Since the Frenchman, Pierre, had taken me to several Abbott and Costello movies on prior school vacations, it was he who received my nod.

With the war's end, Pierre entered the French diplomatic service, to be posted eventually to Philadelphia, where, in the 1950s and '60s, Mother was celebrated as one of that city's leading hostesses. Hobnobbing with prime ministers, prelates, admirals, and captains of industry, she led a life of charm, tumult, media coverage, and much general excitement, remaining Beautiful Basia until her death at sixty-two.

As for me, I was quickly shipped to boarding school to be Americanized, or as Americanized as a nine-year-old could feel with a mother who could not pronounce the th sound, thought the capital of New York State was Alabama, and could not understand why a baseball glove was for the left rather than the right hand. As unprepared for the American boarding-school experience as I had been for my French school in Warsaw, I found my familiarity with the Holy Family to be of little solace in the long lonely nights when I longed for the intimacy of Durnoval. In the absence of further spiritual instruction, Kiki's fragile catechism could not stand up to the abrasions of adolescence, and I set out on the often-trod path of nihilism and agnosticism.

Nor have I received any more street lamps or sausage sandwiches from God. But He did send me an angel. In 1986, at a Unitarian Universalist church service, I met Donna and managed to marry her the following year. Born and raised Catholic, and educated by the sisters, Donna has worked to put me in touch with my Jewish heritage. Though I still have not had one minute of Hebrew instruction, following Donna's leadership we do celebrate various Jewish holidays in our home and share them with my grandchildren whenever we can.

In a quiet church, a quiet temple, I can often hear God speak to me again in the same language that Meesh and I used to use.

Sometimes we just listen to the music together—until people come in and begin fussing in English or Hebrew or Latin. Then God grows still, or maybe He is simply drowned out, and I get fidgety and look for the first pretense to leave.

Sometimes, on a busy street corner, waiting for the light to change, or in a crowded elevator or subway, a stranger and I make eye contact and we suddenly realize that we've both found the same thing funny or poignant, and I feel that God is there with us. Or, in the quiet of my study, God will lay a firm hand over mine and cause the pencil to write things that weren't in my mind a moment ago and that I would not have thought of on my own.

A one-time Air Force navigator and documentary film-maker, I now have three beautiful daughters, two handsome stepsons, seven grandchildren, and, at last count, one lovely great-granddaughter. My wonderful wife Donna and I live in a 104-year-old house in Connecticut where I spend my retirement at what I love best—writing and tennis. Less than a mile away, my mother and grandmother lie in a quiet, suburban cemetery, presumably the only two Jews in that Catholic resting place.